漢英 國際經濟貿易詞典

Chinese - English Dictionary of Economics & International Trade

林燮寰主編

臺灣商務印書館發行

目 錄

前　言

　　由林燊寰教授主編的《漢英國際經濟貿易詞典》，現在與讀者見面了。這本辭典的出版，為全球從事國際經濟貿易的華人，提供了一本較新的實用的工具書，對於溝通世界經濟信息和開拓國際經濟貿易事務都將起重要作用。

　　綜觀全書，我認為這本詞典的特點有三：一是所收集的詞滙比較廣泛，涉及了國際經濟貿易各個主要方面，又比較實用；二是所收集的詞滙比較新，對八十年代以來出現的新詞滙，盡可能收編進來；三是十分注意收香港市場的習慣用語，這不僅使香港讀者感到親切實用，也有助於外地華人對香港用語的了解。

　　林燊寰教授從事國際貿易實際工作和教學工作四十多年，不僅有豐富的專業知識和經驗，而且他的中文、英文均有較高水平。特別值得一提的，是他早年從事過省港經濟新聞工作，對香港特殊用語也頗有研究。因此林教授是主編這本詞典的最理想人選。我與林教授工作相處二十年，對他嚴謹的治學態度，堅韌不拔的毅力，淵博的專業知識，深感欽佩。這本詞典能在較短時間內編纂出版，主要歸功於林教授的努力。參加本詞典收集資料的人員有：邵學言、王力、吳興光、李子江、盧立岩和劉文影。

　　我因工作忙，主要做了一些組織工作，其作用是微不足道的。

　　在本詞典編纂過程中，陳漢華女士做了大量的編排、整理、抄寫工作，如果沒她的辛勤勞動，要完成如此複雜細緻的編纂工作也是不可能的。

　　香港商務印書館編輯在編纂過程中，自始至終給予熱情的指導和幫助，在此表示衷心感謝。

　　由於編纂時間較短，我們能收集到的資料，受條件的限制，加上水平不高，因此錯誤和遺漏在所難免，尚望讀者批評指正。

廣州外貿學院院長、 國際貿易教授

錢益明

1993 年 8 月

體 例 説 明

(一)本詞典係對外經濟貿易專業詞典，可供從事經濟貿易工作者，金融、財會、企業管理從業人員使用。

(二)本詞典共選收詞目約 20,000 條。內容包括國際經濟、國際貿易、國際金融、銀行保險、外滙結算、企業管理、進出口實務、海事仲裁、國際經濟貿易法規和慣例等。並附有「國際經濟貿易縮略語表」、「世界 50 家大銀行」、「世界各國貨幣名稱」三個附表，以供參考。

(三)所選收詞目，除通用、常用者外，特別注意收編近年來國際經濟貿易領域出現的新名詞術語，並對一些繁難或新的詞目，作簡要的釋義説明。

(四)詞目的漢譯，選用通行的、比較規範化的，並考慮香港地區流行的用法。

(五)英語對應詞有兩種以上漢譯或有多個不同含義的譯名，將較常用者、公認者作為正目，放在最前面；其餘的作為參考詞目，並排放在後面，用逗號"，"分開。重要的，另立詞目，以備查閱。

(六)本詞典英文詞語，一般用小寫字母，但人名、機構、公司、地名等，一律沿用大寫字母起首。

(七)為便於查閱，本詞典採用了下列的編排方法：

1. 詞目按繁體漢字第一個字筆畫排列,少者在前,多者在後。

2. 詞首筆畫相同的詞目，則按起筆筆形[、][一][丨][丿]
   [乛](乛包括：乚、乚、丿、乛筆形)的順序排列。以英
   語字母為詞首者，列為"其它"，按英文字母順序排列。

3. 詞首第一個字相同的詞目，按第二個字的筆畫排列；第
   一和第二個字都相同的，再按第三個字的筆畫排列。

(八)符號説明：

　　(　　)圓括號：表示詞目釋義、詞義補充或百科類屬(如運
　　　　　　　　　輸、保險、經濟、法律等)。

　　[　]方括號：代表語種標誌或特殊用法，如：

　　　　　　[拉]：拉丁語
　　　　　　[法]：法語
　　　　　　[德]：德語
　　　　　　[西]：西班牙語
　　　　　　[意]：意大利語
　　　　　　[美]：美國特殊用法
　　　　　　[英]：英國特殊用法

(九)同一詞目而有幾種英譯文者，用逗號"，"分開。

檢字索引

一　畫

[一]

一刀（24 或 25 張同質同大小的紙，稱為一刀）　quire

一人一票　one man one vote

一人公司　one man office

一工分做制　job-splitting

一大筆錢　a round sum

一千萬　ten million

一手（證券，期貨買賣以手計）　lot

一元的本利和　amount of 1

一方所提出的證據　ex-parte evidence

一方得利引起另一方損失的　zero sum

一方當事人在場所作出的仲裁裁決　ex-parte award

一半付現，一半分期付款　half down and half instalment

一切財產留置權，總留置權（涵蓋一切費用或損失的留置權）　general lien

一切海損均不賠償　free of all average

一切險（全險）　all risks

一日（到午夜十二點為止）　legal day

一日對沖，隔日對沖　day-to-day swaps

一包　a parcel; a pack

一包多件的商品包裝　multipack

一打　a dozen (of)

一打裝　pack in dozen

一件　a piece (of)

一式二份　in duplicate

一式三份　in triplicate

一式四份　in quadruplicate

一式五份　in quintuplicate

一式六份　in sextuplicate

一式七份　in septuplicate

一式八份　in octuplicate

一式九份　in nonuplicate

一式十份　in decuplicate

一年一續　one year renewable term

一年內到期之長期債務　current maturity of long-term debt

一次用包裝　non returnable container

一次用完貨品　single-use goods

一次付清　pay in full

一次付清的現金貸款　single payment personal cash loan

一次付清保險費　single premium

一次付款　lump sum

一次因子　first-order factor

一次性收入　lump-sum payment

一次性有效出入境簽證　entry-exist visa valid for a single journey

一次性變動　once-and-for-all change

一次使用信用證　straight letter of credit

一次抽樣單位　primary sampling unit

一次消費　one-time consumption
一次產業　primary industry
一次產業部門　primary industrial sectors
一次稅制　single tax system
一次裝運　one shipment
一次誤差　first-order error
一次償付現值因素　single-payment present worth factor
一次償付複利因素　single-payment compound amount factor
一次償還信貸　non-instalment
一次總付辦法　lump-sum basis
一次總付的保險費　lump-sum premium
一百二十　great hundred
一百萬　one million
一百萬分之一　part per million
一百億　ten billion
一批交貨合同　single delivery contract
一系列的轉賣　series of resales
一角商店(賣便宜貨商店)　dimestore
一位數　one-digit number
一位隨機數　one-digit random number
一宗　a parcel
一定失利　stand to lose
一定贏　stand to win
一夜貸款，隔夜錢　overnight call loan, call money
一律計算的運費(如按重量或體積等)　freight all kinds

一捆　a bundle
一套　a set
一級大銀行　prime bank
一級品率　ratio of first-grade products
一級差別待遇　first-degree discrimination
一級產業　primary industry
一級結果　first-level outcome
一級證券　senior securities
一般分配法　general distribution
一般化國別風險(主要指由於大幅度貨幣貶值：對外國資產的沒收或凍結：法律上的限制，強制性剝奪：嚴重的經濟不景氣：國內騷亂，政變等造成的償債困難)　generalized country risk
一般代理　general agency
一般代理人　general agent
一般用途信用限額(指出口商銀行向進口商銀行提供一定的貸款限額)　general purpose lines of credits
一般交易條件　general terms and conditions
一般作業程序　generalized operating procedure
一般利用率　general availability
一般利率　normal interest rate
一般利潤率　general rate of profit
一般判定　general estimation
一般系統理論　general systems theory
一般系統模擬　general systems simulation

一般投資慣例　normal investment practice

一般均衡　general equilibrium

一般抵押　general mortgage

一般抵押債券(指用來空白抵押公司財產所發行的債券)　general mortgage bond

一般供給過剩　general over-supply

一般押滙質權書　general letter of hypothecation

一般物價水平法　general price-level method

一般物價水平調整　general price-level adjustment

一般物價水平變動　general price-level changes

一般物價指數　general price index

一般信用證　general credit

一般格式　general form

一般背書　general endorsement

一般時效期　overall limitation period, overall time limit

一般租船契約　gencon

一般財產稅　general property tax

一般留置權　general lien

一般消費物價指數　general index of retail price

一般責任保證　general obligation bond

一般現金(指可作日常經營及重置資產用之現金)　general cash

一般基金　general fund

一般貨物運費率　general cargo rate

一般減免　general deduction

一般間接費用　general overheads

一般習慣　general custom

一般稅率　general tariff

一般最惠國條款　general most favoured nation clause

一般經紀人(不加入證券交易所的場外經紀人)　outside broker

一般意外盈餘準備　general contingency reserve

一般債權人　general creditor

一般管理技術　general administration skill

一般管理費用　general administrative expense

一般漲價　general increase

一般質押書　general of hypothecation

一般價格水準　general level of prices

一般銷售費用　general selling expense

一般橫線支票　general crossed check

一般儲備　general reserve

一般營業費用　general expense, general overhead

一般雜貨　general cargo

一般權利　general rights

一個回合(期貨市場，完成購入並沽出套現的交易，或沽出合約後再購入補回的完整過程)　round turn

一致同意的文本　agreed text

一致裁定　unanimous verdit

一致滿意條款(雙方均未履約因而取

銷合約，或僅一方履約而願與對方
另立新約） accord and satisfaction clause

一致銷售法　uniform sales laws

一種木材運輸標準合同格式
Benacon

一堆　lot

一堆貨物單位（碼頭存放，佔地面積
為 120 平方英尺）　lot unit

一貫的政策　consistent policy

一貫性原則，一致性　consistency

一階條件　first order condition

一階通路　one-level channel

一等商業票據　first-class commercial paper

一塊　a piece

一塊地皮　lot of iand

一遇機會即裝運　shipment by first
opportunity

一價定律（認為國際競爭，有把參加
國際貿易的類似商品價格拉平的趨
勢）　law of one price

一錢不值　not a penny worth

一噸位置　a ton by measurement

一齊跌價　all-round decline

一齊漲價　all-round advance

一類抵押債券（指以公司全部財產甚
至將來可能有的財產作擔保的證
券）　first mortgage bond

一籃子貨幣，搭配貨幣　basket of
currencies

一覽表，核對表　check list

一疊鈔票，錢（美俚）　wad

一攬子方案　package arrangement

一攬子交易，整批交易　package
deal

一攬子免責　"catch-all" exceptions

一攬子投資　package investment

一攬子均衡守則（關貿總協定術語）
a balanced package

一攬子易貨，整套易貨計劃　pack-
age barter

一攬子要價（一個大工程項目，由幾
個供應商組織起來共同供應整個項
目所需一切的價格）　package bid

一攬子計劃　package program

一攬子建議　package proposal

一攬子浮動貸款制度（1982 年 7 月起
世界銀行開始實行的一種貸款制
度）pool based variable-rate tend-
ing system

一攬子租賃　master lease

一攬子許可證（技術貿易中以一系列
專利和專有技術的許可證）
blanket licence

一攬子價格（一次交易中購買各種不
同商品總括在一起的價格）
blanket price, flat price, package
price

[丨]

1952 年布魯塞爾關於碰撞事件民事
管轄權若干規則的國際公約
International Convention on Certain Rules concerning Civil Jurisdiction in Matters of Collision
(Brussels, 10 May 1952)

1952年布魯塞爾關於扣押海船的國際公約　International Convention relating to the Arrest of Seagoing Ships (Brussels, 10 May 1952)

1957年布魯塞爾關於海船船東責任範圍的國際公約　International Convention relating to the Limitation of the Liability of Owners of Seagoing Ships (Brussels, 10 October 1957)

1967年布魯塞爾關於統一若干海商留置權與抵押權規則的國際公約　International Convention for the Unification of Certain Rules relating to Maritime Liens and Mortgages (Brussels, 10 April 1926 and Brussels, 27 May 1967)

1968年布魯塞爾關於修改有關提單若干規則的國際公約議定書　Protocol to Amend the International Convention for the Unification of Certain Rules relating to Bill of Lading (Brussels, 23 February 1968)

1955年國際商會國際仲裁庭調解與仲裁規則　Rules of Conciliation and Arbitration 1955

1966年聯合國亞洲與遠東經濟委員會國際商事仲裁規則和調解準則　Rules for International Commercial Arbitration and Standards for Conciliation of the United Nations Economic Commission for Asia and the Far East, 1966

1966年聯合國歐洲經濟委員會仲裁程序規則　under the 1966 ECE Arbitration Rules

1969年美洲商事仲裁委員會程序規則　Rules of Procedure of the Inter-American Commercial Arbitration Commission, 1969

1的累積額　accumulated amount of 1, compound amount of 1

1的現值定期付款　periodic payment with present value of 1

1的複利終值　amount of 1

[一]

69公式（指一筆投資的年利率為 r% 時，則在69/r + 0.35 年時，其本利和將相當於原投資額兩倍）　rule of 69

72公式（按複利計息的投資，其本利和達到原投資額兩倍所需年限的計算公式，即以72除以一項投資的利率）　rule of 72

78公式（金融公司計算月份貸款利息收入使用的公式，將全年利息收入的12/78，分配至一月份：11/78分配到二月份，餘類推）　rule of 78

乙方　second party

乙級（指貨品）　B grade

乙種活期存款　demand deposit "B"

乙類普通股　class B common stock

二　畫

〔一〕

二十四國集團　Group of Twenty-four

二十英尺等量單位（計算集裝箱容積所用的一項標準）　twenty-foot-equivalent unit

二十國委員會　Committee of Twenty

二人票據（有兩人簽署的支票或滙票）　two-name paper

二比一　two-to-one

"二比一"比率（指流動比率）　"two to one" ratio

二手設備　secondhand machinery

二次因子　second order factor

二次抵押權　second mortgage

二次抽樣單位　secondary sampling unit

二次抽樣檢驗　double sampling inspection

二次租賃，轉租　sub-lease, under-lease

二次誤差　second order error

二美元經紀人（即獨立經紀人，名稱來源於初期接受 100 股指令時收費二美元）　two-dollar broker

二重稅　double tariff

二重價格　two-price

二重滙兌市場制　two-tier exchange market system

二倍　bi

二級市場　secondary market

二級抵押市場　secondary mortgage market

二級產品　secondary products

二級產業　secondary industry

二級結果　second-level outcome

"二級"準備金（指商業銀行除原始準備金外，持有的短期有價證券、通知放款等）　"secondary" reserve

二級資料　secondary data

二部徵稅制（即半定半活的徵稅費率）　two-party tariff

二階反饋系統　second order feedback system

二階條件　second order condition

二階通路　two-level channel

二等商業票據　second-class commercial paper

二數列，雙列　bi-serial

二價制　two-price system

二價商店　two-price house

七十七國集團　Group of 77

七大國際石油公司　Seven International Oil Majors

七日入倉條款（指卸貨後 7 天）　seven-day clause

七日通知存款　seven-day notice deposit

十八開金　gold 18 carats pure, 18 carats fine

十之八九　in nine cases out of ten

十天內付款 2% 折扣，三十天內付款無折扣（企業為鼓勵購買者及早付款的一種銷售條件） 2/10, net/30

十、五、三年折舊法（指美國 1981 年實行的加速成本回收制度） ten-five-three depreciation

十足準備計劃 one hundred per-cent (100%)

十足滿載（船舶載量，不論以容積或重量計，均告完全滿載的狀態） full and down

十國集團，巴黎俱樂部 Group of Ten

十進制通貨 decimal currency

十進計時表 decimal time

十進計數法 decimal scale

十進數字法 decimal system

十億 ［美，法］billion

丁字式帳戶 T-account

［丨］

10-K 報告（美國證券交易委員會要求公司形式企業提交的年度報告） 10-K Report

10-Q 報表（企業向證券交易委員會報送的季度財務報表） 10-Q State-ment

［丿］

人力分析 manpower analysis

人力分配法 manpower allocation

人力系統 manpower system

人力利用 manpower utilization

人力投資 investment in human resources, human capital invest-ment

人力財富 human wealth

人力訓練 manpower training

人力規劃 manpower planning

人力資本 human capital

人力資源 human resources, man-power resources

人力資源開發 human resources de-velopment

人力資源會計 human resource ac-counting

人力資源潛力 human potential

人力需求 manpower demand

人力緊壓包 hand press-packed bale

人力輸入輸出分析 manpower in-put-output analysis

人力激發 human motivation

人工小時法 labour hour method

人工工資率標準 labour rate stan-dard

人工分類法 artificial system

人工用量差異 labour usage vari-ance

人工成本 labour cost

人工合成工業 synthetic industry

人工效率差異 labour efficiency variance, labour time variance

人工配搭差異 labour mix variance

人工港 artificial harbour

人工智能 artificial intelligence

人才外流　brain drain

人才存留率　rate of brain retention

人欠　he owes, balance due from

人日（一人工作一天的工作量）man-day

人年（一人一年的工作量）man-year

人名帳戶　personal account

人均，按人口平均計算　［拉］per capita

人均國民收入　national income per capita, per-capita income

人均農產品佔有量　per capita consumption of farm produce

人事心理學　personnel psychology

人事主管　personnel director

人事卡片索引　personnel card index

人事決策　personnel decision

人事考核制度　system of vocational assessment

人事政策　personnel policy

人事保證釋放　replevish

人事部門　personnel department

人事記錄與報表　personnel records and reports

人事組織圖表　personnel chart

人事資料　personnel information

人事新進率　accession rate

人事管理　personnel management, personnel administration

人物行銷　person marketing

人的準動產　chattels personal

人時（一人工作一小時的工作量）man-hour

人員更換成本　personnel replacement cost

人員推銷　personal selling

人員管理　personnel management

人員選擇　personnel selection

人員變動率　turnover rate of personnel

人造系統　man-made system

人造食物　artificial foods

人造絲　artificial silk

人造資源　man-made resources

人造礦物　artificial mineral

人造纖維　artificial fibre

人為干擾　man-made noise

人為低價　artificially low price

人為的供應緊張　man-made shortage of goods

人為的貿易障礙　artificial trade barriers

人為值　artificial value

人為財富　artificial wealth

人為環境　man-made environment

人壽分紅保險　life insurance with dividend

人壽保險　life insurance

人壽保險公司　life insurance corporation

人壽保險費　life insurance premium

人頭稅　poll tax; head tax

人機系統　man-machine system

人機程序圖　man-machine process chart

九九表　multiplication table

九五折　5% off

八小時工作制　eight-hour day, eight-hour system of labour, eight working-hour day

八成　eight-tenths, eighty percent

八份之一點規則（美國證券交易委員會對賣空指令的一條限制性規定，如指令價格不高於前一成交價的 1/8 點，經紀人是不允許執行該指令的）　one-eighth rule

八開　octavo (8 vo)

入市限價（根據國際結算公司或期貨交易所定下之投機者最高入市數限額）　position limit price

入伙紙　occupation permit

入門費與提成支付相結合（技術貿易一種支付方式，合同簽訂後，先由受方支付一定金額的入門費，其餘部分根據利用技術效果，按一定百分比提成）　initial payment and royalty

入門價格，門檻價格　threshold price

入庫保稅品　warehouse bond

入帳　pass entries, pass through accounts

入船塢　docking

入超　import surplus, unfavorable trade balance, excess of imports

入港呈報表　bill of entry

入港稅　port dues

入港費　inward charges, port dues

入港領港費　pilotage inwards

入境地點　points of entry

入籍申請　petition for naturalization

［一］

"三C"信用調查（指信用調查的三個標準：品格 character；才能 capacity；資本 capital，被稱信用三要素）　"three C" credit investigation

三A級（標準及蒲耳氏債券等級的最高級別，符號為 AAA）　triple A

三A級公司債券　triple A corporate issue

三、五、十年折舊法（指美國 1981 年實行的加速成本回收制度，適用該項稅法的固定資產成本，可在三、五、十年內得到回收）　three-five-ten depreciation

三方條款　tripartite tready

三方簽署的票據　three-name paper

三方競爭市場　three market

三元體系　triad

三代店（即代購、代銷、代營店）　triple agency

三合一措施　three-in-one process

三年週期　three-year cycle

三名滙票　three-party draft

三夾板箱　plywood case

三角套滙，三點套滙　three-point

arbitrage in foreign exchange, three-point arbitrage

三角滙兌　three-cornered exchange

三角貿易　triangle trade, three-cornered trade

三角補償貿易(由第三者承擔產品的返銷或承擔提供技術設備。又稱第三國補償貿易)　third country compensation trading

三明治課程(三至六個月短期訓練班，帶薪學習取得一定資格後，仍回原單位工作)　sandwich courses

三重甲板運費制　three decker rate system

三重稅　treble tariff

三度論(威廉‧雷丁提出關於管理人員作風的理論。三度指面向任務、面向關係和面向效果)　3-D theory (3-D 代表 three dimensional)

三級市場(美國術語，指大宗股票的場外交易)　third market

三島式船　three-island type

三差異製造費用分析　three-variance overhead analysis

三帳戶制　three-account system

三堆法　three-bin system

三等證券　third-class paper

三級財貨(指服務)　tertiary goods

三級產業(指服務業)　tertiary production

三料箱制度(以存貨的第三部份作為保險庫存)　three bin system

三階通路　three-level channel

三構面領導理論　Three-Dimension Leadership Model

三點方案　three-pronged program

三聯單　bill in three parts

工人賠償法例　Workmen's Compensation Act

工作因素　work factor; WF

工作場所程序圖　workplace chart

工作獎金制度　premium plan

工作(任務)導向管理　task-oriented management

工時　working hours, man-hours

工時卡　clock card, time card

工時成本　time cost

工時差異　time variance

工時報單　time ticket

工商法規　commercial and industrial law and regulations

工商界　the world of industry and commerce

工商界人士　industrial and commercial figures

工商業所得稅　industrial and commercial income tax

工商業組成指數　index of business formation

工商業稅　business tax, industrial and commercial tax

工商業貸款　business loan

工程施工標準化　construction standardization

工程保險　engineering insurance

工程現值法　project present worth

工程價值分析　value engineering

工程節約，工程經濟學　engineering

economy

工貿結合 integrating industry and trade

工資工時法 Wage and Hour Law

工資分配表 wage allocation sheet

工資率 wage rate

工資率差異 wage rate variance

工資匯總表 wages summary

工業工程 industrial engineering, IE

工業公司 manufacturing establishment

工業民主 industrial democracy

工業生產 industrial production

工業生產指數 index of industrial production, industrial production index

工業生產能力 industrial capacity

工業生產程序 industrial process

工業市場 industrial market

工業市場批發商 industrial market wholesaler

工業自由港 industrial free ports

工業自動化 industrial automation

工業收益債券(美國市政當局發行用以贊助工業發展的債券) industrial bonds

工業地帶 industrial zone

工業危機 industrial crisis

工業投資計劃 industrial investment plan

工業股票 industrials

工業品 industrial goods

工業產品 manufactured products

工業品批發商 merchant wholesaler

of industrial goods

工業品零售價格指數 retail price index of industrial products

工業革命 industrial revolution

工業家,實業家 industrialist

工業時代 industrial age

工業消費者 industrial consumer

工業設計 industrial design

工業產權(指商標、版權、設計、專利權等) industrial property

工業產權制度 industrial property system

工業專業化 industrial specialization

工業停滯 industrial stagnation

工業票據 industrial bill

工業組織 organization of industry

工業進步 industrial progress

工業發展 industrial expansion

工業結構改革 industrial restructuring

工業資本 industrial capital

工業資本主義 industrial capitalism

工業意外 industrial accident

工業債券 industrial bond

工業會計 industrial accounting

工業落後國家 undeveloped countries

工業經濟 industrial economics

工業銀行 industrial bank

工業管理 industrial management

工業質量管理 industrial quality control

工業衛生 industrial health

工業關係　industrial relation

工業蕭條　industrial recession

工業轉移　shift of industries

工業競爭　industrial competition

工會法例　Trade Union Act

工廠　workhouse, factory, mill, plant

工廠平均製造率　manufacturing average rate at factory

工廠成本　factory cost

工廠交貨　ex work, ex factory, ex mill

工廠交貨成本　ex work cost

工廠自動化　factory automation

工廠投資周轉率　plant investment turnover

工廠作業效果指數　plant efficiency factor

工廠負荷　factory burden, shop burden

工廠被市場淘汰　mill was in danger of losing its market

工廠設備　plant equipment

工廠會計　factory accounting

工廠經濟　factory economic

工藝品　art work

工藝流程　technological process

工繳費　processing fees

大小(尺寸)　size

大木桶　barrel

大百,一百二十　great hundred

大百貨公司　emporium

大多數裁定　majority verdict

大折扣　heavy discount

大批承兌　acceptance of batch

大批定貨,巨額訂單　extension order

大來卡(大來集團發行的信用卡,初流行於餐車式小餐館,故亦名迪納爾俱樂部信用卡)　Diners Club Card

大宗土產　staple

大宗存單　tranche certificate of deposit

大宗股票自動交易系統(紐約交易所為促進大宗股票交易而建立的體系)　block automation system

大宗股票買主(美證券市場術語)　block positioner

大法官　Lord High Chancellor

大拍賣,廉價出售　sell at a bargain

"大道"定理(現代西方經濟學用於宏觀經濟增長分析的定理)　the "Turnpike" theorems

大桶(等於 52 1/2 英制加侖或 63 美制加侖)　hogshead

大副收據　mate's receipt

大陸式結算　continental closing

大陸制(指簿記制度)　continental system

大陸橋(海陸聯運中所經過的陸上通道)　land bridge

大陸橋運輸(貨櫃/集裝箱海陸聯運)　land bridge transport

大規模投機　heavy speculation

大量生產　mass production

大量行銷　mass marketing

大量訂購　huge order

大量消費　mass consumption

大量銷售　mass selling

大量購買　mass purchasing

大規模市場　mass market

大規模運輸　mass transportation

大規模廣告　mass advertising

大規模購買力　mass purchasing power

大路貨，普通質量　article of quality

大減價　grand sale, radical reduction, great reduction in price, opening sales

大號　king size, large

大數(分期付款中最後一筆特大數)　balloon

大數目(外滙商人術語，通常指滙率的前三位數)　big figure

大數法則(在隨機現象的大量重複出現中，常呈現幾乎必然的規律)　law of large numbers

大寫金額　amount in words

大噸，長噸　long ton

大賺一筆錢　grab the biz

干預的上下限　upper and lower intervention limits

干預政策　intervention policy

干預貨幣　intervention currency

干預價格　intervention price

干預點差幅　spread between the intervention points

干擾證人　interference with witness

土地收用通知書　notice to treat

土地收回訴訟　ejectment

土地利用及交通最優選擇　land use and transport optimization

土地所有權狀　certificate of possession of land

土地受益人　cestui que use

土地稅　land tax

土地裁判庭　Lands Tribunal

土地復原　land reconversion

土地登記　land registration

土地登記法例　Land Registration Act

土地銀行　land bank

土地增值稅　increment tax on land value

土貨　domestic products, native goods, local products

土產　domestic products, native goods, local products

土產商店　native product shop

土產稅　excise duties

下月　〔拉〕proximo

下定付款　cash with order

下限　lower limit, prescribed minimum, floor level

下書人(保險人俗稱，起源於 13 世紀英國)　underwriter

下降平衡折舊法　declining-balance depreciation

下降趨勢線　downtrend line

下貨港　unloading port

下跌　go down

下等品　low quality

下層甲板　orlop deck

下價貨，廉價貨　low priced goods

[丨]

上午市　morning session

上升行市(用以表示一成交價高於前
一成交價的術語，亦稱＂高市＂)
up tick

上升曲線　ascending curve

上司，老闆　[俗]boss

上市公司(指在證券交易所註冊公開
發行股票的公司，又稱掛牌公司)
listed company

上市的全部股票　list

上市股票(指在交易所掛牌的)　listed
stock

上市股票的總市值　aggregate value
of listed stock

上市股票期權交易　listed option
trading

上市證券，掛牌證券　listed securities

上行式的管理　bottom-up manage-
ment

上岸費　landing charges

上岸碼頭　landing stage, landing
wharf

上限　upper limit

上場商品(指在交易所)　listed brand

上期結轉　carry forward

上選品質　selected quality

上議院上訴委員會　Appellate Com-
mittee of the House of Lords

上級機構　parent body

上等的　superior

＂上等＂信用卡(美國花旗銀行發行對

存款給利息的信用卡)＂Choice＂Card

上等品質　first quality

上等貨　prime quality, super-fine
quality

上期結餘　old balance

口岸檢查機關　inspection office at
the port

口頭定貨　verbal order

口頭協議　oral agreement, verbal
agreement

口頭修正　oral amendment

口頭要約　oral offer

口頭報告　oral report

口頭逮捕令　parol arrest

口頭賒欠　parol credit

口頭諒解　verbal understanding

口頭證據　oral testimony, oral evidence

[丿]

千升(等於1000 litre)　kilolitre

千分之一　[拉]per mille

千瓦　kilowatt

千卡(熱量單位)　kilocalorie

千立方米　kilostere

千米(等於1公里)　kilometre

千伏　kilovolt

千克　kilogram

千噸　kiloton

[一]

小工　unskilled labour

小心瓷器　porcelain with care
小心掉落　do not drop
小心輕放　handle with care
小心標誌　caution mark, care mark
小木桶　keg
小交易所　bucket shop
小件貨物　shipping parcels
小周期　minor cycle
小計和總計　extensions and footings
小型散裝船　mini bulk carrier
小時工資率　pay rate per hour
小衰退　minirecession
小差距滙率幅度安排　narrow margin arrangement
小差距滙率幅度　narrower exchange rate margin
"小蛇"(指比利時、荷蘭、盧森堡三國，1972 年 3 月規定滙率波動在平價上下 0.75% 的一種形象化名稱）"mini-snake"
小販　small trader
小販法例　Hawkers Act
小帳，賞錢　gratuity, tip
小試投機　dable speculation
小商業　petty trade
小陸橋運輸(貨櫃／集裝箱海陸聯運)　mini land brige transport
小量　small quantity
小景氣　［美］boomet
小債務法庭　small debts court
小寫金額　amount in figures
小噸，短噸　short ton
小數　decimal fraction
小數位　decimal place

小數點　decimal point
小額　petty sum
小額股票　stock scrip
小額貸款公司　small-loan company
小額債券　small bond, baby bond
小額錢債審裁處（香港）Small Claim Tribunal
小額優惠　fringe benefit
子公司　subsidiary company
子公司試算表換算　conversion of subsidiary trial balance
子母船　lighter aboard ship (LASH)
已公佈歐洲貨幣貸款額　publicized Eurocurrency credits
已分配利潤　distributed profit
已分配費用　applied expense
已分配製造費用　absorbed manufacturing expense
　［同 absorbed burden, absorbed overhead, applied manufacturing expenses］
已分攤成本　allocated cost
已加工原料　processed materials
已付支票　paid check
已付股利　paid dividend
已付賠款　losses paid
已付價持票人　holder for value
已收入金額　amount received
已收回股份　retired stock
已收回債券　retired bonds
已在倉(指商品已存放於隨時可移送至其他地點或隨時可持合約交收)　in position
已全部折舊資產　fully-depreciated

assets

已全部繳款股份　fully-paid stock

已全部繳款股票　fully-paid shares

已完工批號日記帳　completed jobs journal

已完成會計事項　completed transaction

已完稅　duty paid

已完稅貨物　duty-paid goods

已吸收成本　absorbed costs

已吸收跌價　absorbed declination

已吸收費用　absorbed expenses

已折舊價值　depreciated value

已承兌　accepted

已承兌信用證　accepted letter of credit

已承兌票據　accepted bill

已承兌滙票　accepted draft, accepted bill

已抵除增加額　balanced addition

已抵押資產　pledged assets

已知損失　known loss

已到價合約(指期權交易商品定價低於合約到期時市價的延買期權：或定價高於合約到期時市價的延賣期權) in-the-money

已宣佈股息(利)　dividend declared

已查證帳目(指經會計師證明的) certified account

已耗成本　depleted cost 〔同 expired cost〕

已耗專利權價值　expired patent value

已被拒付的應收票據　notes receivable protested

已核定發票　vouched invoice

已通知還本的公債　called bond

已清償損失額　liquidated damage

已清償債務　liquidated obligation

已清繳保費　paid-up insurance premium

已提出拒絕證書後承兌　acceptance for honour supra protest

已提供押款金額　sum lent on a mortgage

已發生損失　incurred losses

已發在外流通股本　capital stock outstanding

已發行股票　issued stock

已發股本　issued capital, capital stock issued

已發債券　bonds issued

已發證券　securities issued

已結平帳戶　closed account

已結清帳戶　closed account

已貼現票據　discounted bills, discounted notes

已貼現應收票據　notes and bills receivable discounted

已逾時效之規定　statute-barred

已裝船提單　on board bill of lading

已裝船清潔提單　clean on board bill of lading

已裝船海洋清潔提單　ocean clean on board bill of lading

已補進的套滙　covered arbitrage

已催繳股本　call-up capital

已認繳股本　capital stock subscribed

已履行的對價（報酬） executed consideration

已審查憑單　audited voucher

已審查帳目　audited accounts

已實現折舊　realized depreciation

已實現利潤　profit realized

已實現損益　realized gains and losses

已實現增值，已實現漲價　realized appreciation

已撥款項　allotment issued

已獲收益　earned income

已獲利息　interest earned

已獲盈利　profit earned

已獲得的計時利息比率　times-interest earned ratio

已繳　paid in

已繳款股份　paid-up stock

已繳資本　paid-up capital

已贖回債券　retired bond

[、]

方法工程　methods engineering

方便抽樣　convenience sampling

方便旗　flag of convenience

文件的真確證明　authentication of document

文件證據　documentary evidence

文字報告式報表，敍述式報表　narrative form of statement

文據　document, instrument

文據清單　list of documents

文獻調查　literature survey

心理訂價法　psychological pricing

心理訂價戰術 psychological pricing tactics

火車上交貨（價）　free on board train,［美］free on cars

火車快郵　［英］Railex

火車站交貨條款　ex station terms

火車輪渡　train ferry

火災　fire disaster

火災共同保險　fire co-insurance

火災危險　fire peril

火災保單　fire policy

火災保險公司　fire office

火災保險測定　fire insurance surveying

火災保險費　fire insurance premium

火災損失　fire losses

火災損失調整　fire loss adjustment

火災損壞貨物的出售　fire sale

火損　fire damage

火險　fire insurance

火警　fire alarm

[一]

不二價　one price, only one price

不二價政策　one price policy

不二價商店　one price house

不公平　injustice

不公平交易做法　unfair trade practice

不公平競爭　unfair competition

不公開公司　close corporation, private company

不公開出售證券　private offering

不公開招股公司　close corporation, private limited company

不分類定額(指紡織品配額)　basket yardage

不可欠缺的原因　[拉]causa sine qua non

不可分性　indivisibility

不可分開的　pro indiviso

不可分割的份額　undivided share

不可比因素　noncomparable factors

不可平放　never lay flat, not to be laid flat

不可用鈎　use no hooks

不可抗力　force majeure, irresistible force, vis major[拉]

不可拋擲　do not drop

不可保的風險　uninsurable risk

不可倒置　do not turn over

不可廢除的所有權　indefeasible title

不可撤銷、可轉讓和可分割的信用證　irrevocable transferrable and divisible L/C

不可撤銷的保兌信用證　irrevocable confirmed letter of credit

不可撤銷的無追索權信用證　irrevocable without recourse letter of credit

不可撤銷承兌跟單信用證　irrevocable documentary acceptance credit

不可撤銷信用證　irrevocable letter of credit

不可撤銷跟單信用證　irrevocable documentary letter of credit

不可避免成本　unavoidable cost, unescapable cost

不可避免的意外事故　inevitable accident

不可議付的信用證　non-negotiable L/C

不可議付的副本　non-negotiable B/L

不可變更受益人　irrevocable beneficiary

不可控成本　noncontrollable cost, uncontrollable cost

不正常市場　irregular market

不正常交易　queasy transaction

不正常波動　irregular variation

不正當積累　improper accumulation

不正當壓力　improper pressure

不正當競爭　undue competition

不加說明之分錄　blind entry

不平衡　overbalance

不平衡預算　unbalanced budget

不可轉讓信用證　unassignable letter of credit

不收小費　no gratuities accepted

不收租金　rent free

不在市場買賣而按成本計值的投資　investments not traded in the market which were valued at their cost

不交付(不交貨)　non-delivery

不合法付款　illegal payment

不合法的合同　illegal contract

不合併決算之附屬公司　unconsolidated subsidiary

不合格　not qualified, below standard

不合格商業票據　non-eligible commercial paper

不合格票據(在英國，指不能在英格蘭銀行進行貼現的票據，美國也用此術語)　ineligible bills

不合理的差別待遇(關貿總協定術語)　unjustifiable discrimination

不合理的推論　non sequitur

不合理的價格　unreasonable price

不合常規　irregularity

不合程式　want of form

不安指數(官方公佈的失業率和消費價格變動率相加，不計百分比所得出的數字)　Discomfort index

不任職董事　outside director

不折不扣地，恰好地　to a T

不折不扣地履行條款　comply with the provision to a T

不完全市場　imperfect market

不完全的信託　imperfect trust

不完全的義務　imperfect obligations

不完全的關稅同盟　incomplete customs union

不完全貨幣(即名目貨幣)　nonfull-bodied money

不完全標準成本會計法　partial plan of standard cost accounting

不完全競爭　imperfect competition

不良的所有權　bad title

不兌現　non-cashable

不兌現支票，拒付支票，空頭支票　dishonoured cheque

不兌現紙幣　fiat money

不兌換紙幣　inconvertible paper money

不兌換債券　irredeemable bond

不足認購一股之認股權證，零股認股權證　fractional stock warrant

不定比定律　law of variable proportions

不定比率投資法(根據市場的升降決定投資普通的比例)　variable ratio plan

不定值保單　unvalued policy

不定期　irregular dates

不定期存款　irregular deposit

不定期負債　indeterminate-term liabilities

不定期貨輪　tramp vessel

不定期裝運　indefinite shipment

不定期報告　nonperiodical report

不定額公司債　open-end issue bond

不定額投資公司　open-end investment company

不定額抵押　open-end mortgage

不法行為不產生權利　[拉]jus ex

injuria non oritur

不承兌　non-acceptance

不承兌應抗議　protest for non-acceptance

不附條件之背書　unqualified endorsement

不附條件的費率　non-tied rate

不附息票據　non-interest-bearing notes

不爭執條款　non-contest clause

不服評價提起上訴　appeal against valuation

不受限制的(指發行不限量的隨時可兌換現金的股票等)　open-end

不受保資產　non-admitted assets

不受時效限制的權利　imprescriptible right

不受損害　without prejudice

不披露身份的代理　undisclosed agency

不易變動的價格　nonflexible price

不信任　discredit

不指名的代理人　agency unnamed principal

不指定的還款　indefinite payment

不計列資產　inadmissible assets

不計殘值　ignoring residual value

不派作股利的盈餘　surplus not for dividend purposes

不保兌信用證　unconfirmed letter of credit

不相配的到期日(指所籌資金償還日期和貸款或其他資產的到期日不一致)　mis-matched maturity

不活動帳戶　inactive account, dormant account

不恰當要求　unwarranted demand

不相關成本，無關成本　irrelevant cost

不准　not allowed, forbidden

不准手觸　hands off

不准腳踏　no steps

不准轉運　no transhipment permitted

不准轉讓　non-negotiable

不記名支票　check to bearer

不記名有價證券　bearer securities

不記名股份　bearer stock

不記名承兌　acceptance in blank

不記名背書　blank endorsement

不記名寄存單據(在歐洲債券市場，如借款人未獲准發行無記名債券，由牽頭銀行安排發行的一種票證)　bearer depositary receipts

不記名票據　bill to bearer

不記名提單　order bill of lading

不記名資產　impersonal assets

不能自由兌換貨幣　inconvertible currency

不能提前償還的公司債　uncallable bonds

不能堆壓　not to be stowed below other cargo

不能強制履行　unenforceable

不能避免的意外　inevitable accident

不能履行　impossibility of performance

不能變更受益人　irrevocable beneficiary

不流通支票　non-negotiable cheque

不流通期票　non-negotiable note

不凍港　warmwater port, ice-free port

不時發生的損失　sporadic losses

不借債　keep out of debt

不退還的包裝　non-returnable packing

不退還的托盤　non-returnable pallet

不得分運　partial shipment is not allowed

不得反駁　juris et de jure

不得反駁的推定　irrebuttable presumptions

不得用鈎　no hooks

不得作為無效　indefeasible

不得受賄條款　not to benefit clause

不得轉運　transshipment is not allowed

不參加分紅的優先股　non-participating preference share

不健全競爭　pernicious competition

不規定發行價格之無面值股　true no par stock

不規則波動　irregular fluctuations

不通報　failure to disclose

不動本基金，留本基金　nonexpendable fund

不動產　real property, real estate, immovable estate

不動產作保證物　real securities

不動產投資信託　real estate investment trusts

不動產抵押　real estate mortgage, pledge of immovable

不動產抵押貸款　loan on real estate, loan on actual estate, real estate mortgage credit

不動產信用　credit based on real property

不動產凍結　frozen asset

不動產帳　immovable account, real estate account

不動產稅，房地產稅　real estate tax

不動產所有權　titles to real estate

不清潔提單　foul bill of lading, unclean bill of lading, dirty B/L

不累積股息　non-cumulative dividend

不累積循環信用證　non-cumulative revolving credit

不透水　water proof

不透水艙　water tight compartment

不透空氣　air proof

不發行股票　non-issuance of stock certificates

不發達國家　underdeveloped countries

不發達債務國　immature debtor nation

不發達債權國　immature creditor nation

不景氣　depression, slump, hard times

不景氣市場　soft market

不結滙　no exchange surrendered

不結滙進口簽證 imports without exchange settlement

不詳內容條款（載於提單上，對船方的免責條款） contents unknown clause

不當利益 illegal profit

不當特惠 undue preference

不當積累 improper accumulation

不過境 non-transit

不經濟 uneconomical

不認值資產，無清算值資產 inadmitted assets

不管損失比率照賠，單獨海損全賠 irrespective of percentage (I.O.P)

不填數副本 blind copy

不論已否滅失條款（指貨物的已否滅失） lost or not lost clause

不論取得貨物與否均須付款的合同 take-or-pay contract

不論是否同意 〔拉〕nolens volens

不論原因的一切險 all risks whatsoever

不履行 non-fulfilment

不履行支付 non-payment

不履行義務 default, subtraction

不確定性決策 uncertainty decisions

不適當包裝 unsuitable packing

不獨立分店會計制 dependent branch system, centralized branch system

不遵守條件 non-observance of terms

不虧不盈價格 breakeven price

不穩定的市場 queasy market

不穩定性投機 destabilizing speculation

不穩定股票 soft stock

不顧一切的投機家 plunger

不變成本 constant cost

不變美元價值 constant-dollar values

不變資本 constant capital

不變價格 constant price

互有過失之碰撞條款 both-to-blame collision clause

互相交易 reciprocal exchange

互相同意 mutual agreement

互相同意的檢驗報告 mutually agreed survey report

互相抵帳 mutual setting-off of debts

互相查對 mutual check

互相保險 mutual insurance

互相結合 mutual association

互相參照條款（指借款人對其中一個借貸協議違約時，另一個借貸協議亦同時構成違約） cross-reference clause

互助資金 mutual fund

互助資金公司 mutual fund company

互持股權 mutual holding, reciprocal holding

互通有無 mutual exchange of needed products

互買 reciprocal purchase

互惠 reciprocity

互惠互利協議 reciprocal and mutually advantageous arrangement

互惠合作　mutual benefit and collaboration

互惠信託基金　〔英〕unit trust, 〔美〕mutual fund

互惠信貸，互換信貸　credit swaps

互惠待遇　reciprocal treatment

互惠條約　reciprocal treaty

互惠條款　reciprocal clause

互惠通商政策　bargaining policy

互惠貿易　reciprocal trade

互惠貿易協定　reciprocal trade agreement

互惠貿易協定計劃　reciprocal trade agreement program

互惠協定關稅　bargaining tariff

互惠業務　reciprocity

互惠調整（指關稅）　reciprocal adjustment

互惠關稅　reciprocal duties

互換性（指期貨合約有互相替代的特性）　fungibility

互換協定　swap agreement

互賣　reciprocal sale

"五C"信用調查（參見"三C信用調查"條）"five C" credit invesigation

"五P"信用調查（"五P"指 personal, purpose, payment, protect, perspective 五個因素）"five P" credit invesigation

五大銀行（指英國五大銀行）　Big Five

五成折舊法　depreciation-fifty-percent method

五年計劃　five-year plan

天災　act of God, natural disasters

天然收成　fructus naturales

天然特權　natural privilege

天然港　natural harbour

天然產物　natural products

天然橡膠生產國協會 Association of Natural Rubber Producing Countries

切勿平放　never lay flat

切勿受潮　guard against wet

支付　pay, pay out, settle, disbursement

支付人　drawee

支付日　pay day, term day

支付日期　due date, date of payment

支付手段　medium of payment

支付命令　warrants, pay warrants

支付協定　payment agreement

支付股利　dividend warrants

支付股利保證金，股息單　dividend warrants

支付到期的票據　meet a bill

支付能力　ability to pay

支付票據　bills of payment

支付期票期限　usance

支付憑證　payment instrument

支出　disburse, expenditure, outgo, outlay

支出分配數　appropriation allotment

支出表　account of payments

支出帳目　account to give

支出清單　schedule of disbursement

支出項目　item of expenditure

支出單據　payment document

支出傳票 payment vouchers, payment slip

支出預算 appropriation budget

支出預算分類帳 appropriation ledger

支出憑證 pay order, disbursement voucher

支出憑證簿 book of original document for payments

支出應計制 accrued-expenditures basis

支出轉移政策(指貨幣對外貶值導致本國與外國的支出轉移至對本國產品的支出) expenditure-switching policies

支持價格 support price

支配性期貨(指未平倉合約數量最大的期貨) dominant future

支票 〔英〕cheque, 〔美〕check

支票支付 paying by check

支票卡 cheque card

支票出票人 cheque drawer

支票交易(指買銀行支票兌用後再還本付息) cheque trading

支票存根 check stubs

支票存款 check deposit, checking account

支票兌取 check collection

支票兌取人 check collector

支票兌現 check collection

支票利率 cheque rate

支票到期 maturing check

支票持票人 cheque holder

支票託收 check collection

支票帳戶 cheque accounts

支票掛失 cheque lost, check replacement

支票票面值 face of the value

支票貨幣 check-book money

支票清算路線標識 check routing symbol

支票登記簿 check register

支票傳送號碼 check transit number

支票填寫機 check writing machine

支票電託收(收到支票銀行把支票上的金額、地區、銀行和帳戶、支票號碼等信息，通過電訊手段輸送給付款銀行，付款銀行憑以借記客戶的支票帳戶) check truncation

支票磁性墨水識別碼(美國銀行支票下沿的一行奇特字體寫的磁性編碼) magnetic ink character recognition

支票簿 〔英〕cheque-book, 〔美〕check-book

支票簿存根 cheque-book stubs

支票簽字機 check signing machine

支撐困難工業 prop up ailing industries

木屑 saw dust

木條板箱 crate

木桶 cask

木箱 wooden case

尤格拉週期，中期商業週期 Juglar Cycle

尤萊克斯(由計算機輔助進行歐洲債券交易的一個系統，由盧森堡¨尤萊克斯SA¨經營) Eurex

[丨]

中小企業　small and medium-sized enterprise

中午市場　noon market

中木桶　cask

中止運輸(行使停運權)　stoppage in transit

中文電腦　Chinese Computer

中立國船舶　neutral ship

中立船舶證明書，航海證　sea letter

中央銀行　banker's bank, central bank

中位數　median

中和政策(指中央銀行為隔絕該國之貨幣供給受到國際資金流入或流出之影響所採取之行動)　sterilization

中性利率(指＂昂貴的星期四和星期五＂與＂低厘的週末＂的數量相互抵銷的這個時期的歐洲美元利率)　neutral (rate)

中東美元市場　mideast-dollar market

中、長期信貸　medium-term and long-term credit

中非關稅經濟同盟　Central African Customs and Economic Union (UDEAC)

中美洲共同市場　Central American Common Market (CACM)

中美洲自由貿易區　Central American Trade Area (CAFTA)

中美洲經濟合作委員會　Central American Economic Cooperation Committee

中度開發　intermediate in the scale of development

中度開發國家　intermediate developed country

中級品　middlings

中級會計師　semi-senior accountant

中國人民保險公司　People's Insurance Company of China

中國出口商品展覽會(又稱＂廣州交易會＂)　Chinese Export Commodities Fair, 又稱 Canton Fair

中國委員會(1952年成立的巴黎統籌委員會的一個附屬機構，用以加強對中國的＂禁運＂)　China Committee (CHICOM)

中國船舶檢驗局　The Register of Shipping of China

中國國際貿易促進委員會　China Council for the Promotion of International Trade

中國國際貿易促進委員會對外貿易仲裁委員會　Foreign Trade Arbitration Commission of the China Council for the Promotion of International Trade

中國銀行　Bank of China

中間收益　mesne profit

中間消費者　intermediate consumer

中間商　middleman, jobber

中間商人代理商　factor

中間商品　intermediate products, intermediate goods

中間產品　intermediate products

中間港，中途停泊港　intermediate port

中間稅　intermediate tax

中間貿易　intermediate trade

中間業主　mesne lord

中間滙率　medium rate of exchange

中間價格　middle price

中等的　moderate

中等品質　fair average quality

中等貨　middle class goods, medium quality

中等價格　medium-price

中期生產規劃預測　mid-term production-programming forecast

中期多種貨幣放款　medium-term multiple currency loans

中期貸款　medium-term loan

中期資本　medium-term capital

中期資金籌措　intermediate-term financing

中期債券　medium-term bonds

中期歐洲貸款市場　medium-term Eurocredit market

中號的　medium-sized

中標價格，投標價　tender price

中轉利息　transit interest

中轉港，轉運港　port of transshipment

中斷條款（指歐洲貨幣市場貸款契約中規定貸款銀行，在無法再自該市場取得資金時，得要求還款）break clause

中斷租讓合同　annul a concession agreement

中斷程序工業　interruptable process industry

中斷貿易　suspension of trade

中籤債券（以抽籤方式被選中償還的不記名債券）drawn bond

中欄分類帳　centre-ruled ledger

內生變量　endogenous variables

內包裝　internal packing, inner packing

內在付現成本　implicit cash cost

內在缺陷　inherent vice, inherent defect

內在流量　internal liqudity

內在報酬率　internal rate of return

內在價值，實質價值　intrinsic value

內地海關　inland customhouse

內地稅　inland duty

內含利息　implicit interest

內含利息收入　implicit interest revenue

內河航運　inland navigation

內河貨物運輸　carriage of goods by inland river

內河船舶保險　riverhull insurance

內河運輸保險　river transportation insurance

內陸水運　inland water-borne transportation

內陸水運提單　inland waterway B/L

內陸卸貨地點　inland place of discharge

內陸拼裝站　inland consolidation depot

內陸提單條款　inland bill of lading clause

內陸裝卸站　inland depot

內陸運費　inland freight

內陸運輸　inland transportation

內部人員交易（利用內部或特享信息以在市場交易中贏利）　insider trading

內部收益率法（使投資項目的淨現值等於零的折現率，又稱現金流量貼現法）　internal rate of return method (discount cash flow method)

內部回報率（投資者擁有期內投資所能產生按現值計算的回報收益率）　internal rate of return

內部自動審核制度　system of automatic internal audit

內部估價　internal valuation

內部協議　internal arrangement

內部信息　internal information

內部負債　interior liabilities

內部核心貿易　internal core trade

內部報酬率，內含報酬率　internal rate of return

內部資料　internal data

內部會計　internal accounting

內部會計事項　internal transaction

內部運輸　internal transportation

內債（指國家的）　internal debt

內部審計　internal auditing, management audit

內部審計師　certified internal auditor

內幕交易　insider trading

內燃機火車　diesel engine locomotive

日內限額（在交易日內允許外滙經營商持有每一種和各種貨幣頭寸的限額）　intra-day limit

日元基準　Yen base

日元債券　Yenbond

日本工業標準　Japanese Industrial Standard — JIS

日本公債研究所（日本公認的債券評級機構）　Japan Bond Research Institute

日本商事仲裁協會　Japan Commercial Arbitration Association

日本農林規格　Japanese Agricultural Standard — JAS

日本貿易振興會　Japan External Trade Organization

日本預託證券　Japanese Depositary Receipts

日本電氣學會規格　Japanese Electrotechnical Standard — JES

日用品　day-to-day goods, undurable goods, consumer goods, articles in everyday use

日拆　daily money

日夜商店　day-and-night shop

日息　interest per diem

日記帳　journal, day book

日記總帳，日記一分類聯合帳　combined journal and ledger

日率　per diem rate

日結（香港期貨市場為客戶入市後，

會員公司為其每日計算出的賺蝕紀錄） mark to market

日常費用 current expenses, running expenses

日常過帳 day-to-day posting

日常審計 daily audit

日報 daily report

日期填早 dating forward, ante-dating

日期戳記 date mark

日落預算法（係 " 零基預算法 " 之別稱） sunset budgeting

日曆日 calendar day

日曆月 calendar month

日曆年度 calendar year

[丿]

斤（中國市斤 = 0.5 公斤，東南亞斤 = 0.6 公斤） catty

什一稅 tithe

欠人 he trusts, balance due to, balance due others

欠付催繳股款 calls in arrears

欠交訂貨,延交訂貨 back order

欠交訂貨通知單 back order memo

欠交稅款 back duty

欠政府的債 crown debts

欠息 debit interest

欠租 back rent

欠條、借據 "IOU", I owe you

欠帳 outstanding debts

欠單 accommodation kite

欠單交易（即欺詐交易，通常是交易

者協助他人進行的非法買賣） accommodation trading

欠款 debt, arrears

欠款金額證明書 certificate of amount owing

欠款通知 debet memo

欠稅人 defaulter of tax

欠發股利 dividends in arrears

欠發達國家 less developed countries

欠債 owe

欠薪 back salary

公寸 decimetre

公丈 decametre

公分 gramme

公尺 metre

公斤 kilogramme

公升 liters

公引,百米 hectometre

公允反映（審計常用語，表示企業財務報表所使用會計原則與公認會計原則相符合） fair presentation

公允表達 fair presentation

公平工資 fair wages

公平分擔原則 principle of equitable burden-sharing

公平市價 fair market price

公平交易 fair trade, fair dealing

公平交易法 fair trade law

公平利潤 fair profit

公平利潤率 fair rate of profit

公平報酬 fair return

公平價格 fair price

公平價值 fair value

公平競爭 fair competition

公平權益　equitable interest

公司　company, corporation

公司內部價格　intracompany price, intracorporate price

公司分配股份通知書　letter of allotment

公司合併　amalgamation of company

公司利潤率與股東自有資本比率　ratio of profits to stockholder's equity

公司股本　capital stock

公司法　law of corporation, company's act

公司所得稅　corporation income tax

公司政策　corporation policy

公司財政　corporation finance

公司財產　company property

公司條例　companies act

公司盈餘　book surplus, corporate surplus

公司間內部盈餘　intercompany profit

公司間利益　inter-company profits

公司間往來帳　inter-company accounts

公司間費用　inter-company expenses

公司組織大綱　memorandum of association

公司章程　〔英〕articles of association，〔美〕articles of incorporation

公司章程附則　by-law

公司執照　licence of incorporation

公司發起人　company promoter

公司債券　corporation securities, debenture bond

公司債股利　bond dividends

公司債應募人　subscribers

公司董事所作虛偽的報告　false statements by company directors

公司模型　company models

公司標準　company standard

公司證書　certificate of incorporation, corporation charter

公司縱向推銷系統(作為一個單位進行運轉的公司集團，為降低推銷一種或一類貨物所產生的費用而作的縱向聯合)　corporate vertical marketing system

公正無誤　"even and quit"

公共支出決策　public expenditure decisions

公共企業　government enterprise

公共投資　public investment(s)

公共投資計劃　public investment program

公共受託人　public trustee

公共基金　public fund

公共密碼　public code

公共運輸人　common carrier

公共衛生法例　Public Health Act

公共機構　public office

公共機構投資者　institutional investors

公共機構專用認購債券(美國術語，指由證券機構經理人員抽取證券的一定百分比，專供大的公共機構認

購） institutional pot

公共關係,公關 public relations

公共關係部 public relations department

公式投資(當證券價格漲到一定水平,把普通股轉為優先股或公債;而當證券價格一跌時,再把它轉回普通股的投資方法) formula investing

公式翻譯程序語言 FORTRAN (formula translation 的縮寫)

公有財產 government property

公有財產審計 audit of public property

公里 kilometer

公佈的股利 declared dividend

公制 metric system

公兩 hectogramme

公定價格 public price

公海 international sea

公益 public interest

公益金 public welfare fund

公益信託 charitable trusts, public trust

公頃(合十五畝) hectare

公開一般許可證 open general license

公開公司(指股份為多數人所持有,並在市場上公開買賣股份的公司) open corporation

公開分類帳 open ledger

公開市場 public market

公開市場干預活動 open market interventions

公開市場政策 open market policy

公開市場信用 open market credit

公開市場採購 open market purchase

公開市場操作 open market operation

公開市場滙率 open market rate

公開投資公司,股份不定投資公司 open-end investment company

公開投標 open bidding, public bidding

公開拍賣 sell by public auction

公開招標 public tender

公開限期進口許可證 open end import license

公開訊問債務人 public examination of debtor

公開借款 public borrowing

公開帳戶 open account

公開通貨膨脹 open inflation

公開開標 public bid opening

公開發行有價證券 public issues

公開喊價 open outcry

公開報價 public offer

公開買賣 market overt

公開債券 public bonds

公開賣出(將政府債券賣給交易商,用以減少銀行準備金,降低債券價格及調高利率。相對詞為"公開購入") outright sales

公開審計 public audit

公開銷售證券 public offering

公開購入 outright purchase

公開儲備 open reserve

公開競投 competitive bidding

公開競爭　open competition
公設市場　public market
公報　official gazette
公絲　milligram
公款　public money
公眾利益　public interest
公眾妨害　public mischief
公寓招租　apartments to let
公債　public debt, government bond
公債交易　public debt transaction
公債利息　bond yields
公債到期　matured bonds
公債條例　regulations regarding the public debt
公債基金　bonds funds
公債帳戶　bonds account
公債貨幣化(政府將公債交銀行承受，於是財政部在銀行的存款增加)　monetization of the debt
公債發行　public subscription
公債換新　refunding
公債償還　refunding of bond
公債償還資金　public debts redemption
公認資本　authorized capital
公認會計準則　generally accepted accounting principles
公認審計準則　generally accepted auditing principles
公賣　public sale
公噸　metric ton
公錢　decagram
公擔　quintal
公積金　superannuation fund

公營公司　public company
公營經濟事業　public economic enterprise
公斷人　umpire, arbitrator
公斷書　award
公斷裁定　award
公證人　notary, notary public
公證人的證明簽署　notarial acts
公證手續　notarial acts
公證委託書　letter of commitment
公證制度　notary system
公證律師　qualified notary
公證商　superintendent
公證執業會計師　certified public accountant
公證執業管理會計師　certified management accountant
公證證書　notarial deed
公釐　milimetre
分公司，子公司　constituent company
分支代理　subagent
分支組織　branch organization
分出未滿期責任　portfolio ceded
分出再保險　outward reinsurance
分包市場　jobber market
分包商　sub-contractor
分代理　sub-agent
分列(帳戶)　fanout
分合同　sub-contract
分批生產　job production
分批成本，定單成本　order cost
分批成本分類帳　job cost ledger
分批成本計算法　job costing

分批成本單　job cost sheet

分批成本會計　job order cost accounting

分批交貨　partial shipment

分批交貨合同　installment contract

分批折舊　job depreciation

分批法　lot method

分批到貨　split delivery

分批債券　multiple tranche bonds

分批裝船　instalment shipment

分批裝運　partial shipment

分批購買　installment buying

分批償還債券　serial bonds

分步成本計算法　process costing

分步成本會計　process cost accounting

分利式遠期外滙買賣（指客戶與銀行分享所獲贏利的一種遠期外滙買賣和期權結合在一起的做法）　the participating forward

分利優先股　profit participating preferred stock

分派　allotment, apportionment

分派紅利通知書　allotment letter, dividend allotment notice

分（支）店分類帳　branch ledger

分（支）店往來帳　branch office current

分（支）店統制帳戶　branch control account

分（支）店報告　branch office report

分（支）店會計　branch accounting

分店經理　branch manager

分享市場　sharing the market

分享股權貸款　shared equity loan

分股制　stock ownership

分析性成本計算　analytical costing

分析會計學　analytical accounting

分析證明書　certificate of analysis

分保（保險人將所承保保險金額的一部份或全部轉移給其他保險公司，將所得保險費一部份分給分保接受人，亦稱再保險）　reinsurance

分保手續費　reinsurance commission

分保合同　reinsurance treaty

分保安排　placement of reinsurance

分保接受人，再保險人　reinsurer

分保責任準備金　reinsurance reserve

分紅　distribute bonus

分紅利　profit sharing

分紅制　profit sharing scheme

分段利差（歐洲信貸的利率超出LIBOR的利差）　split spread

分段責任制，網狀賠償責任制　network liability system

分段製造費用成本計算　multistep overhead costing

分租　sub-letting

分配　distribute, allocation

分配系統　distributing system

分配係數　distribution coefficient

分配通知書　allotment note

分配通路　distribution channel

分配資金　distribution of fund

分配網　distribution network

分息債券　split-coupon bond

分級運費率　class rates

分部成本　departmental cost

分部直接成本　direct departmental expense

分部會計　departmental accounting

分部邊際貢獻　departmental margin

分組折舊　group depreciation

分組試算，分組結平　sectional balancing

分組資產負債表　sectional balance sheet

分割索取(債項)　splitting of claims

分散分店會計制，獨立分店會計制 decentralized branch accounting, independent branch accounting system

分散定貨　split order

分散資金　proliferation of funds

分期支付的保險費　instalment premium

分期付款　instalment, instalment payment, progressive payment

分期付款中每期應付款付訖　instalment paid

分期付款中最後一筆特大付款　balloon payment

分期付款收據　instalment scrip, instalment receipt

分期付款制　instalment basis

分期付款制會計　instalment basis accounting

分期付款契約　instalment contracts

分期付款信貸　instalment credit

分期付款計劃　instalment plan

分期付款條款　instalment payment clause

分期付款第一期　instalment

分期付款貿易法　instalment trading

分期付款買賣法例　Hire-Purchase Act

分期付款滙票　bill payable by stated instalments

分期付款賒銷　instalment credit selling

分期付款銷售　instalment sale

分期付款銷售　instalment selling

分期付款購買　［英］hire purchase, ［美］instalment buying

分期付款購銷制　instalment systems

分期交貨　delivery by instalments

分期或延期付款債券　partly paid and deferred payment bonds

分期債券　deferred purchase bonds

分期定額折舊法 depreciation-fixed-installment method

分期開單(在一段時期而不是立即向客戶寄出報表的制度)　cycle billing

分期遞減法　reducing installment method

分期認繳股款簿　subscription instalment book

分期還本付息　instalment and interest charges

分期償還債券　instalment bonds

分期攤付　instalment

分期攤還借款　amortization loan

分單位利潤　divisional profit

分單位報表　divisional report

分提單，小提單　delivery order (D/O)

分層抽樣　stratified sampling

分銷集團　selling group

分攤　share ratably

分攤抵押　contributory mortgage

分攤過失　contributory negligence

分錄，記錄　entry, journal entry

分錄憑單　journal voucher

分錄說明　narration

分類日記帳　ledger journal

分類目錄　catalogue raisonne

分類目錄解釋規則　rule for the interpretation of the nomenclature

分類成本制度　class cost system, classified system

分類財務報表　classified financial statement

分類帳　ledger, ledger accounts

分類帳直接轉帳法　ledger transfer

分類帳面資產　ledger assets

分類統制帳　ledger control

分類試算表　classified trial balance

分類費率　class rate

分類廣告　classified advertisement

分類說明　classification manual

(聯產品)分離前成本　before-separation cost

分離後成本　after-separation cost

分攤成本　apportioned cost

分攤配額　allocated quota

分攤稅　apportioned tax

分攤費用　apportioned charges

化為資本　capitalisation

化學分析　chemical analysis

化驗證明　certificate of analysis

手(期貨交易單位)　lot

手工記錄，手工登記　hand-kept

手工勞動　hand labour, manual labour

手工業　handcraft industry

手工藝品　workmanship, articles of handicraft

手段　means

手續　procedure, formality

手續費　costs of formalities, charge for trouble

升水　premium

升值　appreciate

升級條款(契約一方由於成本費用大幅增加，可要求調整合同規定的貨幣數額，作為承擔不合理經濟負擔的一種補救措施)　escalation clause

升華　sublimate into

升達限幅　limit rise, limit up

牛市，多頭市場　bull market

牛皮紙袋　kraft paper bag

牛肉多邊結構協定　Multilateral Framework Agreement of Bovine

月末放款　ultimo loans

月份彙總表　monthly summary

月度分攤數　monthly allotment

月度財務報表，月結表　monthly financial statement

月率　rate per mensem

月終結賬分錄　monthly closing entry

月報　monthly report

月結單　monthly statement

丹尼爾(絲和纖維的纖度單位，重1克長9000公尺為1丹尼爾)　denier

反中介作用(指從金融中介機構提取資金以便直接在金融市場上購買債券的現象)　disintermediation

反向支付(歸還)　reverse payments

反向技術轉讓　reverse transfer of technology

反向持股公司(幾家銀行可共同擁有一家服務子公司的所有權)　reverse holding company

反向兼併(指企業合併後，由較小企業管理合併後的企業)　reverse takeover

反向浮息對沖合約　inverse floating rate hedging instrument

反向貿易　countertrade

反向購買　counter purchase

反向優惠　reverse preference

反托拉斯法　law of anti-trust

反行銷　countermarketing

反面舉證責任　reversed burden of proof

反要求　cross-demand

反要約　counter-offer

反契據　counter-deed

反衰退政策　anti-recession policy

反索償, 反訴　counterclaim

反控　cross-action

反商(除盡為1之數，以其對數相乘得1之數)　reciprocal

反週期政策　anti-cyclical policy

反補貼稅　anti-subsidy duties, countervailing duty

反傾銷　anti-dumping

反傾銷法　anti-dumping act, anti-dumping law

反傾銷政策　anti-dumping policy

反傾銷控告　anti-dumping complaint

反傾銷規則　anti-dumping rules

反傾銷稅　anti-dumping duty

反傾銷訴訟　anti-dumping case

反傾銷調查　anti-dumping investigation

反彈作用　boomering effects

反購規則(交易所規定，到期未交付的股票可由銷售人重新購回)　buying-in regulation

"反濺"效果(亦稱"回波作用"，見該條註釋)　"back wash" effect

反覆換錢　ringing the changes

毛收益率　gross yield

毛利　gross margin, gross profit

毛利率　gross-margin ratio, gross profit ratio

毛利測驗法　gross profit test

毛重　gross weight

毛保險費　gross premium

毛損　gross loss

毛價, 總價　gross price

毛噸位　gross tonnage

勿受潮濕　keep dry

及時性　timeliness

允收品質水準 acceptable quality level

允許的限度 permissible limit

允許分運 partial shipment is permitted

允許轉運 transshipment is permitted

介紹信，推薦信 letter of recommendation

介紹費 middleman fee, procuration

勻期股利 equalizing dividend

勻銷 write off

午盤 noon market

[ㄱ]

比氏吃水線 plimsoll lines

比例 rate

比例分攤 pro rata distribution

比例平等條款(國際融資的標準條款，指借款人的直接的、無擔保的、一般的、無條件的債務，在這些債務之間以及在借款人的其他無擔保權益的債務之間，其清償的次序，按比例平等原則平等排列) pari passu covenant

比例責任再保險 quota share reinsurance

比例稅 proportional tax

比率 ratio

比率分析 ratio analysis

比率不變投資 constant-ratio investment

比率推算法(審計的一種抽樣方法) ratio estimation

比率對沖(在財務期貨交易過程中，通常指期貨對現貨相應比率的計算) ratio hedging

比荷盧關稅聯盟 Benelux Custom Union

比較分析 comparative analysis

比較成本 comparative cost

比較成本定律 the law of comparative cost

比較成本差異 comparative cost difference

比較成本說 comparative cost doctrine

比較利益 comparative advantage

比較財務報表 comparative financial statement

比較國際會計 comparative international accounting

比較最大利益 comparative advantage

比較損益表 comparative income account, comparative profit and loss statement

比較廣告 comparative advertising

比較靜態均衡分析 comparative static equilibrium analysis

比價 comparative price

引伸產品 augmented product

引進外國投資 introduction of foreign investment

引進外資 introduce foreign capital

巴克萊卡(英國巴克萊銀行發行的信用卡，它與美國〝簽證卡〞和法國的〝籃卡〞有密切聯繫) Barclays

Card

巴克萊 B 單位（指 Barclay Bank 融通國際貿易所使用之單位為 US$ 2.4、FFR11.5、SFR7.00、£ ST、GL、 DMK6.00 之 和）Barclays B-Unit

巴拿馬運河航線　Via Panama Canal Shipping Line

巴爾的摩 C 式租約格式　Baltimore Form C

巴爾的摩定期租船合同格式　Baltime

巴爾特紙漿租約格式　Baltpulp

巴爾特煤運租約格式　Baltcon

巴黎俱樂部　Paris Club

巴黎統籌委員會　Coordinating Committee for Export Controls (COCOM)

巴黎證券交易所　Paris Bourse

巴融信心指數（是衡量股票和債券投資者動向的指標，用 10 家信用等級最高公司的債券收益，除以 10 家中等等級公司債券，再乘以 100）Barron's Confidence Index

尺寸不足　short size

尺寸過大　over size

尺碼　measurement

尺碼搭配　size assortment

水尺計重（按船舶吃水的深度計算貨物的重量）　checking weight by draft

水平分析　horizontal analysis

水平貿易（經濟發展水平大抵相同國家間的貿易）　horizontal trade

水分　moisture

水災，洪水　flood

水災保險，洪水保險　flood insurance

水損　damage by water

水腳　freight

水雷和魚雷險　mine and torpedo risks

水運　water way transport

水運條款（指對陸上危險不保）water-borne clause

水漬　water damage, water stain

水漬貨　water damaged cargo

水漬險　with particular average (W.P.A 或 W.A)

水翼船　hydrofoil

水壓機打包　hydraulic press packing

少分配製造費用　underabsorbed burden, underapplied manufacturing overhead

少數股權　minority holding

少數股權股東　minority stockholders

少數權益　minority interest

五　畫

［、］

市（股票市場的開市）　session

市內運送　city terminal service

市況　tone of the market

市況看跌　bearish tone

市政公債　municipal bond

市政會計　municipal accounting

市面冷淡　dull market

市面呆滯　stagnant market, sick market

市面凋零　sagging market

市面清淡　depressed market

市面興旺　booming market

市面蕭條　hard times

市值，市價　market value

市集　bazaar

市場　market, market place, market hall

市場人心　market feeling, market sentiment

市場力量　market forces

市場上可能達到的需求量　potential demand of the market

市場上受歡迎的產品　market is receptive to products

市場上的買空賣空　speculation on the rise and fall of the market

市場干預　market intervention

市場不完全性　imperfections in markets

市場分析　market analysis

市場分配　market sharing

市場分割　market segmentation

市場支配力(指少數買主或賣主影響商品價格的能力)　market power

市場主持者(願意隨時論價買賣某一資產或不斷大量經營某一資產的機構)　market maker

市場可供商品量　availability in market supplies

市場功能　marketing function

市場行銷觀念　market concept

市場份額　market share

市場吸收能力　market absorption

市場佔有率　market share

市場利率　market rate of interest

市場利率低　easiness of money market

市場走勢　market behaviour

市場呆滯　heavy market

市場狂熱　superheating

市場供求情況　market supply-and-demand situation

市場供應緊張　strained market supply

市場明朗度，市場透明度　market transparency

市場波動　market fluctuations

市場阻塞(指市場擠迫現象。空倉雖欲補回，但願套現多倉者不多，亦無新沽家落場)　market congestion

市場定單(以現場內可能取得的任一價格買入或賣出期貨合約的定單)　market order

市場和銷售系統　market and marketing system

市場金融　market finance

市場信息　market information

市場活動　marketing activity

市場活躍　market active

市場政策　marketing policy
市場計劃　marketing plan
市場風險　market risk
市場氣氛　market sentiment
市場氣候　market climate
市場疲跌　bearish market
市場展望　market outlook
市場容量　capacity of the market, market absorption capacity
市場流動性　market liquidity
市場細分　market segments
市場情況　market conditions
市場研究　market research
市場研究與分析銷售潛力　market research and analyze sales potential
市場混亂　market disruption, market chaotic
市場採購　market purchasing
市場稅　lastage, lestage
市場報告, 市況報告　market report
市場發展　market development
市場策略　marketing strategy
市場貼現率　market discount rate
市場結構　market structure
市場堅穩　steady market
市場損失　loss of market
市場業務　marketing function
市場預測　market forecasting
市場滙率　market rate of exchange
市場試銷　test marketing
市場經濟　market economy
市場經濟國家　market economy country

市場劃分　market segmentation
市場需求　market demand
市場需求價格　market demand price
市場銀根鬆　easiness of money market
市場製造者(歐洲債券二級市場參加者向零星顧客標買入賣出價，並可接受任何一種方向的交易)　market makers
市場滲透訂價　market-penetration pricing
市場潛在需求量　market potential
市場概況　market profile
市場價差保證金　market difference margin
市場價格　market price
市場價格變動準備金　reserve for market fluctuation
市場價值　market-value
市場銷售研究　marketing research
市場銷售問題　marketing problem
市場銷售理論　marketing theory
市場銷售管理　marketing management
市場調查　market survey, market research
市場調節　regulation through the market
市場調節器　regulator of the market
市場漲價　appreciation
市場學　marketing
市場聯合　market combination
市場機制　market mechanism

市場蕭條　dull market

市場戰略模擬　marketing strategy simulation

市場操縱　market dominance

市場擴張　market expansion

市場繁榮　brisk market

市場禮遇　market hospitality

市場競爭　market competition

市價　market price, market value

市價比較法　relative market values method

市價正下降　market declining

市價正上漲　market advancing

市價法（指聯合成本的分配）　market price method

市價單（依落訂單時最接近的交易市價成交之指令單，香港稱〝市場定單〞）　market order

市價變動　fluctuation

市場體系　marketing system

永久可重新簽訂的租約　perpetually renewable lease

永久收益　permanent income

永久投資　permanent investment

永久居所原則　principle of permanent residence

永久性協定　permanent agreement

永久性財產　permanent property

永久性籌資　permanent financing

永租權　perpetual lease

永久貸款　perpetual loan

永久資本　permanent capital

永久資產　permanent assets

永久債券　perpetual debentures

永久轉讓　permanent transfer

永續年金，終身年金　perpetual annuity, perpetuities

永續預算　perpetual budget

永續盤存　continuous inventory, perpetual inventory

永續盤存制　perpetual inventory system, balance of stock

永續盤存帳戶　perpetual inventory account

永續實地盤存制度　continuous system of physical inventory

立方公分　cubic centimeters

立方公尺　cubic meters

立方英寸　cubic inches

立方英尺　cubic feet

立方英碼　cubic yards

立即支付的票據　bill payable on demand

立即付現　immediate cash payment

立即付款　at-once-payment

立即交貨　prompt delivery

立即追索　immediate recourse

立即裝船（一個月內）　immediate shipment

立即賠償　immediate compensation

立足收益表之壞帳估計法　income statement approach of estimating uncollectible accounts

立約　make treaty

立約者　contracting party

立約保險　underwrite risks

立章程　to make regulation

立期票　fixing the date of payment

of note

主目標　major heading

主合同　main contract

主任會計師　accountant in charge, in-charge accountant

主約　master contract

主計部　controller's department

主計權責　controllership

主航道　principal channel

主要世界貨幣　major world currencies

主要代理商　main agent

主要市場　staple market, leading market

主要成本　prime cost

主要成本法(指負荷分配的方法)　prime cost method

主要收益　primary income

主要私產權　major regalia

主要技術數據　main technical details

主要附表　leading schedule

主要股東　principal shareholder

主要訂約商　prime contractor

主要負債人　primary debtor

主要港口　main ports

主要帳戶　main account, principal account

主要帳簿　principal book

主要產品　main products, major products, staple products

主要商品批發商　stapler

主要設備　major installation

主要貨幣　principal currency, main currency

主要貿易區　principal trade partners

主要統計值　major total

主要勢差　principal moment

主要嘜頭　main mark

主要標記　main mark

主要關鍵部件　major critical component

主要證據　primary evidence

主管　the boss, the chief

主管官員　officer-in-charge

主管機關　the authorities concerned

主辦　to sponsor

主顧　customer

主權　equity, potestas

主權比率　equity ratio

主權資本　equity capital

主觀的領域原則(指一個國家對於在本國領土內受法律禁止的行為, 即使其影響是在本國領土之外, 也有權依法予以制裁)　subjective territorial principle

半日制　half-day system

半生(美國術語, 指償還大宗債券本金數額的一半之前必須經過的時間)　half-life

半加工的　half black

半平均數　semi-average

半包裝　semi-packed

半自動化　semi-automatic

半自動信息轉接站　semi-automatic message switching centre

半自動控制　semi-automatic control

半官方的　semiofficial

半年一期的分期付款　semi-annual instalments

半年年息　semi-annual coupon

半年的　semiyearly

半年度　semi-annual

半年度報告　semi-annual report

半年保險費　half-yearly premium

半成品　half finished goods

半固定成本　semifixed cost

半耐用品　semi-durable goods

半封閉海　semi-closed sea

半破產狀態　semi-bankruptcy

半掛車　semi-trailer

半專門貿易（指貿易總額減去再出口總額）　semi-special trade

半通貨膨脹　semi-inflation

半貨櫃／集裝箱　semi-container

半貨櫃／集裝箱船　semi-container ship

半稅　half-duty

半週平均值　half-period average value

半就業，半失業　semi-employed

半發達國家　semi-developed nation

半經紀人（股票市場中為經紀人介紹生意，從中賺取佣金的人）half-commission man

半製成品　semifinished product, semi-manufactured goods

半精裝　half binding

半價出售　selling at half price

半熟練工人　semi-skilled labour

半機械化　semi-mechanization

半變動成本　semi-variable cost, partly variable cost

必要生活資料　necessary means of livelihood

必要生產資料　necessary means of production

必要最低利潤　necessary minimum profit

必然發生的成本　inescapable costs

必需品　requirements

［一］

打　dozen

打包　packing, pack up

打包人　packer

打包放款　packing credit

打包信用證，預支信用證　packing credit

打包條款　packing clause

打包商　packer

打包機器　packing press

打開包裝　unpacking

打撈　refloat, salvage

打撈工程　refloating operation

打撈公司　salvage company

打撈船　salvor

打蘭，英錢（衡量單位：常衡 = 1/16 盎斯，合 1.771 克；藥衡 = 1/8 盎斯，合 3.887 克；液量打蘭 = fluidram = 1/8 fluid 盎斯）dram

本人追認代理人所訂合同　ratification of agents' contracts

本地土產　native products

本地批發　local wholesale
本地信用證　local credit
本地貿易　local trade
本年度　current year
本年純益　net profit current year
本年盈餘　surplus for current year
本利　principal and interest, capital and interest
本位貨幣　standard coin, standard money
本金　principal
本金支付機構(歐洲債券術語。指有責任從借款人收取本息並付給最後投資者的銀行)　principal paying agent
本財政年度　current fiscal year
本息票　coupon
本票　promissory note, cashier's check, cashier's order
本國化商品　nationalized product
本國產品出口　national export
本國貨幣滙票　home currency bill
本國製的　home-make
本期　current period
本期生產成本　manufacturing cost for the period
本期收益　current income
本期利息　current interest
本期利潤　profit of the period
本期投資　current investment
本期純利　net profit of the term
本期盈餘　current surplus
本期貨幣性流動資產　current monetary assets

本期損益　current profit and loss
本期營業損益表　current operating income statement
本價　original price
本質性爆炸　inherent explosion
未入帳收入　unrecorded revenue
未入帳存款　unrecorded deposit
未入帳負債　unrecorded liabilities
未入帳費用　unrecorded expenses
未了責任到期滿為止　running off of a portfolio
未上市證券　unlisted securities
未分派利潤　undivided profit
未分配收入　unapplied income
未分配成本　unabsorbed cost
未分配利潤　undistributed profit
未分配利潤稅　tax on undistributed profit
未分配盈餘　undivided surplus
未分配費用　unapplied expenses
未支配預計盈餘額　unappropriated estimated surplus
未支配餘額　unencumbered balance
未平倉合約(香港指未通過抵銷或交代套現之合約數)　open interest
未加工的　in the rough
未付已宣佈股利　unpaid declared dividend
未付工資　unpaid wages
未付支票　unpaid check
未付到期負債　matured liabilities unpaid
未付紅利　unclaimed dividend
未付股本　unpaid stock

未付票據　unpaid bill

未付費用　unpaid expenses

未付資本　unpaid up capital

未付資本帳　unpaid up capital account

未收回成本　unrecovered cost

未收股款　uncalled capital, uncalled shares

未收保費　uncollected premium

未收貨款的賣主　unpaid seller

未收資本　uncalled capital

未成品　unfinished product

未列項目，無其他規定者　not otherwise provided for

未冲銷，未拋補，未保障　uncovered

未決賠款　losses outstanding

未決賠款準備金　reserve for outstanding losses

未完成工程　uncompleted project construction

未完成的合同　uncompleted contract

未完成的訂貨　open order

未完成會計事項　uncompleted transaction

未完成履行的契約　uncompleted contract

未完結交易　open trade

未吸收成本　unabsorbed cost

未吸收費用　unabsorbed expenses

未兌現支票　outstanding cheque, uncashed checks

未折舊原價餘額　undepreciated balance of the cost

未折舊價值，折餘價值　undepreciated value

未軋平頭寸　open position

未來市場　future market

未來成本　future cost

未來行為　future behaviour

未受委託的代理人　negotiorum gestor

未抵押資產　unmortgaged assets, unpledged assets

未卸貨物　goods afloat

未到商品帳戶　goods to arrive account

未到期保險　unexpired insurance

未到期債務　unmatured debts

未到價合約(指期權交易中，預定價高於當時市價之延買期權或預定價低於當時市價之延賣期權)　out-of the money

未押滙信用狀　non-restricted L/C

未查出的誤差　undetected error

未指定用途的現金　unapplied cash

未保留歲出　unencumbered appropriation

未指撥盈餘　unappropriated surplus, free surplus

未能收回的成本　unrecovered cost

未消耗成本　unexpired cost

未清欠帳　open debt

未清股票分割　split

未清借款餘額　outstanding balance of borrowed money

未清帳　open account, unliquidated account

未清算帳目　outstandings

未清償債務　unliquidated claim, unliquidated debt

未清儲備貨幣結餘的整理 consolidation of outstanding reserve currency balances

未得到的收入　unearned revenue, unearned income

未得標商　unsuccessful bidder

未開發國家　undeveloped countries

未掛牌證券　unlisted security

未結平帳戶　open account

未結清期貨合同　open position

未結清權益（指買、賣的期貨合同尚未通過賣出、買進同月份期貨合同而沖銷的權益）　open interest

未發行股本　unissued capital stock

未發行抵押債券　unissued mortgage bonds

未發行債券　unissued bond

未發貨訂單　unfilled orders

未發累積股利　accumulated dividends

未發覺的損失　undiscovered loss

未註明貨種及卸貨港的租船合同 open charter

未貶值貨幣　underpreciated currency

未過期保險費　insurance premium unexpired

未經背書支票　unindorsed check

未解除債務之破產人　undischarged bankrupt

未催繳股本　uncalled capital

未催繳股款　uncalled subscriptions

未領工資　unclaimed wages

未領股利　unclaimed dividends

未滿期保費　portfolio premium

未滿期責任　portfolio assumed

未滿期業務轉出　portfolio withdrawal

未滿期業務轉移　portfolio transfer

未滿載貨櫃／集裝箱　less than container load

未認購股本　unsubscribed capital stock

未認購股本帳戶　unsubscribed capital stock account

未認繳股本　pending subscriptions

未撥用盈餘　uncommitted surplus, unrestricted surplus

未確定損害賠償額　unliquidated damages

未確認信用證　unconfirmed letter of credit

未審核之財務報表 unaudited financial statement

未實現收益　unrealized income

未實現利潤　unrealized profit

未實現資產增價準備　reserve for unrealized increment in assets

未撤銷前有效　good-till-cancelled

未調整借項　unadjusted debits

未調整貸項　unadjusted credits

未擔保剩餘價值　unguaranteed residual value

未償外債　outstanding external debt

未償清長期債款的折扣　unextinguished discount on funded debt

未償貸款　outstanding loan

未償貸款總額　outstanding loan portfolio

未償債務　outstanding debt

未償債權　unliquidated claims

未償擔保信貸　outstanding guarantee credit

未償還提款　outstanding drawing

未繳股本　unpaid-up capital

未攤銷費用　unamortized expense

未攤銷債券折價　bond discount unamortized

未攤銷債券溢價　bond premium unamortized

可分之購股權證　detachable stock warrants

可分派利益　distributive profits

可分配間接費用　assignable indirect charge

可分開契約　severable contract

可分割信用證　divisible credit

可分散風險　diversifiable risk, unsystematic risk

可分屬成本　separable cost

可比性　comparability

可比性概念　comparability concept

可比產品成本　costs of comparable products

可比價格　comparable prices

可支配所得　disposable income

可支配的個人收入　disposable personal income

可支配資金　amount of funds avail-

able for distribution

可可生產國聯盟　Cocoa Producers' Alliance

可用收入　available income

可用作支付股息的利潤　profit available for dividend

可用法律來強制執行的　enforceable at law

可用盈餘　available surplus

可用現金　available cash

可用資金　expendable fund

可用資產　available assets

可用餘額　available balance

可另有保險　other insurance permitted

可加抵押　open-end mortgage

可立即變現資產　quick assets

可以受理的抗辯　admissible plea

可代替的物件　fungibles

可再生產的貨物，可複製的貨品　reproducible goods

可自由支配的收入　discretionary income

可自由支配的開支　discretionary spending

可自由支配的購買力　discretionary purchasing power

可自由動用的收入　disposable income

可自由動用的資本　disposable capital

可自由選擇結算方法　optional modes of settlement

可自動展期存款　automatic renewable deposit

可自動展期貸款　automatic renewable credit

可收回支出　recoverable expenditure

可收回成本　recoverable cost

可收回損失　recoverable loss

可收回價值　recoverable value

可收回優先股　redeemable preferred stock

可在交易所流通　negotiable on the stock exchange

可行性初步研究　pre-feasibility study

可行性標準　standards of feasibility

可行競爭　workable competition

可交付品級(指期貨合同執行交付商品的品級)　deliverable grade, tenderable grade

可交收存貨(指存放在交易所認可倉庫內的存貨，可用該倉庫之收據作交收合約指定之期貨)　deliverable stocks

可交持票人　payable to bearer

可兌換性　convertibility

可兌換放款　convertible loan

可兌換美元債券　dollar convertible debenture

可兌換帳戶　convertible accounts

可兌換黃金的美元短期債券　short-term claims against U.S. gold

可兌換紙幣　convertible paper currency, convertible notes, redeemable paper money

可兌換貨幣　convertible currency, convertible notes

可兌換債券　convertible debenture, convertible bond

可折舊資產之變賣　disposal of depreciable assets

可折疊集裝箱　collapsible container

可承兌性　acceptability

可供分配股利之利潤　profit available for dividend

可供自己支配的資金　funds for use at one's own discretion

可供銷售商品成本　cost of goods available for sales

可供銷售商品數量　volume of marketable goods

可供選擇的方針　alternation policy

可宣告破產的行為　available act of bankruptcy

可保價值　insurable value

可保險權益　insurable interest

可記名收款　payable to order

可能性差額　balance of probabilities

可能達到的國民生產總值(充分就業下的產值)　potential gross national product

可破約遠期外滙交易　the break forward transaction

可動用營業盈餘　available earned surplus

可接受的差異　acceptable difference

可接受品質水準　acceptable quality level

可接受差異範圍　acceptable differ-ence

可控制成本　controllable cost

可控制差異　controllable variance

可替代產品　substitutable product

可替代的貨物　fungible goods

可換股份　convertible stock

可換優先股　convertible preferred

可提前回收優先股　callable pre-ferred stock

可提前償還公司債　call bonds

可貼現票據　bankable bill

可減損失　deductible loss

可貸資金　loanable funds

可貸資金利息論(利率隨可貸放資金的供求關係而波動的理論)　loa-nable funds theory of interest

可買賣的　merchantable

可買賣期權(可轉讓給他人的一種期權)　traded option

可過戶證券　assignable instrument, negotiable instrument

可預見損失　foreseeable losses

可達到成本　attainable cost

可催繳股本　assessable capital stock

可疑債務　doubtful debts

可疑資產　doubtful assets

可遞延成本　postponable cost

可增加抵押(指已抵押財產，尚可增加押數)　open mortgage

可調整平價　sliding parity

可調整的釘住滙率　adjustable peg exchange rate

可調整面值國庫券(巴西首先發行的面值可隨生活指數而調整的國庫券)　readjustable treasury bond

可靠投資　sound investment

可靠性工程　reliability engineering

可靠帳戶　reliable account

可靠債券　gilt-edged bonds

可靠證券　gilt-edged securities

可節省成本　escapable cost

可調換債券　convertible bond

可談判關稅　bargaining tariff

可撤銷信用證　revocable credit

可隨時破產的公司　collapsible cor-poration

可避免成本　avoidable cost, dis-cretionary cost

可獲補償之損失　recoverable loss

可償還股票　redeemable stock

可償還優先股票　redeemable pre-ference shares

可轉售許可證(技術貿易許可證之一，又稱副許可證)　sub-licence

可轉售許可證合同　sub-licence con-tract

可轉換債券　convertible bonds

可轉期權的遠期外滙買賣(指訂立的遠期外滙合同，允許用期權打破它，而利用市場有利形勢進行買賣，只承擔固定滙率與破約滙率之間差額的損失)　forward with op-tion exit

可轉讓定期存單　negotiable certifi-cates of deposit

可轉讓信用證　transferable credit, assignable credit

可轉讓提單　negotiable bill of lading

可轉讓貸款證券　transferable loan instrument

可轉讓提款單帳戶　negotiable orders of withdraw account (NOW A/C)

可轉讓單據　negotiable document

可轉讓期權(持有人可將權利轉讓給第三者的期權或合約)　assignable option

可轉讓證券　negotiable instruments, transferable instruments

可轉讓票據　negotiable paper

可歸屬成本　attributable cost

可證明的破產債務　debts provable in bankruptcy

可續保定期保險　renewal term insurance

可贖回的優先股　redeemable preference share

可贖回股份　callable stock

可贖回債券　callable bond

可變式遠期外滙買賣　the break forward

可變成本　variable cost

可變保證金(期貨市場發出補交保證金通知時繳交之費用)　variation margin

可變限額保證金　variable limit margins

可變息債券　convertible floating-rate notes

可變現淨值　net realizable value

可變動費用　variable expenses

可變動滙率　flexible exchange rate

可變賣的　realisable

變關稅　flexible tariff

平方公寸　square decimeter

平方公分　square centimeter

平方公尺　square metre

平方公里　square kilometre

平方英寸　square inches

平方英尺　square foot

平方英碼　square yard

平市銷售(股票賣空的一種例外情況，指平市可賣空。平市指連續幾次成交價都保持在同一水平上，但必須高於其前最近一次不同的成交價)　selling on even tick

平行條款　parallel clause

平安險　free of particular average (F.P.A.)

平車　flat car

平均　average

平均一般成本　average general cost

平均不變成本　average fixed cost

平均可變成本　average variable cost

平均皮重　average tare

平均生產成本　average production cost

平均出廠品質　average outgoing quality

平均出廠品質界限　average outgoing quality limit

平均收入　average income

平均收益　average revenue, average yield

平均收帳期間 averager collection period

平均吃水(指船舶) average draught

平均成本 average cost

平均成本法 average cost method

平均成本定價法 average-cost pricing

平均存貨水平 average inventory level

平均存貨期 days of average inventory on hand

平均存貨期間，商品存貨可供銷售日數 number of day's sales in merchandise inventory

平均良好品質 fair average quality (f.a.q.)

平均佔用流動資金額 average occupied amount of current capital

平均利潤率 average rate of profit

平均折舊 depreciation straight line

平均股利基金 dividend equalization fund

平均股利準備 dividend equalization reserve

平均投資額 average investment

平均法 average method

平均到期日 average due date, equated maturity, average maturity

平均抽樣檢驗個數 average sample size

平均保險費 average premium

平均保險費率 average rate

平均重量 average weight

平均值 average value, mean value

平均差系數 coefficient of average deviation

平均差額 average balance

平均消費傾向 average propensity to consume

平均進口傾向(反映國民購買進口商品的發展動向) average propensity to import

平均單位成本 average unit cost

平均單價 average unit price

平均報酬率 average rate of return

平均週轉天數 average number of days to turnover

平均資本比率 average capital ratio method

平均資金利潤率 average profit rate on funds, average profit margin, average rate of profit on investment

平均滙率 mid-point-rate

平均需求量 average demand

平均壽命期內的收益(指債券) yield-to-average-life

平均誤差 average error

平均數 average number

平均增長速度 average speed of growth

平均增長率 average rate of growth

平均價格 average price, equilibrium price, mean price

平均價格法 average price method

平放 keep flat

平板式貨櫃／集裝箱 flat containers

平板托盤　plate pallet

平板車式貨櫃／集裝箱拖車　trailer on flat car

平架貨櫃／集裝箱(只有底盤和四角支柱的)　flat rack container

平倉(香港市場指買入或賣出以抵消現有之持倉狀態)　evening up

平倉單(香港恒指市場使客戶離開大市的特別訂單)　stop order

平等互利　equality and mutual benefit

平價　par value, parity

平價以上　above par value

平價兌換　exchange at par

平價制度　par regime

平價政策　parity price policy

平價指數　parity rate

平價條款　parity clause

平價差幅　deviation from par

平價發行　par issue

平價網(歐洲貨幣體系用的術語)　parity grid

平衡　balance, equilibrium

平衡式收益表　balanced form of income statement, account form of income statement

平衡法　equity

平衡法上利益　equitable interests

平衡法上債務讓與　equitable assignment of debt

平衡法上毀壞　equitable waste

平衡法上遺產　equitable assets

平衡法上贖回權　equity of redemption

平衡法抵押　equitable mortgage

平衡股利　equalizing dividend

平衡貸款(分處不同國家的企業互換對方貨幣的貸款)　paralled loan, back-to-back loan

平衡準備　equalization reserve

平衡價格　parity price

平衡線圖　line of balance; LOB

平艙費　trimming charges

正方向變化　change positively

正本　original, original copy

正本條款　original or authentic clause

正式合同　formal contract

正式有資格的獨立檢查人　duty qualified independent inspector

正式收據　official receipt

正式委託代理人　authorised agent

正式通知　formal notice

正式進口　formal entry

正式經紀人　inside broker

正式盤存日期　official inventory date

正品　certified products, quality goods, normal products

正常交易　arm's length transaction

正常交易價格　arm's-length price

正常分配率　normal distribution rate

正常收支　normal revenue and expenditure

正常收益率　normal income rate

正常成本　normal cost

正常存量法　normal stock method

正常折舊　normal depreciation

正常利率　natural rate of interest

正常利潤　normal profit

正常時間　normal time

正常商業交易　arm's-length deal, arm's-length transaction

正常商業談判　arm's-length bargaining

正常損耗　normal loss

正常價格　normal price

正常銷售協定　orderly marketing agreement

正常競爭　normal competition

正規手續　regular procedure

正規批發商　regular wholesale

正規費用率　regulated fees

正商譽　goodwill positive

正斜度收益率曲線（短期利率低於長期利率的一種收益曲線）　positively sloping yield curve

正量　commercial weight

正牌子　standard brand

正資本　capital positive

正當收入　legitimate income

正當成本　legitimate costs

正當交易　bona fide transaction

正當持票人　holder in due course

正當商業利益　legitimate commercial interests

正當業務　legitimate business

正價　nominal price, net price

左右手程序圖　right and left-hand chart

左右市場價格的公司股票　barometer stocks

末行數字（企業年終結算的損益表中最末一行是損益數字）　bottom line

末期股息　final dividend

石油工業　petroleum industry

石油美元　petro-dollar

石油美元再循環　recycling of petro-dollars

石油設施　petroleum installations

石油標價　petroleum posted price

石油輸出國組織　Organization of Petroleum Exporting Countries (OPEC)

世界出口貿易公平比率　equitable share of world export trade

世界市場　world market

世界市場參考價格　reference world market price

世界性通貨膨脹　world inflation

世界知識產權組織　World Intellectual Property Organization

世界貨幣秩序　world monetary order

世界貨幣制度　world monetary system

世界貿易　world trade

世界貿易中心聯合會　World Trade Centres Association

世界經濟　world economy

世界銀行　World Bank

世界銀行集團　World Bank Group

功能折舊，效能折舊　functional depreciation

瓦楞紙箱　corrugated case

布雷頓森林協定　Bretton Woods Agreement

布雷頓森林制度　Bretton Woods System

布雷頓森林會議　Bretton Woods Conference

《布魯塞爾估價公約》　Brussels Convention on Valuation

布魯塞爾稅則目錄　Brussels Tariff Nomenclature (BTN)

示範工廠　demonstration plant

示範，商品宣傳　demonstration

示範項目　demonstration project

示範效果　demonstration effect

巨額交易　extensive transaction

巨額折價債券　deep discount bond

巨額定單　maxiorder

[丨]

以毛作淨　gross for net

以用戶檢驗為最後依據　user's inspection to be final

以代理人資格簽署　sign "per pro"

以有艙位為準（無艙位時，可取消合約）　subject to shipping space available

以即期頭寸抵補遠期頭寸　spot against forward position

以投資為目標的項目　investment-oriented project

以股易股，股本轉移　split-off

以股票付股息　stock dividend

以股票作紅利　share bonus

以物為證　take something as a pledge

以美元買入遠期法郎　buying francs forward for dollars

以前有代表性的時期　a previous representative period

以起岸重量為準　landed weight final

以貨付款　in kind

以貨易貨制　barter system

以國庫券為唯一公開市場工具之政策　The "Bill-only" policy

以船運費最廉的航線裝運　shipment by cheapest route

以買方檢驗為最後依據　Buyer's inspection to be final

以＂期＂換＂現＂（商品交易所術語）　against actuals

以期貨換現貨（期貨市場交投者把相同數量的多倉期貨合約轉讓給沽家，購入現貨的交易過程）　exchange of future for cash

以華爾街名義（美國術語，指以經紀人、銀行或其他第三者的名義登記證券，而不用證券所有者的名義，目的是便於管理）　Wall Street name

以裝船重量為準　shipping weight final

以滙票為擔保的證券　bill on deposit

以新債券取代舊債券　rollover, refunding

以廉價吸引顧客的商品　price leader

以廣招徠　in order to promote patronage or sales

以暫時股票付紅利　scrip dividend

以銷售為目的果菜園　market garden

以鄰為壑(在對外貿易中，一國以損害他國而利己的一些做法)　beggar-my-neighbour

以鄰為壑政策　beggar-my-neighbour policy

以應收票據擔保　notes receivable as collateral

以證券為擔保的借款者　giver-on

以證券為擔保的貸款者　taker-in

以簽訂契據為條件　subject to contract

以權益為證券計價之依據　equity basis of security valuation

北大西洋公約組織　North-Atlantic Treaty Organization

北大西洋航線　North-Atlantic shipping line

北京理算規則(是中國理算共同海損的暫行規則)　Beijing Adjustment Rules

甲方　first party

甲板貨　on deck goods

甲板貨提單　on deck bill of lading

甲板貨運費率　deck cargo rates

甲級　grade A

用戶　users, consumers, purchasers, subscriber

用戶第一主義　consumerism

用戶調訪　canvass customer opinions

用於生活費的收入　income that can be used as living expenses, income used for living expenses

用於積累的購買力　purchasing power for accumulation

用抽查法證實　verification by " test and scrutiny "

用料清單　bill of material

用料彙總表　summary of materials consumed

用途　usage

用途別(成本，費用)報表　objective statement

用貨櫃／集裝箱運　containerize

用量差異　usage variance

用硬幣支付　payment in specie

用鋼筆過帳　pen-and-ink posting

四八〇公法(美國會 1954 年通過之農產貿易援助法案)　Public Law 480

四分之一　quarter

四分之三碰撞責任條款　three-fourths runing down clause

" 四季青 " 保證(國際借貸協議中，貸款人要求借款人所作的説明與保證在簽協議時和在整個借貸協議有效期間，始終保持其正確性)　ever-green warranties

四捨五入　round off

由我方負擔　be covered by us

由我方選擇　at our option

由法院所定　per curiam

由託運人負擔危險　at shipper's risk

由貨主負擔危險　at owner's risk

由買方自行當心，貨物出門不換 [拉]caveat emptor

由買方選擇　at buyer's option

由稅收支付　charge upon revenue

由最先開航的船裝運　shipment by first available vessel

由運貨人負擔危險　at carrier's risk

由賣方自行當心，包退包換 [拉] caveat venditor

由賣方選擇　at seller's option

由機動董事解決方式(投資爭端解決的一種方式，指由一個雙方都接受的局外人擔任有決定權的董事) the swing-man director

由簽署人自行當心(指一經簽署不得翻悔) [拉]caveat subscriptor

卡車　freight car

卡車上交貨　free on truck

卡車運輸　truckage

卡特爾　cartel, kartell

卡特爾價格　cartel price

目的地　destination

目的地交貨　free on board destination

目的協調原則　principle of harmony of objective

目的港　port of destination

目的港船上交貨　ex ship

目的港碼頭交貨　ex quay, ex wharf

目的港碼頭交貨，關稅由買方負擔 ex quay, duties on buyer's account

目的港碼頭交貨，關稅已付　ex quay, duty paid

目標市場　target market

目標成本　target cost, standard cost

目標成本管理　target cost management

目標行銷　target marketing

目標利潤　target profit

目標利潤原則　target return principle

目標函數的約束條件　bound for objective function

目標訂價法　target pricing

目標管理　management by objectives (MBO)

目標價格　target price

目標導向行為　goal-directed behaviour

目錄　contents, catalogue, index, inventory

目錄表　list

目錄價格　catalogue price

申報失實　misleading declaration

申報股本　stated capital

申報金額　amount declared

申報價值　declared value

申報關稅　customs declaration

申請付款書　requisition for payment

申請外滙　application for exchange

申請單(鮮活、易壞貨物申請迅速通關卸貨)　request note, requisition

申請破產　voluntary bankruptcy

申請書　application, request note

申請書格式　form of application

申請專利　application for patent

申請費 application fee

申請註冊 application for registration

申請裝船單 application for shipment

叫價(期貨買家報出買入價) bid

[ノ]

包 bale

包工 job work, by contract

包工工資 contractor's pay for piece work

包工制 piece work system

包工程 engineering contract

包用 guaranteed suitable

包括一切費用價格 all-round price

包括起貨費用價格 landed price

包括清理及平艙費在內的離岸價格 free on board stowed and trimmed

包括裝卸費在內的運費 free in and out

包租(對車、船等) charter

包退包換 guarantee to exchange returned as unsuitable

包船 chartered vessel

包裝 package

包裝工業 packaging industry

包裝方式 manner of packing

包裝不全 incomplete packing

包裝不良 insufficient packing

包裝不完備 faulty packing

包裝不符 variation in packing

包裝不能適應海運 insufficiently packed for ocean voyage

包裝內容 packing content

包裝用布 packing cloth

包裝用品，包裝物料 packing material

包裝成本 packing cost

包裝政策 packaging policy

包裝信用證 packing credit

包裝革命 package revolution

包裝紙 packing paper

包裝破損 packages in damaged condition

包裝排列 packing for display

包裝設計 package design

包裝費用 packing charges

包裝標準化 standardization of packing

包裝蔴繩 pack twine

包銷 have exclusive selling rights, underwrite (用於有價證券的發行)

包銷人 sole agent

包銷辛迪加(歐洲債券的承銷集團) underwriting syndicates

包銷團，銷售集團 selling group

包裹運費率 parcel rates

包機運輸 chartered carrier, chartered flight

付方 credit side, credit

付出代價 pay a price

付出利息 interest paid

付保證金購買 on margin, buying on margin

付息 payment of interest

付息日之間之債券估價 bond valuation between interest dates

付息期間　interest payment period

付息保障倍數（用以衡量企業支付其合同規定的利息的能力，又稱＂總付息保障率＂）　times interest earned

付訖支票，註銷支票　cancelled check, paid check

付清　pay off, pay in full, clear a bill, pay up

付清欠帳　pay off a debt

付清帳款　account squared

付貨通知單　shipping order

付現成本　out-of-pocket cost, outlay cost

付現自運　cash and carry

付現折扣　cash discount

付現條件　cash terms

付現款　payment in cash, pay cash

付款人　payer, drawee

付款日　cash day, day of payment

付款日程表　payment schedule

付款不足　payment insufficient

付款申請書　requisition for payment

付款交單託收方式　documents against payment (D/P)

付款命令　payment order

付款到期日　date on which payment becomes due

付款條件　terms of payment

付款流動值，付款流動期　disbursement float, payment float

付款通知書　notice of payment

付款給來人　pay to bearer

付款給抬頭人　pay to order

付款給持票人　pay to bearer, payable to bearer

付款給執票人　payable to holder

付款滙單　documentary payment bill

付款銀行　paying bank

付款寬延期限　moratorium

付款憑單　payment voucher, payment certificate

付款證據　evidence of payment

付稅單　duty memo

失去市場　lose the market

失去控制市場能力　lose ability to control the market

失去通貨資格　demonetization

失去買賣機會　lose one's market

失物自理　not responsible for anything lost

失均衡　overbalance

失事船　wrecked ship

失事船浮出的貨物　flotsam

失重　loss of weight

失信用　break faith, loss credit

失真之現金餘額　distorted cash balance

失效　lapse

失效支票　stale check

失效提單　stale bill of lading

失時效的債務　stale debt, outlawed debt

失業守恒規律　law of conservation of unemployment

失業津貼　unemployment dole

失業保險費　unemployment in-
surance expense

失業恐慌　fear of unemployment

失業率　rate of unemployment, job-
less rate

失業救濟　unemployment benefit,
unemployment relief

失業救濟工程　relief works

失察　oversight

失調　imbalance, dislocation

失實記錄　blind entry

失竊貨物　stolen goods

失竊票據　stolen bill

失蹤　disappearance

失蹤船　missing ship

失蹤被保險人　lost policy holder

代用券　token

代用品　substitute articles

代用貨幣　substitutionary coinage

代用傳票　substitute voucher

代決性戶口(由經紀人可代為買入或
賣出商品或證券的客戶)　dis-
cretionary account

代收款　agency receipt, collection for
others

代收貨款　collection of trade charges

代收滙兌　collection of domestic
drafts and bills

代行債務　delegation of duties

代位權(保險人在償付海損的保險賠
償後，向被保險人要求的一種權
利，即取代被保險人的地位)　the
right of subrogation

代物清償　performance by accord
and satisfaction

代放款項　loan made on behalf of
others

代客買賣股票　jobbing

代售　sale on commission

代售佣金　sale commission

代售商　commission merchant

代理人　agent, proxy, mandatory

代理人的侵權行為　agent's torts

代理人留置權　agent's lien

代理人酬金　agent's renumeration

代理支店　sub-agent

代理中間商　agent, middleman

代理手續費　agency commission

代理收租　rental agency

代理佣金　agent commission

代理委託　commission order

代理委任書　power of attorney

代理招租　letting agency

代理約定書　agency agreement

代理處　agency

代理商, 行紀人　factor, commercial
agent

代理商行　correspondent

代理商佣金　factorage

代理區域　scope of territory repre-
sented

代理貿易　commission trade

代理貿易商　commission agent

代理經理　acting manager

代理業　factorage

代理業務　agent service

代理債務　vicarious liability

代理銀行 agent banks, correspondent bank

代理銀行追詢書 correspondent tracer

代理權 franchise, agency right, procuration, power of attorney

代理權期滿 expiration of agency

代產包銷制度 putting-out system

代買代賣帳單 bought and sold notes

代替式定期利率交易(香港地鐵公司於1986年的集資方法) fixed interest rate substitute transaction

代替效應 substitution effects

代電 lettergram

代墊款項 advance money for

代銷 sale by proxy

代銷貨 consigned goods

代價 purchase money, price

代價收訖 value received

代價券 scrip

代辦人 commission agent

代辦行 commission house

代辦律師 attorney

代辦商 commission merchant

代辦帳戶 indent account

代購人 purchasing agent

代購商店 indent house

代購貨品 indent goods

代簽 per pro (per procuration)

外包裝 outer packing

外生變數(外界產生的變數) exogenous variable

外行 layman, out of one's line

外在的酬賞 extrinsic rewards

外交特權 diplomatic privileges

外交豁免 diplomatic immunity

外地集裝箱回空 overland transit empty (OT)

外地裁判庭證據法例 Foreign Tribunals Evidence Act

外地裝箱回送 overland transit full (OF)

外股 silent partners, sleeping partner, dormant partner

外來投入 external input

外來事故 external causes

外來貨幣(外滙經營術語，指主要國際金融市場上不存在的一種貨幣，如印尼盾、埃及鎊等) exotic

外來資金 external funds

外表良好 in apparent good order and condition

外界董事(指非股東董事) outside director

外國一般代理商 foreign general agent

外國人的雇用 alien employment

外國子公司 foreign affiliates

外國公司 foreign corporations

外國支票 foreign check

外國判決互惠執行法例 Foreign Judgment Reciprocal Enforcement Act

外國投資 foreign investment

外國投資淨額 net foreign investment

外國法人 foreign juridical person

外國法律　foreign law

外國股份　foreign equity holding

外國股票的場外交易　over-the-counter dealings of the foreign stock

外國政府公債　foreign government bond

外國和國際債券市場　foreign and international bond markets

外國借款　foreign borrowing

外國借款人　foreign borrowers

外國商行, 洋行　foreign firm

外國貨物進口報單　application for import of foreign goods

外國港口間貿易　cross-trade

外國稅收　foreign revenue

外國貸款　foreign loan

外國滙票　foreign bill of exchange

外國債券　foreign bond

外國債券市場　foreign bond markets

外國資本　foreign capital

外國資本流量　foreign capital flows

外國資產的往來　transactions in foreign assets

外國滙票　foreign bill

外國僑民　foreign nationals

外國銀行票據　foreign bank bill

外國證券　foreign securities

外部投入資本　outside venture capital

外部經濟負效果　external diseconomy

外部經濟效果　external economy, externalities

外部審計　outside audit

外部證據　extrinsic

外埠付款票據　domicile bill

外埠同業存款　outport bank deposit

外埠同業透支　overdraft by outport correspondents

外現利息　explicit interest

外港(參見＂僻地港＂條)　outport

外貿中心　foreign trade centres

外貿依存度　ratio of dependence on foreign trade

外貿乘數　foreign trade multiplier

外貿槓桿作用　the role of foreign trade as a lever, leverage effects

外貿機構　foreign trade agency

外圍倉庫制度　terminal receiving system

外圍業務(指銀行在離岸市場上只能做市場所在國以外的業務)　out-out business

外債　external debt, foreign debt, external loan

外債清償　external debt servicing

外資　foreign capital

外資企業　full foreign-owned enterprises

外資流入　foreign capital inflow

外資產業　enterprises owned by foreign capitalists

外滙　foreign exchange

外滙升水　exchange premium

外滙分成, 外滙留成　share the foreign currency earnings, sharing of

foreign exchange earnings, keep part of the foreign exchange earnings

外滙幻覺 foreign exchange illusion

外滙出售核定單 authorization sheet for sales of exchange

外滙市場 foreign exchange market

外滙市場機制 mechanics of the foreign exchange market

外滙平準基金 exchange stabilization fund

外滙平價 foreign exchange parity

外滙申請書 application for exchange

外滙收入 foreign currency earnings, foreign exchange receipt

外滙收支 foreign exchange receipt and disbursement

外滙收支順差 favourable balance of foreign exchange earnings and outlays

外滙交易 foreign exchange transaction

(銀行)外滙交易員 foreign exchange trader

外滙批發市場 foreign exchange wholesale market

外滙投機 foreign exchange speculation

外滙波動保險 foreign exchange fluctuation insurance

外滙官價 official exchange rate

外滙指定銀行 authorized bank for dealing in foreign exchange

外滙契約統一規則(國際商會於1983年5月通過) Uniform Rules for Foreign Exchange Contracts

外滙保值協定 Agreement on Exchange Guarantees

外滙保留條款 exchange proviso clause

外滙信貸 credit in foreign exchange

外滙風險 exchange risk

外滙風險轉移 transfer of foreign exchange risk

外滙風險暴露的測定 foreign exchange exposure measurement

外滙風險暴露管理 foreign exchange exposure management

外滙限額 exchange quota

外滙配給,外滙配售 rationing of exchange

外滙配額制度 exchange quota system

外滙許可證 foreign exchange licence, foreign exchange permit

外滙票證 foreign exchange instrument

外滙稅 exchange tax

外滙貼水 exchange discount

外滙貼水率 exchange discount rate

外滙集中制度 foreign exchange concentration system

外滙結存 foreign balance

外滙結算 foreign exchange settlement

外滙結算協定 exchange clearing

agreement

外滙期貨　foreign exchange futures

外滙期貨市場　forward exchange market

外滙買賣損益　profit or loss on exchange

外滙報價　foreign exchange quotation

外滙經紀人　foreign exchange broker

外滙滙率　foreign exchange rate

外滙零售市場　foreign exchange retail market

外滙資金短缺　limited reserves of foreign exchange

外滙資產　foreign exchange assets

外滙業務　foreign exchange transaction

外滙牌價　foreign exchange rate, exchange rate quotation

外滙銀行　foreign exchange bank

外滙管制　foreign exchange control

外滙管理　foreign exchange management

外滙管制法規　foreign exchange control regulation

外滙管制當局　exchange control authorization

外滙傾銷　exchange dumping

外滙緩衝　foreign exchange cushion

外滙頭寸，外滙持有額　foreign exchange position

外滙戰　foreign exchange warfare

外滙購買核定單　authorization sheet for purchase of exchange

外滙儲備　foreign exchange reserves

外運加工　outward processing

外幣支付憑證　foreign currency payment instruments

外幣存款　foreign currency deposit

外幣存款戶　foreign currency deposit account

外幣折合率　foreign currency conversion rate

外幣折算風險，換算風險　translation risk

外幣折算損益　translation gain or loss

外幣兌換　foreign currency exchange

外幣兌換水單　exchange memo

外幣兌換業執照　money exchange's licence

外幣持有額　foreign currency holdings

外幣信貸　foreign currency credit

外幣兌換指定代理處　authorized agency for foreign currency exchange

外幣期貨　foreign currency futures

外幣期貨期權　options on foreign currency futures

外幣期權　foreign exchange option, foreign currency option

外幣債券　foreign currency debentures

外幣滙票　foreign currency bill

外銷　export sales

外銷貨　export goods

外銷機構　export organization

外觀 appearance

生命週期成本 life cycle cost

生命週期成本法 life cycle costing

生活必需品 necessity of life, daily necessities

生活的第一需要 life's prime want

生活津貼 living allowance

生活素質極高化 maximization of living standard

生活費用指數 cost of living index

生活費用價格總指數 total price index of living costs

生效日期 effective date

生息合格債務(指附有利息的) interest-bearing eligible liabilities

生息資本 interest-bearing capital

生產 produce, output

生產力 productivity

生產人工成本法 productive labour cost method

生產工程 production engineering

生產方式 methods of production, mode of production

生產支出 productive expenditure

生產成本 cost of production

生產合作 productive cooperation

生產因素 factors of production

生產收益 proceedings from production

生產自動化 production automation

生產系統 production system

生產者風險 producer's risk

生產者價格 producer price

生產放款 productive loan

生產性積累 productive accumulation

生產函數(表示一定數量的各種必要投入物所能生產的最大可能的產量) production function

生產(工作、作業)定額 job rates, job rating

生產要素 factors of production

生產要素—價格邊緣 factor-price frontier

生產指數 production index

生產指數單位成本 production index unit cost

生產能力 capacity

生產能力比率 productivity ratio

生產能力利用率 capacity utilization rate

生產能力過剩 overcapacity

生產能量比率 capacity ratio

生產能量成本 productive capacity cost

生產流水線 production line

生產流程 flow of production

生產效率 production efficiency

生產設備 production facility

生產過剩 over-production

生產寬容度 tolerance level in production

生產資料轉移價值 transferred value of the means of production

生產經理 production manager

生產資源 resources for production

生產管制 production control

生產管理 production management

生產線平衡　line balancing

生產概念（或導向）　production concept or orientation

生產價格　production prices

生產標準　production standard

生產調整準備成本　setting-up cost

生產調整準備費用　setting-up expense

生產機制　production mechanism

生產額　volume of production

生意興隆　booming business, roaring business

生意興隆的商人，善於經營的商人　prosperous merchant

生意蕭條　business depression

生態會計學　ecological accounting

生豬玉米比率　hog-corn ratio

生豬玉米的週期循環　hog-corn cycle

白手拿魚（指未花錢而賺得利潤的股票買賣）　free riding

白色貨物（指大型、價高的家用電器或白色織物）　white goods

白信用卡（美國使用較廣的信用卡之一，可在全世界的民航、很多大旅館、高級飯店使用）Carte Blanche

白票　white paper (= clean bill)

白領階級　white collar class

瓜分市場　sharing the market

[一]

台（機器）　unit

出入口銀行　export and import bank

出入往返權　ingress, egress, regress

出口　export, exportation

出口支出　export debit

出口加工區　manufacture and export zone

出口卡特爾　export cartel

出口市場　export market

出口申報書　export declaration

出口外滙　export exchange

出口包裝費由買方負擔　export packing for buyer's account

出口代理商　export agent

出口代辦行　export commission house

出口行　export house

出口收入　export earnings

出口收滙方式　manner of collecting export proceeds

出口多樣化　the diversification of export

出口投標防止風險期權（規定如客戶中標，在滙率不利時可得到保障；如未中標，則銀行退回預繳費用的半數）　export tender risk avoidance

出口定單　export order

出口投資　export financing

出口押滙　outward documentary bill, bill purchased

出口招標　export tender

出口信用擔保制度　export credit guarantee scheme

出口信用證　export credit

出口信貸　export credit

出口信貸利率　export credit rate

出口信貸保險　export credit insurance

出口信貸擔保　export credit guarantee

出口津貼　export bounty, export subsidy

出口協會　export association

出口限額　export quota, ration export

出口託收　foreign collection

出口盈利指數　export profit index

出口淨值　net export value

出口流動函數　export flow function

出口財務　export financing

出口特許證　special permission export

出口退稅　export rebate, export drawback

出口商　exporter, export trader

出口商品結構　export mix, line up of export commodities

出口商品流動費用　circulation cost of export commodity

出口商品進貨成本　purchasing cost of export commodity

出口商信貸　exporter's credit

出口商貸款　exporter's advance

出口貨款保收業務　export factoring

出口商的銷售價　exporter's sales price

出口部　export department

出口部門　export division

出口部經理　export manager

出口寄銷商品　merchandise outward on consignment

出口許可證　export licence

出口授權書　export authorization

出口量　export volume

出口稅　export duty

出口港　port of exit

出口貿易　export trade

出口貿易法　Export Trade Act

出口貸款　loan for export

出口提單　export bill of lading

出口跟單匯票　documentary export bill, outward documentary bill

出口結滙　bill to purchase

出口發票　export invoice

出口單據　export documents

出口報關單　export declaration

出口鼓勵　export incentives

出口預付　export advance

出口滙票　export bill

出口補貼　export subsidy, export bounty

出口傾銷　export dumping

出口管制　export control

出口獎勵金　export bounty

出口增加帶動經濟增長　export-led growth

出口價格指數　export price index

出口艙單　export manifest, outward manifest

出口融資保險　export finance insurance

出口檢驗合格證　certificate for export

出口優勢 trump-cards in the export of, export superiority

出生地主義 ［拉］ jus soli

出立保單 issue a policy

出示單據 surrender of the document

出市經紀（在交易所內為客戶或本身進行交易的經紀人） floor broker

出多入少法 more-out-than-in method

出更高的價錢 overcall

出租 to hire out

出租人 lessor, renter

出租房屋的閑置率 vacancy rate in rental housing, rental vacancy rate

出租財產 leasing asset

出納 receive and pay out money or bills

出納員 cashier, pay clerk, teller, purser, treasurer

出納科 cashier's department

出納機 cash register

出帳，沖銷，轉銷 charge off

出產 output, yield

出產地 place of origin, country of origin

出產率 rate of output

出票人 drawer, check drawer, remitter

出票日 date of draft

出票後若干日付款的滙票 bill drawn payable at a certain time after date

出票條款 drawn clause

出售投資證券 sales of investment securities

出售物 offering

出售債券 offering of bonds

出售證券 sale of securities

出售證券收入 securities proceeds

出售證券協議 negotiated offering

出貨編序系統 stock locator systems

出超 export surplus

出進口比率 export-import cover ratio

出（保）單公司 issuing company

出港申報表 bill of clearance

出港通知 clearance notice

出港費 clearing fee

出港證 clearance permit

出發港 port of departure, port of sailing

出境 leave the country

出境回執 exit receipt

出境簽證 exit visa

出廠品質條件 factory quality terms

出廠價格 ex-factory price, factory's price, producer price

出廠數量 factory's quantity

出價 bid, make an offer

出價人 bidder

出質資產 pledge assets

出險通知（損失通知書） loss advice

母公司 parent company, parent corporation, parent firm

幼稚工業 infant industry

幼稚工業保護説（一種保護貿易理論） infant industry argument

加工出口 export processing

加工出口區 export processing zone

加工出口用料 processing material for export

加工成本 conversion cost, processing cost

加工品 finished goods

加工廠商 processor

加工稅 processing tax

加工進口貿易 improvement trade for import

加工貿易 processing trade, improvement trade

加工費 processing charge

加工裝配工業 assembly industry

加工標準 process criterion

加成 mark-up

加成訂價法 mark-up pricing

加利(指成本加利變成售價) mark-on, mark-up

加收利息 interest surcharges

加侖 gallons

加重關稅 dual tariffs

加班 overtime

加班工資 overtime pay (or wage)

加班津貼 overtime (and shift) premium

加班費 overtime pay

加拿大出口商會 Canadian Exporters Association

加拿大進口商協會 Canadian Importers and Traders Association

加拿大商會 Canadian Chamber of Commerce

加拿大經濟委員會 Economic Council of Canada

加倍定率遞減折舊法 depreciation-double-declining balance method

加勒比海共同市場 Caribbean Common Market

加勒比海共同體 Caribbean Community

加勒比海自由貿易區 Caribbean Free Trade Area

加勒比海自由貿易協會 Caribbean Free Trade Association

加勒比海航線 Caribbean Sea Shipping Line

加添抵押 adding mortgage

加速折舊 accelerated depreciation

加速到期 acceleration

加速還款條款(凡買賣合同屬分期付款者，如任何一期未償付，則全部貨款視同到期) acceleration clause

加速攤銷法 accelerated amortization method

加蓋火漆印的契約 specialty

加價 hike, raise a price, mark up

加碼 increase position

加權平均法 weighted average method

加權資本市值法 weighted market capitalization method

民主管理 democratic management

民用航空線 civil aviation lines

民法 civil law

民事財產關係 civil property relations

民事責任保險　civil liability insurance

民事訴訟　civil action

民事訴訟程序法例　Civil Procedure Act

民事債務　civil debt

民間貿易　nongovernment trade

民營事業　private enterprise

司法手續　judicial proceeding

司法受託人　judicial trustee

司法受託人法例　Judicial Trustees Act

司法判斷　judicial decision

司法補償　judicial remedies

司法管理法例　Administration of Justice Act

司法調查　judicial investigation

司法權法例　Judicature Act

司庫, 財務主任　treasurer

六　畫

[、]

交叉加算　cross-adding

交叉核對　cross-check

交叉責任(計算船舶碰撞事故賠償責任的一種方法)　cross liability

交叉貿易(技術貿易中, 一方的使用技術對另一方使用技術的交換)　cross trade

交叉發價　cross offer

交叉報酬率　intersection rate of return

交叉滙兌　cross exchange

交叉滙率, 套滙滙率　cross rate of exchange

交叉違約(指違約不能償還貸款時, 貸款銀行得向該借款所屬集團的其他任何成員追索還款)　cross default

交叉補貼　cross-subsidization

交叉需求彈性　cross-elasticity of demand

交叉對冲　cross hedge

交叉彈性　cross elasticity

交叉總計, 橫總計　cross-footing

交互承兌　cross acceptance

交互計算　running account

交付定金　down payment

交付股金　payment of shares

交付定貨　execute an order, fill an order

交付拍賣　put up to auction

交付契據　delivery of a deed

交付現金　cash payment

交出物權　cessio in jure

交收月(期貨合約指定為交收結算之月份)　delivery month

交收文件(期貨市場指倉庫收據或付運單證等)　delivery instrument

交收通知(期貨市場沽家表示願在指定日期內交付未平倉空頭期貨合約商品的書面通知)　delivery notice

交收價(指交收時結算期貨合約的價

格，由結算公司釐定） delivery price

交收點（由商品交易所指定執行合約、交收期貨合約商品的地點） delivery points

交易　transaction

交易人　negotiator

交易日　market day

交易市場　trading market

交易成本　transaction cost

交易券　trading stamp

交易所　exchange, bourse

交易所外市場　off-board market, kerb market

交易所外價格　off-board price

交易所席位　seat on the exchange

交易所掛牌證券　listed securities

交易所術語　stock exchange expression, stock exchange parlance

交易所登記股票　listed stock

交易所經紀人費用　exchange brokerage

交易室（美國商品交易所中的交易室），現場　pit

交易突然湧躍　spurt

交易風險，交易暴露　transaction exposure

交易限額　trading limit

交易活躍　brisk trade

交易速度　transactions velocity

交易量　volume of business, volume of trade

交易場，交易廳（交易所內的） floor, trading floor

交易單位　trading unit

交易貸款　trade credit

交易圈（指交易所內的圓形場地） ring or pit

交易損失　trade loss, normal loss

交割延期　backwardation

交錯抽樣　zigzag sampling

交錯總和　alternating sum

交易額　trading volume

交通銀行　Bank of Communications

交貨　delivery

交貨不到險（特別附加險之一） failure to delivery

交貨日期　date of delivery

交貨付現，貨到付款　cash on delivery

交貨地點　delivery points

交貨收款銷售　cash on delivery sales

交貨前付現　cash before delivery, payment prior to delivery

交貨後付款　payment after delivery

交貨時間　time of delivery

交貨港　port of delivery

交貨期限　time of delivery

交貨短量　short delivery

交貨數量　delivered quantity

交接證明書　certificate of completion of handling over

交割日　settlement day, prompt day, pay day

交割日的前一天　ticket day

交割延期，交割延期費　backwardation

交割延期費　backwardation, contango

交割限期日　continuation day, contango day

交換分保　exchange of reinsurance

交換支票(為換回現金或另一張支票而開出的支票)　exchange check

交換技術信息協議　exchange of technical information agreement

交換物　〔拉〕quid pro quo

交換使用專利權　cross licensing

交換的廣度和深度　scope and depth of exchange

交換條件　terms of exchange

交換許可證(許可證貿易，雙方以價值相當的技術互惠互換，不需支付費用的許可證)　cross license

交換經紀(商品交易所成員，通常是經紀行經紀。代其他經紀或客戶交換部份或全部交易)　carrying broker

交換銀行，清算銀行　clearing bank

交替成本　alternative cost

交替收放的應變經濟政策　〔英〕stop-go policy

交替供給　alternative supply

交替需求　alternative demand

交替輪班　split shift

交際費　entertainment

"交鑰匙"工程項目　"turn-key" project

"交鑰匙"方式(指成套包建)　"turn-key"

"交鑰匙"合同　"turn-key" contract

"交鑰匙"條件　"turn-key" terms

充分平均利潤率　full average profit rate

充分表達，充分揭露　full disclosure

充分提供資金　full funding

充分就業　full employment

充分就業下的產值　full employment output

充分就業，失業率　full-employment unemployment rate

充分就業條件的平衡　full employment balance

充分競爭條件　fully competitive conditions

充足理由　sufficient reason

充足資本　abundant capital

字母數字記帳機　alphanumeric bookkeeping machine

字據　written evidence

安全存貨　safety inventories

安全存量　safety quantity, safety stock

安全係數　safety coefficient, safety factor

安全率　factor of safety

安全國際多式運輸　safe international multimodal transport

安全港　safeport

安全資本　security capital

安全裝載量　safety carrying capacity

安全標誌　safe mark

安全邊際(指售價超出成本的數額)　margin of safety

安排信貸償還　scheduled repayments on credit

安第斯共同市場　Andean Common Market

安裝費, 裝配費　erection cost

沖帳　strike a balance, reverse an entry

沖銷　charge against

沖銷壞帳　write off uncollectible account

沖轉盈餘　surplus charge

次入先出法　next-in first-out method

次日報價　unknown prices, next calculation

次生帳戶　secondary account

次要收益　secondary income

次要週期　minor cycle

次級方案　subprogramme

次級市場　secondary market

次級抵制　secondary boycott

次級資料　secondary data

次級債券　subordinated debenture

次　貨　throw-out, inferior quality, second quality goods

次等票據　second class paper

次等普通股票, 紅利後取股　deferred ordinary shares

次等證券　junior securities

次等權益(對一項財產較低等級的權益)　subordinated interest

次數　frequency

次數分配(把大量經濟資料整理分類, 壓縮精簡的一種統計方法)　frequency distribution

次適化　sub-optimization

次優方法　second best measure

次優化　sub-optimization

決策　decision-making

決策差別成本　discretionary cost

決策配制(根據已有的備選辦法的相互關係、相對重要性並根據既定參數來確定進一步方針的過程)　decision formulation

決策時滯　decision lag

決策會計　decision accounting

決策價格　policy price

決策點　decision point

決策樹(意指決策的來龍去脈, 有如樹枝分布狀)　decision tree

決策參數　decision parameters

決策程序　decision-making process

決算　final settlement of account, actual budget

決算日　closing day, tick day

決算表　final statement

決算帳戶　final account

決算審計　audit of returns

決標　award of bid

冰凍保險單　freezing insurance policy

冰凍條款　ice clause

冰雹保險　hail insurance

江輪　river steamer

守約　follow treaty

守約方　observant party

〔一〕

存入　deposit

存入保證金　margin (security) deposited with the bank

存入關棧報關單　entry for warehousing

存放同業　due from banks

存放於陰涼地方　store in a cool place

存放國外商品　goods in foreign countries

存放款比率　deposit loan ratio

存取時間　access time

存單　certificate of deposit

存根（指票據等）　counterfoil

存倉　deposit in godown

存倉費用　storage expenses

存海關未完稅貨物　bonded goods

存貨，現貨　goods in stock, inventory

存貨之平均成本計算　average costing of inventory

存貨收入憑單　stock debit notes

存貨交易　stocklot transaction

存貨估價　valuation of inventory

存貨抵押　field warehousing

存貨的後進先出計價法　last-in first-out method of inventory costing

存貨定價法　method of inventory pricing

存貨降為市價損失　loss on reduction of inventory to market

存貨統制卡　stock control card

存貨短缺成本　stockout cost

存貨週期　inventory cycle

存貨週轉率　inventory turnover ratio, rate of stock turnover

存貨損益　inventory holding gain or loss

存貨銷售比率　inventory-sales ratio

存貨盤點　inventory taking

存款　deposit, bank deposit

存款人　depositor

存款不足　not-sufficient-funds

存款不足支票　not-sufficient-funds check

存款收據　deposit receipt

存款利息　interest on deposit

存款利息所得稅　income tax on interest

存款利率　deposit interest rate

存款利率／貸款利率差價制（歐洲貨幣交易標價方法）　bid/offer spread

存款法定準備金　required reserves

存款到期日　expiry

存款金額　amount deposited

存款保證保險　depositary bonds

存款帳戶　deposit account

存款通貨　deposit currency

存款貨幣　deposit money

存款週轉率　deposit turnover

存款銀行　bank of deposit

存款餘額　outstanding deposit

存量　stock

存量決策（指人們希望以其他的資產來替代國內貨幣而改變社會之資產組合的一種決策）　stock decisions

存量管制　stock control

存摺　check book, pass book, deposit book

存摺保管證 passbook custodian certificate

存儲港，轉口港 entrepot port

死亡保險 death insurance, life insurance

死亡率 death rate, mortality rate

死者的遺產 estate of deceased person

死帳 dead loan

死資產 dead assets

死艙（算容積但不載貨的艙位） dead space

老本 original capital

老主顧 regular customer

老帳，舊帳 old account

老婦人（俗稱英格蘭銀行） old lady

百元，百鎊（鈔票） century

百分比 per cent (%)

百分比定額制 percentage quota system

百分比資產負債表 percentage balance sheet

百分率 percentage

百分率表 percentage statement

百分率耗減法 percentage depletion

百分誤差 percentage error

百分數 percentage

百分數表 percentage table

百分數效用損失 percentage utility loss

百分點 percentage points

百貨公司 department store

百萬卡（美國萬事達集團同日本東海銀行聯繫，以後者名義發行的信用卡） Million Card

百貨批發商 general line wholesaler

地方行銷 place marketing

地方批發市場 local wholesale market

地方稅 local tax

地位已確立之證券 seasoned security

地位表（資產負債表的新名） position statement

地契 crown lease, title deed

地租 ground rent

地產 land estate, land property

地產公司 real estate agency

地產經紀人 real estate broker

地區證券交易所 regional stock exchange

地價成本 cost of floor space

地價高漲 soaring estate

地價稅 assessment tax

地積比率 plot ratio

地點條款（海上保險中，限制承保人對那些已積存某一地點的貨物所承擔的責任） location clause

有支付能力的社會需求 effective social want, social needs with purchasing power

有支付能力的購買力 effective purchasing power

有外滙價值的有價證券 securities that have foreign exchange value

有市價證券　marketable securities

有付償能力聲明　declaration of solvency

有收益的資產　active assets, earning assets

有全權　plenipotentiary

有利可圖　lucrative, profitable

有利投資　good investment, lucrative investment

有利的貿易差額　favorable balance of trade

有利滙兌　favorable exchange

有利價格　remunerative price

有形供應(期貨市場術語，指持牌貨倉內的商品供應，包括已在途及產區內之"可見"供應)　visible supply

有形財產　corporeal property, visible assets, material property

有形貨物　tangible goods, material goods

有形產品　tangible products

有形設備成本　tangible equipment costs

有形貿易　visible trade

有形貿易差額　visible trade balance

有形資本　material capital

有形資產　tangible assets

有形滅失　physical loss

有形損耗　material wear and tear, physical depreciation

有投票權的股票　voting stock

有投票權的認繳款項　subscriptions carrying voting rights

有批註的滙票(指滙票上訂有條款，詳細指明所使用滙率或其他情況的滙票)　claused bill of exchange

有表決權股份　voting stock

有抵押品的公司債券　mortgage debenture

有抵押品的票據　bills with collateral securities

有抵押擔保之債權人　secured creditor

有法定時間限制的息票　statute barred coupon

有政府擔保的可靠股票　gilt-edged shares

有面值股票　par value stock

有附帶聲明的購股選擇權　qualified stock options

有毒　poison

有限公司　limited company

有限市場　limited market

有限合作　limited cooperation

有限合夥　limited partnership

有限兌換　limited convertibility

有限制之股份認購權　restricted stock option, qualified stock option

有限制的股票承購權　restricted stock option

有限制的物權　qualified property

有限股東　limited partner

有限的禁止令　limited prohibition

有限的競爭　restricted competition

有限品種商店　limited-line store

有限保證　limited guarantee

有限浮動滙率　limited floating rate

有限責任　limited liability

有限責任合夥　limited partnership

有限責任合夥人　limited partner

有限責任合夥營業法例　Limited Partnership Act

有限責任股東　limited shareholder

有限價格廉價百貨商店　limited price variety store

有限償債責任　limited liability

有限權利　limited interest

有限鑄幣制　limited-coinage system

有背簽擔保償還的債券　indorsed bond

有紀錄清償　satisfaction on the roll

有保證債權人　secured creditor

有效　valid

有效分散(投資)策略　efficient diversification strategies

有效分權　efficient departmentalization

有效生產　efficient production

有效佔有　effective possession

有效估計　efficiency estimation

有效利息率　effective interest rate

有效信貸　effective credit

有效保險　insurance in force

有效保護(指關稅保護不僅取決於對一種商品的名義關稅率，也取決於對在生產中用作進料的一切商品課徵的名義關稅率)　effective protection

有效時間　substantial time

有效率外滙市場　efficient foreign exchange market

有效現金成本　effective cash cost

有效控制(一般要擁有一個公司有表決權股票的51%，才能對該公司實行有效控制，但實際上，由於股票相當分散，就有可能擁有不到50%的所有權，即可實行有效控制)　working control

"有效能赤字"(世界經濟衰退期由美、西德、日本擴大進口，帶動各國經濟復甦。這樣出現的貿易赤字，被稱為有效能赤字)　virtuous deficit

有效期　validity, period of validity

有效期已滿的專利　expired patent, lapsed patent

有效貸款償還期結構　maturity structure of effective loan

有效滙率(指以各國與本國之貿易量佔本國之總貿易量的比重為權數所計算出來的本國與各國雙邊滙率的加權平均滙率)　effective exchange rate

有效資產　efficient portfolio

有效需求　effective demand

有效競爭　effective competition, workable competition

有能力償債證明書　affidavit of means

有條件出口　conditional export

有條件出售協議　conditional sales agreement

有條件交貨　conditional delivery

有條件免稅進口　conditionally duty-free

有條件承兌，部份承兌　qualified acceptance

有條件的允許　qualified consent

有條件的清償能力（僅能在某種條件下運用的）　conditional liquidity

有條件的最惠國條款　conditional most favoured nation clause

有條件的資金供應　conditional financing

有條件的證明書　qualified certificate

有條件契約　escrow

有條件清盤　conditional liquidation

有條件債券　escrow bond

有條件銷售　conditional sale

有條件轉讓契約（債券）　escrow agreement (bonds)

有條件釋放　conditional discharge

有息即期存款　interest-bearing demand deposit

有息貸款　lend money at interest

有缺陷的支票　lame check

有秩序銷售協議　orderly marketing arrangement

有追索權　with recourse

有追索權信用證　with recourse credit

有追溯力的　［拉］ex post facto

有專利權　patented

有清算值資產　admitted assets

有組織的市場　organized market

有組織的決策過程　organized decision-making process

有組織的證券交易所　organized security exchange

有過失　［拉］in delicto

有意欺騙　being calculated to deceive

有疑義時從寬　［拉］in dubio, pars mitior est sequenda

有獎儲蓄公債　premium savings bonds

有對價的報酬　for valuable consideration

有價抵押證券　documentary securities

有價證券　valuable securities, securities

有價證券市場　security market

有價證券投資　portfolio investment

有價證券和交易所法　securities and exchange law

有價證券和交易所委員會　Securities and Exchange Commission

有價證券所有權　titles to securities

有價證券的國外投資　portfolio foreign investment

有價證券選擇　portfolio selection

有價證券損益　profit and loss on buying and selling stocks, bonds (investments)

有價證券管理　portfolio management

有銷路的　merchantable

有撤銷的意向　［拉］animus revocandi

有廢除的意向　animus cancellation

有擔保負債　secured liability

有擔保帳款　secured account

有擔保貸款　secured loan

有擔保債券　secured bond

有錯當查，差錯待查，錯漏除外　errors and omissions excepted

有關成本，相關成本　relevant cost

有關係廠商　affiliated makers

有關當局，主管當局　appropriate authority

有優先權之債權人　preferred creditor

有權主張權利的人　person entitled to make a claim

再一次滲入市場的產品　second penetration product

再分股票　sub-divided share

再分保　retrocession

再分配　redistribution

再加工成本，繼續加工成本　cost of future processing

再出售(進口商無力付款提貨，只好在進口地點減價出售)　resale

再生產，複製　reproduction

再生產成本　reproduction cost

再生產投資　reproductive investment of capital

再生產價值　reproduction value

再生資源　renewable recources

再行銷　remarketing

再吸收成本　reabsorbed costs

再投資　reinvest

再投資用的利潤　plough back profit

再投資利潤　plow back earnings

再投資的收益　reinvested earning

再投資率　reinvestment rate

再估價　revaluation

再保險，分保　reinsurance

再保險佣金　reinsurance commission

再保險單　reinsurance policy

再訂貨，重新訂貨　re-order

再訂購點　reordering points; ROP

再開票公司(由跨國公司資金部設立的貿易中介公司)　reinvoicing company

再進口　re-import

再測信度　test-retest reliability

再裝船　re-shipment

再貼現　rediscount

再貼現票據　bills rediscounted

再發盤　repeat offer

再報價　repeat offer

再檢驗，再查對　re-examine

灰市(稀有貨品，以不尋常方法高價買賣，但不違反法律者為灰市，或稱半黑市)　gray market

灰領工人(指自動化工廠中觀察儀表的人)　gray-collar

灰份　ash

在工廠交貨　at factory

在出口點的美元價值　dollar value at point of exportation

在外股票數(指發行股票減庫存股票數)　outstanding stock

在交易所出售　sale at an exchange

在交易所掛牌　listing on the exchange

在交易所登記　listing on the exchange

在岸金融市場　onshore financial market

在啟運港憑單據付現　cash against document at port of shipment

在貨棧交貨　at godown

在船位，待裝船　on the berth

在運現金　cash in transit

在運商品　goods in transit

在製人工　labour in process　〔同 labour in progress〕

在製帳戶　manufacturing account

在製製造費用　burden-in-process, manufacturing expenses-in-process

在關棧貨物　goods in bond

在同一銀行轉讓轉帳　bancogiro

扣存準備金　deposit retained

扣押　distress, distraint

扣押令(指送達第三債務人的)　garnishee order

扣押抵債　foreclose, foreclosure

扣押申請人　distrainor

扣押財物　distraint, seizure of property

扣押財物估價　commission of appraisement

扣押財物的出售　distress sale

扣押船舶　seizure of the ship

扣除　deduct, subtract

扣除赤字　offsetting the deficit

扣除折舊前淨利　net income before depreciation

扣除折舊後淨利　net income after depreciation

扣除所得稅前淨利　net income before income taxes

扣除所得稅後淨利　net income after income taxes

扣除物價上漲因素　allowing for price rises

扣除預支　deduct prepayment

扣留　embargo, withhold

扣留貨物　detained goods

扣留船舶　arrest of ship, detention of vessel

扣留權　right of retention

扣貨留置權　possessory lien

扣款清單　withholding statement

扣價條款　deduction clause

扣繳　withhold

扣繳所得稅　withholding income tax

扣繳稅捐　taxes withheld

扣繳義務人　withholding agent

扣繳聯邦所得稅　federal income tax withheld

托盤(運輸用的木製平台或平板，一般為 32×48 英寸到 40×48 英寸)　pallet

托盤化組合裝運，托盤化單元運輸　palletized unit load

托盤化貨物　palletized cargo

托盤化運輸　palletized transport

托盤包裝，托裝　pallet packing

托盤貨物　pallet cargo

托盤裝運　pallet shipment

托盤運輸船　pallet ships

西伯利亞大陸橋運輸　Siberian land bridge transport

西伯利亞聯運（貨櫃／集裝箱）trans-Siberian container service

西非國家經濟共同體　Economic Community of West African State

西非清算所　West African Clearing House

西非貨幣聯盟　West African Monetary Union

西非關稅聯盟　West African Customs Union

西歐共同市場　European Common Market

共用權　right of common

共同市場　common market

共同主權　common sovereignty

共同成本，聯合成本　common cost, joint cost

共同合併　amalgamation

共同收益　community income

共同佔有（在一定時期內的合夥）joint tenure

共同投資　joint venture, joint financing

共同投標　joint bidding system

共同所有權　common ownership, joint-ownership

共同承兌人　co-acceptor

共同協商　joint consultation

共同放款　participation loan

共同事業　joint enterprise

共同信託基金　common trust fund

共同負債　joint and several liabilities

共同保險　co-insurance

共同保證　joint guaranty

共同財產　common property

共同借款人　co-borrower

共同海損　general average

共同海損分配　general average apportionment

共同海損分攤額　general average contribution

共同海損理算　general average adjustment

共同海損理算書　general average statement

共同海損擔保函　general average letter of guaranty

共同海損費用　general average expenditure

共同海損費用保險　general average disbursement insurance

共同海損犧牲　general average sacrifices

共同租賃　tenancy in common

共同租賃人　joint tenants

共同配額　common quotas

共同產品　joint products

共同票據　joint note

共同單位分析，同型分析　common-size analysis

共同發票人　co-drawer

共同過失　both-to-blame

共同資本　joint stock

共同債務人　co-debtor

共同農業政策　common agricultural

policy

共同農業基金　common agricultural fund

共同經營，權益聯營　pooling of interests

共同經營法，權益聯營法　pooling of interests method

共同需要　joint demand

共同對外關稅　common external tariff

共同實物計量單位　common physical unit of measure

共同關稅　common tariff

共有物主　part owners

共有財產　joint property

共有財產原則　community-property principle

共有基金投資　mutual fund investment

共享專利協定　patent-pool agreement

式樣　design

式樣不符　different type

〔｜〕

同一日內透支（指每日清算之前CHIPS系統成員銀行的付大於收的差額）　intraday overdraft

同一日期的　of even date

同一責任制　uniform liability principle

同一項目連續性收入　continuing nature relating to the same item of income

同工同酬　equal pay for equal work

同方向不同比例　same direction but in different proportions

同方向同比例　same direction and proportion

同步行銷　synchromarketing

同步指標　coincident indicator

同步現金流轉　synchronizing cash flows

同步增長　grow in step with, grow in phase with

同附貼樣品嚴格一致　strictly same as per attached sample

同品質樣品　same quality sample

同等利潤線　iso-profit line

同等級債權　debts of equal degree

同業公會　gild, guild, trade council, trade association

同業合併，水平合併　horizontal combination

同業存款　due to banks, deposit due to other banks

同業折扣　trade discount

同業協議　trade agreement

同業競爭　horizontal trade competition

同種期權（指同一形式，同種證券的購進或銷售的期權合約）　class of options

同樣品相似　similar to sample

同樣品大致相同　about equal to sample

早已到期　long past due

早已過期　long past due

早交貨　prompt delivery of goods

回升，復甦　recovered

回本期(衡量投資回本期間)　pay-back period

回扣　brokerage, rebate

回收　recovery

回收成本　cost recovery

回收折舊　recapture of depreciation

回收價值　returned value

回收期法，歸本年期法　payback period method

回收期倒數法，歸本年期倒數法　payback reciprocal method

回佣　return commission, rebate

回波作用(指不發達國家犧牲國內工業增長和農業工業化而將重點放在出口貿易所引起的不利狀況。貿易的回波作用比貿易的刺激作用更強烈)　backwash effect

回租(出售產權同時長期租回使用)　lease-back

回執，收據　acknowledgement of receipt

回單　acknowledgement

回單圖章　acknowledgement stamp

回程　return journey

回程租賃(指擁有使用設備的公司，將其設備賣給租賃公司，然後再從租賃公司租回該設備使用)　sale and leaseback lease

回程貨物　return cargoes

回程運費　back freight

回復所有　reduction into possession

回復的權利　reversionary interest

回購　buy-back, counter purchase

回購交易　buy-back deal

回購補償貿易　buy-back (compensatory) trade

回歸分析(從已知的自變量數值預測一個因變量數值的一種經濟分析方法)　regression analysis

回歸方程式(表示兩個或多個變數間關係的一種方程式)　regression equation

回歸係數　regression coefficient

回籠貨幣　withdraw surplus paper money, recall part of the currency issued, returns of the money

曲折下降　irregular lower

曲線回歸　curvilinear regression

曲線相關　curved correlation

因延遲給付而發出之傳票　default summons

因素分析　factor analysis

因素比較法　factor comparison system

因素成本　factor cost

因變量(一個變量的數值是由別的變量所決定)　dependent variable

此處開啟　open here

此處舉起　heave here

此端向上　this side up

吊上、吊下方式　lo-lo (lift-on and lift-off)

吊鈎，索具　tackle

"吊鈎到吊鈎"規則　"tackle to tackle" rule

吊裝（指貨櫃的吊裝） lo-lo shipment

吊裝船　lo-lo ship

吊裝貨　lo-lo cargo

吊裝貨櫃／集裝箱船　lo-lo container ship

吊銷土地使用證書　withdraw the land use certificate

吊橋　suspension bridge

光票（信用滙票）　clean bill, clean draft

光票信用證　clean letter of credit

光票託收　collection on clean bill

光票滙款　clean remittance

光船租賃　bareboat charter, demise charter

光顧　patronage

[丿]

件　piece

件號　package number

件數　number of package

休假工資　vacation pay

休假津貼　vacation allowance

仿造的　counterfeit

仿製品　imitation product

仲裁　arbitrage, arbitration

仲裁人　arbiter, arbitrator

仲裁立法　arbitration legislation

仲裁法　arbitration act

仲裁法庭　arbitration court

仲裁委員會　arbitration commission

仲裁長　umpire

仲裁協議　arbitration agreement

仲裁條款　arbitration clause

仲裁裁決　arbitration award

仲裁程序　arbitration proceedings

任意支配所得　discretionary income

任意決定信託（受託人有絕對自由運用信託的資金和入息）　discretionary trust

任意仲裁　voluntary arbitration

任意折舊法　depreciation-arbitrary method

任意折舊計算　free depreciation

任意背書　facultative endorsement

任意徵稅　arbitrary taxation

任意償還（指在寬限期過後，發行人可以任意償還債券的全部或一部份）　optional redemption

任選目的港　optional destination, optional ports

任選港交貨　optional delivery

任選港附加費　optional charge, option fee

任選港貨物　optional cargo

任選港提單　optional bill of lading

任選港裝船　optional shipment

任選發放方式的股利　optional dividend

自己保險　own insurance

自由土地保有人　freeholder

自由土地保有權　freehold

自由外滙　free foreign exchange

自由外滙市場　free exchange market

自由市場滙率　free market rate

自由企業制度　free enterprise system

自由兌換　free convertibility

自由兌換貨幣　freely convertible currency

自由投資　free investment

自由的多邊貿易　free multilateral foreign trade

自由保有地產　freehold property

自由信貸　untied loan

自由浮動(滙率)制度　freely floating system

自由浮動滙率　freely floating exchange rate, free exchange rate

自由配額　unilateral import quota

自由港，免稅口岸　free port

自由進入市場　liberal market access

自由貿易　free trade

自由貿易主義　manchesterism

自由貿易區　free trade zone

自由準備金　free reserve

自由運費率　open rates

自由經濟　free economy

自由關稅區　tariff-free zone

自由償還制度　free redemption

自由競爭　free competition

自主性交易　autonomous transactions

自主性投資　autonomous investment

自主管理權　self-management

自主關稅　national tariff; autonomous tariff

自平預算　balanced budget

自行申請破產　voluntary bankruptcy

自有資本　equity capital

自我目標管理形　self-fulfilment management style

自我投入　ego involvement

自我服務　self-service

自我風險　own risk

自我實現的需求　needs for self-actualization

自助商店　self-service store

自助零售　self-retailing

自保　self-insurance

自保保險公司(大企業成立為本系統服務的保險公司)　Captive Insurance Company

自限協定　self-restraint agreement

自動化　automation

自動化存貨管理系統　automated inventory control system

自動化銀行業務　automated banking

自動化辦公室設備　automated office equipment

自動支付　voluntary payment

自動出口配額制　voluntary export quotas, autonomous export quota, voluntary restraint of export

自動外滙分配　automatic foreign exchange allocation

自動代碼(電子數據處理用語，指能把符號語言翻譯成機器語言的代碼)　autocode

自動承保　automatic cover

自動信託　active trust

自動限制出口　voluntary restriction of export

自動限額　voluntary ceiling

自動保險　voluntary insurance

自動展期貸款　automatically renewable credit

自動記錄器　self-recorder

自動售貨　automatic selling

自動售貨機　automat

自動清算所(用電腦磁帶或磁盤代替紙支票的託收系統)　Automated Clearing Houses

自動清償貸款　self-liquidating loan

自動進口限額　automatic import quota

自動結束　voluntar winding up

自動結算轉帳系統　Clearing House Automated Transfer System

自動提款機　[美]cashomat[英]cashpoint

自動提繳保費貸款　automatic premium loan

自動補充存貨　automated replenishment

自動補足保額條款　automatic reinstatement clause

自動資金轉帳　automatic fund transfer

自動線　autoline

自動銷保(當戰爭爆發時)　automatic termination cover

自動調節　self-adjustment, self-regulation

自動調節經濟機制　mechanism whick regulates the economy automatically

自動撤銷　voluntary withdrawal

自動數據處理　automatic data processing

自動擱淺　voluntary stranding

自動獲准進口配額制　automatic import quota system

自動櫃員機　automatic teller machine

自動轉帳存款，自動撥款帳戶(儲蓄帳戶與支票帳戶相聯繫的一攬子帳戶)　automatic transfer service account

自動續保　automatic reinstatement

自買(拍賣人出高價自己購買)　bid in

自然失業率　natural unemployment rate

自然因素　natural causes

自然利率　natural rate of interest

自然風險　natural risk

自然損耗　natural losses, natural wastage, ordinary wear and tear

自然資源　natural resources

自然價格　natural price

自然增值　natural increase of value

自然營業年度，自然會計年度　natural business year

自備外滙　self-provided foreign exchange

自給自足　autarchy, autarky

自給率　degree of self-sufficiency

自給經濟　self-sufficing economy

自銷　self-sale

自燃　spontaneous combustion

自燃險　risk of spontaneous combustion

自營公司　operating company

自營商(證券交易中作為主體而不是充當代理人的個人或公司)　dealer

自營商業　do business on one's account

自償性(指信用本身具有清償能力)　self-liquidating

自願限制協定　self-restraint agreement

自願連鎖系統　voluntary chain

自變息債券(浮息債券。當市場利率超過預計水平,可按預先確定的利率自動變為定息債券)　drop-lock bonds

自變量(一個變量的數值不由別的變量所決定)　independent variable

多元回歸相關分析　multiple regression-correlation analysis

多元利益　multiplicity of interest

多元分析　multivariate analysis

多元共同性(指許多經濟時間數列,因共同的原因,隨時間而同時擴大或收縮的趨勢)　multicollinearity

多分配(數),多攤配數　overabsorption

多分配費用　overapplied expense

多付　overpay

多用途倉庫　multipurpose warehouse

多用途貨倉　multipurpose godown

多用途貨船　multipurpose vessel

多用途貨櫃船／集裝箱船　multipurpose container

多用途散裝船　multipurpose bulk carrier

多列,多計,誇大　overstatement

多次往返有效的出入境簽證　multiple entry-exit visa

多次抽樣檢驗　multiple sampling inspection

多次消費　multitime consumption

多式聯運,陸海空聯運　multimodel transport

多式聯運人　multimodel operator

多式聯運系統　multimodel transport system

多式聯運術語　multimodel parlance

多式聯運單據　multimodel transport document

多式聯運經營人　multimodel transport operator

多角化　diversification

多角化投資公司　diversified investment company

多角化控股公司　diversified holding company

多段式收益表　multiple-step form of income statement

多重稅　multiple tax

多重稅制　multiple taxation

多重循環　multi-cycle

多重關稅　multiple tariff

多品牌策略　multibrand strategy

多計總額　overfoot

多借　over-borrowing

多級分組　multi-step grouping

多級加工　multistage process

多級抽樣　multistage sampling

多級管理　multiple management

多倉合約數（香港指具體期貨市場持有多倉權益或合約之數目）　long interest

多倉客（香港市場係指"多頭"、"做多頭的人"）　long

多倉套戥，多頭套戥　long position in futures

多國公司　multinational corporation

多國性企業　multinational business, multinational organization

多國貨幣調整　multinational currency realignment

多國銀行　multinational bank

多國銀團　multinational banking consortia

多買　over-bought

多買地位　over-bought position

多等級倫敦銀行同業拆放利率（根據銀行信譽不同而有差異的 libor）　multi-tier LIBOR

多種貨幣干預　multicurrency intervention

多種貨幣措施　multiple currency practices

多種貨幣貸款　multicurrency loan

多種貨幣儲備制度　multicurrency reserve system

多種滙率　multiple exchange rate

多種滙率的外滙管理制度　multiple-rates system of exchange control

多賣　oversold

多賣地位　oversold position

多樣化經營　diversifying operations

多數股東　majority stockholders

多數股權　majority holding, majority interest

多數權利（指股東而言）　majority interest, controlling interest

多餘準備金　excess reserve

多層營業（指分層管制的股權公司等機構）　multiple-level operation

多頭　long position, bull, over-bought position

多頭戶　long side

多頭市場，牛市，好市　long market, bull market

多頭平倉，平倉　liquidation

多頭套期保值　long hedge

多頭帳戶　long account

多頭清理　long liquidation

多頭買家　long buyer

多頭操縱　long manipulation

多邊支付　multilateral payments

多邊技術援助　multilateral technical assistance

多邊承諾　multilateral commitment

多邊保障系統（關貿總協定用語）　multilateral safeguard system

多邊條約　multilateral treaty

多邊借貸　multilateral lending

多邊清算 multilateral clearing, multilateral compensation

多邊貿易 multilateral trade

多邊貿易協定 multilateral trade agreement

多邊貿易承諾制度 system of multilateral trade commitments

多邊貿易談判 multilateral trade negotiation

多邊稅務條約 multilateral tax treaty

多邊援助 multilateral aid

多邊農產品貿易機制 multilateral agricultural framework

多邊關稅談判 multilateral tariff negotiations (MTN)

多欄式日記帳 analytical journal, columnar journal, divided column journal, multi-column journal

多欄式分類帳 tabular ledger ［同 Boston ledger］

多纖貿易協定 Multi-Fibre Arrangement

血本 hard-earned capital

血統主義 jus sanguinis

行市記錄 quotation record

行市標準 basis of quotation

行李保險 baggage insurance

行使假文件 uttering forged document

行使期權（利用期權合約規定的權利，購入或賣出商品） exercise option

行使偽幣 uttering false coin

行政性保護 administrative protection

行政管理 administrative management

行家話 expert remark

行情 market quotations, tone

行情自動顯示器 ticker, ticker tape

行情表 tabular quotations

行為會計 behavioral accounting

行業盈利情況 industry-wide profit levels

行業暗語 lingo

行銷努力 marketing effort

行銷系統 marketing system

行銷信息系統 marketing information system; MIS

行銷促進 marketing promotion

行銷組合 marketing mix

行銷研究 marketing research

行銷通路 marketing channel

行銷溝通組合 marketing communication mix

行銷預算 marketing budget

行銷試驗 marketing experimentation

行銷管理 marketing management

行銷管理哲學 philosophy of marketing management

行銷稽核 marketing audit

行銷環境 marketing environment

丟失貨物 missing package

向外發展政策 outward-looking development policy

向外籌措資金 external financing

向承運人索賠　claim against carrier

向前連鎖效果　forward linkage effect

向前連鎖率　forward linkage

向前整合　forward integration

向後連鎖效果　backward linkage effect

向後連鎖率　backward linkage

向後整合　backward integration

向責任第三方追償　recourse against the responsible third party

合同　contract, indenture

合同上的收益　contractual revenue

合同成立地國家法律　〔拉〕lex loci contractus

合同有效期間　duration of contract

合同安排　contractual arrangement

合同前言　preamble

合同規定股利　contractual dividend

合同授權　contract authorization

合同期限　contract period

合同期滿　contract expires, expiration of the contract period

合同費率和非合同費率制度　contract rate and non-contract rate system

合同當事人指定適用合同的法律　prescriptive designation (by the parties to a contract of the law applcable to their contract)

合同價　contract price

合同慣例　contractual practice

合同數量　contract quantity

合成工業　compound industry

合成商品　composite commodity

合成謬誤　fallacy of composition

合作社　co-operatives

合作商店　cooperative stores

合作開發　joint exploitation

合作經營　cooperative business operation

合併　amalgamation, merger

合併收益　consolidated income

合併法例　Consolidation Acts

合併政策　consolidation policy

合併盈餘　consolidated surplus

合併留存收益表　consolidated statement of retained earnings

合併財務報表　consolidated financial statement

合併商譽　consolidated goodwill

合併訴訟　consolidation of actions

合併集團　consolidated group

合併溢值　consolidated excess

合併債務　consolidation of debts

合併損益表　combined income statement, consolidated income statement

合併資產負債表　aggregate (or amalgamated, or consolidated) balance sheet, combined balance sheet

合併裝運　consolidated shipment

合併銷售成本　consolidated cost of goods sold

合法之舉債幅度　legal debt margin

合法收入　lawfully-earned income

合法佔有　possessio

合法的　lawful

合法持有人　holder in due course

合法持票人　lawful bearer

合法債務差額　legal debt margin

合法證券　eligible papers

合法權益　lawful rights and interests

合計,總計,直加總記　footing

合約　contract, agreement

合約生命期(指具體期貨交易開始至交易期滿的一段時間)　life of contract

合約市場(指符合具體商品交易法規定買賣合約的交易委員會)　contract market

合約完成毛利計算法　complete contract method

合約品級(交易所正式批准可用於交收、結算期貨合約的商品等級)　contract grades

合約根基　root of agreement

合約單位(指具體期貨合約規定的商品實數)　contract unit

合約價格　contract price

合格上市證券　securities eligible for market operations

合格票據　eligible papers

合格證書　certificate of competency

合理的注意　reasonable care

合理的原因　reasonable grounds

合理時間內　within reasonable time

合理漲價　justified raise

合資企業　joint enterprise, joint venture

合資投資　joint venture investment

合資事業公司　joint venture com-pany

合資經營　joint venture

合資經營法　joint venture law

合資經營協議　joint venture agreement

合夥　partnership

合夥人　partner

合夥人薪金　partner's salary

合夥人權益變動表　schedule of change in partners' equity

合夥文據　partnership instrument

合夥企業　partnership

合夥法例　Partnership Act

合夥股東　part-owners

合夥契約　partnership agreement, articles of co-partnership

合夥條款　articles of partnership

合夥租賃　joint tenancy

合夥寄售　joint consignments

合夥會計　partnership accounting

合夥解散　partnership dissolution

合辦企業　joint enterprise

合營各方　parties to a joint venture

合營企業所得稅　joint venture income tax

全名　full name

全成本定價法　full cost pricing

全式提單　long form bill of lading

全面成本管理　overall cost control

全面沖淡之每股盈利　full diluted earning per share

全面回報率(投資者評定物業吸引力之方法)　overall rate of return

全面保付代理,全面貸款保收　full

factoring

全面通貨膨脹　generalized inflation

全面經濟效果　overall economic effect

全面質量管理制　total quality control; TQC

全面盤存　complete inventory, wall-to-wall inventory

全面盈餘觀點　clean surplus concept

全能代理人　universal agent

全值保險　full value insurance

全套單據　full set of documents

全套提單　full set of bill of lading

全通甲板船　flush deck vessel

全部付款　full payment, payment in full

全部成本，總成本　complete cost

全部負債　full liabilities

全部保險費　in-full premium

全部損失　actual total loss

全部審計，全部審核　complete audit, full audit

全部實際資本　stock of real capital, real capital stock

全部繳清的股份　full-paid stock

全球性分保合同　world-wide treaty

全球性行銷，總括市場(內外貿易)　global marketing

全球性經濟衰退　global recession

全球流通手段　global liquidity

全球配額，統括配額　global quota

全球進口配額　global import quotas

全球補償貿易　global compensation

全球銀行間金融電訊協會(1973 年 5 月由西歐、北美 200 多家銀行聯合組成)　Society for Worldwide Interbank Financial Telecommunication (SWIFT)

全球談判　global negotiation

全參與優先股　fully-participating preferred stock

全國營貿易　full state trading

全國證券市場體系(一種把上市證券成交行情傳遞到各地證券市場的通訊體系)　National Market System

全國證券交易商自動報價協會(美國)　National Association of Securities Dealers Automated Quotations (U.S.A.)

全責聯運提單(適應集裝箱運輸的新式提單，具有保險單和提單合一性質，又稱"保險提單")　full liability through B/L

全貨櫃／集裝箱專用船　full container ship

全程多種方式聯運　through multi-modal transport

全程單據　through document

全程運費　through freight

全程運輸　through transit, through carriage

全損　total loss

全損賠償　free of all average

全損險　total loss only (T.L.O.)

全蜂窩式貨櫃／集裝箱船　fully cellular container ships

全衡背書　indorsement in full

全數檢驗　one hundred percent inspection, 100% inspection

全額分期付款　installment in full

全額付清　full paid

全額付款租賃　full-pay-out lease

全額共同保險　full coinsurance

全額利潤分成　sharing the entire profit, sharing the total profit

全額保險　full insurance

全額累進稅制　taxation system based on progressive rates

全權代理人　universal agent

企業　enterprise

企業主報酬　entrepreneur's salary

企業自有資金　funds at the disposal of enterprises

企業自然年度　natural business year

企業投資　investment in enterprise

企業使命　business miss

企業政策　business policy

企業界　business circles

企業計劃　proposition

企業家　entrepreneur, enterpriser

企業倫理　business ethics

企業倒閉　business failure

企業責任　business responsibility

企業基金　enterprise fund, business fund

企業組織設計　business forms design

企業策略　business strategy

企業集團　business conglomerate

企業預測　business forecasting

企業道德　business ethics

企業精神　spirit of enterprise

企業聯合　cartel

各自負責協議（指保險）　knock for knock agreement

各別的　several

各別租借　severalty, several tenancy

各別責任　several liability

各別擔保　several guarantee

各國共同採用的法律　［拉］jus gentium

各期間價值變化　period-to-period value changes

各種債權人　sundry creditors

名產　staple

名牌產品　famous-brand products

名義上的所有者　nominal owners of

名義上原告　nominal plaintiff

名義上賠償　nominal damages

名義上營業支出　nominal expenditure

名義支付　payment for honour

名義收入　nominal income

名義收益　nominal earning, nominal yield

名義成本　nominal cost

名義有效匯率　nominal effective exchange rates

名義合夥人　ostensible partner, nominal partner

名義利率　nominal interest rate

名義利潤　nominal profit

名義作價　nominal allowed price

名義所得　nominal income

名義美元　nominal dollar

名義負債　nominal liability

名義託運人　nominal shipper

名義帳戶，虛帳　nominal account

名義國民收入　nominal national income

名義票面價格　nominal par

名義貼現率　nominal discount rate

名義報價　nominal quotation

名義資本　nominal capital

名義資產　nominal asset

名義董事　honorary director

名義滙率　nominal rate

名義價格　nominal price

名譽，信譽　reputation

先行經濟指標(指那些在總的經濟活動達到高點或跌到低點之前先出現高點或低點的指標)　leading indicators

先行經濟指標綜合指數(美商務部編製的)　composite index of leading indicators

先例　precedents

先例約束力的原則　rule of precedent

先受償債權人(指受償順序上得以排列在其他債權人之前，優先得到清償，又稱先位債權人)　senior creditor

先進先出法　first-in, first-out method

先進國家　advanced country

先期交稅票據　tax anticipation bills

先期承兌　anticipated acceptance

先期償還債券溢價　call premium

先買權　preemption, preemptive right

先徵啟用費(世界銀行從貸款生效日起收取的費用)　front-end-fee

先驅企業(指被確認為國家發展極需的企業)　pioneer enterprises

先驗估計數(不是通過計算以最後形式出現的參數估計數，而是利用從現有樣本資料中得不到的某些有關的經濟情報所作出的參數估計數)　priori estimates

先驗概率　prior probability

年成本比較法　annual-cost method of comparison

年利率　annual interest rate, rate of interest per annum

年金　annuity

年金折舊法　depreciation-annuity method, compound interest method

年金信託帳　annuity trust account

年金現值　present value of annuity

年度決算　annual accounts

年度財務報表　annual financial statement

年度配額　annual quota

年度結帳　annual closing

年度結算　annual reckoning

年度預算　annual budget

年度審計　annual audit

年度虧損　annual loss, losses in a year

年度總報告　general annual report

年保險費　annual premium

年訂貨成本　annual ordering cost

年息　annual interest

年租　annual rental

年終決算書　annual balance sheet

年終股利　year-end dividend

年終滙總　year-end summarization

年終審計　year-end audit

年終調整　year-end adjustment

年率表示的遠期外滙報價　forward quotation in annual percentage terms

年累積增長率　cumulative annual rate of growth

年報　annual report

年增長係數　annual improvement factor

年數總和折舊法 sum-of-years-digits depreciation method

年頭　the begining of a year

年關　new year's eve

年儲存成本　annual holding cost

年額　annual amount

年鑑　annual

印定條款(提單上的印刷條款，又稱免責條款，對比 stamp clause) printed clause

印花稅　stamp duties, stamp tax

印花稅法　stamp tax act

印花稅票　fiscal stamp, revenue stamp

印戳條款(又稱批註條款，對比印定條款) stamp clause

印鑑證明書　letter of indication

危害條款(歐洲貨幣協定中的一項條款) jeopardy clause

危險分佈　distribution of risk

危險分級　classification of risk

危險性質變更　change in nature of risk

危險度　degree of risk

危險品　dangerous articles

危險品標誌　dangerous mark

危險訊號　danger signal

危險責任的起期　attachment of risk

危險貨物　dangerous goods

危險經理(大企業設立主管危險認識、測定、處理的主管人員) risk manager

危險點(美國稅則委員會對每項進口商品的最低稅率) peril point

危險類別　class of risk

危險藥物條款　dangerous drugs clause

成文法　written law

成文法上的留置權　statutory lien

成文契約　literal contract

成本公式　cost formula

成本分析　cost analysis

成本分配　cost distribution, cost allocation

成本分類　cost classification

成本分攤　allocation of costs, cost assignment

成本加利(合同訂明買方同意對賣方支付的金額，取決於賣方生產所售貨物和勞動的成本加上一定百分率或固定金額的利潤) cost-plus

成本加利計價法　cost-plus pricing

成本加保險費價　cost and insurance

(C.&I.)

成本加值　cost markup

成本加運費　cost and freight — C. &F., CFR

成本加價基礎　cost plus basis

成本平衡模式　cost balancing model

成本收入分析　cost-revenue analysis

成本收回法　cost-recovery method

成本收益分析　cost-benefit analysis

成本收益比率　cost-benefit ratio

成本收益估價　cost-benefit evaluation

成本收益差額帳戶　margin account

成本回收期　period of cost recovery

成本因素　cost factor, cost element

成本決定　cost determination

成本同等差　equal difference in cost

成本吸收活動　cost-absorbing activities

成本估計　cost estimate, cost estimating

成本利潤率　rate of profit based on the cost of production, profit rate on costs

成本定率折舊法　depreciation-fixed percentage of cost method

成本的極小化　cost minimization

成本降低計劃　cost deduction program

成本計算　costing, cost calculation

成本計算表　costing schedule

成本計算基礎　bases of costing

成本指數　cost index number

成本，保險費加運費，到岸價格　cost, freight, insurance (C.I.F.)

成本流動　cost flow

成本流量　cost flow

成本效益分析　cost-benefit analysis

成本效率　cost-efficiency, cost-effectiveness

成本差異　cost variance

成本帳戶　cost account

成本控制　cost control

成本推動的通貨膨脹　cost-push inflation

成本累積法　cost accumulation method

成本會計　cost accounting

成本會計規程，成本手冊　cost manual

成本會計準則聲明　statement of cost accounting

成本對銷售價格的比率　ratio of cost to selling price

成本與營業收入相配合　matching cost with revenue

成本審計　cost audit

成本膨脹　cost inflation

成本證明　proof of cost

成份　composition

成份百份率財務報表　common-sized financial statement, percentage statement

成交　make a bargain, conclude a transaction

成交通知書　advice note

成交量　volume of business

成交確認書　sale confirmation

成交價與市價背離大的期權　deep out-of-money option

成交價與市價略有背離或背離很大的期權　slightly out or deep out-of-money options

成交價格　transaction price

成果共享　gain sharing

成果管理　result's management

成品油管道　product oil pipeline

成套設備　complete plant, complete sets of equipment, complete factories

成套設備出口　complete plant export

成套轉讓　package transfer

成組化貨運　cargo unitization

成組裝運,單元裝運　unit load

成數分保合同　reinsurance treaty

[一]

劣品　inferior quality

劣貨　low grade goods, faulty goods

劣幣　bad coin

收入　income, revenue, proceeds, earning

收入水平　income level

收入分配　income distribution

收入利息　interest received

收入政策　income policy

收入效應　income effect

收入速度　income velocity

收入項目　items of receipt

收入債券(發行公司在賺到一定收入時才派息的債券)　income bonds

收入彈性　income elasticity

收入總額　gross income, gross receipts

收方(簿記)　debit, debit side

收支　revenue and expenditure, income and expenses

收支不平衡　payments inbalance

收支平衡　balance between income and expenditure, balance of income and outlay, maintain a balance between receipts and payments

收支平衡點　receipt and disbursements breakeven point

收支表　statement of income and expenditure

收支相抵　revenues and expenditures are in balance, expenses balance receipts

收支差額　gap between revenues and expenditures, balance of payment

收支滙總表　summary of receipts and expenditures

收支範圍　division of the revenue and expenditure boundaries

收支憑證　receipt and payment documents

收市訂單(要求在收市價範圍內買賣商品合約的訂單)　market on close

收市執行（表明以官方確定之收市價執行之訂單）on close, execcution at the close

收市報價，收市行情　closing quotation

收市價　closing price

收付實現基礎　cash basis

收回投資　recouping the capital outlay

收回股份基金　stock redemption fund

收回非法扣留動產　replevin

收回的票據　retired bill

收回租借　re-entry

收回（成本）基礎　discovery basis

收回貸款，催收貸款　call in a loan, recall loans, recover loans

收回資本　capital recovery

收回資金之時間標準　recovery guideline

收回債券　retire bonds

收回價值，殘值　recover value

收回優先股票準備　reserve for redemption of preferred stock

收回舊欠　collect outstanding accounts

收回壞帳收益　income from recoveries of bad debts

收取的利率　interest charges

收訖　received, paid, payment received, received in full

收訖章　received stamp

收益　income, yield, constand return

收益力　earning power

收益之實現　revenue realization

收益及支出明細表　statement of income and expenditure

收益支出　revenue expenditure, income charges

收益決定　income determination

收益曲線（某種證券到期日和收益之間的關係，正收益曲線表示期限越短，利息越少；期限越長，利息越多）yield curve

收益表　earnings statement, income statement

收益表比率　income sheet ratio

收益表帳戶　income-statement accounts

收益受益人　income beneficiary

收益能力　earning power

收益率　earning rate, earnings yield

收益帳戶　income account

收益減除數　income deductions

收益掉期法（賣掉持有的低收益債券，買入另一高收益債券）yield pickup swap

收益資本化價值　earnings capitalized value

收益債券（即收入債券）revenue bond, income bond

收益預測　earnings forecast

收益對風險比率　reward-to-variability ratio

收益遞減　diminishing returns, decreasing profits

收益遞增　increasing returns

收清　received in full

收貨人　consignee

收貨人倉庫　consignee's warehouse

收貨員　goods clerk

收貨候裝　received for shipment

收貨費用　receiving expenses

收貨憑單　consignment sheet

收帳政策　collection policy

收帳流動值，收帳流動期　collection float

收帳期　collection period

收帳費用　collection expense

收得量差異　yield varance

收款　make collections

收款人　payee

收款員　receiving teller

收款率(指帳款回收率)　collection rate

收款傳票　receipt voucher

收款銀行　due bank

收買權　pre-emption

收稅官　tallagers

收稅單　duty paid certificate

收債人　debt collector

收盤　closing quotation

收盤上漲，高價收盤　closing high

收盤叫價　closing call

收盤滙率　closing rate

收盤價，收市價　closing price

收據，收入　receipt

收縮包裝　shrink packing

收購價格　procurement price

如上所述　〔拉〕ut supra

如下所述　〔拉〕ut infra

如有錯誤，可以更正　errors & omission excepted

如所指示　〔拉〕ut dictum

如期的　punctual

好友，多頭　bull, long side

好市，看好市場　〔美〕long market, 〔英〕bull market

奸商，投機商人　profiteer

孖展(即保證金，香港市場對客戶按給經紀作擔保的金額，或經紀按給結算公司作擔保的金額叫做＂孖展＂)　margin

七　畫

〔、〕

良好平均品質　fair average quality

良好銷售品質　good merchantable quality

良性循環 benign cycle between, sound cycle of economic activities

辛廸加投標　syndicated tender

辛廸加貸款，銀團貸款　syndicated loan

序列分析　sequential analysis

序列生產過程　serialization

序列抽樣　sequential sampling

序列程序機　sequence program machine

序列債券　serial bonds

序時帳簿 chronological book, book of chronological entry

序時記錄 chronological record

完工百分率制 percentage-of-completion basis

完工百分率制之存貨估計 percentage-of-completion inventory valuation

完工程度毛利計算法 degree-of-completion method, percentage-of-completion method

完全上層建築船 complete super structure vessels

完全公開(公司為發行證券向公眾報價前，將公司全部情況向證券交易委員會公開申明) full disclosure

完全公開原則(證券管理原則之一) principle of full disclosure

完全成本法 absorption costing, full costing

完全承保 full coverage

完全消耗係數 complete consumption coeficient

完全破產 strong broke, dead broke

完全責任 full liability

完全規範化決策 completely specified decision

完全國營貿易 full state trading

完全競爭 pure competition

完全競爭市場 perfect competition market

完全獨佔 perfect monopoly

完全關稅同盟 complete customs union

完好貨物 sound goods

完好貨物到達時淨值 net arrived sound value

完稅 pay tax

完稅後交貨 delivered duty paid

完稅貨價 duty paid price

完稅進口報關單 entry for home use

完稅價格 dutiable price, duty-paid value

完稅證明，完稅憑證 duty-paid proof

完整性 completeness

完整背書，正式背書 full endorsement

完整租借 entire tenancy

完整條款 entire agreement clause

宏觀分析 macro-analysis

宏觀決策 policy-making in a macrocosmic sense

宏觀結構 macrostructure

宏觀資金融通率(指一國當年年初官方儲備總額，國內金融機構外滙資產淨額，從國際金融市場能獲得最高貸款額，和該國當年商品、勞務出口收入對該國當年商品、勞務進口總額、外債支付額和到期的外債償本額的對比) macro economic financing ratio

宏觀會計 macroaccounting

宏觀預測 macro-forecast

宏觀經濟清償率(根據一國當年所需支付的外債還本付息額，同它所能獲得的短期資金總額進行對比，以分析該國清償能力的方法) macro economic liquidity ratio

宏觀經濟模式 macroeconomic model

宏觀經濟學 macroeconomics

宏觀經濟變量 macroeconomic variable

社會分工 division of labour in society

社會分攤資本 social overhead capital

社會平均成本盈利率 profit ratio on the basis of the average social cost

社會成本 social costs

社會共同需要 common needs of society

社會保險 social insurance

社會風險 social risk

社會傾銷(指利用工資低、勞動時間長等惡劣條件而降低生產成本，以低廉價格向外國推銷其產品) social dumping

社會福利事業保險 social welfare insurance

社會福利函數 social welfare function

社會機會成本 social opportunity cost

社會總產品 total social product, aggregate social product, gross social product

社會總資本的再生產和流通 reproduction and circulation of aggregate social capital

社會主義市場 socialism market

社會財富 social wealth

社會目標 social goals; social objective

社會行銷觀念 societal marketing concept

社會保險 social security

社會技術系統方法 sociotechnical system approach

社會計量法 socimetry

社會需求 social needs

社會福利 social welfare

社會固定成本 social overhead infrastructure

社會契約 social contract

社會價值 social value

社會經濟技術 sociometric technique

社會經濟(學)的 sociometric

社會經濟革命 socio-economic revolution

社會機會成本 social opportunity cost

社經變數 socioeconomic variables

社團法人 juridical person of an association

兌付禮券 gift coupons cashing

兌成現金 cashing

兌換 exchange, convert, agiotage

兌換不利 exchange against us

兌換平價 conversion parity

兌換有利 exchange for us

兌換收益 exchange profit

兌換佣金 exchange commission

兌換折價 exchange discount

兌換商　money dealer, money exchanger

兌換率　rate of change

兌換現金　exchange for cash, exchange for ready money

兌換紙幣　exchange of paper currencies

兌換票據　exchange of a bill

兌換期票　bill for a term

兌換損益　exchange gain or loss

兌換溢價　exchange premium

兌換憑單　exchanging slip

兌現　pay cash, redemption, cash note

兌現支票　cash check

兌現紙幣　redeemable paper money

冷門股票　low-price issues

冷背商品　unsaleable

冷軋鋼板　cold-roll steel sheets

冷氣設備　air-conditioning equipment

冷氣通風貨櫃/集裝箱　ventilated enclosed container

冷凍食品　frozen foods

冷凍貨(冷藏船裝運華氏30°以下貨物)　frozen cargo

冷凍貨櫃/集裝箱　refrigerated enclosed container

冷凍連鎖　cold chain

冷貨(冷藏船裝運保持華氏30°-40°貨物)　chilled cargo

冷藏車　refrigerator-car, reefer

冷藏條款　refrigeration clause

冷藏庫,冰箱　refrigerator

冷藏船　refrigeration ship, reefer

冷藏貨　refrigerated goods

冷藏貨艙位　reefer space

冷藏貨櫃/集裝箱　refrigerated container, reefer container

冷藏艙　refrigerated compartment

冷藏險　risk of frozen products

沉入成本，旁置成本，已投入成本　sunk cost

沉沒　sinking

汽車互撞免賠協定　knock for knock agreement

汽車行　garage

汽車車身保險　motor hull insurance

汽車保險　motor car insurance, automobile insurance

汽車乘客險　motor vehicle passenger insurance

汽車第三者責任保險　motor vehicle third party insurance

汽車責任保險　motor car liability insurance

汽車貨櫃/集裝箱　auto container

汽車貸款收益證券(以汽車貸款作抵押並提供收益的投資證券)　certificate of automobile receivables

汽車運輸　motor vehicle transportation

汽墊船　hovercraft

沒收　forfeiture, confiscate

沒收走私貨物　seize smuggled goods

沒收股本盈餘　surplus from forfeited stock

沒收股份,作廢股　forfeit stock (share)

沒收股款 forfeited stock subscription

沒收法例 Forfeiture Act

沒收物的處置 disposal of forfeits

沒收押品 forfeited securities arising from loans

沒收性賦稅 confiscatory taxation

沒收財產 forfeiture, confiscation of property

沒收貨物 confiscated goods

沒收擔保品 foreclosure

沒收擔保品價值 foreclosure value

沒有限定的權利 indefinite right

沒銷路 unsaleable

判決的豁免 immunity from judgement

判決產權歸屬 quiet title

判決確定的費率 judgement rates

判決確定的債務 judgement debt

判決確定的債務人（法院判決需償還款項的人） judgement debtor

判決確定的債權人（依據法院判決得到債權的人） judgement creditor

判決應付款項 judgement payable

判決應收款項 judgement receivable

判斷市場機會 assess market opportunities

判斷抽樣 judgement sampling

判斷預測 judgement forecasts

[一]

批 lot

批改條款，批單（附加更改內容的） endorsement, rider

批准 approved, ratified

批註 endorsement

批量生產 job-lot manufacturing, batch production

批量保付代理，批量貨款保收業務 bulk factoring

批發 job, wholesale, sale in bulk

批發中間商 wholesale middleman

批發市場 terminal market

批發折扣 trade discount, distributor discount

批發物價指數 wholesale price index

批發商 wholesale merchant, wholesaler, jobber, warehouse-man

批發帳戶 wholesale account

批發貿易 wholesale trade

批發價 at wholesale price, trade price

批發銷售 wholesale sales

投入 input

投入產出分析 input and output analysis

投入產出比率 input-output ratio

投入資本 equity capital, invested capital, paid-in capital, venture capital

投入資本所得率 rate of return on invested capital

投放 release by

投放市場 release

投股說明書 prospectus

投保　cover

投保價值　insured value

投郵主義（英美法關於承諾的規則，即受要約人把承諾通知投入郵箱便生效。）　deposited acceptance rule

投郵生效原則　mail-box rule

投資　investment

投資中心　investment centre

投資中間人　investment middleman

投資支出　investment outlays

投資公司　investment company, investment corporation, investment house

投資公司股票（指投資公司以共同基金名義出售其股票）　investment company shares

投資比例　ratio between investments in

投資分析　investment analysis

投資分類帳　investment ledger

投資市場　investment market

投資失當　investment dislocation

投資回收期　payback period

投資托拉斯　investment trust

投資決策　investment decision

投資收益　income from investments, income on investment

投資收益率　rate of return

投資利息　interest on investment

投資估價　investment appraisal

投資係數　investment coeffients

投資於股票　invest in stock

投資於企業　invest in an enterprise

投資於新企業的資本　equity capital

投資協會　investment association

投資承諾　investment commitment

投資前方案　pre-investment programmes

投資前的研究　preinvestment studies

投資前活動　pre-investment activity

投資前項目　pre-investment project

投資前基金　pre-investment fund

投資前援助　pre-investment assistance

投資信用（指長期信用）　investment credit

投資信託　investment trust

投資信貸　investment credit

投資計劃　investment plan, investment programs

投資函數　investment function

投資盈餘率　rate of return

投資刺激　investment incentives

投資保險　investment political risks insurance

投資保證　investment guarantee

投資能力　ability to invest

投資淨收入　net investment income

投資淨收入稅　tax on net investment income

投資淨收入現值　net present value of income from investment

投資淨額　net investment

投資特性　investment feature

投資高指標　bigger investments

投資高漲　investment boom

投資時滯　investment lag

投資乘數　investment multiplier

投資帳　investment account

投資率　investment rates

投資開支　investment expenditure

投資組合　investment portfolio

投資組合風險　investment portfolio risk

投資組合管理　investment portfolio management

投資研究　investment research

投資專家　investment expert

投資貨幣　investment currency

投資費用　investment cost

投資稅收抵免（美國對投資者在購買設備後，可從其應稅利潤中扣除購買價格的一定百分比）investment tax credit

投資景氣　investment boom

投資策略　investment strategy

投資報酬率　rate of return on investment

投資結構　pattern of investment, structure of investment, composition of investment

投資週轉率　investment turnover rate

投資資本　investment capital

投資損失　investment loss

投資意向　investment intention

投資傾向　propensity to invest

投資補助金　investment grant

投資債券　investment bond

投資經紀人　investment broker

投資業務　investment portfolio

投資過剩　over-investment

投資預算支出　below-the-line expenditure

投資經營者　investment manager

投資銀行　investment bank, investment-banking

投資賦稅優惠　investment tax credit

投資價值　investment value

投資報酬率定價法　rate-of-return pricing

投資實得率　yield rate

投資醞釀階段　gestation period of investment

投資優待　investment incentive

投資購買　investment buying

投資總規模　volume of total investment

投資總量　aggregate investment

投資總額　gross investment

投資環境　investment climate

投資證券的市值　market value of investment securities

投資證券買賣　investment securities traded

投資顧問　investment adviser (or consultant)

投資權益　investment interest

投棄貨物（船舶遇險時投棄的貨物）jetsam

投標　tender, submission to

投標人、競買人　bidder, tenderer

投標日　tender date

投標中分擔權益的期權（銀行把期權賣給招標人，招標人再把它轉賣給各投標人，費用由各投標人分攤，

中標者自動獲得期權） share currency option under tender

投標手續 tender procedures

投標出價 tender offers

投標保函 tender guarantee, bank's guarantee for bid bond

投標保證金 bid bond, tender bond

投標契約 bidding contract

投標訂價法 sealed bid pricing

投標書（工程主代投標人擬定的一般有規定格式的文件） form of tender

投標須知 instruction to bidders

投標期間買滙期權 tender to contract option

投標價格 price tendered

投機 speculation

投機市場 speculation market

投機交易 speculative transaction, speculation

投機交易所 bucket shop

投機者 speculator

投機者有意抬高市價（指在交易所內交易） rigging

投機性約期套購 straddle

投機性需求 speculative demand

投機事業 speculation business

投機活動 profiteering

投機倒把 engage in speculation

投機動機 speculative motive

投機商人 gambler

投機買賣 speculative trade

投機資本 risk capital, venture capital

把日期遲填 post date

把支票劃上橫線 cross a check

把握機會 grasp a chance

折半信度 split-half reliability

折合 equivalent to

折扣 deduct, discount, abatement, rebate

折扣收入 discount earned

折扣商店 discount store

折扣習慣 customary discount

折扣發行（債券） issue bonds at discount

折扣期間 discount period

折扣損失 discount loss

折扣價格 prices at a discount

折扣額 deduction

折耗 depletion

折耗成本 depletion cost

折射指數 index of refraction

折現因子 discount factor

折現偏好 discount preference

折算風險暴露，折算暴露 exposure to translation risk, translation exposure

折算率 conversion rate

折算為現值 discount to present value

折算損益（指外幣折算的） translation gain or loss

折算調整（指貨幣的） translation adjustment

折價 convert into money, evaluate in term of money

折價保值 assessment of value in monetary terms and the maintenance of value

折價物　trade-ins

折價停板　（香港金銀貿易場規定，若即市價較前節市公價差達黃金保證金限額時，貿易場便會宣佈停止交易）　suspend trading

折價累積　accumulation of discount

折舊　depreciation

折舊不足　underdepreciation

折舊方法　method of depreciation

折舊—分期定額法　depreciation-fixed instalment method

折舊—分期遞減法　depreciation-reducing instalment method

折舊—任意決定法　depreciation-arbitrate method

折舊—估價法　depreciation-appraisal method

折舊—年金法　depreciation-annuity method

折舊—重置成本法　depreciation-replacement method

折舊—直線法　depreciation-straight-line method

折舊—原始成本定率法　depreciation-percentage of original cost method

折舊效能　efficiency of depreciation

折舊率　depreciation rate

折舊費用　depreciation expense

折舊基金　depreciation fund

折舊基數　depreciation base

折舊準備　depreciation reserve

折舊複利法　compound interest method of depreciation

折舊餘值變率法　changing percentage of cost less scrap of depreciation

折舊餘額遞減法　declining balance method of depreciation

折舊償債基金法　sinking fund method of depreciation

折讓，津貼　allowance

折讓及折扣　allowance and rebate

折讓準備　allowance reserve

抗拉強度　tensile strength

抗稅　refuse to pay tax

抗衡性投資　defensive investment

抗壓強度　compressive strength

抗彎強度　flexible strength

拋空基差(期貨市場術語，指沽出即期商品時，手中無貨，但已購入期貨合約對冲的一種交易)　short the basis

拋售……的投機活動　speculate against

拋售貨物　sell large quantities of goods, undersell

拋售儲存　stock-releasing

拋棄和浪打落海（貨物）　jettison and washing overboard

拋錨，停泊　anchored

找零備用金　change funds

找零錢　change, to give change

扭轉性行銷　conversional marketing

技術分工　technical division of labour

技術引進　introducing of technology from abroad

技術生命週期　technology life cycle

技術合作　technical cooperation

技術交流　technical exchange

技術投入係數　technical input coefficient table

技術吸收　the absorption of technology

技術性回升(指交易所市場本身條件變化，導致價格變動)　technical railly

技術差距　technology gap

技術專利　technical monopoly

技術專家控制體制　technostructure

技術密集工業　skill-intensive industries

技術密集的　technology-intensive

技術密集的投資　technology-intensive investment

技術訣竅　technical know-how

技術訣竅市場　technical know-how market

技術訣竅協議　technical know-how agreement

技術訣竅費　technical know-how fee

技術援助　technical assistance

技術援助協議　technical assistance agreement

技術貿易　technology trade

技術貿易支付方式　payment of technology transfer

技術預測　technical forecasting

技術擴散　true diffusion international

技術轉移　technology transformation

技術轉讓　technology transfer

技術簽證　technical visa

技術壟斷　technical monopoly

技術繼續援助和反饋權(技術貿易協議上規定輸出方的任何技術改進須提供給輸入方；而輸入方的任何技術改進也須隨時提供給輸出方，前者叫做"技術繼續援助"；後者叫做"反饋")　continuing assistance and grant-back right

技術鑑定　technical expertise

杜邦系統　Du Pont System

材料分配　distribution of stores

材料成本　cost of material

材料交換　stores swap

材料供應　material supplies

材料周轉率　material turnover

材料缺乏　materials shortage

材料消耗　material consumption

材料核算　material accounting

材料採購　material purchases

材料清單　bill of material

材料搬運　material handling

材料管理　material management

材料需求規劃　material requirement planning

材料盤存　material inventory

材料調劑　material adjustment

材料調撥　material appropriation

均方差(測定標誌值之間差異程度之重要指標)　variance and standard

deviation

均等分攤法　equal instalment system

均等向量　equalized vector

均等等價調期(美國術語，指賣出一宗債券的同時，又買進同名同等數量的另一宗債券，而不考慮現金淨差額)　even par swap

均等機會　equal chance

均衡平價區　equilibrium parity zone

均衡利率　equilibrium rate of interest

均衡削減保護措施(關貿總協定用語)　balanced reduction of protective measures

均衡值　equilibrium value

均衡條件　equilibrium condition

均衡理論　equilibrium theory

均衡滙率　equilibrium exchange rate

均衡價格　equilibrium price

均衡補償準備　equalization reserve

更正分錄，改錯分錄　correcting entry

更正條款　amendment clause

更正通知　correction advice, advice to correction

更正記帳　correction entry

更正記帳憑證　correction voucher

更正憑單　correction voucher

更正圖章　correction chop

更改　alteration

更改支票　altered cheque

更改目的港　alteration of destination

更改航程　change of voyage

更改票據　altered bill

更改提單　altered bill of lading

更換公債　renewal bond

更新成本　renewal cost

更新投資　replacement investment

更新固定資產　renovation of fixed assets, renewal of fixed assets

更新基金　renewal fund

更新設備周期　cycle for updating equipment

更新換代(指產品)　replace the older generations of products by new ones

更新選擇權　renewal option

否定追索權　recourse repudiation

否認合同有效　repudiate a contract

否認仲裁員管轄權的抗辯　plea as to the arbitrator's jurisdiction

否認仲裁庭管轄權的抗辯　plea as to arbitral jurisdiction

否認法院管轄權的抗辯　plea as to the jurisdiction of the court

否認債務　repudiation

形式上的差別　phenomenal difference

形式決算表　proforma statement

形式效用　form utility

形式原因　formal cause

形式產品　formal product

形式售貨清單(寄售的)　proforma account sales

形式發票　pro forma invoice

形成價值實體的量　value-creating

sustance

赤字　deficit, red ink

赤字財政　deficit financing

赤字記錄　red-ink entry

赤字開支　deficit spending

赤字發行　reckless issuing of bank-notes

赤字提貨單　red bill of lading

赤字預算　deficit budgeting

赤字餘額　red balance

走私　smuggle, owling

走私者，走私犯　owler, smuggler

走私船　smuggler

走私貨　smuggled goods

走私販私活動　smuggling and sale of smuggled goods

走私集團　smuggling ring

克拉(寶石重量單位，一克拉等於二百毫克)　carat

克萊頓法(美國一系列反托拉斯法中補充最初的《謝爾曼反托拉斯法》的一項法律)　Clayton Act

求償權　right of claim, right of recourse

車站交貨　delivery at the railway station

車站搬運工　[美]red cap

車馬費，交通津貼　transportation allowance, transportation fee

車禍保險　accident insurance

車運費用　trucking expenses

車輛保險　car insurance

巫術經濟學(美國布什總統供應學派理論的貶稱)　voodoo economics

[丨]

快信　express mail

快速收回的貸款　quick loan

快速貨櫃／集裝箱船貨運服務(船只停基本港口)　express container service

快速報價帶(交易所的報價帶)　fast tape

快捷信貸(萬國寶通銀行 1989 年推出的一種透支服務)　ready credit

快運公司　express company

快運貨車　red ball

快運貨物　express goods, express consignment

快運費　expressage

快裝費　dispatch money

快遞費　express fee

快餐　quick lunch

吸收合併　consolidation by merger

吸收存款　take deposits, attract deposits

吸收貨幣　absorb currency

吸收理論(運用凱恩斯的宏觀理論分析國際收支問題的一派理論)　absorption approach

吸收游資　absorb idle funds

吸取先進技術　utilize the advanced technology

吸納成本法　absorption costing

足金　pure gold, solid gold

足價　full price

足價成本計算法　full price costing

呆帳，壞帳　bad debts, doubtful accounts, uncollectible accounts

呆帳比率（指呆帳與銷貨淨額之比）　bad debts ratio, ratio of bad debts to credit sales

呆帳準備　bad debt provision, bad debt reserve

呆帳損失　bad debt loss

呆帳劃銷　bad debt written off

呆滯市場　stagnant market, sluggish market

呆滯存貨　inactive stock, slow moving inventory

呆滯貨品　drug in the market

呆滯資產　slow assets

町　cho

里程碑，里程碑法　milestone

里程碑排程　milestone scheduling

里程碑預算　milestone budget

刪去　delete, cross out

刪除條款　deleted clause

刪除帳面值　write-off

串味　tainted by odour

串味險（被保險的食用物品等貨物在運輸過程中，因受其他物品影響而引起的串味損失）　risk of odour

串通圍標　collusive bidding

串通舞弊　collusion

貝氏決策理論　Bayesian Decision Theory

貝塔係數（計量證券風險的一項指標，其係數為 1.0 表示證券的風險是正常，即其變化幅度與證券市場行情的平均變化相等，如果大於 1.0，表示該證券有較大的風險）　beta coefficient

貝塔風險（通過抽樣調查，推斷某一帳戶的餘額無誤差，但對該帳戶的餘額進行總體檢查後，卻證明其存在相當大的誤差）　beta risk

貝塔誤差　beta error

見票即付　on demand, at sight

見票即付支票　bearer cheque, bearer check

見票即付票據　bill at sight, demand note

見票即付滙票　bill payable at sight, bill drawn payable at sight

見票後　after sight

見票後……（天數）……付款或承兌　after sight

見票後付款滙票　bill payable after sight

見票後定期付款滙票　bill payable at a fixed date after sight

見票後若干日付款滙票　bill drawn payable at a certain time after sight

見票後遠期付款票據　bill payable at long sight

見單據付款　cash against document

見跌即止期權　down-and-out option

見漲即止期權　up-and-out option

見證條款　attestation clause

步陞定息債券（1988 年 2 月香港"地鐵"委託獲多利融資安排發行的債券）　step-up fixed rate bonds

步增成本　step cost

囤戶　hoarder

囤積　hoard, buy up

囤積居奇　corner the market, hold the market

囤積居奇者　cornerer

[丿]

我方存款　nostro deposit

我方帳戶　nostro account

我方餘額　balance in our favour

吞吐量　volume of freight handled, cargo handling capacity, loading and unloading capacity, volume of incoming and outcoming freights

妥協，折衷，和解　compromise

妥協條例　compromise act

利市，生意興隆　prosperous trade, a good market

利用外資　introducing foreign investment

利用收益的調換（指銷售大量債券，用其收益購另一種大量債券）　applied proceeds swap

利用係數　utilization coefficient

利用差異　utilization variance

利用效率　utilization ratio

利好、利多　bull

利好市場　bullish market

利空，利淡　bear

利空市場　bearish market

利物浦原棉交易所　Liverpool Cotton Exchange

利息　interest, hypothetical cost

利息收入，利息收益　interest income

利息平價（在遠期交易中，以貼水或升水直接表現的兩種貨幣的不同利差）　interest parity

利息平準基金　interest equalization fund

利息平衡稅　interest equalization tax

利息成本　interest cost

利息回扣　interest rebate

利息低，銀根鬆　ease of money

利息的資本化　capitalization of interests

利息津貼　interest subsidization

利息津貼基金　interest subsidy fund

利息條款　interest clause

利息套戥（香港期貨市場稱〝套利〞為〝利息套戥〞）　interest arbitrage

利息差額　interest differential

利息基金　interest fund

利息帳　interest account

利息單　interest note

利息稅　interest tax

利息費用，利息支出　interest expenses, interest charges

利息費用與銷貨比率　ratio of interest expense to sales

利息預扣稅　interest with holding tax

利息準備　interest reserve

利息補貼，利息津貼　interest subsidization

利息債權，利息要求權　interest

claim

利息暫記　interest suspense

利差幅度　interest margin

利率　rate of interest, interest rate

利率平價　interest rate parity

利率的期限結構　term structure of interest rates

利率政策　interest rate policy

利率差幅　split margin, split spread

利率敏感資產負債表（把銀行的資產負債對市場利率變化的敏感程度進行劃分對照的一種資產負債餘額表）　rate sensitive balance sheet

利率期貨　interest rate futures

利率期權　interest rate option

利率結構　interest rate structure

利率調換交易（雙方在一定數額的本金基礎上，交換不同利息收入的交易，又稱利率掉期）　interest rate swap transaction

利得，利益，收益，盈益　gains

利得稅　profit tax

利量比率（利潤銷貨額比率）　profit-volume-ratio, contribution ratio

利潤　profits

利潤分享有價證券　profit-sharing securities

利潤分配　appropriation of profit

利潤再投資　reinvest profits, plough back

利潤扣除額　profit allowance

利潤股息比率　dividend cover

利潤率　profit margin, profit rate

利潤邊際　profit margin

兵險　war risk

兵險附加費　war risk surcharge

兵險條款　war risk clause

告退股東　retired partner

告發　information

告發人　informer

告貸　ask for a loan

告貸無門　unable to borrow

系列化產品　serialization products

系列期權（指具有相同到期日和協定價格的期權合約）　series of options

系列債券（指企業發行的一組到期日和利率均不相同的債券）　series bond

系列預測法　series forecasting method

系統化　systematization

系統化售貨管理　systematized sales management

系統性風險（又稱"普遍的市場風險"，指因受宏觀經濟因素或不測事件的影響，整個股市發生全面性波動）　systematic risk, general market risk, marketwide risk

系統抽樣　systematic sampling

系統的選擇方法　system alternatives

系統設計　systematic design

系統開發　system development

系統程序設計　system programming

系統管理　systematic(al) management

系統管理學派　system management school

系統審計　operational audit

私人支票　personal check, individual check

私人企業，私營企業　individual enterprise, private enterprise

私人投資　private investment

私人股份　private shares

私人物品　personal effects

私人直接投資　private direct investment

私人協議　private treaty

私人信託款　private trust-fund

私人專利　private monopoly

私人密碼　private code

私人短期資本流動　private short-term capital movement

私人貸款　private loan

私人債務　private debt

私人運輸業　private carrier

私人廠牌　private brands

私人簽署　private seal

私自下貨　ship goods without permit

私自起貨　land goods without permit

私有財產　private property

私逃　abscond with money

私貨　run goods, smuggled goods

私運進口　smuggle goods into a port

私營公司，股份不公開公司　private corporation (or company)

私營銀行　private bank

每一單位積累額　accumulated funds of each enterprise

每人，人均〔拉〕　per capita

每人平均國民收入　per capita national income

每人計算　per capita calculation

每千〔拉〕　per mille (‰)

每日　per diem

每日升水　daily premium

每日分期付款　daily instalment

每日利息　daily interest

每日津貼　per diem allowance

每日貼水　daily premium

每日費用　per diem expenses

每日價位變動限幅　daily limit of price changes

每日價格限幅　daily price limit

每日價格變動限幅　daily limit of price changes

每月　per mensem

每百　per centum (%)

每百美元積累的新增國民收入　sum of newly gained national income provided by accumulation per 100 dollars

每年　per annum

每年成本等值　equivalent annual cost

每年收益　annual earning

每年利潤　profit perannum

每年利潤率　annual rate of profit

每年免稅額　annual allowance

每年遞增　an average annual increase of

每美元外幣價　foreign currency per U.S. dollar

每股收益，每股盈利　earnings per share

每股盈餘　per-share earnings

每股帳面價值　book value per share

每季保險費　quarterly premium

免付利息　no interest, waiving interest

免付速遣費　free despatch

免收利息　free of interest (FOI)

免所得稅　free of income tax

免於追索　without recourse

免拆驗　exemption from customs examination

免除(債務、捐款等)　remission

免除條款(例外情況可解約的條款)　escape clause

免除責任背書　endorsement without recourse

免除部份責任　partially exempt obligation

免除債務證書　quittance

免責條款　memorandum clause

免費　free of charge, gratis, cost free

免費服務　free service

免費試用　free trial

免費搬運　free-haul

免費運輸　free-hauled traffic

免稅　duty-free, free of tax, exemption of tax, tax evasion

免稅出口貨　free exports

免稅投資　tax-free investment

免稅利潤　tax-free profit

免稅放行　release without payment of duty

免稅服務　free service

免稅待遇的凍結　zero-duty bindings

免稅貨物　duty-free goods, nondutiable goods, goods exempt from taxes

免稅貨物進口報關單　entry for free goods

免稅執照　duty-free certificate

免稅單　exemption certificate, duty free slips, bill of sufference

免稅期　tax holiday

免稅進口貨　tax free imports, free imports

免稅進口貨單　free list

免稅證券　tax-exempt securities

免運費回扣(指租船)　free of address

免賠額，免賠限度(海上貨物保險，規定保險人對損失之逾越約定限度者，始就全部損害予以賠償)　franchise

免賠額(率)條款　franchise clause

免償債務　forgive a debt, exemption of debt, remit a debt

免繳保險費　waiver of premium

免驗　exempt from customs examination

免驗放行　pass without examination

免驗證　laissez-passer

含有支付命令的授權書　written authorization containing payment orders

含佣金價　price including commission

含金量　gold content

低水位線　low water mark

低收入低消費政策　low-income, low-consumption policy

低收入國家　low-income country

低收入集團　low-income groups

低收益折讓　low-income allowance

低成本　low cost

低成本自動化　low-cost automation

低成本技術　low-cost technologies

低成本、高收益投資　low-cost high-return investment

低行銷　demarketing

低估稅　undervaluation duty

低估價值　undervaluation

低利借款　cheap money

低利率　low interest rate

低利貸款　low interest loans

低於票面價值　below par, par low-at a discount

低於標準險(保險)　substandard risk

低於橋高　below bridges

低所得寬免額　low income allowance

低型跨式載運車　low profile straddle carriers

低度均勢　low equilibrium

低度折舊　sub-normal depreciation

低度相關　low correlation

低度開發國家　less developing countries, underdeveloped countries

低級　low class

低級品　low quality

低級債券　junior bonds

低息貨幣政策　cheap money policy

低牽連反應模式　low-involvement response model

低溫運輸系統(新鮮食品的運輸)　cold chain

低落　recede

低運費貨物　low-paying cargo

低滙傾銷　low-currency dumping

低價位股票　low-priced stock

低價售賣令　venditioni exponas

低層堆場(貨櫃／集裝箱的)　low elevation stacking area

低標準統一賠償責任制度　low-level uniform liability system

低檔貨物　inferior goods

佈點圖法　scattergraph method

作投機生意　play the market

作股票投機　stocks speculation, gamble in stocks

作抵押(以房屋)　on mortgage

作抵押品的地產　estate in gage

作業　activity

作業成本　cost of activity

作業成本計算　activity costing

作業性規劃　operational planning

作業特性曲線　operating characteristic curves; OC Curves

作業研究　operations research

作業試驗　performance testing

作業管理　operations management

作業會計　activity accounting

作業標準　performance standard

作廢　repeal

作廢支票　spoilaged check

作廢股　forfeited stock

佣金　commission, premium

佣金中間商，佣金商　commission

merchant

佣金代理商　commission agent

佣金代銷商　commission seller

佣金代購商　commission buyer

佣金制　commission system

佣金保險　commission insurance

佣金率　rate of commission, scale of commission

佣金經紀　commission broker

"何來何去"表（即資金來源和運用表）　"where-got where-gone" sheet

估定保險費　assessment insurance

估定稅額　assessed tax

估定價格　estimated price

估計市價　estimated market value

估計可變現價值　estimated realizable value

估計啟航時間　estimated time of departure

估計殘值　estimated scrap value

估計資產負債表　estimated balance sheet

估計壞帳　estimated bad debt

估損（保險）　appraisal of damage

估損人　claims assessor

估量　approximate measurement

估稅人　assessor

估稅率　assessment percentage

估算成本　imputed cost

估算利息　imputed interest

估算資本值　imputed capital value

估算錯誤　estimate error

估價　appraised price, assessment, estimate price

估價折舊　depreciation appraisal

估價基礎　valuation basis

估價慣例　valuation convention

伸縮加成定價法　flexible markup practice

伸縮性貨幣政策　flexible monetary policy

伸縮性基礎利率　flexible prime rate

伸縮性滙率，彈性滙率　flexible exchange rate

伸縮性價格　flexible price

伸縮條款　escalator clause

伸縮關稅　flexible duty, flexible tariff

佐證書　letter of support

住宅自動化　house automation

住宅貸款信託債券　trust of housing loan bonds

住宅貸款銀行　home loan banks

住房津貼　house allowance

伯爾尼聯會（即國際信用保險聯會）　Berne Union

伯奧利分配（統計）　Bernoulli distribution

伯羅船（一種多用途的新式定期貨輪，既能裝石油及散裝乾貨，也能運輸集裝箱）　BORO

佔用費　fee for possession and use of, fee charged for the use of, occupancy expenses

佔用資金付費原則　principle of payment for the use of funds

佔有　possession

佔有、保有及管有　possession, custody and control

佔有物　thing possessed

佔有性的留置權　possessory lien

佔有的實現　realization of appropriation

佔有動產(指一切實際可佔有之財產)　choses in possession

佔有統治地位的公司　dominant firm

狂跌　slump

狄龍回合(關稅貿易總協定的輪談判)　Dillon round

延付貨款　deferred payment

延付催繳股款　calls in arrears

延派股利　deferred dividends

延長信用證有效期　extend letter of credit

延長索賠期限　extend the time limit for filing clause

延長期限　extension

延度　ductility

延後　postpone

延期　prolongation, respite, defer

延期手續費　extension commission

延期付息股票，紅利後取股(比普通股後分配公司紅利的股票)　deferred stock, deferred shares

延期付款　payment respite, deferred payment

延期付款信用證　deferred payment credit

延期付款貿易　deferred payment trade

延期回扣　deferred rebates

延期回扣制度(運費同盟為爭取貨運，對已收運費經過一定時期後，給予5-10%的回扣)　deferred rebates system

延期合約　extension agreement

延期交貨　back order

延期交貨負債　deferred performance liabilities

延期折扣　deferred rebate

延期利息　interest on arrears

延期海難抗辯書(船長呈交公證行的)　extended protest

延期索償同意書　letter of licence

延期費　deferred charges, demurrage, extension fee

延期裝船　delay in shipment

延期過帳　delayed posting

延期寬限日　days of grace

延期償付法　moratory law

延期償付債券　extended bonds

延期償付權　moratorium

延期償還　moratoria

延遲互換交易權責日　deferred swap accrual date

延遲附加費(運費)　delayed surcharge

刨花　excelsior

[一]

防火　fire prevention, fireproof

防火建築　fireproof construction

防火費　fire protection expense

防火牆　fire wall

防止貪污法例　Prevention of Corruption Acts

防止貿易的技術壁壘法規　Code for Preventing Technical Barriers to Trade

防止詐欺法　Statute of Frauds

防波堤　pier

防止損失　loss prevention

防漏　leakage-proof

防撞艙壁　collision bulkhead

防衛條款，保障條款（歐洲共市對抗日本貨進口的條款）　safeguard clause

改正記錄　correcting entries

改組　reorganization

改組現有企業　revamping existing enterprises

改裝，重新包裝　repacking

改良修理貿易　improvement and repair trade

改良費用　improvement expense

改變生產方向　reorient production

即時出售　prompt sale

即時付現　immediate cash payment, prompt cash payment

即時回覆單（期貨市場一種必須立即完成，否則要立刻回覆客戶的訂單）　kill-or-fill order

即時交付　pay down

即時交貨　prompt delivery, immediate delivery

即時定貨單　immediate order

即時信息處理系統　real-time information-processing system

即時消費　immediate consumption

即時結算　speedy clearance

即時管理情報系統　real-time management information system

即時辦公室（由規模大的商業中心開辦方便客戶租作辦公、開會的辦公室）　Instant Office

即期　delivery on spot, on demand, at sight

即期支票　prompt check

即期付款　payment at sight, cash down

即期付款交單　document against payment-sight

即期存款　deposit at call, demand deposit

即期外滙　spot foreign exchange

即期承兌　immediate acceptance

即期信用狀　sight letter of credit

即期票據　bill at sight, bill payable on demand, note on demand

即期與即期的次日對做（即期賣出一種貨幣的同時買入即期交割日後一天交割的同一種貨幣，或反之）　spot next

即期債務　debt at call

即期滙票　sight draft, demand bill, demand draft

即期滙率　spot exchange rate

局部均衡　partial equilibrium

局部要價　partial bid

局部喪失能力　partial incapacity

局部認付　partial acceptance

局部履行　part performance

局部審計，短期查帳　limited audit

忍痛補買的空頭　squaring bears

忍痛補賣的多頭　squaring bulls

尾數　balance, arrears

尾數四捨五入的累加數　round-off accumulating

門戶開放政策　open-door policy

門市　sell retail over the counter

門面　storefront

門到門貨櫃/集裝箱運輸　door-to-door container

門到門運輸　door-to-door transport

門到站（貨櫃/集裝箱運輸）　door to CFS (container freight station)

門到場（貨櫃/集裝箱運輸）　door to CY (container yard)

門板（貨櫃/集裝箱的）　door sheet

門庭若市　roaring business

門鎖桿（貨櫃/集裝箱的）　door lock rod

門鎖托架（貨櫃/集裝箱的）　door lock rod bracket

"門檻"協議（英國用詞，即按生活指數自動調整工資的條款）threshold agreement

門檻（貨櫃/集裝箱的）　door sill

門檻價格（西歐共市為實施共同農業政策所制定的用於穀物進口最低限價，又稱閘門價）　threshold price

君子協定　gentlemen's agreement

災後損失保險　consequential loss insurance

災害保險　casualty insurance

妨害公共秩序罪　offences against public order

妨害名譽　offences against personal reputation

妨害信用　offences against personal credit

妨害商務　injurious to trade

八　畫

［ 、 ］

法人　artificial person, legal person, juridical person, legal entity

法人身份　status of a legal person

法人稅　corporation tax

法人團體　body corporate, corporate body

法令　decree, laws and decrees, statute

法令限制　statute of limitations

法治　rule of law

法例　act, act of parliament

法官　judge

法定已獲盈餘準備金　legal earned surplus reserve

法定支付期　legal term, term time

法定公債　bonds authorized

法定皮重　legal tare

法定用途　legal appropriation

法定代理人　statutory agent

法定平價　mint par of exchange, mint parity

法定交收點(指交易所授權交收期貨合約之銀行、倉庫、碼頭倉庫等地點)　approved delivery facility

法定利息　legal interest

法定利率　state rate

法定延誤期間　legal delay

法定股本　legal capital, capital statutory

法定抵押(通過法律程序辦理的抵押)　legal mortgage

法定的認繳股金　subscriptions authorized

法定含金量　official gold content, legal gold content

法定淨重　legal net weight

法定重量　legal weight

法定責任　legal liability

法定專利　legal monopoly

法定動產　legal personalty

法定清盤　legal liquidation

法定稅率　national tariff, statutory tariff

法定準備　legal reserve

法定準備金　legal reserve fund

法定最低利率　official minimum rate

法定最低資本額　minimal capital required by law

法定貼現率　official discount rate

法定貶值　official devaluation

法定資本　authorized capital

法定滙兌平價　official par of exchange

法定滙價,官方滙率　official rate of exchange

法定債款償金　legal tender

法定價值　legal standard of value

法定擔保　statutory guarantee, legal securities

法定總預算　legal consolidated budget

法定證券(商品期貨交易署條例第一條二十五點指定之證券)　approved securities

法定權利　legal rights

法律上的業主　legal owner of property

法律上的幫助　legal aid

法律上負責　legally responsible for

法律所不容許　not tolerated by the law

法律的推定　presumption of law

法律制裁　legal sanction

法律牴觸　conflict of laws

法律責任　legal obligation

法律強制性規定　imperative provisions of the law

法律程序　legal procedure

法律補救方法　legal remedy

法律環境　legal environment

法庭收回地產令　cape

法庭保釋　court bail

法庭逮捕令〔拉〕　capias

法庭費用　court fees

法警　catchpole

法國船級局　Bureau Veritas

法幣,法定貨幣　legal tender

河口港　estuary port

河流貿易　river traffic

河流監測　monitoring of rivers

河運　inland water transportation

河運提單　river waybill

河運運費，內河水腳　river freight

波及效果（對外貿易對國民經濟其他部門的影響）　spread effect

波動　fluctuations

波動平價　fluctuating par

波動行市　fluctuating market

波動條款（契約上規定在特殊情況下，賣方得變更售價之條款）〔英〕fluctuation clause,〔美〕escalator clause,〔日本〕slide clause

波動幅度　fluctuation spread

波動滙率　fluctuation exchange rate

波羅的海航運交易所（設在倫敦的世界最大租船市場）Baltic Mercantile & Shipping Exchange（簡稱：Baltic Exchange）

沿用貸款抵押品　conventional collateral for loans

沿岸海床經濟區域　coastal sea-bed economic area

沿海水域　coast waters

沿海航運　coasting shipping

沿海航線　coasting shipping line

沿海貿易　coastwise trade, coasting trade

沿海漁業　coast fisheries

沿海管轄權　coastal jurisdiction

沽出對冲　the selling hedge, the short hedge

沽家市場（貨源緊缺，沽家有較好條件以較高價格推售商品之市場又稱賣方市場）　seller's market

沽家喊價　seller's call

沽家期權（沽家在合約指定時間內，選擇交收商品的質素、交收時間及交收地點之權利）　seller's option

注目字句　catch phrase

注重價格的市場　price market

注重標誌　care mark, caution mark

注意　〔拉〕nota bene (N.B.)

派生收入　derivative revenue

派生存款　derived deposit

派生的統計數字　derived statistics

派生指數　derivative index

派生貨幣　derivative money

派生需求　derived demand

派生價值　derived value

派股通知書　letter of allotment

派息率　dividend payout ratio

泊位用率　berth occupancy

泊位生產量　berth throughput

泊位條款　berth clause

泊位費　berthage, quayage

泊位裝貨條件　berth charter

泊位裝船貨租船合同　berth charter party

泊船　anchor a vessel

泊船章程　regulations for mooring vessels

油污　oil pollution, oil contamination

油商　oil man

油漬　oil stain

油漬險　risk of oil damage

油輪　tanker

泡沫橡膠　foam rubber

初步系統　rudimentary system

初步審計　preliminary audit

初級市場　primary market, basic-level market

初級生產　primary production

初級產品　primary commodities, primary products

初級商品價格　commodity price

初級資料　primary data

初級證券市場　primary securities market

初付費　initial lump sum

初次加工　prior processing

初次分配　primary distribution of the national income

初步分析　preliminary analysis

初步平衡　rough balance

初步折扣　initial allowance

初步概算　initial budget estimates

初值　initial value

初級生產　basic-level production

初級生產要素　primary factor of production

初級抵押市場　primary mortgage market

初級產品出口國　primary exporting country

初級產品與製成品世界出口價格指數 world export price indexes of primary commodities and manufactured goods

初級產業　primary industry

初級債券（只答應定期付息及還本而無安排抵押品的債券）junior bonds

初期市場佔有率　initial market share

初期存貨　initial inventory

初期保險費　initial premium

初期盈餘　initial surplus

初期撥款　initial issue, initial appropriations

官方市場牌價　official market quotation

官方外滙市場　official exchange market

官方外滙資產　official foreign exchange assets

官方持有外滙　official foreign exchange holdings

官方統計　official statistics

官方開發援助　official development assistance

官方清償赤字　official settlements deficit

官方註冊　official register

官方短期資本流動　official short-term capital movement

官方結算差額　official settlements balance

官方滙率　official exchange rate

官方債務　official debts

官方擔保的出口信貸　officially guaranteed export credit

官方檢查　official inspection

官方儲備　official reserve

官方儲備收支平衡　official reserve transactions balance

官方儲備交易　official reserve transactions

官用發票　official invoice

官定貼現率　official discount rate

官定最低利率　official minimum rate

官定滙兌平滙　official par of exchange

官價　official price, official rate

官價上下限（指中央銀行對外幣規定的最高、最低買賣價）　upper and lower intervention limits

空白　blank space

空白支票　blank check

空白本票　blank note

空白收據（未經簽字的收據）　blank receipt

空白表　blank table

空白承兌，不記名承兌　acceptance in blank

空白定單　blank order forms

空白背書　blank endorsed, endorsement in blank

空白背書滙票　bill endorsed in blank

空白滙票　bill of exchange in blank

空白票據　blank bill

空白提單　blank bill of loading

空位　filler

空倉（未平倉合約中沽空後尚未補回之合約）　short

空倉補回　short covering

空船年度租約　bareboat charters on annual contract

空船吃水線　light draught

空船租賃　bareboat charter

空船排水量　light displacement

空閒時間工資　idle time pay

空閒時間補充率　idle time supplementary rate

空郵提單　airmail bill of lading

空運　air transportation

空運代理　air freight forwarder

空運代理行提單　house air waybill

空運協會　air transport association

空運到岸價　cost, insurance, freight by plane

空運保險　insurance for air transportation, air risks

空運旅途平安險　insurance against air trip accident

空運航線　airways

空運組　air transport service division

空運貨物　airborne goods, air cargo

空運貨櫃/集裝箱　igloo

空運貿易　airborne trade

空運提單　airway bill of lading, air consignment note

空運集裝箱　air container

空過股利（在一時期應分派而未分派之股利）　passed dividend

空餘艙位運費　filler cargo rate

空頭　short position, bear, oversold

空頭支票　rubber cheque, bad check, accommodation bill, bounced check, dishonoured check, dud check, fictitious paper, kiting cheque

空頭方補進　covering by short

空頭市場，熊市　bear market

空頭交易合同　short contract

空頭回補，軋空頭　short covering, cover short

空頭者　short interest

空頭借入　borrowing short to lend

空頭套期保值　short hedge

空頭帳戶　short account

空頭票據，欠單　accommodation kite

空頭被迫受損，空頭忍痛補倉　short squeeze

空頭猛跌（指銷售股票、商品或貨幣的浪潮，通常含有在賣方之間有協調一致之意）　bear raid

空頭提單　accommodation bill of lading

空頭買賣　dummy job

空頭補進（香港稱為＂補倉＂）　short covering, bear covering

空頭補進受損　short covering at a loss

空艙位（運費按實佔艙位計時損失的艙位）　broken space

空艙費　dead freight

空額信用證　blank credit

定金，定錢　purchase money, earnest money, bargain money, handsel, margin, down payment

定性分析　method of qualitative analysis

定則投資（一種投資技術，將投資基金有比例地分配在股票和債券上）formula investing

定息　fixed interest, fixed rate of interest on capital

定息債券　fixed interest securities

定息與恒生指數掛鈎牛熊債券（香港1987年7月由百利達亞洲融資發行的債券）　fixed rate index linked bull and bear bonds

定值美元　constant-dollar values

定值保險單　valued policy

定值過低貨幣　undervalued currency

定值過高貨幣　overvalued currency

定率減價折舊　depreciation fixed percentage of diminishing value

定率遞減折舊法　depreciation-diminishing-provision method

定貨單　order for goods, order sheet

定貨管理　order control

定基（指固定基期）　fixed base

定基指數　fixed base index

定基價比　price relative of fixed base

定單，定貨　order, indents, order form, contract for goods, value favour

定單控制，定貨管理　order control

定量　quantitative

定量分析　quantitative analysis

定量作業管理　task management

定期　at fixed period, fixed due date

定期付款　periodical payments, payment on terms

定期付款滙票　bill payable on a stated date

定期收入　fixed income

定期任用　fixed term appointment

定期交易　time bargains

定期交貨　delivery on term, time delivery

定期年金　limited annuity

定期存款　fixed deposit, time deposit, dated deposit

定期存款單　time certificate of deposit

定期泊位計劃(新加坡港務局開辦對定期船舶使用舶位的合約)　time slot scheme

定期抵押　term mortgage

定期信用證　time letter of credit

定期保險　fixed term insurance, time insurance

定期保險單　time policy

定期保險展期　renewal term insurance

定期船　liner

定期票據　fixed bill, period bill, day bill

定期集市　fair

定期集市法例　Fairs Act

定期貸款　term loan, time loan, time money

定期債券　term bond

定期滙票　date draft, time draft, time bill

定期資產負債表　periodic balance sheet

定期審計　regular audit

定期擔保貸款　secured time loan

定期償還　mandatory redemption

定期償還債券　time-payment debts

定期攤付法　fixed instalment method

定稅和評價法例　Rating and Valuation Act

定幅度的遠期外滙買賣(客戶簽合同時，規定滙率幅度的上、下限，在此幅度內，如滙率升，可享受好處，下降也可得到保障)　the range forward

定程租船　voyage charter

定期租船契約　charter by time, time charter

定程連續租船　consecutive voyage charter

定製品　articles made to order

定價　price making., list price, set price

定價目標　pricing objective

定價成本　costs involved in determining price

定數比例折舊法　depreciation-proportional method of fixed base

定購股份單　share contract note

定購單　buying order

定點概率向量　fixed probability vector

定額分保　quota share reinsurance

定額分期付款　fixed instalment

定額序列複利因素　uniform-series compound amount factor

定額投資公司　closed-end company

定額備用金　imprest cash, imprest fund

定額補貼　setting quotas for subsidies

定額銀行專戶 imprest bank account

店鋪交貨 ex store

店鋪門前交貨 store-door delivery

底價 floor price

夜工 night work

夜市 night market

夜班 night shift, night watch

夜間輪班 graveyard shift

房地產 real estate, real property, realty

房地產公司 real estate agency

房地產代理商 real estate agent

房地產抵押 mortgage on real estate

房地產稅 real estate tax, housing and land tax, house property tax, house duty

房地產提存金 land and building sinking fund

房地產買賣 sales and purchase of real properties

房地產經紀人 real estate broker, realtor

房地產管理 management of properties

房契 title deeds for house, house lease

房屋介紹人 house agent

房屋出租 premises to let, house for rent

房屋招租 house for rent, house to let

房屋服務費用 building service expense

房屋和設備 building and equipment

房屋裝修 house improvement & betterment

房捐 house tax

房租 house rent

房租保險 rent insurance

房租津貼 lodging allowance

房產 premises

房產稅 building tax

盲目上項目 rashly launching new projects

盲目競爭 blind competition, unbridled competition

放任式領導 laissez-faire leadership, permissive leadership

放任管理 drifting-management, permissive management

放押款者 scrivener

放射性污染 radioactive contamination

放高利貸者 jew

放息資本 loan capital

放陰涼處(包裝標語) keep in cool place

放款 lending

放款人 money-lender

放款方案 lending programme

放款收益 income from loans

放款利率 lending rate, interest upon loans

放款業務 lending operations

放款銀行 loan bank

放款標準 lending criteria

放款機構 lending institution

放款競爭　lending race

放債　lending, lend money on usury

放棄交易，停業　giving up a business

放棄金本位　off the gold standard

放棄要求　waiver claim

放棄條款，棄權條款　waiver clause

放棄索賠權　waiver of the right of indemnity

放棄訴訟　non-suit

放棄購貨保留權(指在交易所合同規定期限內按約定價格購貨的權利)　abandonment of option

放棄權利　renunciation of right

放棄驗貨權　waiver of inspection of goods

放寬利率　liberalization of interest rate

放寬政策　implement policies more flexibly, adopt more liberal policies, in easing restrictions to allow individual merchants to run their business

放寬條件　soften the terms

放寬貸款條件　easy credit terms, liberalize the conditions of loans

放盤　clearance sales

放鬆銀根　easier money

放鬆銀根政策　easy money policy

炒家(交易所現場的投機客，在同一交易日內持倉時間極短，頻頻買入或沽出。香港稱為〝炒家〞)　scalper

炒貨(利用市價波動頻頻買入或賣出之薄利倒賣活動)　scalping

[一]

來人支票　check payable to bearer, bearer check, bearer cheque

來人債券(所有權假定由持票人擁有的債券)　bearer bond

來人滙票　bearer draft

來回程租船契約　return voyage charter

來件裝配　assembling parts supplied by clients

來取即付的滙票　sight bill, draft on demand, bill payable on demand

來往帳戶　current account, bank account

來往帳目　open account

來料加工　processing with imported material, processing with supplied material

來帳(以外國銀行名義在本國開立的本國貨幣帳戶)　[拉]vostro(意為〝你的〞)

來路貨　imported goods

來源不一致性　source incongruity

來源可信度　source credibility

來源證　certificate of origin

來牌定貨　order with customer's brand

來圖加工　processing with supplied drawings

來賓止步，不許進入　no entry

來樣加工　processing with supplied designs

來樣定做　order with supplied sample

來樣定貨　order with customer's sample

披露文據　discovery of documents

披露事實　discovery of facts

拍板成交　strike a bargain

拍賣　auction, auction sales

拍賣人　auctioneer

拍賣人的小槌　auctioneer's hammer

拍賣人的佣金　auctioneer's commission

拍賣市場　auction market

拍賣行　auction room

拍賣條件　conditions of auction

拍賣時不出價的秘密協議　"knock out" agreement

拍賣清單　statement of auction

拍賣場　auction mart, bidding block

拍賣價格　auction price

抽身債券（由債務國向債權銀行發行以替代債權銀行應向債務國提供新信貸的一種債券）　exit bond

抽查　tests at random, test audit, test check, spot check

抽查法檢查　test-basic examination

抽逃資金　spirit one's money away

抽稅　levy taxes

抽象法　means of abstaction

抽審　audit at random

抽樣方法　sampling method

抽樣規模　sampling size

抽樣單位　sampling unit

抽樣程序　sampling program

抽樣誤差　sampling error

抽樣調查　sampling survey

抽樣檢驗　sampling inspection

抽點存貨　inventory testing

抽緊銀根　tighten the money in circulation

抬高市價　jack-scrowing, jacking up price

抬高利潤　profiteering

抬頭人　addressee, payee, in favour of

抬頭人支票　order check

抬價　force up commodity price, at high price, at exorbitant prices

押金，孖展，保證金　margin, cash pledge

押金存款　margin deposit

押房　mortgage a house

押契　mortgage deed

押借限額　loan value

押船契約（船長以船作抵押的借據）　bottomry bond

押款　sum lent on a mortgage

押貨　mortgage goods

押運　escort goods in transportation

押滙申請書　application for negotiation of draft under letter of credit

押滙信用證　documentary credit

押滙滙票　documentary bill (draft)

押滙總質押書　general letter of hypothecation

押標金　bid bond

抵制　boycott

抵制同盟　hartall

抵岸重量　landed weight

抵岸價格　landed price

抵免額　creditable amount

抵押　mortgage, hypothecate, pledge, impawn, collateralize

抵押人，出押人　mortgager, pledger

抵押市場　mortgage market

抵押合同　mortgage contract

抵押合併　consolidation of mortgage

抵押延期償付權　mortgage moratoria

抵押放款　secured loan, loan on collateral security, loan on security

抵押放款浮息債券　mortgage-backed floating rate notes

抵押品　lending stock, hypothecated goods

抵押品被沒收　mortgage forfeit

抵押信用　mortgage credit

抵押保險　hypothecation insurance

抵押契約，典約　deed of mortgage

抵押負債　mortgage liability

抵押條款　mortgage clause

抵押借款，抵押貸款　mortgage loan

抵押票據　mortgage note

抵押訴訟　mortgage action

抵押債券　mortgage bonds, mortgage debentures

抵押債務　mortgage debt

抵押資金　mortgage money

抵押資產　mortgage assets

抵押經紀人　mortgage middleman

抵押銀行　mortgage bank, hypothec bank

抵押銀行債券　mortgage bank debenture

抵押據　letter of hypothecation

抵押優先清償　tacking mortgage

抵押證券　securities held in pledge (pawn)

抵押權　mortgage, hypothecate, pledge

抵押權人　mortgagee

抵港　arrival at port

抵銷　compensating, offset

抵銷分錄　elemination entry

抵銷性錯誤　compensating errors

抵銷信貸　offset credit

抵銷記入　cross entry

抵銷帳戶　offset account

抵銷稅　countervailing levy

抵銷數　offsetting deductions

抵銷權　right of set-off

抵賴　repudiate

抵償　compensate for, give something by way of payment for

抵償交易　compensation transaction

抵償貿易　compensation trade

拆股　splitup

拆放　loan at call

拆放同業　banker's call loan

拆卸　dismantled

拆卸代理人　break bulk agent

拆卸分裝出口　knock-down export

拆卸分裝裝運　knock-down

拆息　native interest

拆款　day to day loan, call money

拆箱分卸（對貨櫃／集裝箱貨物）　de-consolidation

拆箱作業　deconsolidation service

拆遷成本　removal cost

拆檢　overhaul inspection

拆櫃交、整櫃接　less (than) container load/full container load (LCL/FCL)

拉丁美洲自由貿易協會　Latin American Free Trade Association

拉丁美洲自由貿易區　Latin American Free Trade Area

拉丁美洲共同市場（由瓜地馬拉、哥斯達黎加、薩爾瓦多、洪都拉斯、尼加拉瓜等中美洲五國組成）Latin American Common Market

拉弗曲線（美國拉弗假設的一條曲線，說明稅收隨稅率而增加，但稅率高至某一點，投資和儲蓄隨之放緩，致稅收反而減少）　Laffer Curver

拉美美元市場　Latin-American-dollar market

拉鏈條款（集體談判協議規定的條款，在協議期間，任何一方不得提出重新談判之要求）　zipper clause

招人領取公債券金額　call a bond

招股　raise capital by floating shares, call for capital

招股章程　prospectus

招租　house to let

招牌　signboard, placard, ambassador of good will

招商局　China Merchants Steamship Company

招募股份　subscription

招募股、債說明書　prospectus

招標　invite to tender, invite bid, submit public bids, call for bid, call for tender

招標公告　announcement of tender

招標制　competitive-bidding system

招標條件　terms of tender

招標採購　open tender

招聘　invite applications for a job, advertise for

招請引水員旗號　pilot flag

招攬生意　canvass business orders, drum up trade

拒付　non-payment, dishonour

拒付支票　protest check, dishonour check, rejected check

拒付欠款　repudiate a debt

拒付通知書　notice of dishonour, protest notes

拒付票據　dishonoured notes

拒付滙票　bill dishonoured

拒付應收票據　notes receivable dishonoured

拒付證書　notarial protest certificate

拒收品質水準　rejectable quality level; RQL

拒收承兌證書　protest for non-acceptance

拒保　declinature

拒絕支付抗議書　protest for non-payment

拒絕出售　refusal to sell

拒絕交易　boycott

拒絕承兌　refusal to accept, non-acceptance

拒絕接受特別提款權分配額的權力　out opting

拒絕登記　refusal of registration

拒絕發運　refusal to deliver

拒絕購買　sales resistance

拒絕償還債務　recourse repudiation

拒絕賠付　repudiation of claims

拒絕賠償　refuse to indenmify

拒絕履行契約　lying down

拒賠　claims rejected

拖欠，尾數(指欠款的)　arrears

拖欠比率(在整個業務量中，過期未還貸款相對於還本付息貸款總額的比率)　delinquency rate

拖欠分期付款　delinquent instalment

拖欠利息　arrears of interest

拖欠紅利　arrears of dividends

拖欠稅款　default of tax payments

拖欠債券　defaulted bonds

拖欠應收款項　delinquent receivables

拖船　towing boat, tug boat

拖帶航程　towing voyage

拖帶費用　towage, towing charges

拖運費　haulage

拖網漁船　trawler

軋出，退關(指貨物之軋出或退關)　shut out S/O)

軋平，拋補，補進，補空　cover the position

軋平頭寸　cover position

軋空　short squeeze

軋空頭(迫使賣空者用高價補進，或稱“殺空頭”)　bear squeeze, squeeze the shorts

軋進頭寸　take position

到期日付款　payment at maturity

到岸重量　landed weight, landing weight

到岸品質　arrival quality

到岸價格　cost, insurance and freight

到岸價格加內河運費價　cost, insurance, freight inland waterway

到岸價格加佣金及利息價　cost, insurance, freight, commission and interest

到岸價格加利息價　cost, insurance, freight and interest

到岸價格加卸貨價　cost, insurance, freight landed terms

到岸價格加結關費用價　cost, insurance, freight cleared

到岸價格加滙費及目的港價　cost, insurance, freight, exchange and port of destination

到岸價格加關稅價　cost, insurance, freight duty paid

到岸價格淨價　cost, insurance, freight net

到岸輪船吊鈎下交貨價(成本、保險費、運費至輪船吊鈎下交貨價)　cost, insurance, freight under ship's tackle

到岸輪船艙底交貨價　cost, insurance, freight ex ship's hold

到貨日價格　day of arrival price

到貨兌現滙票　arrival draft

到貨通知　advice of arrival

到港船　arrived ship

到港提單　port bill of lading

到期　mature, maturity

到期日　maturity date, due date, expiry date, settlement day

到期支票　matured cheque

到期未付票據　overdue bill

到期未付債務　matured liabilities unpaid

到期本金　matured principal

到期全部付清　be paid in full at the appointed time

到期付款　payable at maturity

到期利息　interest due

到期股金和股息　due share capital and dividends

到期前付款　pre-maturity payment

到期負債　matured liability

到期值　matured value

到期通知書　expiration notice

到期票據　matured bill, matured note

到期滿日為止的收益(指債券的)　yield-to-maturity

到期應償付的債券　bonds due for payments

到達,抵港　arrival, arrival at port

到達日,入港日期　date arrival

到達主義(大陸法關於承諾的規則,承諾須到達相對人才生效,又稱到達生效原則)　received the lettter of acceptance

到價市價單,牌價定單(如市價到達定單要求的價位,該定單就成為市價單)　market-if-touched order

其他一切危險　any other perils

其他收益　other revenue

其他負債　other liabilities

其他資產　other assets

其他權利不受損害　[拉]salvo jure

其次最佳法規　next best rule

事主　client, clientele

事件　event

事先平衡　planned balance

事先安排的預算　planned budget

事先防止損失　take measures to prevent losses in advance

事先磋商　prior consultation

事先監督　supervision in advance

事故防止條款(海上保險)　sue and labor clause

事故保險　accident insurance

事故頻率　accident frequency

事前審計　pre-audit

事後日期　post dated

事後審計　post-audit

事後監督　subsequent supervision

事項　particulars

事業機構會計　institutional accounting

花式貨　fancy goods

花色齊全　nice selection

花紅　bonus, premium

花冤枉錢　pay for a dead horse, to spend money to no avail

花債券(美國財政部的長期庫券)

flower bond

花錢少，見效大 require less money, earn more profit

芝加哥商人交易所 The Chicago Mercantile Exchange

芝加哥國際貨幣市場 International Monetary Market of Chicago

芝加哥期權交易所 Chicago Board of Option Exchange

芝加哥農產品交易所 Chicago Board of Trade Exchange

亞克米商品及用語密碼（美國 A.C. Meisenback 1923 年編製的世界通用商業用語電碼） ACME commodities and phrases code

亞克米電碼補編 ACME supplement

亞非經濟合作組織 Afro-Asian Organization for Economic Co-operation (AAOEC)

亞洲大米貿易基金 Asian Rice Trade Fund

亞洲及太平洋經濟社會委員會 Economic and Social Commission for Asia and the Pacific

亞洲及遠東經濟委員會 Economic Commission for Asia and the Far East

亞洲再保險公司 Asia Reinsurance Company

亞洲美元 Asiandollar

亞洲美元市場 Asian dollar market

亞洲美元債券 Asian dollar bonds

亞洲開發基金 Asian Development Fund

亞洲開發銀行 Asian Development Bank

亞洲清算同盟 Asian Payment Union

亞洲清算貨幣 Asian Clearing Dollar

亞洲貨幣單位 Asian Monetary Unit

長打（十三個） long dozen

長度 length

長途運輸 line haul

長期 long-range, long-term

長期分析 long-run analysis

長期分期付款 long-term instalment

長期平均成本 long-term average cost

長期市場前景 long-term market out-look

長期失業 chronic unemployment, long-term unemployment

長期合同 long-term agreement

長期合約會計處理 long-term (construction) contract accounting

長期交稅債券 tax anticipation bills

長期利率 long-term interest rate

長期投資 long-term investment, permanent investment

長期投資決策 capital investment decision

長期均衡 long-run equilibrium

長期的限價證券 long tap

長期信用 long credit

長期信貸發放 long-term credit delivery

長期信貸銀行　long-term credit bank

長期保險　long-term insurance

長期負債　long-term liability

長期借債　long-term borrowings

長期租約　long-term lease

長期租賃　long-term lease

長期基金　long-term fund

長期票據　long-term note

長期單　long bill

長期期票　long bill

長期期貨合約（可長達 5 年的期貨交易）　long-term forward contract

長期貸款　long-term loan

長期資本　long-term capital

長期資本損益　long-term capital gain or loss

長期資金融通　long-term financing

長期資產　long-lived assets

長期債券　long-term bonds

長期債券利率　long-term bonds rate

長期債務　long-term debts

長期債務對資本總額比率　long-term debt to capitalization ratio

長期債款　funded debt

長期債權人　long-term creditor

長期預測　long-term forecast

長期賒帳便利　long-term credit facility

長期償付能力　long-term solvency

長期購買　long purchase

長期趨勢　long-time trend, long swings

長噸（英制噸，每噸 2240 磅）　long ton

長臂法案（美國各州訂立的法令，用以確定法院對不居住在美國的被告是否有對人的管轄權的標準）　Long-Arm Statute

奇貨可居　hoard as a rare commodity

奇零價格（指產品訂價為單數與零數）　odd price

杰森條款（遇險時拋棄貨物的條款）　Jason clause

或有年金　contingent annuity

或有折舊　contingent depreciation

或有利得　contingent gain

或有利潤（未來不肯定發生的經濟業務所實現的利潤）　contingent profit

或有負債（假定由某一特定業務所發生的負債）　contingent liability

或有費用　contingent charge

或有損失　contingent loss

或有資產（指一項資產的存在，價值和所有權決定於某一特定業務的發生或不發生）　contingent asset

東西方貿易　East-West trade

東京回合　Tokyo round

東非共同體　East African Community

取代進口貨工業　import-substituting industry

取代債權人　subrogation

取代舊債券　refinancing

取決於市價定單（交易所經紀持有之定單以當時市價為準，低於市價時買入，高於市價時賣出）　resting

order

取回股份　reacquired stock

取回被扣押財物　replevy

取回債券　reacquired bond

取得交換價值　acquisition of exchange value

取得成本　acquisition cost

取得利潤　securing of the profit, extraction of the profit

取得時效　acquisitive prescription

取得額調整數　acquisition adjustment

取款憑單　bill of credit

取銷支票　cancel a cheque

取銷合同　cancel a contract, rescind a contract

取銷判決　reversal of judgment

取銷歧視待遇　elimination of discrimination treatment

取銷股利　rescission of dividends

取銷抵押品贖回權　foreclosure

取銷定單　cancel an order, cancellation of order

取銷前有效　good-till-cancelled

取銷登記　cancellation of registration

取銷報價　withdraw an offer

取銷債務　debt cancellation

取樣檢驗　take a sample for examination and test, inspection by sampling

直立安放　to be kept upright

直航　direct route

直接分配　direct distribution

直接以貨幣支付的成本　explicit costs

直接以貨幣支付的利息　explicit interest

直接出口　direct export

直接包裝　immediate packing

直接成本　direct cost

直接成本法　direct cost method

直接存取（指在電子計算機中存、取一部份信息時，不必通過全部的存儲資料，亦稱＂隨機存取＂）　direct access

直接交易　direct transaction

直接交貨　direct delivery

直接收益　direct yield

直接安排（債券發行方式之一，指債券發行者直接將其債券全部售與法團投資者）　〔美〕direct placement, 〔英〕private placement

直接行銷　direct marketing

直接沖銷法　direct charge-off method

直接投資　direct investment

直接投資——發展週期（英國 J. H. Duning 提出，又稱＂直接投資發展 U 形曲線＂）　investment-development cycle

直接投資流動　direct investment flows

直接折舊法　straight-line depreciation method

直接函件廣告　direct mail advertising; DM Advertising

直接信用證，一次使用信用證　straight letter of credit

直接易貨　direct barter

直接持股　direct holding

直接後果　immediate consequence

直接負債　direct liability

直接計價　direct pricing

直接指數化　direct indexation

直接借入　direct debiting

直接借出　direct lending

直接原因　immediate cause

直接原料成本　direct material cost

直接套利　direct arbitrage

直接產品　direct products

直接稅　direct tax

直接費用　direct expenses, direct charges

直接貿易　direct trade

直接提單(指定收貨人，不能轉讓提單)　straight bills of lading

直接過帳　direct posting

直接結算法　direct closing method

直接滙兌　direct exchange

直接滙票　direct draft

直接零售商　direct retailing

直接運輸規則　rule of direct consignment

直接對外投資　direct foreign investment

直接銀行保證　direct bank guarantee

直接需求　direct demand

直接需要品　goods of first order

直接調查　direct observation

直接價格　direct price

直接銷售　direct sale

直接銷售價　direct sales price

直接標價法　direct foreign exchange quotation

直接擔保品　direct securities

直接償付　direct obligation

直接籌資　direct financing

直接變動成本　direct variable cost

直接攤還法　straight line method of amortization

直達船　direct vessel

直達港　direct port

直達航空線　direct air route

直達提單　direct bill of lading

直達滙票　straight arrival bill

直運提單　straight bill of lading

直線式程序　linear programming

直線式銷售組織　linear sales organization

直線折舊法　depreciation-straight line method

直接信用證　straight credit

雨淋保險　pluvious insurance

雨淋淡水險　rain and freshwater damage

雨淋損失　rain water damage

雨傘基金(指在一個"母基金"下，再組成若干個"成分基金"，允許投資者將其投資從一個成分基金轉移到另一個成分基金)　umbrella funds

兩(中國及亞洲東部一些國家的衡量單位)　tael

兩可地帶　zone of indifference

兩用帳戶　two-way account

兩合公司　limited partnership

兩次稅制　double tax system

兩年預算週期　biennial budget cycle

兩角套滙　two-point arbitrage in foreign exchange

兩段投標（國際承包工程方式之一）two-stage bidding

兩訖　on the balance

兩級抽樣　two-stage sampling

兩差異分析　two-variance analysis

兩差異製造費用分析　two variance overhead analysis

兩部式收益表　two-section income statement

兩價制　two-price system, two-tier price system

表外業務（指銀行沒有在"資產負債表"上完全反映出來的業務）off-balance-sheet business

表式帳簿，多欄式帳簿　tabular book

表決權（指股東對公司事務進行表決的權力）voting rights

表面危險同所在權一起轉移　risk prima facies passes with property

表面狀態　apparent condition

表面供應量　apparent availability

表面消費量　apparent consumption

表面價值　face value, nominal value

表面證據　prima facie evidence

表首　heading

表現股（指迎合某一時代潮流，但未必能適應另一時代潮流，致其市價呈巨幅起伏之股票）performance stock

刺激作用，波及效果　spread effect

刺激經濟　stimulate the economy

刺激經濟的政府投資　pump priming

刺激經濟政策　pump priming policy

刺激需求　demand promotion

〔 丨 〕

岸上火險條款　fire risk ashore clause

性向測驗　aptitude tests

性別差異　sex difference

性能　efficiency

帕舍指數（德國赫爾曼·帕舍編的，用以衡量實際購買數量的價格變化的指數）Paasche index

協作貿易　cooperating trade

協定　agreement

協定稅則　agreement tariff, conventional tariff

協定稅額　conventional tax

協定費率　tariff rate

協定關稅　conventional duty

協商和解　settlement by agreement

協會　association, institute

協會貨物條款（倫敦保險商協會的條款）Institute cargo clause

協會貨物條款（全險）Institute cargo clause (All risks)

協會貨物條款（單獨海損不賠）Institute cargo clause (F.P.A.)

協會貨物條款（單獨海損賠償）Institute cargo clause (W.A.)

協議貨物　conference cargo

協議區域　agreed territory

協議運費率　conference freight rate

協議價格　negotiated prices, agreed-upon prices

肯尼迪回合　Kennedy round

典契　deed of mortgage

典當　pledge, pawn, impawn

典當商　pawn operator

典質證書　instrument of pledge

尚待履行的合同　executory contract

歧視性貨幣安排　discriminatory currency arrangement

歧視性滙率，差別滙率　discriminatory exchange rate

歧視待遇　discrimination treatment

歧視關稅　discriminating duties

具有兩次表決權的記名股票　double vote registered shares

具有業務償債能力　business solvency

具保　find surety

具結　pledge, binding over

具體項目　specific items

易手　to change hands

易引起誤解的標記　misleading indications

易貨　barter

易貨合同　barter contract

易貨交易　barter deal, barter transaction

易貨協定　barter agreement, barter arrangement

易貨制度，易貨方式　barter system

易貨貿易　barter trade, barter versus

易貨滙兌　barter exchange

易售性（在某確定價格下對一種特定金融資產需求的程度）　marketability

易碎　fragile

易腐貨物，易壞貨物　perishable goods, perishable cargo

易銷貨物　marketable goods

易燃　inflammable

易變情況下的決策　decision-making under uncertainty

易變現金的財產　liquid assets

味道　taste, smell

呼救信號（國際通用的船舶、飛機等的呼救）　SOS

旺市，牛市　bull market

旺季　peak season, peak selling period

明示條件　express condition

明示擔保　express warranties

明約　express contract

明信片　postcard

明細分類帳　subsidiary ledger

明細科目　classification item

明細記錄　itemized record, subsidiary record

明智投資　prudent investment

明買明賣，公開交易　open transaction

明電　plain telegram

明語　plain language

明碼　ordinary telegraph code, listed price

明碼售貨　put goods on sale with the prices clearly marked, sell at market prices

固有性質　inherent nature

固有瑕疵，內在缺陷　inherent vice, inherent defect

固有價值　intrinsic value

固定比例分成收入　fixed ratio shared revenue

固定比率　fixed ratio

固定生產成本　fixed cost of production

固定平價　fixed parity

固定收入　fixed income

固定成本　fixed cost

固定地點佈置　fixed position layout

固定投入　fixed input

固定投資　fixed investment

固定佣金　dead commission

固定利差的遠期外滙買賣（指就遠期兩種貨幣的存款利率差額簽訂遠期外滙合同，如到期時利差擴大，由銀行承擔損失）　the forward spread agreement

固定利息投資　fixed interest investment

固定利息證券　fixed interest bearing securities

固定利率抵押　fixed rate mortgage

固定利率貨幣互換交易　fixed rate currency swap

固定股利　regular dividend

固定美元計算數字　constant dollar estimates

固定負債　fixed liability

固定保險費　fixed premium

固定訂購存貨系統　fixed-order-size inventory system

固定費用　standing charges

固定滙兌平價　fixed par of exchange

固定滙率制度　fixed exchange rate system

固定資金　consolidated fund

固定資產　capital asset, fixed asset

固定資產重估利益　profit from revaluation of fixed assets

固定資產租賃制　leasing system for fixed assets

固定資產與固定負債比率　ratio of fixed assets to fixed liabilities

固定資產與長期資本比率　ratio of fixed assets to long-term capital

固定預算　fixed budget

固定製造費用標準　fixed manufacturing overhead standard

固定製造費用預算差異　fixed overhead budget variance

固定製造費用能量差異　fixed overhead capacity variance

固定製造費用價格差異　fixed overhead price variance

固定製造費用數量差異　fixed overhead quantity variance

固定樣本調查　panel survey

固定價格　fixed price, regular price

固定數額貸款　fixed volume credit

固定證券價格　pegging

固封艙　strong compartment

忠誠保證保險　fidelity insurance, fidelity bond

非人名帳戶　impersonal account

非上市股　outside share (or stock)

非上市股票交易特權(在有些交易所，非上市股票無須公司本身事先申請，只要應交易所的某一成員要求即可在交易所交易)　unlisted trading privileges

非工程計劃性投資　non-project investment

非公會會員的航運公司　non-conference line

非分期付款信貸，一次償還信貸　non-instalment credit

非互惠性優惠　non-reciprocal preference

非互惠性貿易優惠　non-reciprocal trade preference

非互惠待遇　non-reciprocal treatment

非正式招股章程(指未明白表明募股之計劃書，又稱紅魚招股章程)　red-herring prospectus

非可控成本　non-controllable cost

非生產(性)資本　unproductive capital

非市場經濟　non-market economy

非本意投資　involuntary investment

非成員國　nonmember countries

非再生資源　non-renewable

非牟利公司　non-profit company

非牟利機構　non-profit making organization

非守則項下的非關稅措施(關貿總協定術語)　non-tariff measures not the subject to code

非技術支助　non-technical support

非技術支援　non-technical backstopping

非系統性風險(指由某種具體的、特定的因素引起的個別公司的特定風險)　unsystematic risk, firm specific risk

非歧視待遇　non-discriminatory treatment

非歧視原則的例外(關貿協定術語)　exceptions to the rules of non-discrimination

非歧視地實施數量限制　non-discrimination administration of quantitative restriction

非完整合約數量(指不按每筆期貨合約數量的零散交易)　job lot

非居民　non-resident

非居民兌換　non-resident convertibility

非居民借款人 non-resident borrower

非居民帳戶　non-resident account

非股份公司　non-stock corporation

非法交易　unlawful trading

非法利潤，超額利潤 exorbitant profit

非法倒買倒賣外滙　illegal dealings in foreign currencies

非法貿易　illicit trade

非法毀滅　fraudulent destruction

非法價格　exorbitant price

非固定進口稅　variable import levy

非承運人的聯運人 noncarrier multi-model transport operator

非東道投資國　non-host investor

非直線回歸　non-linear regression

非直線相關　non-linear correlation

非直線趨勢　non-linear trend

非抽樣誤差　nonsampling error

非金融公司債務　the debt of nonfinancial corporation

非股權投資(指以專利權、商品牌號、商標及經營管理的知識和才能作價入股，取得專利權、特許費、各種勞務費的一種靈活投資方式) non-equity investment

非耐久消費材料　non-durable consumer goods

非耐用消費品　non-durable consumer goods

非洲中央銀行聯合會　Association of African Central Bank

非洲石油進口國阿拉伯特別基金會 Special Arab Fund for African Oil Importers

非洲經濟委員會　Economic Commission for Africa

非美元國家　non-dollar countries

非約束性條款　permissive provision

非盈利事業　non-profit business

非保兌信用證　unconfirmed letter of credit

非契約收入　non-contractual income

非契約性責任　noncontractual liability

非契約索賠　noncontractual claims

非要素勞務　non-factor services

非純粹租賃(租賃的一段時期內資產的所有權與使用權相分離，但實際之承租人卻負擔着所有權所帶來的一切風險和利益，非純粹租賃，美國稱為"有條件銷售")〔英〕Hire Purchase,〔美〕conditional sale

非個人聯絡銷售　non-personal selling

非借入儲備　non-borrowed reserves

非流通期票　non-negotiable note

非流動資產　non-current assets

非流動債權　nonliquid claims

非常收入　extraordinary revenue

非常收益　extraordinary gains, abnormal gains

非常危險　abnormal risks

非常利益　extraordinary profit

非常折舊　abnormal depreciation

非常狀態　abnormal condition

非常損失　abnormal losses

非參加優先股　non-participating preference share

非參與投資　non-participating investment

非參與股份　non-participating stock

非商事合同　non-commercial contracts

非開放港口　non-open port

非現金項目　non-cash item

非現金費用　non-cash charges

非通貨膨脹性工資增長　noninflationary wage increase

非掛牌股票　unlisted stock

非掛牌證券　unlisted securities, over-the-counter security

非貨幣化效應　demonetization effect

非貨幣化硬幣　demonetized coins

非貨幣投資　non-monetary investment

非貨幣性負債　non-monetary liabilities

非貨幣性黃金　non-monetary gold

非貨幣性項目　non-monetary items

非累積股息　non-accumulative dividend

非累積優先股　non-accumulative preferred stock

非累積償債基金　non-accumulative
sinking fund

非連續複利計算　discrete com-
pounding

非減讓性官方貸款　non-concessional
official lending

非減讓性資金流動　non-concessional
flows

非項目貸款 non-project lending, non-
project loans

非貿易支付　non-trade payment

非貿易帳戶　non-trade account

非貿易國際結算　international settlements in connection with non-
trade transaction

非程序決策　non programmed de-
cision

非貼現滙票　non-discountable bill

非循環信用證　non-revolving credit

非極化歸零記錄法　nonpolarized
return-to-zero recording

非零效果　non-zero effect

非會員銀行　nonmember bank

非經常收益　non-recurring income

非經常利益　non-recurring gain

非資產負債表所列業務 out-of-bal-
ance-sheet services

非傳統出口商　non-traditional exporter

非傳統出口商品　non-traditional exports

非違禁品　non-contraband

非銀行背書　non-bank endorsement

非銀行機構　non-banking concerns

非徵稅支出　non-tax payment

非劃線支票，普通支票　uncrossed
check

非談判性關稅　non-bargaining tariff

非線性分析　nonlinear analysis

非線性回歸　nonlinear regression

非線性估計　nonlinear estimation

非線性相關　nonlinear or non-recti-
linear correlation

非線性規劃　nonlinear program-
ming

非線性最佳化　nonlinear optimization

非線性預測　nonlinear prediction

非實物資產　non-physical assets

非價格競爭　non-price competition

非標準材料　non-standard material

非標準產品　non-standard product

非標準集裝箱　non-standard con-
tainer

非請勿進　no admittance

非擔保證券　unsecured notes

非營利的　non-profit

非營業支出，非營業費用　non-operating expenses

非營業收入　non-operating revenue

非營業收益　non-operating earnings

非營業成本　non-operating cost

非營業所得　non-operating income

非營業控股公司 non-operating holding company

非營業項目　non-operating item

非營業損失　non-operating losses

非獨佔區域　non-exclusive territory

非關稅干擾　non-tariff distortion

非關稅手段　non-tariff device

非關稅貿易干擾手段 non-tariff trade distortive devices

非關稅措施守則　non-tariff measures codes

非關稅壁壘　non-tariff barriers (NTBs)

非競爭的價值規律 law of value without competition

非競爭集團　non-competing groups

昂貴　long price, long figure

[ノ]

爬行式固定滙率，浮動釘住　crawling peg

爬行固定滙率，滑行式固定滙率 crawling peg exchange rate, sliding peg exchange rate

爬行通貨膨脹　creeping inflation

金牛浮息債券　bull floating rate instrument

金本位制　gold standard

金本位貨幣　gold currency

金平價　gold parity

金字塔式交易法（股票投機的一種買賣方法，即當股票價格上漲時，使用保證金帳中產生的新增資產淨值購買更多股票，而不必增加現金投資）　pyramiding

金字塔式控制　pyramid control

金字塔式控制股權　pyramid holding

金字塔式推銷　pyramid selling

金條　gold bar

金庫　treasury, vault

金庫審計　audit of treasury

金塊　bullion

金塊本位制　gold bullion standard

金滙兌本位制　gold exchange standard

金銀比價　ratio between gold and silver

金銀市場　bullion market

金幣　gold coin

金幣條款　gold coin clause

金磚　gold brick

金融人士　financial figures

金融中心　financial centre

金融中心地點承兌信用證　financial centre acceptance credit

金融中界物　financial intermediary

金融公司　financial company

金融市場　monetary markets, money market

金融市場鬆動　easing of money rates

金融市場證書(美國住宅金融機構發行的類似 CD 的小額證券) money market certificate

金融交易　financial transactions

金融托拉斯　money trust

金融同質化(指各國普遍推行的專業化金融體系已被金融創新所衝垮，金融機構業務日益交叉，走向多樣化、綜合化，提供同樣的或類似的產品和服務) financial homogenization

金融危機　financial crisis

金融投機　monetary speculation

金融政策　monetary policy

金融服務革命　financial service revolution

金融制裁　financial sanction

金融界　financial community, financial circle, financial world, moneyed interest

金融家　moneyman

《金融時報》100 種股票交易指數(是1984 年開始根據倫敦股票市場挑選出的 100 家公司上市股票市值編製的指數，基數定為 1000) Financial Times——Stock Exchange 100 Share Index (簡稱: FT-SE 100 Index)

《金融時報》工業普通股票價格指數(英國《金融時報》根據 30 種熱門工業普通股票的平均價格計算的指數，又稱"30 種工業指數"，基期: 1935 年 7 月 1 日 為 100) Financial Times Index of Industrial Ordinary Shares (OR30-Share Index)

《金融時報》世界敏感商品價格指數 Financial Times Index of Sensitive World Commodity Price

《金融時報》固定利率精算指數 Financial Times Actuaries Fixed Interest Indices

《金融時報》股票價格指數(英國《金融時報》根據英國 150 種股票行情編製的指數) Financial Times All-Share Index

《金融時報》綜合精算股票指數(根據從倫敦股票市場上挑選出的 40 多組，700 多種股票市值統計出的綜合股票價格指數，基期: 1962 年 4 月 10 日 為 100) Financial Times Actuaries All-Share Index

金融混合聯合　financial conglomerate

金融期貨　monetary future

金融期貨市場　monetary future market

金融創新　financial innovation

金融資本　financial capital

金融業者　financier, moneyed interest house

金融滙率　financial rate

金融寡頭　financial oligarch

金融影響　monetary effect

金融融通　monetary facilities

金融機構　financial organ, financial

facilities

金融機構投資者　institutional investor

金融環境　financial environment

金錢來源　pecuniary resources

金錢損失　pecuniary loss

金錢萬能[美俚]　money talks

金錢賠償　relief in the form of money, pecuniary reparation

金錢懲罰　pecuniary fine

金衡制　troy

金衡盎司　ounce troy

金礦股票　gold issues, gold shares

金邊股票（尤指有政府擔保的股票）　gilt-edged shares

金邊債券（即優質債券，主要指英國政府的債券，也包括信用卓著的大公司債券）　gilt-edged bonds

金邊債券買賣商　gilt-edged jobbers

金邊證券（英國政府定息債券）　gilt-edged securities

金屬貨幣制度　metallic monetary system

委付　abandon

委付者　abandoner

委付書　abandonment, letter of abandonment

委付權　right of abandonment

委任理算人　appointment of an adjuster

委任書　letter of appointment

委託　instruct to, entrust, commission, consignment, mandate

委託人　mandator, consignor, bailer

委託人對受託人行為負責的原則　principle of respondeat superior

委託加工出口　processing deal for export

委託加工材料　outside processing materials

委託付款證　authority to pay

委託取款背書　endorsement for collection

委託書，代理權　proxy, trust deed

委託書制度　proxy system

委託商店　commission shop, commission house

委託貿易　commission business

委託銷售　sales on commission

委託撥款證　letter of authority

委託購買(書)，國外訂貨單　indent

委託購買證　authority to purchase

委託競爭（指在董事選舉會上，為爭取更多選票，盡量爭取較多的簽字委託書的做法）　proxy fight

爭奪市場　seize markets, contend for markets

受約束稅率　bound rates of duty

受領(貨物)　take delivery

受股人　transferee of stock

受抵押人　mortgagee, pledgee

受委託人　mandatory

受約人　promisee

受限制之現金　restricted cash

受限制之留存收益，受制盈餘　restricted retained earnings (or surplus)

受限制之資產　restricted assets

受限制的股票 restricted stock

受要約人 offeree

受託人 bailee, consignee, fiduciary, trustee

受託人代客保險 bailee's customers' insurance

受託人條款 bailee clause

受託人資格 fiduciary capacity

受害人 victim

受害方 injured party, aggrieved party

受益人 beneficiary

受益所有人 beneficial owner

受益者權利 rights of beneficiaries

受益值 benefit value

受益權益 beneficial interest

受票人, 付款人 drawee

受貨人 consignee, recipient of goods

受款人, 收款人 payee, accepter

受援國 recipient country, benefit country

受損失程度 extent of damage

受損後價值 damaged value

受損狀況 condition in damaged

受損貨物 damaged goods

受損貨物市價 damaged market value

受損貨物報告書 damaged cargo report

受載通知和待卸通知 notice of loading readiness

受補貼的出口 subsidized export

受補貼的進口 subsidized import

受僱人員酬金 compensation of employees

受潮 wetting

受潮受熱險 risk of sweating and/or heating

受影響最重的國家 "M" countries

受驚的錢 fright money

受讓人 assignee, transferee

卸岸 unloading ashore

卸貨 landing, discharging

卸貨人 discharger

卸貨日 date of discharge, lying days

卸貨申請書 application to unload

卸貨地點 landing place

卸貨收據 discharge receipt

卸貨港口 port of discharge, unloading port, port of debarkation

卸貨費用 landing charges, discharging expenses

卸貨報告 outturn report

卸貨準備完成通知書 notice of readiness

卸貨碼頭 discharging quay

卸箱指示(指卸貨櫃 集裝箱) general discharging instructions

制止令 inhibition

制止背信原則(證券管理原則之一) principle of anti-fraud

制裁 sanction

制裁後活動 activities after sanctions

制裁對象 object of sanctions

所有人 owner

所有制結構 pattern of ownership

所有權 ownership, proprietary rights, proprietorship, title

所有權及風險 title and risk

所有權文據 document of title

所有權的移交 transfer of title

所有權保留 retention of ownership

所有權契據 title deed

所有權益 ownership equity

所有權獨有條款 sole and unconditional ownership clause

所有權優勢（發展中國家對外直接投資的一個決定因素） ownership advantages

所有權轉移 transfer of property

所有權證據 evidences of title

所有權權利 proprietary rights

所在地法律 ［拉］lex loci rei sitae, lex situs

所在國 host country

所持有的有價證券 securities portfolio

所得，收益 income

所得政策 income policy

所得效果 income effect

所得稅，溢利稅 income tax

所得額來源資料 information at source

物件所有權 title to property

物件歸還 restitution of property

物有所值 good value for money

物物交易條件 barter terms of trade

物物交換，易貨貿易 barter

物的準動產 chattels real

物品敍述 description of property

物料 materials

物產保險 fire and marine insurance

物理檢驗法 physical testing

物資 material assets, resources

物資交流 material exchange

物資損失 material damage

物業水火保險 fire and marine insurance

物業不動產 real estate

物業交付文據製作 conveyancing

物業法法例 Law of Property Act

物業稅 property tax

物質文明 material civilization

物質利益 material gains, material interests, material benefits

物質資本 material capital, physical capital

物質資源 material resources, physical resources

物質權益 material equity

物價 prices of commodities

物價上漲 inflation of prices

物價回降 price reductions, price decreases

物價政策 price policy

物價波動 price fluctuation

物價指數 price indices, price index

物價指數債券 indexed bond

物價飛漲 skyrocketing prices, soaring prices, steep increase in prices, rocketing prices

物價管制 price control

物價與所得政策 prices and incomes policy

物價總水平 general level of market prices

物價總指數 general price index

物價趨漲 prices tend upwards

物價螺旋上升　price spiral
物歸原主　revesting
物權　real right
物權擔保　security interest
返還財產　restoration of property
近似成本　approximate cost
近似值　approximate value
近似現金的資產　near-cash assets
近似貨幣　near-money, quasi-money
近洋航線　near-sea shipping line
近海石油開發保險　offshore oil exploration insurance
近期交貨　near delivery
近期決策　near term decision
近期兌現資產　near-liquid assets
近期貨(指距交收月份最近之期貨合約)　nearbys
季度股利　quarterly dividend
季報　quarterly report
季節性失業　seasonal unemployment
季節性流動資金　seasonal loans for circulating funds
季節差價　parities according to season, seasonal price difference
季節調整　seasonal adjustments
季節變動　seasonal fluctuation, seasonal variation
乳膠袋　latex rubber bag
彼得遜世界商業電碼　Peterson international code
往來存款　bank account
往來抵押透支　overdraft on current account secured

往來帳戶　current account
往來資產　quick assets
往來銀行　bank with credits opened
往返運輸　out and back haul
往帳(本國銀行在國外銀行所持有的外幣帳戶)　[拉] nostro (意為"我們的") account
併股　reverse stock split, reverse split-up
依約照付　pay as may be paid
依法宣佈無效　ipso jure avoidance
依法律觀點　in the eye of the law
依法准許　duly admitted
依法給欠債人的延期償付權　moratorium
依法懲處　impose punishment in accordance with the law
依附關係　relations of dependence
依約廢止　denunciation
依限付款　pay on due date
依限提出　due presentment
依率計徵　taxation according to fixed rates
依期付款　payment in due course
依照入息支付　pay-as-you-earn
依照先例　stare decisis
依照票面價格　at par
使用人(最後使用人)　end user
使用年限　service life, useful life
使用借款　loan for use
使用稅(版權、專利權等的使用稅)　royalty
使用率　usage rate
使用費　charge for use

使用資本　use capital

使用價值　use value

使有效　giving effect to

例外分析　routine analysis

例外原則　exception principle

例外清單　exception list

例外管理　management by exception

例外檢查　routine inspection

供不應求　the supply is unable to meet the demand

供求律　law of supply and demand

供求情況，供求關係 supply-demand situation

供求價格　price based on supply and demand, supply-and-demand price

供參考外型　reference pattern

供貨人發票　supplier's invoice

供給曲線　supply curves

供給過多，供過於求　oversupply, overstock

供給與需求自動均衡　automatic equilibrium of supply and demand

供給彈性　elasticity of supply

供過於求　supply exceeds demand, pile up in excess of requirement

供過於求市場，買方市場　buyer's market

供需法則　law of demand and supply

供需總量　total supply and demand

供確認的樣品　sample for approval or confirmation

供應不足　supply has failed

供應方信貸　supplier's credit

供應價格　supply price

供應範圍　scope of supply

供應短缺　short supply

服務上門　door-to-door service

服務成本　cost of service

服務性租賃　service leases

服務性設施　service facilities

服務性勞動　service-type labour

服務能量　service capacity

服務產出折舊法　service output method

服務部門　service department

服務商標　service mark

服務業　service industry

股本　capital stock, share capital, equity

股本面值　par-value capital stock

股本定額不足　under capitalization

股本定額過大　over-capitalization

股本投資　equity investment

股本折價　stock discount, discount on capital stock

股本持有比例　capital shares apportionment

股本盈利　premium on capital stock

股本值　value of capital stock

股本資本　equity capital

股本與淨值比率　ratio of capital stock to net worth

股本溢價　premium on capital stock, stock premium

股本轉移　split-off

股份，股票　［英］share,［美］stock,

［法］action

股份不公開公司（即不公開招股的公司）　"close" corporation

股份不定投資公司　open-end investment company

股份公司 stock company, joint stock company

股份公開公司　open corporation, public corporation

股份分割　stock split up

股份平均數　stock averages

股份有限公司　limited company, limited liability company, company limited by shares, joint stock company limited, incorporated company

股份交換　exchange of stocks

股份兩合公司　joint stock limited partnership

股份固定投資公司　closed-end investment company

股份制度　joint stock system

股份紅利　stock bonus

股份信託證券　stock trust certificate

股份保險　joint stock insurance

股份稀釋，股權削弱　stock dilution

股份資本　share capital

股份資本化　stock capitalization

股份與股票　stocks and shares

股份銀行　joint-stock bank

股份認購　stock subscription

股份認購權　qualified stock option

股份儲蓄銀行　stock saving bank

股份轉讓　transfer of share

股份轉讓簿　stock transfer book

股利，股息　dividends, stock dividend, dividends earned

股利及公司債　stock and bonds

股利支付表　dividend payment sheet

股利支付率　dividend payout ratio

股利支付簿　dividend payment book

股利支票　dividend check

股利平衡基金　dividend equalization fund

股利平衡準備　dividend equalization reserve

股利收入　dividends earned

股利免税額　dividend exemption

股利股份　dividend stock

股利股票　dividend share

股利股票臨時憑證　dividend stock scrip

股利政策　dividend policy

股利除外，股利未付　ex-dividend

股利票，息票　coupon, dividend coupon

股利累積，拖欠股息 dividend in arrears

股利簿　dividend book

股東　stock holder, share holder

股東大會　general meeting of share holders

股東分戶帳 stock ledger, stockholders' ledger

股東主權，股東自有股份 shareholder's equity

股東主權報酬率　return on stockholder's equity

股東合夥人　equity partner

股東自有股份　shareholder's equity

股東自有資本　equity

股東年度報表　stockholder's annual report

股東名單　list of share holders

股東財產淨值　stock holder's equity

股東登記簿　register of members

股東優先認購權　privileged allocation to stockholders

股東權利　stockholder's right

股東權益　stockholder's equity

股東權益表　statement of stockholder's equity

股息　dividend

股息再投資計劃(股票派息不直接付給股東現金，而自動為股東購買本公司的增資股票)　dividend reinvestment plan

股息收益　dividend yield

股息委託書　dividend mandate

股息限度　dividend limitation

股息率　rate of dividend

股息帳　dividend account

股息基金　dividend fund

股息掉換券　talon

股息單　dividend warrant

股息稅　dividend tax

股息準備金　dividend reserve

股票　share, share certificate, stock certificate, equity security, stock, capital stock certificate

股票上漲　ballooning

股票升水　premium on capital stock

股票分票　fractions of shares

股票分割　stock splip, stock split-up

股票市值　shares: market value

股票市場　stock market

股票出售收益　gain on sale of stock

股票出售權(在一定期限以一定價格交售一定數量股票的選擇權)　put

股票合併　share consolidation

股票交易　stock deals

股票交易所　stock exchange

股票交易所指數　stock exchange index

股票交易所牌價　stock exchange list

股票交易所週轉量　turnover on stock exchange

股票交易所經紀　stock jobber

股票交易所證券　stock exchange securities

股票交易清算　stock exchange settlement

股票交割日前的一天　ticket day

股票行情表　stock quotation

股票更換　change of shares

股票投資　equity investment

股票投資信託　stock investment trust

股票投機　speculation in stock

股票投機狂　tickerosis

股票投機商　〔英〕stock-jobber

股票投機商代理人　takers-in

股票估價　stock valuation

股票抵押借款　stock collateral loans

股票抵押貸款利率　loaning rate on stocks

股票紅利　stock bonus

股票指數期貨　stock index futures

股票指數期貨合約　stock index future contract

股票指數期權　options on stock indexes

股票留置權　lien on shares

股票販子　share pusher

股票組合保險交易(在股市看跌或看漲時，為彌補現貨可能的損失而沽出或買入股票指數期貨的一種程序交易)　portfolio insurance trades

股票票面價值　shares nominal value, face value of share

股票發行溢價　share premium

股票登記　share registration

股票登記簿　share register, register of shares

股票期貨　stock future

股票欺詐　stock swindle

股票貸款　stock loan

股票報酬　stock compensation

股票買賣成交量　turnover

股票買賣特權　stock option

股票買賣權(約定在指定時期內，按一定價格買賣規定數量股票)　straddle

股票期權　share option

股票過戶　transfer of title

股票過戶代理人　stock transfer agent

股票過戶稅　transfer tax on stock

股票過戶證　deed of stock transfer

股票經紀人　stock broker, stock jobber

股票經紀人貸款　stockbroker's loans

股票溢價　premium on capital stock

股票管理　regulation of stock

股票價格　share price

股票價格限制　stock price restraint

股票價格指數　stock price index

股票價格規定　regulation of stock price

股票調換　stock swap

股票購買證書　stock purchase warrant

股票優惠權　stock right

股票轉手率　stock turn

股票轉讓　stock transfer, transfer of share

股票轉讓中間人　transfer agent

股票轉讓授權書　stock power

股票轉讓權　right to transfer stock

股票臨時收據，臨時股票　scrip

股票簿　stock certificate book

股票證券　share certificate

股票攙水　stock watering

股款付還　repayment of shares

股款催繳通知　call, notice of call

股數不定(投資)公司　open-end investment company

股權公司　holding company

股權出售　rights offering

股權委託，股權信託　voting trust

股權信託書　voting-trust certificate

股權資本　equity capital

股權價值　value of stock rights

［一］

附加人工成本　additional labour costs

附加股息　supplementary dividend, extra dividend

附加金額　surcharge value

附加值,增值　added value

附加稅　surtax, additional tax, additional duty

附加費用　extra charges, surcharge, additional charges

附加資本　additional paid-in capital

附加罰款　surcharge

附加險　additional risk, accessory risk

附件　enclosure; inclosure

附有各種權利　cum all

附有股利(銷售股票價格中包括下期的股利)　cum dividend

附有條件的合同　tying contract, conditional contract

附有條件的提單　claused bill of lading

附有條件的銷售　conditional sales

附有條件的證明　qualified certificate

附有息票(指在證券交易中，買方有權獲得下一次到期的利息付款)　cum coupon

附有說明之財務報表　descriptive financial statement

附有說明書的發盤　offer by description

附有認股書的歐洲債券　Eurobonds with equity warrants

附股合夥人　subpartners

附則　supplemental provision, supplementary provision

附限股制　restricted share

附條件承兌　qualified acceptance

附條件背書　conditional endorsement, qualified endorsement

附條件查帳報告　qualified report

附條件動產抵押據　conditional bill of sale

附帶成本　incidental cost

附帶交易　incidental transactions

附帶的損失　incidental damage

附帶條件貸款　tied loan

附帶條款　institute clause

附帶提存,附抽簽權　cum drawing

附帶期票　collateral note

附帶損害　collateral damage

附帶催繳股款　cum call

附帶權益　carried interest

附從合同(指不經談判由一方事前制定的)　contract of adhesion

附得利益　boot

附息票據　interest-bearing note

附息票債券　coupon bond

附息貸款　lend money on interest

附息滙票(在票面上記載利息條款之滙票)　interest bill

附息銀行債券　interest-bearing bank debenture

附貼樣品　attached sample

附擔保品借款 loans on collateral

附擔保品票據 bill with collateral securities

附擔保貼現票據 bill discounted with collateral securities

附樣品發盤 sampled offer

附繳資本 additional paid-in capital, capital surplus, paid-in surplus

附繳超定值資本 additional paid-in capital in excess of stated value

附屬公司，子公司 sub-company, subsidiary company

附屬付款承諾 subordinated

附屬協定 collateral agreement

附屬的法律 subsidiary legislation

附屬負債人 debtor paravail

附屬帳戶 adjunct account, absorption account, auxiliary account

附屬商店 tied shop

附屬債券 subordinated debts

附屬擔保品，擔保債券 collateral security

附權（股票中附有按一定折扣購新發股票的權利） cum right

阿克塞斯卡（英國四大銀行發行的信用卡） Access card

阿拉伯石油輸出國組織 Organization of Arab Petroleum Exporting Countries

阿拉伯共同市場 Arab Common Market

阿拉伯貨幣基金組織 Arab Monetary Fund

阿拉伯數字 Arabic numerals

阻擾價值 nuisance value

居民 resident

居民儲蓄 household savings

居留證 residence permit

居間股權公司 intermediate holding company

承付人，承兌人 acceptor, accepter

承付日期 date of acceptance

承付票據通知 advice of bill accepted

承付貸款的票面值 face value of loan commitments

承包商，小包工 sub-contractor

承兌 acceptance

承兌支票 honor a check

承兌日期 date of acceptance

承兌手續費 acceptance commission

承兌市場 acceptance market

承兌付款 payment by acceptance

承兌交單託收方式 documents against acceptance (D/A)

承兌收據 binding receipt

承兌（票據）利率 acceptance rate

承兌拒付滙票 acceptance supra protest

承兌押滙票 documentary acceptance bill

承兌信用 acceptance credit

承兌信用證 acceptance letter of credit

承兌限額 acceptance line

承兌商行 acceptance house

承兌責任 liability for acceptance

承兌通知書 accepted bill advice

承兌票據 acceptance bill

承兌票據到期紀錄 acceptance maturity record

承兌提示 presentment for acceptance

承兌滙票 acceptance bill, acceptance draft

承兌費 acceptance charge, acceptance fee

承兌銀行 accepting bank

承押人，受押人 mortgagee, pledgee

承受抵押條款 mortgage clause

承受背書票據人 endorsee

承受滙兌風險 exposure to exchange risk

承前 brought down, brought forward

承保 underwrite, cover

承保人 underwriter

承保辛廸加 underwriting syndicate

承保的風險 perils insured against

承保盈利 underwriting profit

承保信貸限額 cover for line of credit

承保限額 underwriting limit

承保通知書 cover note

承租人 leasee, renter, tenant

承運人 carrier, haulier

承運人代理 carrier's agent

承運人責任保險 carrier's liability insurance

承運人艙單 carrying capacity

承運船隻 carrying vessel

承認仲裁裁決 recognition of the award

承認判決 recognition of judgements

承認負債 acknowledgement of debt

承認責任 admission of liability

承認債權(指對方的債權) recognize a claim

承銷 consignment-in

承銷人預付款 advances of consignees

承銷人記錄 consignee's entries

承銷品 goods on consignment-in

承銷證券 underwrite

承諾 undertaking, promise, accept

承諾或未平倉合約 commitment or open interest

承擔未滿期責任 portfolio assumed

承擔抵押貸款 assuming the mortgage

承擔負債(間接負債) assumed liabilities

承擔費(指借款人按協議籌措資金而未能按期使用貸款，應向貸款銀行支付的一種賠償性費用) commitment fees

承諾的貸款 loan commitments

承諾書 letter of commitment

承辦人 undertaker

承繼公司債券(指一公司發行由另一公司繼承的債券) assumed bonds

姐妹船條款(同屬一個船主的船隻相撞後，保險公司亦應賠償損失) sister-ship clause

九　畫

[、]

為未償還借款重新籌集的資金　refinancing of outstanding borrowings

為在國內使用資金而在國外發行的債券　out to in external bond

為在國外使用資金而在國外發行的債券　out to out external bond

為償付債務開支再籌資　refinancing of debt service payments

美元危機　dollar crisis

美元災　dollar glut, dollar overhang

美元均衡定期投資法(一種購股技術，每隔一定時期以一定數額的美元購買證券的一種體制)　dollar cost averaging

美元荒　dollar shortage

美元差額，美元缺口　dollar gap

美元區　dollar area

美元偏好　dollar preference

美元黃金本位　dollar-gold standard

美元票據的支付期　dollar usance

美元集團　dollar bloc

美元遠期交易　dollar forward transaction

美元衝擊　dollar shock

美元總庫　dollar pool

美元購買力　dollar's buying power, dollar's purchasing power

美中貿易委員會　National Council for U.S.-China

美式計息法(在分期付款銷售中計算利息的一種方法)　United States rule

美孚石油公司　Mobil Oil Corporation

美制加侖　U.S. gallons

美洲國家商務仲裁委員會　Inter-American Commercial Arbitration Commission

美洲開發銀行　Inter-American Development Bank

美洲銀行卡(1977年改名為"簽證卡")　Bank Americard

美國1921年反傾銷法　Anti-dumping Act of 1921 (U.S.A.)

美國1962年擴大貿易法　Trade Expansion Act of 1962 (U.S.A.)

美國1966年公平包裝和標簽法　Fair Packaging and Labeling Act of 1966 (U.S.A.)

美國1968年貸款利率真相法(一種消費信貸保護法)　Truth in Lending Act of 1968 (U.S.A.)

美國1974年貿易法　Trade Act of 1974 (U.S.A.)

美國1974年商品期貨交易委員會法　Commodity Futures Trading Commission Act of 1974 (U.S.A.)

美國1988年綜合貿易法　Omnibus Trade Act of 1988 (U.S.A.)

美國土耳其國外貿易銀行 American Turkish Foreign Trade Bank

美國大豆協會 American Soyabean Association

美國反國外行賄法案(美國會 1977 年通過的一個法案) Foreign Corrupt Practices Act U.S.A.

美國中期國庫證券 treasury notes

美國出口用語定義 American Export Definitions

美國平準基金 American Stabilization Fund

美國市場營銷協會 American Marketing Association

美國全國對外貿易協會 National Foreign Trade Council

美國仲裁協會 American Arbitration Association

美國材料試驗協會規格 American Society for Testing Materials — ASTM

美國均等信用機會法(禁止貸款人在種族、宗教、原國籍別、年齡、性別、婚姻等方面對申請貸款人的歧視) Equal Credit Opportunity Act (U.S.A.)

美國亞太商會 Asian Pacific American Chamber of Commerce

美國的商品交易所 commodity exchange in the United States

美國股票證書 American share certificate

美國長期國庫券 treasury bond

美國食品藥物管理條例 Food & Drug Administration — F.D.A.

美國保管收據(即美國預託證券) American depositary receipt

美國海上貨物運輸法 (1936 年) Carriage of Goods by Sea Act, 1936 U.S.A.

"美國條件"平安險 free of particular average American conditions

美國航運局 American Bureau of Shipping

美國商務仲裁協會 American Arbitration Association (AAA)

美國商會 American Chamber of Commerce

美國國家安全委員會 National Safety Council

美國國家安全條款 national security clause

美國國庫券 treasury certificate

美國國庫債券(美國政府為吸收游資而發行的債券) tap bond, tap issue

美國國際合作總署 U.S. International Cooperation Administration

美國國際貿易委員會 International Trade Commission U.S.

美國國際開發總署 Agency for International Development, U.S.A.

美國清算所銀行同業支付系統(該系統連結 139 家最大銀行的電腦) Clearing House Interbank Payment System

美國售價制度(美國廠商對產品的定價。政府據以規定同類產品進

口稅額) American Selling Price System

美國進出口商公會 American Exporters and Importers Association

美國進出口銀行 Export-Import Bank of the United States

美國無面值股票 "no par value" shares

美國短期國庫券 treasury bill

美國電子協會規格 Electrotechnical Industry Association—EIA

美國電機製造協會規格 National Electrical Manufacturer's Association—NEMA

美國運通信用卡(美國五大信用卡之一，係以發行旅行支票聞名的運通公司發行的) American Express (AMEX)

美國會計學會 American Accounting Association

美國會計師協會 American Institute of Accountants

美國執業會計師協會 American Institute of Certified Public Accountants

美國預託股份 American Depositary Shares

美國預託證券(美國人投資外國公司股票的一種代用證書，外國股票託存美國銀行，由美國銀行發行的一種代用票據) American Depositary Receipts

美國對外貿易定義 American foreign trade definitions

美國製造商出口信用保險公司 American Manufacturers Foreign Credit Insurance Exchange (AMFCIE)

美國銀行家協會 American Bankers Association

美國製造商出口信用保險協會 American Manufacturers Foreign Credit Insurance Exchange

美國標準 United States Standards (USS)

美國標準協會 American Standards Association

美國聯邦儲備通訊系統80(簡稱FRCS-80，係美國聯儲計劃中心的現代化通訊網絡) Federal Reserve Communications System for the Eighties

美國總商會 American Chamber of Commerce

美國關稅委員會 Tariff Commission, U.S.

美國證券交易所 American stock exchange

美援 U.S. Aid

美噸(等於2000磅) short ton

美國總統輪船公司 American President Lines

前市 morning session

前門交易 "front door" deal

前定變量 predetermined variable

前期收益調整數 adjustment of earnings of prior periods

前期股利 preceding dividend

前期損益調整　prior-period adjustment

前期滾結帳目　brought forward account

前期滾結損益　loss and gain brought forward

前景調查　anticipation survey

前端信貸(指出口信貸按合約金額的15%部分由買方自行籌措，銀行對這部分進行融貸，稱前端信貸)　front end finance

前端費(在貸款開始時收取的佣金、費用或其他付款)　front end costs

前轉嫁(指生產企業可將稅款包括在價格之中，轉嫁給消費者)　shifting forward

首先留置權　first lien

首先進入市場　first-to-market

首批訂貨　initial order

首要準備金　primary reserve

首航(船東保證在冰封港凍結後首先進入港口)　first open water (F.O.W.)

首席銷貨員　star salesman

首期付款，定金，現付款額　down payment, initial payment

突降　bust

穿梭運輸　shuttle service

穿越證券(指以不動產抵押貸款為後盾的債券，本金和利息由最後借款人傳送至最後貸款人的管道，故名)　pass through securities

宣佈日期　date declaration

宣告合同無效　to declare the contract avoided

宣告判決　pronouncement of judgment

宣告破產　declare bankruptcy, adjudication of bankruptcy

宣告無力償債　declaration of inability to pay

宣告無效　declaration of avoidance

宣告無效的債券　invalidated bonds

宣傳品　promo

宣傳推廣資料　promotional literature

宣誓發票(指商業發票經出口商加註宣誓內容正確無訛文句)　sworn invoice

客戶分類帳，應收客帳　customer's account, debtor's ledger, sales ledger, accounts receivable ledger

客戶存入款　deposit by customers

客戶定金，存入保證金　customer's deposit

客戶預付款　advances from consumers

客車　passenger car

客船　passenger boat

客商　investor

客貨輪　passenger-cargo vessel, combination vessel

客運　passenger transport

訂金(尤指分期付款購貨的首次付現部份)　down payment

訂貨　order goods, place an order

for goods

訂貨代理人　indent agent

訂貨成本　ordering cost

訂貨單　order for goods, order form, order sheet

訂貨追踪　follow up the order

訂貨時付現金　cash with order

訂貨時機　ordering opportunity

訂貨週期時間　order cycle time

訂貨確認書　confirmation of order

訂載營業所　booking office

訂價　pricing

訂價先導，訂價領先　price leadership

訂艙　booking space, booking cargo space, chartering space

訂艙單　booking memo, booking note

訂購　purchase order

訂購商品　goods on order

訂購量　order quantity

計入成本之利息　interest charged to cost

計件工資　piece wage

計件折舊法 unit depreciation method

計件制　piece-rate system

計件超額工資　above-norm piece-work wages

計年土地租借人　tenant for years

計時工資　time wages

計時利息　time interest

計時制　daywork system

計息前淨收益　net income before interest charges

計息後淨收益　net income after in-terest charges

計量分析　quantitative analysis

計量方法　quantitative approach

計量抽樣檢驗　sampling inspection by variables

計量值　variable

計量經濟學　econometrics

計劃　plans

計劃平衡　planned balance

計劃成本　planned costs

計劃性功能廢舊 planned functional obsolescence

計劃性材料廢舊　planned material obsolescence

計劃性廢舊　planned obsolescence

計劃評核術 program evaluation and review technique (PERT)

計算每股收益　computing earnings per share

計算帳戶平均餘額　averaging of accounts

計算貨幣　money of account

計算課稅所得額時之除外項目　tax exclusions

計算機處理之數據文件 computer-ized data file

計價(外滙商行話，表示一種滙率水平，意指滙率的末兩位數為"00") figure

計價高於成本之發貨 shipments billed above cost

計價帳戶　valuation account

計價備抵　valuation allowance

計價準備　valuation reserve

計價對銷帳戶　contra valuation account

帝國特惠制　imperial preference

派生收入　derivative revenue

派生利息　derivative interest

派生性活期存款　derived demand deposit

派生所得　derivation income

派生指數　derivative index

派生貨幣　derivative money

派生需求　derived demand

派發股份　allotment of shares

派遣時期和停留期間　time of despatch and period of stay

"洞蛇"制，"蛇"體系(歐洲共市成員國間滙率波動的較小幅度和史密森協定規定的較大幅度兩者間關係的形象化名稱)　"snake in the tunnel" system

洛美協定(歐洲共市優待亞非某些國家貿易的協定)　Lome Convention

洛倫茨曲線(用來描述任何分配性質的一種曲線)　Lorenz Curve

活性資產　active assets

活性債務　active debt

活重(指活牲畜重量)　live weight

活頁存款單　loose-leaf demand certificate

活動成本　cost of activities

活動帳戶　active account

活動資本　liquid capital, active capital

活動資產　active assets

活動債券　active bonds

活動債務　active debts

活期支票帳戶　current checking account

活期存單　demand certificate

活期存款　demand deposit, current deposit

活期存款帳戶　current account

活期利息　current interest

活期利率　rate of call

活期抵押放款　call loans secured

活期放款　demand loan

活期放款及透支　demand loan and overdraft

活期信用放款　cash credit

活期通知借款／拆款　call money

活期通知貸款　call loan

活價合同　pricing contract

活躍市場　liven up the market, buoyant market

活躍的需求　buoyant demand

活躍產品　dynamic product

染污　stain

施行　go into effect, put in force

施行細則　rules for implementation

施救條款　sue and labour clause

施救費用　sue and labour charges

施救費用理算　adjustment of salvage loss

[一]

面積　area

面額一百美元股票　full stock

面額二十五美元股票　stock quarter

面額五十美元股票　half stock

面額股本　par-value capital stock

面額證券公司　face-amount certificate company

面向出口的工業　export-oriented industry

面向市場生產　market-oriented production

面值　face value, nominal value, par value

面值股票　par value stock

面值證書　face-amount certificate

面試　interview

要因分析圖　cause and effect analysis chart

要求付款　claim for payment

要求退款　claim for refund

要求減價　claim for reduction

要求確立產權的訴訟　petitory action

要求報酬率　required rate of return

要求賠償　claim indemnity, claim compensation

要求賠償書　claim letter

要求賠償損失權　right to claim for damages

要求償還　claim for reimbursement

要況報告　flash report

要約　offer

要約人　offeror

要約引證　invitation for offer

要徑　critical path

要徑會計　critical-path accounting

要素成本　component cost

要項控制　key area control

要價　the price asked, quote

要價過多　surcharge

厚利多銷　large profits and quick turnover

厚利資本　lucrative capital

厚度　thickness

"春播秋收"貸款　"seed-time for harvest" lending

查抄財產令　order for seizure of property

查封已查抄的財產　impounding of property seized

查封財產　attachment, seal up and confiscate property

查封債項　attachment of debts

查勘　survey

查帳,審計　audit, check account

查帳方法　audit techniques

查帳附註　exception

查帳員責任　auditor's liability〔同 auditor's responsibility〕

查帳程序　audit program

查帳備忘錄　audit memorandum, audit notebook

查帳報告　accountant's report〔同 auditor's report〕

查帳範圍　scope of audit

查帳標準,審計標準　audit standards

查帳線索,核數索引　audit trail

查帳證明　attest

查帳證明書　attest certificate

查帳權　inspection of licensee's account

查稅　tax inspection

查閱文據　inspection of documents

查點財產　inspection of property

查證通函　circular for confirmation

查證請求　confirmation request

政府大宗採購　government bulk-buying

政府干預　government intervention

政府公債　government bonds

政府地稅　crown rent

政府有價證券　government securities, government papers

政府估定價值　assessed value

政府投資　government investment

政府投資計劃 public investment program

政府法律官員　law officers of the crown

政府股票　government stock

政府放款　government loan

政府的證人　queen's evidence

政府信用保證　government credit guarantee

政府律師　Crown Solicitor

政府財政　government finance

政府許可證　government license

政府間信用證　letter of credit of government to government

政府專利　government monopoly

政府貿易代表團　government trade mission

政府貿易協定　governmental trade agreement

政府援助　government assistance

政府補助金　government subsidy

政府會計　government accounting

政府債券　government bonds

政府債務　government obligations

政府債務交易　public debt transaction

政府經紀人（在英國證券交易所任命的經紀人）　government broker

政府預算　government budget

政府預算赤字　government budget deficit

政府管制　government restriction

政府擔保債券　government-guaranteed bond

政府雙邊貸款　government bilateral loans

政府證券　government security

政策性成本　policy cost

政策性折舊　policy depreciation

政策性因素　factors resulting from policies

政策性補貼　subsidies granted for policy considerations

政策性變數　policy varial

政策配合　policy mix

契約　contract

契約上的收益　contractual revenue

契約文字　contractual language

契約生效　execution of contract

契約收入　contract revenue

契約自由（合同法的一項基本原則）　freedom of contract

契約式合資企業　contractual joint

venture

契約式垂直行銷系統　contractual VMS

契約有效期間　duration of contract

契約見證人　attesting witness

契約性投資　contractual investment

契約要素　essence of the contract

契約條件　conditions of contract

契約終止　termination of contract

契約規定佣金　stipulated commission

契約規定股利　contractual dividend

契約規定的義務　contractual obligation

契約規定航線　contractual route

契約規定準備金　contractual reserve

契約落空　frustration of contract

契約當事人　contracting parties

契約運費制度　contract rate system

契約運輸業　contract carrier

契約履行期限　contract date

契約標的　subject-matter of contract

契約價格　contract of price

契稅　contract tax, deed tax

契據　escrow, deed

契據本文　body of deed

契據的履行部份　operative part of a deed

契據副本　antigraphy

怡底支付法(抵銷反傾銷稅的一種辦法：以高價出售給進口商，另外暗中給進口商支付一筆回扣，使進口國無法認為是在價格上進行傾銷)

kick backs under the table payment

相互合作　mutual cooperation

相互承兌　mutual acceptance

相互抵銷　repeal by implication

相互約束　reciprocal bond

相互保險　mutual insurance

相互保險公司 mutual insurance company

相互核對　mutual check

相互控股　mutual stock holding

相互透支　mutual swing credit

相互貿易協定法　Reciprocal Trade Agreement Act

相互債務　cross liabilities

相互需求　reciprocal demand

相反效果　boomerang effect

相抵錯誤　errors of compensation

相約取消期(租船時規定船舶到港裝貨的期限)　cancelling date

相當二十英尺長單位(指貨櫃/集裝箱之長度)　twenty-foot equivalent unit

相對往來帳戶　reciprocal accounts

相對銷售價值法 relative sales value method

相鄰效應　neighborhood effects

相鄰等級　adjacent rank

相關　correlation

相關成本　relevant cost, related cost

相關係數(是衡量一種股票與整個市場之間相互關係的統計數字，數值由 0 開始，表示無相關；至 1，表示關係極完善)　correlation coefficient

相應的百分比　corresponding percentage

相應數額　matching amount

耐久性有形資產　permanent tangible property

耐用年限　service life

耐用品　durable goods; hard goods

耐用消費品 durable consumer goods

苛刻的交易　hard bargain

英尺　foot

英里　mile

英兩,盎司　ounce

英制加侖　Imperial Gallons

英帝國化學工業公司 Imperial Chemical Industry

英美煙草公司 British-American Tobacco

英畝　acre

英國 1956 年限制性貿易措施法 Restrictive Trade Practice Act 1956 (UK)

英國 1964 年租購法案規定的默示條件與保證義務　hire purchase contracts: conditions and warranties 1964 (UK)

英國 1965 年租購法　Hire Purchase Act 1965 (UK)

英國 1973 年公平交易法　Fair Trading Act 1973 (UK)

英國工程標準協會　British Engineering Standard Association

英國出口局　British Export Board

英國汽車公司　British Motor

英國政府債券(由英格蘭銀行直接發行的債券)　tap stock

英國保險協會　British Insurance Association

英國海上保險法　Marine Insurance Act 1906

英國海上貨物運輸法(1924)　Carriage of Goods by Sea Act 1924, U.K.

英國條件平安險　free of pacticular average English conditions

英國海外貿易局　British Overseas Trade Board

英國財政部債券 treasury bill, treasury bond

英國商船法案　Merchant Shipping Act

英國商船隊　red ensign

英國船級社　British Corporation

英國貨運碼頭局　British Transport Docks Board

英國貨幣　sterling

英國貿易部　Board of Trade

英國勞埃德商船註冊協會　Lloyd's Register of Shipping

英國標準　British Standards

英國標準規格 British Standard Specification

英國聯合電氣工業公司　Associated Electrical Industries

英國儲蓄公債 British savings bonds

英碼　yard

英擔　hundredweight－CWT

英噸(等於 2200 磅)　long (gross)

ton, English ton

英聯邦特惠制(英國和英聯邦成員國之間在貿易上彼此給予優惠關稅待遇的制度) Commonwealth Preference System

英聯邦特惠關稅　British preferential tariff

英鎊　sterling, [英俗] quid

英鎊危機　sterling crisis

英鎊區　pound area, sterling area

英鎊結存　sterling balance

英鎊集團　pound bloc

英鎊遠期價格　sterling forward price

英鎊證券　sterling bonds

南太平洋航線　South-Pacific shipping line

南北貿易　South-North trade

南北對話　North-South dialogue

南北談判　North-South negotiations

南非航線　South-Africa shipping line

南南合作　South-South cooperation

南南會議　South-South Conference

南美航線　South-America shipping line

封閉工廠　lockout

封閉式公司　closed corporation

封閉式遮蔽甲板船　closed shelter-decker

封閉性系統　closed system

封閉型小型貨櫃/集裝箱　enclosed small container

封閉港　closed port

封閉區域　closed area

封鎖　blockade

封鎖外滙制度　aski system

封鎖帳戶　blocked account

封鎖貨幣　blocked currency

封鎖禁運　blockade and embargo against

封鎖經濟　closed economy

故意傷害　intentional injury

故障貨物　goods in bad order

故障檢修　corrective maintenance

玻璃工業　glass industry

玻璃保險　plate glass insurance

頁數欄, 單據號數欄　folio column

指示式債權　claim to order

指示票據　order paper, order instrument

指示提單　order bill of lading

指示滙票　bill drawn to order

指示傳票　summons for directions

指示價格　indication price

指定人支票(俗稱"抬頭人支票")　order check, order cheque

指定人提單(又稱"指示提單")　order bill of lading

指定日期　appointed day

指定目的地完稅後交貨(價)　delivery .... duty paid

指定用途留存收益　appropriated retained earnings

指定用途盈餘, 撥定公積　appropriated surplus, earmarked surplus

指定外滙銀行　authorized foreign exchange bank

指定地付款　payment domiciled

指定式背書　endorsement to order

指定式滙票　bill drawn to order

指定存款　designated deposit

指定仲裁員的機構　appointing authority

指定的訂單轉換系統(紐約證券交易所由電腦指揮訂單的買進和賣出) Designated Order Turn-around System

指定受益人信用證　straight letter of credit

指定差距跨期單(一種跨期買賣常見訂單，在特定的差距內，進行相反買賣兩個不同月份的合約)　basis order

指定貨幣　designated currency

指定銀行　designated bank

指定遺贈　specific legacy

指定遺囑執行人　executor

指定邊境地點交貨(價)　delivery at frontier.......

指數　index numbers

指數化　indexation

指數化貸款　indexed loan

指數化債券(又稱"穩值債券")　indexed bond (stabilied bond)

指數本位幣制　monetary system with the price index as the standard

指數成份股　component stocks, underlying stocks

指數法(企業評價)　index method

指數值　index value

指數基　base index

指數變化　index movement

指標　index mark

指標股票(指市價可顯示一般狀況的股票)　barometer stock

指標價格　target price

指導價格(歐洲共同市場農業政策使用的價格系統，以決定是否徵稅和徵多少稅的一種辦法)　guide price

持平分析　breakeven analysis

持有多數股權之附屬機構　majority-owned subsidiary

持有損益　holding gains or losses

持有證券　securities owned

持作抵押品　hold in pledge

持股公司　proprietary company; holding corporation

持倉　position

持倉者　position trader

持倉限額　position limit

持票人　check holder, bearer

持牌小販　licensed stallholder

持牌倉庫(指交易所批准之倉庫)　licensed warehouse

持證人簽名　holder's signature

持續要約(在撤銷前一直有效的要約)　standing offer

持續保險 preliminary term insurance

持續策略(一商號持續利用同一市場層次、渠道、價格和推銷方法的銷售政策)　continuation strategy

持續期間　time of duration

持續貸款　perpetual loan

持續增長　sustainable growth

拼裝(指貨物集裝成貨櫃)　consolidation

拼裝作業　consolidation service

拼裝承運商　consolidator

拼裝承運商提單　consolidator's B/L

拼裝站　consolidation slation, consolidation depot

拼裝場　consolidation shed

拼櫃交，拆櫃接（指貨櫃/集裝箱在裝
貨港拼裝，在卸貨港拆卸）LCL/
LCL (less than container)

拼櫃交，整櫃接（指貨櫃/集裝箱在裝
貨港拼裝，在卸貨港整卸）LCL/
FCL (less than container load/full
container load)

拼櫃裝（指貨櫃/集裝箱零貨拼箱裝
卸）LCL (less than container
load)

拼櫃裝貨物（用貨櫃/集裝箱拼箱裝卸
的貨物）LCL cargo (less than
container load cargo)

拼櫃裝運費率（貨櫃/集裝箱拼裝運費
率）LCL rate (less than container load rate)

按人口平均消費水平　level of aver-
age per capita consumption

按人口平均計算，人均〔拉〕per
capita

按人口平均計算的國內生產總值，人
均國內總產值　per capita gross
domestic product

按人口平均計算的國民生產總值，人
均國民生產總值　per capita gross
national product

按人口平均計算的國民所得，人均國

民收入　national income per capita

按人口平均計算的實際所得，人均實
際收入　real income per capita

按人口平均計算的總產值，人均總產
值　per capita gross product

按毛利分配　distribution on gross
profit

按比例　pro rata

按比例分攤　pro rata distribution

按比例平均　pro rata average

按比例收費　proportional charges

按比例註銷　pro rata cancellation

按比例增加或減低　scale up or down

按日放款　day-to-day-loan

按月分期付款銷售　monthly install-
ment sale

按月循環信用狀　monthly revolving
credit

按日分期付款額計息　interest based
on each installment

按不變價值美元計算　in constant
dollar value

按生活指數調整指數化　indexation

按市場價格計算的國民生產總值
gross national products computed
at market price

按市價　at market price

按市價兌換的債券　debenture con-
vertible at current price

按市價折舊　depreciation at market
price

按成本　at cost

按成本與市價孰低　at the lower of
cost or market

按成果付酬 compensation by the result

按件生產 jobbing production

按年攤付 yearly instalments

按批生產 batch production

按批折舊法 depreciation-job method

按序存取(指在電子數據處理中，對一個輸入輸出媒體，和磁帶中所存儲的數據必須按順序地存取。與"直接存取"詞義相對) sequential access

按股分紅 sharing profits according to contributions

按使用年限折舊法 depreciation-service life method

按金 margin, margin deposit

按金證書 certificate of deposit

按兩者中較低者計算 whichever is lower

按兩者中較高者計算 whichever is higher

按指數計算的貸款 indexed loan

按指數償付的債券 indexed bond

按航次計費租船 charter by voyage, trip charter

按值交保證金 ad valorem deposit

按值徵稅 ad valorem duty

按容積噸計算運費法 measurement ton method

按國民生產總值固定加權指數 GNP fixed weighted price index

按部門的投資分配 sectoral distribution of investment

按規定日期付款的匯票 bill drawn payable at a fixed date

按商品現狀 tel quel, tale quale

按船舶能裝速度供應貨物裝船(租船合同用語) as fast as can

按產量折舊法 depreciation-output method

按買方發貨通知 delivery on call, delivery on request

按勞付酬 pay according to work

按揭組合參與工具(是一種由多家銀行參與的"按揭證券"，銀行把其部份樓屋按揭貸款組合起來，把應收帳以一定面額的證券形式售給其他銀行) mortgage portfolio participation facility

按期盤存制 periodic inventory system

按資本額推算的利息 imputed interest

按當時購買力之財務報表 current purchasing power statement

按概率比例抽樣 sampling with probability proportionate to size

按價格水平調整的貸款 price level adjusted loan

按總收益提成折舊法 depreciation-gross earning method

按體積計算運費 measurement freight

[丨]

冒用商標 infringement

冒充貨 adulterated goods

冒牌 imitation brand

冒險　gamble

冒險投資　reckless investment

冒險事業會計　venture accounting

背負式運輸（鐵路平車裝運載有貨櫃的汽車、拖車、半拖車的運輸方式）piggy back

背約　breach of contract

背信（為債務）encumbered with debts

背書　endorse, back, endorsement

背書人　endorser, backer

背書不符 endorsement irregular (E/I)

背書支票　endorse a check

背書責任　liability for endorsement

背書票據　back a bill

背對背信用證　back to back credit

背對背貸款（指由一國以一種貨幣向另一國另一種貨幣提供貸款）back to back loan

哄抬物價　price-jacking

哈瓦那憲章　Havana Charter

哈特法（美國 1893 年制定的海上運輸法）Harter Act

品級　grade

品脫（容量單位，在美國乾量等於0.5505 公升；液量等於 0.47315 公升。在英國等地，乾量或液量均等於 0.56793 公升）pint

品種分類　assortment

品質　quality; brand

品質大致同樣品相同　quality to be considered as being about equal to the sample

品質欠均勻　lack of uniformity

品質不符　different quality

品質成本　cost of quality

品質有缺點　defective quality

品質低劣　inferior quality

品質免賠限度　quality franchise

品質按買方樣品 quality as per buyer's sample

品質按賣方樣品 quality as per seller's sample

品質保證　guaranteed qualities

品質差幅　quality latitude

品質較差　inferior quality

品質試驗證明書　certificate of quality test

品質管制　quality restriction

品質標誌　quality mark

品質擔保條款 quality warranty clause

品質檢驗書 inspection certificate of quality

品質優良　fine quality

品質覆驗　checking of quality

品質證明書　quality certificate

削減進口　import curtailment

削減關稅　reduction in tariff

削價　price cutting

削價競爭　price-cutting competition

削髮融資（美國術語。指以證券作擔保品的一種借款，借款額為證券價值 80%，由於另 20% 被當作頭髮削掉，故名）haircut finance

恰當授權　just authority

[ノ]

風災　windstorm

風災險　windstorm insurance

風險　risk

風險下的決策　decision-making under risk

風險大的保險戶　poor for insurance

風險分析　risk analysis

風險由貨主負擔　at owner's risk

風險性決策　risk decision

風險率　risk ratio

風險減至最小限度　risk minimization

風險資本　risk capital

風險資產　risk assets

風險與收益特性　risk-return characteristics

風險補貼　risk premium

風險溢價　risk premium

風險隔離　isolation of risk

風險調整折現率　risk-adjusted discount rate

風險調整報酬率　risk adjusted return

盈利比率　profit ratio

盈利佣金　profit commission

盈利能力　profitability

盈利能力指數　profitability index

盈利敏感度（指盈利在經濟上受限制的程度）　profit sensitivity

盈利敏感率（用國民總產值的變化除共同盈利的變化而得的比率）　profit sensitivity ratio

盈利稅　business profit tax

盈利對利息的倍數　times-interest earned, interest coverage ratio

盈餘帳戶　surplus account

盈餘撥抵折舊法　depreciation-appropriation method

盈餘調節　surplus reconcilement

盈虧平衡分析　breakeven analysis

盈虧平衡點，盈虧臨界點（交易所股票交易量的基數點，超過此點就會實現盈利，反之則虧）　breakeven point

盈虧通知書（期貨經紀給予未平倉客戶的清單）　difference account

版稅　royalties

版權　copyright

科學管理　scientific management

負因素　negative factor

負利息　negative interest

負投資　negative investment

負抵押（一種貸款條款，規定不經貸款人許可，不發行有利於以後債權人的證券）　negative pledge

負所得　negative income

負所得稅（指政府對低收入的個人家庭所進行的一種補助，也稱"有保障的年收入"）　negative income tax

負約　break an agreement

負信用　negative credit

負相關（指一個變量的增加伴隨着另一個變量的減少的相關關係）　negative correlation

負效用　disutility

負差異　negative variance

負差幅，反向差幅　negative spread

負現金流量（指一個企業或項目的現金流入量少於流出量）　negative

cash flow

負斜度收益率曲線（指短期利率高於長期利率的收益率曲線） nega-tively sloping yield curve

負量　negative quantity

負商譽　badwill, negative goodwill

負債　liability, incur debts, indebt-edness

負債人無力清償債款聲明　declar-ation by debtor of inability to pay his debts

負債率（各種形式的長期債務，除以一公司的資本總額） debt ratio

負債淨額　net indebtness

負債帳戶　liability account

負債準備金　liability reserve

負債管理　liability management

負債對資本比率　liabilities to capi-tal ratio

負債對銷帳戶　contra-liability ac-count

負債證明書　liability certificate

負資本（指借款，存款） negative capital

負資產　negative asset

負資產帳戶　negative asset account

負增長　negative growth

負擔代替　novation

負擔系數　dependency coefficient

負擔攤派　contribution

負邊注　marginal note

急電　[英]urgent cable，[美]urgent telegram

急逼債務　immediate indebtedness

看跌　bear

看貨買賣，驗貨後買賣　sale by in-spection

看漲　long, bull

看漲貨幣　bull currency

香港上海滙豐銀行　Hongkong and Shanghai Banking Corporation

香港民安保險公司（由中國人民保險公司投資 5000 萬港元在香港註冊成立） Min An Insurance Company of Hongkong

香港恒生指數（選取 33 種上市股票以加權資本市值法計算的指數） Hang Seng Index

香港指數（由聯合交易所以香港 49 種股票為成份股編制的指數） Hong Kong Index

香港商品交易所　Hong Kong Com-modity Exchange

香港貿易發展局　Hong Kong Trade Development Council (HKTDC)

香港期貨交易所　Hong Kong Fu-tures Exchange

香港期貨保證有限公司　The Hong Kong Futures Guarantee Corpo-ration Ltd.,

香港預託證券　Hong Kong Deposi-tary Receipts (HKDR)

香港聯合交易所有限公司 The Stock Exchange of Hong Kong Ltd.

香港總商會　Hong Kong General Chamber of Commerce (HKGCC)

香港優質產品標誌（1978 年後推行） HK Q-MARK

香蕉出口國聯盟(1974年9月成立) Union of Banana Exporting Countries

垂直行銷系統 vertical marketing system

垂直貿易(經濟發展水平不同國家間的貿易) vertical trade

垂直整合 vertical integration

重工業 heavy industry

重大過失 gross negligence

重大違約 fundamental breach

重出租人 underlessor

重生策略 recovery strategy

重合經濟指標(指衡量那些與總的經濟活動同時間、同方向變化的經濟活動的一種指標) coincident indicators

重合經濟指標綜合指數(美國商務部編製) composite index of coincident indicators

重估價 revaluation

重估價盈餘 revaluation surplus, reappraisal surplus

重估價稅 tax on revaluation

重估價調整數 revaluation adjustments

重利盤剝 exorbitant usury

重取得股份 reacquired stock

重取得債券 reacquired bond

重定資本, 調整資本 recapitalization

重油輪 dirty ship

重招標(合約市場容許結算公司接受交收通知的合約持有人沽出期貨合約, 把交收通知交還結算公司發給

其他多倉客, 香港稱為"重招標") retender

重要錯報 material misrepresentation

重訂租約 renew a lease

重訂還債期限 debt rescheduling

重計價盈餘 revaluation surplus

重計價程序 revaluation process

重商主義 mercantilism

重商主義者 mercantilist

重量及尺碼標誌 weight and measurement mark

重量貨物(每長噸不超過四十立方呎的貨物) dead weight cargo

重量噸 dead weight ton

重量檢驗書 inspection certificate of weight

重量證明書 certificate of weight

重貼現 rediscount

重承租人 underlessee

重租(按年計的租借人或承租人, 把租來的土地或房屋, 轉租給他人) underlease

重複發盤 repeat offer

重複需求 repeat demand

重複發價 repeat offer

重置成本 replacement cost

重置折舊法 depreciation-replacement method

重置基金 replacement fund

重置會計 replacement accounting

重置價值 replacement value

重置價格法 replacement price method

重置成本, 更新成本 replacement cost

重置資本，抵補資本 replacement capital

重置價值，更新價值 replacement value

重新打包 repacking

重新安排付款期限 rescheduling of payment

重新安排償還期 rescheduling

重新估價 revaluation, revalorization

重新釘好 renailing

重新進貨 restock

重新裝載 reloading

重新發盤 renew offer

重新遞盤 renew bid

重新擁有的貨物 repossessed goods

重新包裝 repacking

重新談判條款（在合同中規定在什麼情況下雙方需重新談判之條款）re-opener clause

重穀（指玉米、小麥、黑麥在1894年英國海商法中被列為重穀，而大麥，燕麥為輕穀）heavy grain

重購入股份 repurchased stock

重獲股份 reacquired stock

重點集體面談話法 focus group interview

迫售價格（價值）forced sale value

敍述式報表 explanatory statement

敍述式損益表 narrative form of profit and loss statement

秋季貨品 fall goods

食物添加劑 additives

食品法典委員會 Codex Alimentarius

律師 solicitor, lawer

律師公會 law society

律師出庭 audience of solicitor

律師意見書 legal opinions

衍生部門 derivative departments

衍生組織結構 flat organization structure

衍生價值 derived value

待付款 obligation

待收 due in

待發 due out

待結帳戶，過渡帳戶 clearing account

待履行的對價 executory consideration

後入先出法 last-in first-out method

後工業社會 post-industrial society

後生成本（指銷售後繼續發生的成本）after-cost

後決條件 condition subsequent

後延 carry forward

後抵押 subsequent mortgage

後派息股 deferred shares

後取息股 deferred stock

後保債券 junior bond

後受償債權人（又稱次位債權人）subordinated creditor

後受償債權協議（指借款人的某些債權人同意，在該借款人的其他債權人的債權得到全部清償前，他不得要求清償）subordination

後受償債權信託 subordination trust

"後門"（英國術語。指英格蘭銀行按市場利率而不按"最低借款利率"向貼現行提供貸款）"back door"

後門融通資金　backdoor financing

後艙　after hatch

後續投資　follow-up investment

後續服務　follow-up service

後驗概率　posterior probability

修正後的價格指數　price indices corrected

修正條款　amending clause

修正統一責任制　modified uniform liability system

修改手續費　amendment fee

修改事項　particulars of amendment

修改通知　amendment advice

修理及保養　repairs and maintenance

修理通知單　repair order

修理設備　repairing equipment

修理費　repairing charges

保付支票　certified check; accepted check

保付代理人　confirming agent

保付代理業務，承購應收帳款（指購買貿易債務，通常不附有追索權）factoring

保付貨款合同　del credere contract

保付貨款代理人佣金　del credere commission

保付貨款代理人　del credere agent

保付貨款協議　del credere agreement

保存貨樣　keeping a sample, file sample

保存證據　perpetuation of testimony

保守秘密　private and confidential

保全會計　custodial accounting

保兌文句　confirming clause

保兌的不可撤銷信用證　confirming irrevocable letter of credit

保兌信用證　confirming credit

保兌銀行　confirming bank

保持平放（包裝外表標誌）　keep flat

保持同一水平　keep on an "even keel"

保持完整　be kept perfectly

保持原始價格　keep aboriginal

保持涼爽（包裝外表標誌）　keep cool

保持豎直（包裝外表標誌）　be kept upright

保持優勢　hold on to our favourable position in

保留存貨區位系統　reserve-stock locator system

保留利潤　retained profit

保留所有權　with retained ownership, title retention

保留押金信用證（埃斯克羅信用證）escrew credit

保留條款　saving clause

保留盈餘　retained earning

保留追索權　reserve the right to recourse

保留進口　retained import

保留意見　qualification

保留權利　rights reserved

保留權限　reserved authority

保息股票　guaranteed stock

保售協議　del credere agreement

保稅加工廠　bonded factory

保稅卡車　customs bonded vehicle

保稅倉庫　bonded warehouse

保稅區　bonded area

保稅貨物　bonded goods, goods in bond

保稅運貨商　bonded lighterman

保稅運輸　bonded transportation

保稅關棧　bonded store; bonded warehouse

保稅關棧費　bonding fee

保單負債　warranty liabilities

保單滿期　expiration of policy

保溫貨櫃／集裝箱（內部有隔熱裝置但無冷凍裝置的貨櫃）　insulated container

保費準備金利息　interest on premium reserve

保管人　custodian

保管提單　custody bill of lading

保管費　possession money

保障條款（歐洲共市對抗日本進口的條款）　safeguard clause

保險　assurance, insurance

保險人　assurer, insurer

保險不足　under-insurance

保險公司　insurance company

保險代理商　insurance agent

保險市場　insurance market

保險合同　insurance contract

保險回扣　insurance rebate

保險交易所　insurance exchange

保險佣金　insurance commission

保險投保單　cover note

保險利益　insurable interest

保險利益由保險單證明　policy proof of insurance

保險批單（保險單上所加的變更保險範圍的條款）　endorsement

保險折舊　depreciation insurance

保險折舊法　depreciation-insurance method

保險法　assurance law; insurance law

保險事業　insurance business

保險金額　amount insured, risk insured

保險金額未確定保單　unvalued policy

保險金額自動恢復條款　automatic reinstatement clause

保險客戶　policy holder

保險信託　insurance trust

保險要素（指構成保險關係的主要因素，如保險人、被保險人、保險標的期限、責任、金額等）　essence of insurance

保險契約　contract of insurance

保險保障　insurance cover

保險庫　vault

保險條件　insurance conditions

保險條例　insurance act

保險倉庫　safe deposit

保險條款　insurance clauses

保險託管　safe deposit

保險起期　inception of insurance

cover

保險索賠　insurance claim

保險帳戶　underwriting account

保險國有化　nationalization of insurance

保險基金　insurance fund

保險率表　premium tariff

保險清單　schedule of insurance

保險副單　alternate policy

保險稅　insurance tax

保險單　insurance policy, insurance certificate

保險單一般條件　general policy condition

保險單的再生效　revival of policies

保險單持有人　policy holder

保險單退保值(保險人中途放棄保險時）　surrender value

保險單據　insurance documents

保險單證明權益　policy proof of interest

保險責任終止　termination of risk

保險費　premium, insurance premium, insurance expense

保險費另議　premium to be arranged

保險費收條　premium receipt

保險費借款　premium loan

保險費率　rate of premium

保險費準備金　premium reserve

保險費總額　gross premium

保險統計　actuarial

保險準備　insurance fund reserve

保險準備基金　insurance reserve fund

保險經紀人　insurance broker

保險經紀人公司　corporation of insurance brokers

保險業計算標準　actuarial basis

保險種類　kind of benefits

保險箱　safe deposit box

保險標的物　insurable subject matter

保險價值　insurance value

保險賠款　insurance indemnity (compensation), insurance proceeds

保險範圍　insurance cover, insurance coverage

保險憑證　insurance certificate

保險擔保書　guarantee of insurance

保險鑑定人　insurance appraiser

保險櫃　vault

保險類別　branch of insurance

保賠協會，船東責任保險協會　Protection and Indemnity Association

保價信　insured letter

保證人　guarantor; bondsman

保證支付　guarantee pay

保證比率(指證券經紀人向銀行借款額佔其所提供作抵押證券價值的比率）　margin requirement

保證交換　guarantee to exchange

保證函　letter of guarantee (L/G)

保證股　guaranteed stock

保證金　margin, security money, guarantee deposit

保證金下限　maintenance margin

保證金要求(對客戶用經紀人貸款購買股票時必須付出部份費用的要求）　margin requirement

保證金要求收市價(交易所設立的為保證金要求提供計算基礎的每日期權收市價)　closing call price

保證金維持規則(當保證金購買的股票價格下跌,如客戶股票全部賣出還去經紀人貸款後所剩餘額不足股票市值的 25%,經紀人必須向客戶提出增加保證金的規則)　margin maintenance rule

保證金額　guarantee sum

保證紅利　guaranteed dividend

保證退款　money back guarantee

保證品質　guaranteed quality

保證保險　guarantee insurance

保證書　guaranty

保證條款　warranty clause

保證責任　liability on guarantee

保證基金(通常保證每年利息不少於 5% 的投資基金)　guaranteed fund

保證發行　guaranteed issue

保證期限　period of guarantee

保證期票　principal note

保證貸款　loan on guarantee

保證債券　guaranteed bonds

保證債權人提出立刻履行　guarantee on first demand

保證滿意　full satisfaction guaranteed

保證履行合同　guarantee performance

保證價格　guaranteed price

保釋　bail out

保釋保證書(出具給法院以求釋放被扣留船隻的保證書)　bail bonds

保護工業產權巴黎公約　Paris Convention for International Protection of Industrial Property

保護工業產權國際同盟　International Union for the Protection of Industrial Property

保護主義　protectionism

保護性入口關稅　protective import duty

保護性出口稅　protective export duty

保護性稅則(關稅)　protective tariff

保護性關稅　protective duty

保護關稅(為消除不平等的競爭條件對進口貨徵收的關稅)　safeguarding duties

保護貿易　protection

保護貿易主義　protectionism

保護貿易主義者　protectionist

保護貿易主義政策　protectionist policy

保護貿易法令　protective legislation

保護貿易制度　protective system

保護貿易論者　protectionist

保護標誌　protective mark

侵吞公款　embezzle public funds

侵佔財產(指不動產)　disseizin

侵犯商標　infringement of trade mark

侵犯商標權,商標冒用　trade mark infringement

侵權行為　tort, act of tort

侵權行為的賠償責任　tort liability

促進出口　export promotion

促進投資　investment promotion

促進貿易性運費率　promotional freight rate

促進對外貿易　foreign trade promotion

促銷　sales promotion

促銷組合　promotion mix

便士股票(指低價發行，具高度投機性股票，在美國常每股低於一美元出售。又稱"低價股票") penny stock

便利(表述銀行各種服務詞語，尤指貸款服務)　facilities

便利功能　facilitating functions

便利品　covenience goods

便宜貨　good buy, bargain

信用　credit

信用公司債　debenture bonds

信用分析　credit analysis

信用比率　credit ratio

信用卡　credit card

信用交易　deal on credit

信用危機　credit crisis

信用投資　fiduciary investment

信用放款　fiduciary loan

信用狀況　credit standing, credit status

信用制度　credit system

信用政策　credit policy

信用便利,信用服務　credit facilities

信用限度　credit limit

信用昭著　credit is good

信用限額　limited credit, credit line

信用保險　credit insurance

信用保證制度　credit guarantee sys-

tem

信用流通　credit circulation

信用第一　credit first

信用通貨　credit currency

信用貨幣　fiduciary money, credit money

信用貨幣化(由銀行貸款而形成存款，從而使貨幣量增加) monetization of credit

信用票據　credit instruments

信用透支　credit facility, fiduciary overdraft

信用發行　fiduciary issue

信用期限　credit period

信用程度　creditability

信用等級，信譽等級　credit rating, quality rating

信用創造　credit creation

信用欺詐　credit fraud

信用買賣　credit business

信用風險　credit risks

信用循環　credit cycles

信用資本　debenture capital

信用債券　debenture bonds

信用滙票　credit bill

信用滙款　credit remittance

信用經濟　credit economy

信用管理　credit management

信用管制　credit control

信用緊縮　credit contraction, credit squeeze

信用線(指銀行對某一借款人放款的最高限額) line of credit

信用調查，資信調查　credit information

信用標準　credit standards

信用膨脹　credit inflation

信用諮詢公司　credit bureau, credit agency

信用機構　fiduciary institution

信用額度　line of credit

信用擺動額　swing credit

信用轉讓　credit transfer

信用證　letter of credit

信用證申請書　application for letter of credit

信用證受益人　credit beneficiary

信用證券　credit paper, credit document, trust bonds

信用證統一慣例　uniform customs for credits

信用證"軟性條款"（規定貨物在通過海關後，或由主管當局批准後，信用證項下款項才能支付）　credit with "soft clauses"

信用證費　letter of credit charges

信用證轉讓申請書　application for transfer of letter of credit

信息，資料，資訊，情報　information

信息化時代　information age

信息加工　information process

信息成本　information cost

信息系統　information system

信息社會　information society

信息來源　information source

信息速率　information rate

信息處理　information processing

信息貯存　information storage

信息密集工業　information-intensive types of industries

信息產業　information industry

信息資源　information resources

信息編碼　information encoding

信託，委託　trust

信託人，託管人　trustee

信託公司　trust company

信託存款　trust deposit

信託收據　trust receipts

信託投資業務　trust and investment business

信託契約　deed of trust

信託保證金　trust deposit

信託財產　trust estate

信託基金　trust fund, fund-in-trust

信託週轉基金　trust revolving fund

信託銀行　trust bank

信託證書　trust certificate

信託債券　trust bonds

信託會計　fiduciary accounting

信託業務　fiduciary work

信託資產　trust assets

信託證書　trust certificate

信貸文件　credit instruments

信貸支持的信貸（貸款人憑另一筆信貸所發放的貸款）　credit supported by other credit

信貸市場　credit market

信貸交易　credit transaction

信貸份額　credit tranche

信貸限制　credit restriction

信貸協定　credit agreement

信貸承諾　credit commitment

信貸保密保付代理　confidential factoring

信貸條件　credit terms

信貸配給　credit rationing

信貸接受人　credit receiver

信貸期以前　precredit

信貸最高限額　credit ceiling

信貸銀行　credit bank

信貸管理　credit management

信貸擴張　credit expansion

信貸儲備　credit reserve

信貸額　credit amounts, credit volume

信貸額度　line of credit

信滙　mail transfer (M/T)

信號效果（指中央銀行的干預，會改變人們對利率、滙率的預期）　signal effect

信頭（信箋上端所印商號，地址等）letter-head

信賴度　reliability

信賴度工程　reliability engineering

信賴區間　confidence interval

信譽　good reputation, good-will

信譽保險單　honour policy

牲畜貨櫃／集裝箱　cattle container, livestock container, pen container

牲畜運輸保險　livestock transit insurance

牲畜運輸船　cattle carrier

〔 一 〕

架橋票據（指臨時過渡性票據）bridging over bill

建立公司期中利息　interest during corporation

建立需求和供給曲線　statistical construction of demand and supply curve

建設週期　construction cycle

建築物保險　building insurance

建築物租約　building lease

建築時期觀念（工程項目專設的一條會計原則：在項目建設期間的一切費用，應准予作資本支出）construction period concept

建議價格　suggested price

紅色空運單　red air waybill

紅色條款（信用證附加條款，允許受益人在全套單據齊備前可預支部份款項）red clause

紅色條款信用證　red clause credit

紅利　bonus, dividends earned

紅利公司債　bonus bond

紅利分配　profit sharing

紅利分配追溯法　retropective bonus plan

紅利未付　ex dividend

紅利股　bonus dividend, bonus stock

紅利限度　dividend limitation

紅利政策　dividend policy

紅利後取股（比普通股後分配公司紅利的股票）deferred shares

紅利帳戶　bonus account

紅利基金，紅利集成　bonus pool

紅利債券　bonus debentures

紅利總帳　bonus ledger

紅利準備金(提存) dividend reserve

紅魚招股章程(指一種初步印發的證券説明書) red-herring prospectus

紅提單(指兼具保險單作用的提單) red bill of lading

約克—安特衞普理算規則 York-Antwerp Rules

約束性成本(在一個項目進行過程中, 管理人員不能影響的成本) committed cost

約定(公司債券證書, 抵押契約或合同條件中一種具有法律強制性的諾言或限制) covenant

約定皮重 computed tare

約定全損(保險) compromised total loss

約定利率 contract rate of interest

約定股利 contractual dividend

約定授信額度 agree on the ceiling of credit

約定準備 contractual reserve

約定價值 agreed value; commitment value

約計 approximately

約期套利 straddle

約期選擇售賣 put

約當完工產量 equivalent full units

約當產量 equivalent product

飛行適航證書 certificate of airworthiness

飛漲 skyrocketed, soaring

飛漲價格 skyrocketing price

飛機一切險 aircraft all risks

飛機上交貨價 free on plane, free on aircraft

飛機地面險 ground risks

飛機旅客保險 aircraft passenger insurance

飛機意外事故 aircraft accident

飛機機身險 aircraft hull insurance

飛機機艙內交貨(價) free on board plane

降低(價格等) knock down

降低平均價格購買法(一種投資技術, 股價下跌時持續買進, 以降低所購股票的平均價格) averaging down

降低生產成本 reduce production costs, cut back production costs, lower production costs

降低生產增長速度 holding up the growth of production

降低成色 debasement

降低物價 cut the prices

降低原料消耗 cut down the consumption of raw materials

降低帳面價值扣除(英國對資本投資項目一律按 25% 逐漸降低所購置設備的帳面價值) writing down allowances

降低等級 downgrade

降低貸款利息 marking down loans

降值 depreciation

限制 constraint

限制用途的現金 restricted cash

限制性分配 restricted distribution

限制性投標 restricted tender

限制性背書 restrictive endorsement

限制性信貸政策　restrictive credit policy

限制性條款(合同中規定不允許從事的行為)〔拉〕proviso, 即restrictive convenant

限制性措施　restrictive practice

限制性商業措施　restrictive commercial practice

限制性商業慣例 restrictive business practices

限制性援助　tied aid

限制性貸款　tied loan

限制承兌　qualified acceptance

限制信用證　restricted credit

限制貿易　restrain trade

限制議付信用證　restricted negotiable letter of credit

限期滙票　tenor draft

限價　ceiling price, limit price

限價平倉單(在市價達到平倉限價時, 即可作有限價的買入或賣出平倉) stop-limit order

限價定單　limit order, limited price order

限額　quota norm, restrained limit

限額分配　ration

限額抵押債券　closed mortgage bond

限額基金　closed-end fund

限額進出口制　quota system

限額輸入　import quota

限額輸出　export quota

限虧止單(香港稱"限價平倉單", 投機者為避免市況不利時損失過大,

吩咐經紀人在達到某一價位時了結其交易)　stop loss orders

省時商品　time-saving commodities

省錢　save money

"屋普鐵馬"卡(美國運通公司1987年6月發行的一種新信用卡, 利率訂為13.5%, 只發給使用運通卡已一年以上信譽良好的客戶)Optiam Card

十　畫

〔丶〕

容忍風險　risk-bearing

容忍疵品比率 lot tolerance percentage defective

容許界限　tolerance limit

容量　cubic measure

容量包裝　capacity packing

容量重量證明書　certificate and list of measurement and (or) weight

容積　capacity

容積法　measurement ton method

容積貨物　measurement goods

容積運費　freight by measurement

容積噸　measurement ton

家庭收益　family earnings

家族合夥　family partnership

家庭抵押債務 household mortgages

家庭電器用具　home appliances

家庭經濟　family economy, household economy

家庭經濟調查　means test

案卷　file

高入先出法　high-in first-out method

高工資　higher-grade pay, high wage

高分子合成工業　high polymer synthesis industry

高估　overestimate, overrate

高利外債　high-interest foreign loans

高利率，高息借款　dear money

高利率政策　dear money policy

高利貸　high interest rate

高利貸者　usurer, vampire,〔美俗〕loan shark

高利貸款　lend money on usury, high-interest loans

高利資本　usurer's capital

高位集團　higher groups

高低點法　high-low point method

高於票面價值　above par value

高科技產品　high-tech products

高度投機性之投資　take a flier

高度相關　high correlation

高度現代化生產工具　sophisticated instruments of production

高品質銷貨(貢獻邊際效率高的銷貨)　high-quality sales

高級主管發展計劃　executive development programm

高級品質　high quality

高級常務董事　senior managing director

高級債券　senior bonds

高級會計師　senior accountant

高級證券，優先證券　senior security

高效率的　high-efficiency

高效型產業結構　efficient production structure

高息率息票　high coupon

高速分理閱讀機(閱讀支票上磁性編碼數據的計算機，可在事先編好的程序控制下，以每分鐘一千張的速度對票據進行分類處理)　high-speed sorter-readers

高速存儲器　high-speed memory

高速進位　high-speed carry

高速電子計算機　high-speed electronic computer

高速電碼系統　high-speed coding system

高速資本　high-geared capital

高階層管理　top management

高價　long price, top price dear price, high price

高價收購(近年美國企業吞併競爭對手最常使用的方法：在股票市場上公開用高價收購股票，以取得對對手企業的控制權)　take over bid (TOB)

高價位魅力股　high flying glamour stock

高價購買　give a long price for

高槓桿比率(指項目建設主要依靠貸款來籌措資金的方式)　high leverage

高檔品，精製品　fancy goods

高檔商品　expensive commodities,

high-grade products

高壘堆放(貨櫃/集裝箱)　high elevation stacking

衰退　decline, slump, recession, slowdown

衰退期　decline phase

站到站運輸　station to station transport

託付　apply for remittance

託收　collection, apply for collection

託收中款項　cash item in process of collection

託收手續費　collection charge, collection commission

託收成本　collection cost

託收委託書　collection order, advice for collection

託收背書　endorsement for collections

託收現款　collection of cash

託收票據　bill for collection

託收票據費　collection fees

託收項目　items sent for collection

託收款項　bills sent for collection

託收款項情況通知　advise of fate

託收滙票　bill of collection

託收銀行　remitting bank

託收價值　value in collection

託運人,貨主,發貨人 shipper, consignor

託運人所報貨物(提單批語) shipper's description of goods

託運人負擔甲板貨風險　shipped on deck at shipper risk

託運人負擔風險　shipper's risk

託運人裝櫃和封閉(指對貨櫃/集裝箱) shipper's pack and seal

託運人裝櫃和點件(指對貨櫃/集裝箱) shipper's pack and count

託運單　consignment note, booking note

記名公司　registered firm

記名支票　check to order, specific check

記名股票 registered share, registered stock

記名背書　special endorsement, endorsement to order

記名貨船　named vessel

記名票據　notes to order

記名提單 named bill of lading, straight bill of lading

記名債券　registered bond

記名證券 incribed securities, incriptions

記有船名的海運保單　named policy

記要書　memorial

記帳　keep accounts, charge to an account

記帳交易　transaction for account, open account

記帳貨幣　money of account

記帳符號　tally

記帳結算　settlement on account

記帳錯誤　errors of book entry

記帳證券(美國術語，指證券的發行不以單據形式，而採用在銀行登記入帳的形式)　book-entry security

記錄　record

記錄拒兌滙票　noting a bill

記錄處　enrollment, registry

記錄錯誤　clerical error

記憶法（電腦為帳戶或存貨分類法的一種記憶部）　memorial system

記憶室（電腦）　memory cell

記憶調查法　memory test

討價還價　price haggling, price bargain, prig, huckster over

討價還價的能力　bargaining power

旅行支票　traveller's cheque, circular note

旅行住宿費　lodging expenses

旅行社　tourist agency, travel agency

旅行信用證　traveller's letter of credit

旅行執照　travel warrant

旅行推銷員　travelling salesman

旅行意外險　travel accident insurance

旅行艙位　travel accommodation

旅行護照　travelling passport

旅客行李保險　tourist luggage insurance

旅客責任險　passanger liability insurance

旅客運送費　passage money

旅客險　passanger risks

旅遊　tour

旅遊者　tourist

旅遊業　tourism

旅遊團　tourist party

旅館管理　hotel management

效用　utility

效用分析　utility analysis

效用曲線　utility curve

效用函數　utility function

效用指標　utility index

效用遞減律　law of diminishing utility

效用虧損與貨幣虧損比較　utility versus money loss

效果　effectiveness

效能　effectiveness

效能收益　efficiency earning

效益成本分析　benefit-cost analysis

效益成本比率　benefit-cost ratio

效益成本關係　benefit-to-cost relationship

效率　efficiency, power efficiency

效率限界　efficiency of frontier

效率差異　efficiency variance

效率標準　efficiency standard

差少補貼（銀行等給出納的補貼）　risk money

差別工資　differential wages

差別化　differentiation

差別成本　differential cost

差別利益法則　law of differential advantage

差別利潤率　differential profit ratio

差別定價壟斷　discriminating monopoly

差別計件工資　differential piece rate

差別稅則　differential tariff

差別報酬　differential returns

差別會計　differential accounting

差別滙率　discrimination exchange rates

差別價格　differential price, discriminatory price

差別關稅 differential duties, discriminating duty

差相關　difference correlation

差異分析　variance analysis

差異行銷　differentiated marketing

差異界限　threshold of divergence

差異報告　variance report

差量分析　differential analysis

差量成本　differential cost

差量收益　differential earning

差價進口稅　variable import levy

差錯遺漏待查　errors and omissions excepted

差額　balance difference

差額收入　difference income

差額收入調節稅　regulatory tax on differential

差額利潤比率 difference profit ratio

差額所得　difference gain

差額稅　variable levy

差額補貼　deficiency payment

差額賺得　differential earning

兼任執行人　plural executives

兼任董事會制　interlocking directorate

兼併　merger

兼容信息系統　compatible information system

兼理出口商(為不只一家製造商充當出口推銷部的獨立出口商號) combination export manager

逆向市場(交割日期遠的貨物價格低於交割日期近的貨物價格出現逆向變化的商品期貨市場，又稱倒掛市場) inverted market

逆利率　negative interest

逆指標　inverse indicator

逆差　deficit

逆差國家　deficit country

逆貼水　disagio

逆滙　adverse exchange

逆傾銷(將某種商品以高於國內價格同時在國外出售) reverse dumping

逆經濟系列(與經濟週期運動方向相反的一些經濟週期指標) reverse economic series

逆選擇(指不利於保險人方面的對契約的選擇) adverse selection

逆優惠，反向優惠 reverse preference

逆轉嫁(指在不可能實現"前轉嫁"情況下，批、零商將稅負轉回歸生產企業負擔) shifting backward

送達　service

送達地址　address for service

送達的背書　indorsement of service

送達通知書　service of notice

送達傳票　service of summons

送達證明書　certificate of service

送閱商品　goods on approval, sales on approval

准許裝貨單　shipping permit

准許證　permit

准進口證　import permit

准運證　navicert

准購證　purchase permit

淨支出　net disbursement

淨出口　net export

淨出口國　net exporter

淨付款　net settlement

淨收入　net proceeds

淨收益分配表　statement of appropriation of net income

淨收益對資本淨值比率　ratio of net income to net worth

淨收益對資產總額比率　ratio of net income to total assets

淨收益對實發股本比率　ratio of net income to outstanding common stock

淨收益對銷售比率　ratio of net income to net sales

淨成本　flat cost

淨自由準備金　net free reserve

淨利, 純利　net income, net profit

淨利比率　profit margin ratio

淨利潤分配額　net profit quota

淨利潤對資本比率　ratio of net profit to capital

淨投資　net investment

淨易貨貿易條件　net barter terms of trade

淨重　net weight

淨盈利, 淨收益　net earnings

淨負債　net indebtedness

淨保險費　net premium

淨相關　net correlation

淨相關係數　net correlation coefficient

淨息　net interest

淨值　net worth, net value

淨值交易事項　equity transaction

淨值收益率 income to net worth ratio

淨值帳戶　net worth accounts

淨值週轉率 net worth turnover ratio

淨借入準備金　net borrowed reserve

淨效用　net utility

淨效率　net efficiency

淨租船(船方除航運外, 不負擔一切港務裝卸費用) net charter

淨流動資產　net current assets

淨差額　net balance

淨貨(指包裝完整未受損害的貨物) clean cargo, fine cargo

淨國外投資　net foreign investment

淨帳面值　net book value

淨現金流量　net cash flow

淨現值　net present value

淨現值扣息法(投資可行性研究) net present value method

淨產值　net output

淨清償差額　net liquidity balance

淨進口　net import

淨貼水　net premium

淨發股本, 外發股本　outstanding capital stock

淨殘值(指海難後的殘貨值)　net salvage

淨運用資本週轉率　turnover of net working capital

淨資產, 資產淨額　net assets

淨週轉率　net turnover rate

淨遠期　outright forward

淨價　net price

淨價法　net price method

淨賣家(指賣多於買的) net seller

淨銷價法 net selling price method

淨噸位(指船舶載貨的) net tonnage

淨營運資金 net working capital

淨虧 net deficiency

淨額 net amount

淨變(交易所當日與前一日收盤價之差) net change

淨變現價值 net realigable value

涼貨(冷藏船裝運保持華氏 40°-60° 貨物) air cooling cargo

凍結工資 frozen wage

凍結存款 blocked deposits, frozen deposits

凍結信貸(由於債務人的經濟狀況不好，債權人因而暫停貸款) frozen credit, frozen loans

凍結物價 freezing price

凍結帳戶 blocked accounts, frozen account

凍結貨物 frozen goods

凍結貨幣 blocked currency

凍結資金 frozen fund, blocked fund

凍結資金銀行證明 blocked funds attestation

凍結資產 blocked assets, frozen assets

凍結債款 frozen loan

海上交通線 sea route, sea-line

海上風險 perils of the sea

海上保險 maritime insurance

海上保險期(海上保險用語，包括船舶停港期和航行期) at and from

海上封鎖 naval blockade

海上貿易 maritime trade

海上碰撞 collision at sea

海上遇險信號 signal of distress

海牙仲裁公約 Hague Arbitration Convention

海牙規則 Hague Rules

海水損害條件 sea damage-S.D.

海外私人投資公司 Overseas Private Investment Corperation

海外投資 oversea investment

海外投資信貸 oversea investment credits

海外貿易 ocean commerce

海外傾銷 dumping field

海事仲裁委員會 maritime arbitration commission

海事法 maritime law, admiralty law

海事法院 admiralty court

海事留置權 maritime lien

海事報告 sea report

海事管轄權 maritime jurisdiction

海事審判權 admiralty jurisdiction

海底油田 seabed oilfield

海底資源 seabed resources

海洋公約 maritime convention

海洋沿海貿易 maritime coasting trade

海洋船殼保險 marine hull insurance

海洋運送 carriage by sea

海洋運輸保險法 maritime insurance law

海洋權 maritime rights

海員保險證書 crew's insurance certificate

海員留置權 seaman's lien

海區 sea zone

海船碰撞 collision between seagoing vessels

海商法　maritime law, marine law

海商法上的抵押　maritime mortgage

海商法上的債權　maritime claim

海琴(即套期保值)　hedging

海琴條款(美國表示不承認者的術語，拒絕來自外部諸如市場通訊等信息的準確性承擔法律責任)　hedge clause

海港檢疫　quarantine of sea-port

海損，海水漬　sea damage, average

海損保費單　average policy

海損條款　average clause

海損理算書　average statement

海損理算師(係海洋法和海損方面裁決的權威)　average adjuster

海運　sea transportation

海運法　[美]Merchant Marine Act

海運事業　shipping interest

海運信件　sea mail

海運保險法(1906年改訂的英國海運保險法)　Marine Insurance Act, 1906

海運留置權　maritime lien

海運貨物法例　Carriage of Goods by Sea Act

海運費，海運水腳　ocean freight

海運碼頭　sea terminal

海蜂式駁船　seabee ship

海關　custom house, custom office

海關手續和準則 customs procedures and norms

海關卡，海關房　customs shed

海關合作理事會稅則商品分類目錄 Customs Co-operation Council Nomenclature

海關扣留　customs detention

海關再進口憑證　customs re-entry permit

海關收據　customs receipt

海關免稅倉庫　customs free depot

海關估價 customs valuation, customs appraised value

《海關估價法規》Customs Valuation Code

海關巡邏艇　customs cruiser

海關法　customs laws

海關法庭(美)　Customs Court

海關封條　customs seal

海關律師 customs attorney, customs lawyer

海關保稅，海關罰款　customs bond

海關保管　customs custody

海關倉庫　customs warehouse

海關退稅　customs drawback

海關退稅憑單　customs debenture

海關配額　customs quota

海關許可證　customs permit

海關規章，海關條例　customs regulation

海關規費　customs fees

海關通路　customs route

海關貨棚　customs shed

海關稅收　customs revenue

海關稅則　customs tariff

海關稅則分類　customs nomenclature

海關發票（報關用的發票） customs invoice

海關過境單據 customs transit document

海關監督區 customs supervision zone

海關監管 superintendent of customs

海關緝私官員 customs preventive officer

海關擔保制度 customs guarantee system

海關檢疫 customs quarantine control

海關檢查，驗關 customs inspection

海關檢查人員 surveyor of customs, customs examiner, searcher

海關檢查站 customs inspection post

海關疆界 customs boundary

海關驗貨單 customs examination list

海嘯 sea quake

海難 perils of the sea

海難抗辯書 sea protest

海難救助 salvage at sea

海難救助作業 salvage operation

海難救助費 salvage charges

海難搶救損失 salvage loss

流水帳 day-to-day account, current account

流水線 assembly line

流行品存貨單 model stocklist

流行計數 fashion count

流行貨，暢銷貨 articles in great demand

流動公司債券 floating debentures

流動比率（指流動負債與流動資金的比率） current ratio, liquid ratio

流動支票 circulating cheque

流動存款 floating deposit

流動投資 current investment

流動性 liquidity

流動性比率 liquidity ratio

流動性偏好 liquidity preference

流動性陷阱（認為當利率降到某種水平時，對於貨幣的投機需求就會變得有無限彈性） liquidity trap

流動狀況分析 current position analysis

流動負債 circulating liabilities, floating debts

流動保險單 floating policy

流動費用 floating charge

流動基金 current funds

流動集裝箱／貨櫃 floating container

流動資本 circulating capital, fluid capital, working capital

流動資本週轉率 working capital turnover

流動資本總額 gross working capital

流動資金 circulating funds

流動資金全額信貸 acquisition of all circulating funds through credits

流動資金週轉率 turnover period for circulating funds

流動資產 circulating assets, current asset, liquid assets

流動資產淨額 net liquid assets

流動資產動態 movement of current assets

流動資產循環 current asset cycle

流動資產與固定資產比率 ratio of current assets to fixed assets

流動資產與總資產比率 ratio of current assets to total assets

流動質權債券 floating debenture

流動證券 liquid securities

流通支票，可轉讓支票 negotiable check

流通手段 medium of circulation

流通市場 circulation market

流通利潤 profit through circulation

流通股 floating stock

流通票據 negotiable instruments, negotiable papers

流通期票 negotiable note

流通渠道 circulation channel

流通硬幣 coin circulation

流通證券 negotiable instruments

流量 flow

流量分析 flow analysis

流量決策（指人們希望目前的開支大於目前的收入的一種決策） flow decisions

流程程序圖 flow process chart

流程圖，程序圖 flowchart

流轉率，流轉速度 rate of flow

流轉環節 intermediate links

浮吊 floating crane

浮式鑽井船 floating drilling vessel

浮拖貨櫃/集裝箱 floatainer

浮息票據 floating rate notes

浮船塢 floating dock

浮動工資 floating wages

浮動小數點項目 floating-point item

浮動利率 floating interest rate

浮動利率存單 floating interest rate certificate of deposit

浮動利率貸款 floating-rate loan

浮動投票 floating vote

浮動供給（指有大批證券或商品以備在市場立即銷售或購買） floating supply

浮動抵押 floating mortgage

浮動保單 floating policy, 通稱 open policy

浮動庫存 floating stock, floating supply

浮動貨幣 floating currency

浮動滙率 floating exchange rate

浮動滙率制度 floating rate system

浮動滙率票據 floating-rate notes

浮動碼頭 floating pier

浮動擔保 floating charge

消除失業 eliminate unemployment

消除外滙風險 eliminate foreign exchange risk

消除貿易障礙 removal of barrier to trade

消帳 cross off account

消費水平 consumption level, standards of consumption

消費不足 underconsumption, inadequate consumption

消費主義（以消費刺激經濟） consumerism

消費失調 imbalance of consumption

消費合作社 consumer's co-operative society

消費品　consumer goods

消費投資成本　outlay cost

消費者心理因素 customer mentality

消費者分期付款信貸　consumer instalment credit

消費者目標市場 consumer orientated market

消費者至上，顧客至上　consumers' sovereignty

消費者行為　consumer behavior

消費者的倒帳　consumer bad debts

消費者的特徵 consumer characteristics

消費者協會　consumers' association

消費者信用卡保條 consumer credit-card slips

消費者信用保險 consumer credit insurance

消費者風險　consumer's risk

消費者保障　consumer protection

消費者偏好,消費者的優先選擇 consumers' preference

消費者偏好測驗　consumer preference test

消費者貨物　consumer goods

消費者動機　consumer motivation

消費者運動　consumer movements

消費者需求　consumer demand

消費者滿足極大化　maximization of consumer satisfaction

消費者調查　consumer survey

消費者態度　consumer attitude

消費者聯盟　consumer union

消費者購買力 consumer purchasing power

消費物價指數 consumer price index

消費函數(把消費水平與國民收入水平聯繫起來的一種函數)　consumption function

消費信貸(指對消費者賒帳，分期付款購買等)　consumer credit

消費信貸公司 consumer finance company

消費品價格指數 consumer price index

消費稅 consumption duty, consumption tax, outlay tax

消費無差異曲線(表示某兩種商品之各種不同數量的組合，均對消費者提供同等的滿足)　consumption indifference curve

消費貸款　consumer loans

消費傾向　propensity to consumer

消費壓制　underconsumption

消極平衡　negative equilibrium

消極因素　negative factor

消極保證條款(國際借貸中，由借款人向貸款人保證不在其資產或收入上設定任何抵押權、擔保權、質權或其他擔保物權的條款)　negative pledge clause

消極效果　negative effects

庫存　stock, reserve

庫存平衡表　balance-of-stores sheet

庫存股份(公司收買自己的股票或由股東贈給公司的股票，股款已照票面全部繳足)　treasury stock

庫存股份盈餘　treasury stock surplus

庫存物資　stock in storage, good kept in stock

庫存指數　inventory index

庫存現金　cash holdings, cash on hand, vault cash

庫存商品　merchandise inventory

庫存商品的價格變動　fluctuations in prices of merchandise inventory

庫存週轉率　inventory turnover

庫存債券　treasury bonds

庫存銷售比率　inventory-sale ratio

庫西普號碼系統（美國用於鑑別證券發行的一種標準字母號碼）　Cusip Number System

庫茨涅茲循環（指平均週期為 15-25 年的景氣循環）　Kuznets cycle

疾病保險　insurance during a period of illness

疲軟　bearish tone

疲軟市場　weak market, soft market

粉狀貨物　powdered goods

粉狀貨貨櫃/集裝箱 free flowing bulk material container

[一]

真不二價　never quote two price

真正平衡價格　true equilibrium price

真正成本　true cost, bona fide cost

真正收益　true earning

真正利潤　true profit

真正價格　true price

真正價值　true value

真材實料　real stuff, real thing

真空包裝　vacuum-packing

真值　sterling worth

真實中位數　true median

真實平均數　true average, true mean

真實成本　real cost

真實利率　real interest rate

真實美元價值　real-dollar values

真實持有人　bona fide holder

真實常數　true constant

真實票據　real bill

真實票據主義　real-bills doctrine

真實發票　definite invoice

真實眾數　true mode

索債, 討債　dun, dun for debts

索債人, 討債鬼　dunner

索價, 取費　charge

索賠　claim, claim settlement

索賠人　claimant, claimer

索賠委員會 claims commission, claims board

索賠清單　claims statement

索賠期限　time limit for payment of claim

索賠報告　claim report

索賠損失　claim for damages

索賠證件　claims documents

索償的背書　indorsement of claim

索償陳述　statement of claim

草袋　straw bag

草簽文件　initial a document

起泡包裝　blister packaging

起岸費 landing charges, landing expenses, landing hire

起岸後品質條件　after landing quality terms

起岸重量　landing weight

起岸駁船　landing barge

起岸證明書　landing certificate

起重機　crane, derrick, hoist

起重機使用費　cranage

起租　on hire

起息日(外滙或歐洲貨幣市場術語)　value date, end-end

起貨　discharge, unload goods

起貨上岸代理行　landing agent

起貨港　port of discharge, port of unloading

起貨棧單　landing account

起貨碼頭　landing pier, landing stage

起貨證　permit to land

起動成本　start-up costs

起動價格,觸動價格　trigger price

起動價格方式,觸動價格方式　trigger price mechanism

起期(保險)　attachment

起訴　institute proceedings

起訴者　suitor

起算　initial cycle

起算日　initial day, zero date

起錨　weighing anchor

套利　interest arbitrage

套利公司　arbitrated house

套利基金,套頭交易基金　hedge fund

套利帳,套滙帳　arbitrage account

套利貸款(指在低利市場借款,滙至高利市場應用,同時用與借款期同的遠期滙兌以轉移滙率風險)　international interest arbitrage loans, 俗稱 arbi loans

套利選擇權　straddle option

套做股票　stocks for margin trading

套期保值(買賣商品、證券和貨幣的手段。旨在減少由於不利的價格波動導致交易者贏利下降的風險)　hedge, hedging

套期保值條款　hedge clause

套戥(香港期貨市場稱套期保值為"套戥",有時亦稱為"戥倉")　hedge, hedging

套滙,套做　arbitrage of exchange

套滙交易　arbitrage tansaction

套滙商　arbitrageur

套滙帳　arbitrage account

套滙滙率　arbitrage rate (of exchange)

套裝軟體　software package

套算滙率　cross rate

套算滙率差距　break in cross rates

套購人　arbitrage dealer

套購股票　arbitrage in stock

套購金銀　arbitrage in billion

套購保值條款　hedge clause

套購證券　arbitrage in securities, stock arbitrage

格子箱,板條箱　skeleton, crate

格雷欣法則("劣幣驅逐良幣"的一項貨幣流通定律)　Gresham's law

核心產品　core product

核心商品　core commodity

核心報表　core statement

核定股本　authorized capital stock

核定股份　authorized share (stock)

核定承兌滙票　approved acceptance

核定計劃　approved programme

核定資本　authorized capital

核定預算　approved budget

核定概算　approved estimates

核准帳目　approval of account

核准發行　approved for release

核准發行的債券　authorized bonds

核對　check

核對帳目　verification of account, checking account

核對無過帳數字　check figures in posting

核算生產成本　work out the cost of production

核算單位,核算點　business segment

核實的物價指數　price indices verified by

核實的數字　verified figures

核數簡報　short-form report

核數試算表　working trial balance

核證人　certifying officer

株式會社(日本的股份有限公司)　kabuskiki kaisha

校正,校對　collate

校對無誤　collated correct

校對電報　collated telegram

根本好轉　fundamental turn for the better

根本性不平衡　fundamental disequilibrium

根本性逆差　fundamental deficit

根本違反合同　fundamental breach

根據公平合理原則作成的仲裁裁決　award made ex aequo et bono

根據和解作出的仲裁裁決　award upon settlement

根據法律　[拉]secundum juris (or legem)

根據定期合同規定的牌價(交易所用語)　price for account

根據契約的訴訟　[拉]action ex contractu

根據侵權行為的訴訟　[拉]action ex delicto

根據時效的抗辯　plea based on prescription

根據規定　[拉]secundum requlam

根據慣例　[拉]secundum usum

根據標準樣品　according to standard sample

捆包工程　packing engineering

捆紮物鬆落(提單批語)　bands off

捆裝　bundle

捆裝鬆弛(提單批語)　bundle slacken

挫折解除契約　discharge of contract by frustration

捐助　offer financial assistance, donate

捐稅　taxes and levies

捐款　contribute money

捐款人　subscribers, donor

捐贈　donation

捐贈地產　donated land

捐贈地產準備　donated land reserve

捐贈股份　donated stock

捐贈盈餘　donated surplus

捐贈帳戶(記載捐贈股票的貸方帳戶) donated account

捐贈國　donor country

捐贈資本　donated capital

捐贈運用資本 donated working capital

挪威船級社　Norske Veritas

原子能工業　atomic energy industry

原支票(指未背書的)　original check

原本的副本　duplicate original

原皮貨櫃/集裝箱　hide container

原本單證　original documents

原本證據　original evidence

原投資本　original capital

原投資額　original investment

原始毛利率　original gross rate

原始加價　original mark-up

原始投資　initial capitalization

原始股本　original capital

原始押金，原始保證金　original margin

原始信用證　original credit

原始效用　original utility

原始記錄　original records, original entry

原始責任　original responsibility

原始產品　primary products

原始單據　source documents

原始資料　primary data

原始傳票　original voucher

原始數據　initial data

原始憑證　original evidences

原受益人　original beneficiary

原油管道　crude oil pipeline

原料代用物　raw material substitute

原料生產國組織　raw material producers' organizations

原料成本　material cost

原料成本差異　material cost variance

原料缺乏　material shortage

原料消耗　material consumption

原料差異　material variance

原料過剩　material overstock

原料盤存　material inventory

原產地　country of origin

原產地名稱　appellation of origin

原產地交貨價　ex point of origin

原產地證明書　certificate of origin

原票據(指未背書的)　original bill

原棉等級　grades of raw cotton

原煤　unprocessed coal, raw coal

原運貨人　original carrier

原價　original cost, old price, cost price

原課稅　original taxation

馬力　horsepower

馬利華禁令(英國法院對某項爭議管轄權，命令被告不得把特定財產轉離其管轄範圍的禁令)　Marreva injunction

馬票　parimutuel ticket

馬斯洛需求階層理論 Maslow's Need Hierarchy Theory

馬歇爾曲線(指英國學者馬歇爾用來分析國際價值的曲線) Mashallian Curves

馬歇爾計劃　Marshall Plan

馬錶測時法　stopwatch time study

破冰船　ice-breaker

破約滙率（見"可轉期權外滙買賣"條）
break rate

破產　bankruptcy, insolvency

破產人　bankrupt, brokee

破產戶之債權人　creditor of bankruptcy

破產申請　bankruptcy petition

破產行為　act of bankruptcy

破產企業財產清理價值　break up value

破產法例　Bankruptcy Act

破產事務官　Official Receiver

破產財團　bankrupt estate

破產帳　bankrupt account

破產程序　bankruptcy proceedings

破產通知書　bankruptcy notice

破產清算人　assignee in insolvency

破產訴訟　liquidation or bankruptcy proceedings

破產債權人　creditors of a bankrupt estate

破產管理人　trustee in bankruptcy, administrator in a bankrupt estate

破產銀行　〔美〕failed bank

破裂　rupture

破損　breakage

破損折扣　breakage allowance

破損險　risk of breakage

破損險條款　breakage clause

破壞行規　job stealer

破壞性檢驗　destructive inspection

破壞罷工　strike-breaking

恐慌　panic

恐慌價格　panic price

恐嚇　intimidate

恐嚇信（以"高價收購"股票作恐嚇手段，如悄悄收購一家公司5%的股票，然後寫一恐嚇信，要求其在限期內將這5%股票以高價購回）
Greenmail

埃克森公司　Exxon Corporation

致損原因　cause of damage

珠算　reckoning by the abacus, abacus

珠寶　jewellery

珠寶保險　jewellery insurance

珠寶商　jeweller

班船條件租賃　berth charter

班輪　liner, schedule steamer

班輪公會　shipping conference

班輪公會忠誠信約制度　conference loyalty regime

班輪公會運費率　conference rates

班輪公會與非班輪公會運費　conference freights and outside freights

班輪條件（租船合同名詞。指租船運輸主要條件應與班輪運輸同樣商品的正常條件一致）　liner term

班輪運輸　liner transport

班輪運輸條件　liner terms

班輪運輸航線　liner trade route

班輪運輸提單　liner bill of lading

班機運輸　scheduled airline

配合度檢定　goodness of fit test

配合假設（原則）　matching assumption (or principle)

配合慣例(費用與收益相配合的慣例) maching convention

配套工程　parts and accessories for imported equipment, auxiliary projects

配套生產 form a complete production network

配套件　parts and auxiliary equipment

配套能力 ability to provide the auxiliary items

配消商品牌　distributor's brand

配貨單　order blank, invoice

配船計劃　cargo planning

配搭極佳　well assorted

配搭誤差　maching error

配額　quota

配額分配　quota allocation

配額市場　allocation market

配額制　quota system

配額權利　quota rights

酌情處理　act at one's discretion, settle a matter as one sees fit

酌情管理(是一種管理方法，強調在各種各樣情況下的一種最佳解決途徑)　contingency management

[丨]

員工指導人　employee director

員工需求指數　coefficient of personnel demand

員工福利　employee welfare

骨幹工程　backbone projects, major projects

骨幹企業　key enterprises

骨幹帳戶　skeleton account

盎斯，英兩(常衡等於 1/16 磅；金衡、藥衡等於 1/12 磅，即 31.103 克；液量，英制，等於 1/20 pint；美制，等於 1/16 pint)　ounce

閉口抵押權(指公司以全部固定資產作抵押發行第一優先順位公司債後，不得再發行第一順位公司債)　closed end mortgage

閉口訂貨單(指定供應廠商的外國訂購單)　closed indent

閉市後市場　after hours market

閉市後交易　after hours trading

閉市後價格　after hours value

閉港　closure of port

閉路電視　closed circuit T.V.

閉關自守　cut oneself off from the outside world, closing the door to the outside world

閉關自守經濟 closed economy, autarky

閉關政策　exclusion policy, policy of "closed-door"

問題分析　problem analysis

問題解決　problem solving

問題說明　problem definition

剔除 disallowance, rejection, charge off, pick out

剔除貨，次品　rejection

時效已告完成 prescription which has taken effect

時效期　prescriptive period

時值會計法　current value accounting

時區　time zone

時間分享(指兩個或兩個以上企業購買或租賃電子計算機)　time sharing

時間事件分析　time-event analysis

時間的風險　time risk

時間限制　time bar

時間相關　time relationship

時間偏向參數　time-bias parameter

時間偏好學說(解釋利息發生的原因起於時間偏好)　time preference theory

時間研究　time study

時間損失　loss of time

時間管理　time management

時間數列　time series

時間價值　trend of the times

時間標準　time standard

時間衡量單位 time measurement unit, TMU

時滯　time lag

時髦　fashionable

時樣,流行款式　fashion style

時價　current price, market value

時價率　average rate

財力　financial resources, financial capacity, financial ability

財力負擔限度　limits of financial capacity

財力壟斷　financial monopoly

財政公開 make public the administration of finance

財物扣押令　distress warrant, fieri facias

財物沒收　forfeiture of property

財政收入　financial revenue

財政收支平衡　balancing budgetary revenues and expenditures, fiscal balance

財政年度　fiscal year, financial year

財政年度貨幣折算調整　translation adjustment for fiscal year

財政充裕　financial sufficiency

財政危機　fiscal crisis

財政赤字　financial deficit

財政金庫　financial treasury

財政金融危機　financial and monetary crisis

財政或貨幣措施　fiscal or monetary action

財政和貨幣政策　fiscal and monetary policies

財政性貨幣發行　issuance of money for financial purposes

財政政策　fiscal policy

財政信貸　financial credit

財政刺激　fiscal incentive

財政貨幣混合政策　fiscal-monetary mix

財政稅收　fiscal levy

財政資助　financial support

財政實力 financial solvency, financial strength

財政關稅　revenue tariff

財務公司　finance company

財務分析　financial analysis

財務比率　financial ratio
財務代理協議（公開發行債券的）Fiscal Agency Agreement
財務代理商　fiscal agent
財務成果　financial outturn
財務收益　financial return
財務狀況　financial position
財務狀況表　statement of financial position
財務計劃　financial planning
財務指標　financial index, financial target
財務結構　financial structure
財務結算　financial settlement
財務混亂　general chaos in bookkeeping
財務報告　financial statement, financial report
財務報告分析　financial statement analysis
財務會計　financial accounting
財務會計制度　financial and accounting rules
財務槓桿　financial leverage
財務管理　financial management
財務審計　financial audit
財務調查　financial investigation
財務調整　financial adjustment
財產付與　disposition
財產收回　recovery
財產交託命令　vesting order
財產自然增益　accession of property
財產的分配　distribution of property

財產所有權的讓渡　livery
財產股利　property dividend
財產保險　property insurance
財產留置權　possessory lien, encumbrance
財產租賃所得　income from leasing property
財產清單　inventory
財產管理人　receiver
財產管理權　right to administer properties
財產轉讓書　assurance
財產繼承權　right to inherit
財產權利等的受讓人　cessionary
財產權利等的轉讓　cession
恩格爾法則（指隨家庭收入增加，收入中用在食物上的開支的比例，就越來越少）　Engel's Law
恩惠　favour, benefit
恩惠日，寬限日期　day of grace

[丿]

乘數表　multiplication table
乘數原理（由凱恩斯所創，用以說明國民所得與投資間的函數關係）principle of multiplier
乘數理論，增殖理論　theory of multiplier
乘機漁利　profiteering
息差年率（指兩種貨幣利息的年差率）interest differential
息票　coupon, interest coupon
息票利率（在一種債券發行時所定的

利率，按債券面值一定百分率支付） coupon rate

息票到期日 due date of coupon

息票調換券（附於債券息票上的一種附券） talon

息票登記簿 coupon register

息票債券（即不記名債券，還本付息時以債券及其息票為憑） coupon bond

息債 loan on interest

息摺 interest pass-book

租用外輪 charter foreign vessels

租回已售出產業 leaseback

租地 lease

租地人 tenant, leaseholder

租地契約 land lease agreement

租地權 tenant right

租金 rent

租金收入 rental income

租金負擔 rent-charge

租金費用 rent expense

租約 lease agreement

租借 lease

租借人 tenant

租借地 leased territory

租借合約 tenancy agreement

租借法案 lend-lease act

租借物業 leasehold property

租借屋宇 tenement-house

租借契約 contract of tenancy

租借期限 period of lease

租借購買 lease purchase

租借權 leasehold

租借權終止 termination of tenancy

租借權繼續 continuance of tenancy

租船 chartering

租船人 charterer

租船人支付費用 charterer pays dues

租船主 chartered owner

租船代理 chartering agent

租船市場 chartering market

租船合同 charter party, affreightment

租船合同提單 charter party bill of lading

租船承運商 charterer's operator

租船委託書 charter order

租船按時計費，時租 charter by time, time charter

租船按航次計費，程租 charter by voyage, voyage charter

租船期 charter period

租船費 charterage

租船經紀人 chartering broker

租船運輸 shipping by chartering

租船證書 charter certificate

租期 lease term

租賃 lease, rent, hire

租賃人 leaseholder, hirer

租賃合併 consolidation by lease

租賃固定資產 lease fixed assets

租賃財務公司 lease finance company

租賃財產 leasehold property

租賃貿易 leasing trade

租賃期間 lease term

租賃籌資 lease financing

租賃權益保險 leasehold interest insurance

租購（未付清購價時作為租賃） hire

purchase

租購法　hire purchase system

租購信用保險　hire purchase credit insurance

租購信貸公司 hire purchase company

租讓合同　concession agreement

租讓合同承租人　concessionaire

秘密投標　sealed tender, sealed bid

秘密協議　confidential agreement

秘密理財　backdoor financing

秘密貿易(受到法令禁止但仍私下進行的貿易)　clandestine trade

秘密準備　secret reserves

秘密資產　nonledger assets

留成外滙 retain a portion of foreign exchange

留成資金　retention funds

留存收益表　statement of retained earnings

留存利潤　retained profits

留存盈餘　retained earning

留存現金　cash on hand

留住貨物(美國商法中買方違約時賣方可以採取的一種補救方法) withholding the goods

留置物　retained thing

留置權(債權人在債務未償清前對擔保品的扣押權)　lien

留置權書　letter of lien

倉至倉條款 warehouse to warehouse

倉位(期貨市場用語)　position

倉租 storages charge, godown charges

倉庫成本,倉棧費用 warehouse cost

倉庫交貨　ex godown, ex warehouse

倉庫存貨　warehouse stock

倉庫收據　warehouse receipt

倉庫型商店　warehouse store

倉庫業者　warehouseman

倉庫標誌　warehouse mark

倉庫憑單　warehouse certificate

倉單　godown warrant

倉單條款　warehouse receipt clause

倉儲　warehousing

倉儲成本　carrying cost

倉儲管理 warehousing management

拿出拍賣　put up for auction, send to the hammer

拿高薪　get good wages

拿樣品賣貨的人　tally man

缺口分析　gap analysis

缺貨單　want slips

缺貨價格(指限制產量以保證利潤的價格)　scarcity price

缺項滙票(缺少某項內容的滙票) inchoate bill

缺額　vacancy

矩陣(將經濟數據寫成列和行的矩陣列。行,表示一個經濟變量的分佈;列,表示另一經濟變量的分佈) matrix

矩陣式組織　matrix organization

矩陣法會計(用縱橫棋盤式的對照表表示出業務的借貸科目)　matrix approach accounting

矩陣管理制　matrix management

矩陣簿記　matrix bookkeeping

氧化劑(包裝外表標誌) oxidizer, oxidizing agent

氧氣轉爐 oxygen converter

釘住黃金的貨幣 gold-pegged currency

釘住滙率,掛鈎滙率 pegged exchange rate

釘住滙率制度 pegging rate system

航行次數 voyage number

航行通知書 ordering of vessel

航行錯誤除外 navigational error exception

航行權 right of navigation

航次租船契約 voyage charter

航空人身意外保險 aviation personal, accident insurance

航空公司總提單 master airway bill

航空分運提單 house airway bill

航空急件傳送 air express

航空責任險 aviation insurance

航空貨運 airfreight

航空港 airport

航空提單 airway bill of lading

航空運送 carriage by air

航空運輸險 air transport insurance

航空線 airways

航空聯運 through air transport

航海 navigation, voyage

航海證明書 navicert

航程中止條款 frustration clause

航程往返時間 round-trip time

航程保險 voyage insurance

航程保險單 voyage policy

航程挫折 frustration of the insured voyage

航程挫折條款 frustration clause

航運交易所 shipping exchange

航運企業 shipping enterprise

航運企業家 shipping entrepreneur

航運倉單 shipping manifest

航運設施 shipping facilities

航運業,航運界 shipping business, shipping interests

借 debit

借入 borrow

借入股票 borrowed stock

借入資本 debt capital, borrowed capital, loan capital, debenture capital

借入資本成本對借入資本的比率 ratio of cost of capital borrowed to borrowed capital

借支 ask for an advance on one's pay

借方 debit side, debtor

借方欠戶 debit customers

借方銀行 debit bank

借方對銷 contra debit

借方餘額,借差 debit balance

借外債 contract a foreign loan

借入款利息 interest on loans

借條 note of hand

借約(指以服務償債務的) due bill

借項 debit item, debit entry

借項通知單 debit memorandum

借項憑單 debit memo

借款 borrowing, raise a loan, borrow money

借款人 borrower

借款市場 loan market

借款安排 borrowing arrangements

借款企業 borrowing venture

借款利息 loan interest

借款股份　debenture stock

借款契約　loan agreement

借款能力　borrowing capacity

借款條件　condition of a loan

借款票據　loan bill

借款費用　borrowing costs

借款期限　life of loan

借款證　loan note, receiver's certificate

借款權限　borrowing power

借貸　debt and credit

借貸利息　loan interest

借貸股票　lending stock, loan stocks

借貸記帳法　debit-credit plan

借貸對照表　financial statement

借債　get into debt

借債抵押品　security for a loan

借債能力　ability to borrow

借新債還舊債　refunding

借錢　borrow money

借據　due bill, debt on bond

個人人身意外傷害保險　personal accident insurance

個人支出　personal outlays

個人支票，私人支票　personal cheque

個人至上決策　personalistic decision

個人企業　individual enterprise

個人免稅　personal exemption

個人所得　personal income

個人所得稅　personal income tax

個人金融公司　personal finance company

個人信用　personal credit

個人信用貸款，個人抵押貸款　loan on personal security

個人保證貸款　loan on personal guarantee

個人財產　personal wealth, personal property

個人消費　personal consumption

個人責任　personal liability

個人責任保險　personal liability policy

個人（小額）貸款　personal loan

個人儲蓄　personal savings

個別合同　specific contract

個別折舊法和分組折舊法　unit and group bases of depreciation

個別風險　unique risk, unsystematic risk

個別許可證　individual licence

個別鑑定法　special identification method

個別鑑定存貨計價法，辨認法　identification method

候帳　wait for the account

候審　pending trial

倫巴德人街（倫敦的銀行街，是英國的金融中心）　Lombard Street

倫巴德利率（以證券作抵押的抵押放款利率）　Lombard rate

倫巴德貸款（英格蘭銀行給商業銀行的證券抵押貸款）　Lombard loan

倫敦外滙市場　London foreign exchange market

倫敦加權（為補償在倫敦工作人員支付較高的居住和交通費用而給予的津貼，亦稱倫敦津貼）　London weighting

倫敦仲裁法庭　London Court of Arbitration

倫敦承保人協會（倫敦海上保險公司的一個協會）　Institute of London Underwriters

倫敦金屬交易所　London Metal Exchange

倫敦到岸價格條件　London landed terms

倫敦城　city of London

倫敦黃金市場　London gold market, London bullion market

倫敦商品交易所　London Commodity Exchange

倫敦國際金融期貨交易所　London International Financial Futures Exchange

倫敦貼現市場　London discount market

倫敦預託證券　London depositary receipts

倫敦銀行同業拆放息（指倫敦銀行貸款給第一流銀行的利率，它用於決定大多數歐洲信貸所支付的利率）　London interbank offered rate (LIBOR)

倫敦銀行清算所　London Bankers' Clearing House

倫敦價格（指美國股票在倫敦的價格）　London price

倫敦糖業終端市場　London sugar terminal market

倫敦證券交易所（成立於1773年）　London Stock Exchange

倫敦證券交易所服務員　waiter

倫敦證券交易所理事會（有會員46名）　Council of the Stock Exchange

條件　conditions, terms

條件不明的契約　open contract

條例　regulation, ordinance

條約生效　treaty valid

條約批准　treaty ratification

條約保障　treaty protection

條約義務　treaty obligation

條約簽字　sign treaty

條款　provision, article, clause

倒扣盈利　plow back the earnings

倒收利息　negative interest

倒軋成本法　reversal cost method

倒逆購回協定（中央銀行在公開市場中將債券賣給交易商並在指定的日期和價格上購回）　match sale-purchase agreement

倒閉　failure, bust

倒閉銀行　cash in closed banks

倒帳　insolvency, become bankrupt, bad debts

倒掛市場　invert market

倒填日期　antedate

倒填提單日期（裝船日期已超過信用證期限，船公司將提單上裝船日期倒退填寫到信用證期限之內）　back date of B/L

倒填日期票據　back date bill, antedated bill

倒算　seize back confiscated property

倒數　reciprocal

倒轉生息曲線(指短期債券利率比長期債券利率高的情況)　inverted yield curve

倒簽提單(指貨物由於實際裝船日期遲於信用證規定裝船日期，而在提單上按信用證規定日期倒簽)　anti-dated B/L

值得　worth, to be worth it

值得信貸的　creditworthy

值得信貸的程度　［美］creditworthiness

倍率，百分率　percentage

倍數　a multiple, multiplier

倍增　multiplication

徒步購物區　pedestrain malls

追求最大利潤　maximize profit

追加支付　additional payment

追加股息　supplementary dividend

追加股款　supplementary calls

追加押金　call margin, additional margin

追加定貨　additional order

追加所得稅　supplementary income tax

追加的購買力　added purchasing power

追加信貸　supplemental credit

追加保險　additional insurance

追加保證金　call margin

追加條款，批單(保險)　rider

追加借款限制　additional debt restriction

追加稅　additional tax

追加預算　additional budget, supplementary budget

追加運費費率　incidental fee tariff

追加概算　supplementary estimates

追加撥款　supplementary appropriations

追加擔保品　additional collateral

追加關稅　additional duty

追回　recovery

追回欠債　recovery debts

追回全部款項　recover funds in full

追回款　recoveries

追回贓物　recover stolen property

追計加入　retroactive admission

追索訴訟　recovery action, recourse action

追索權　right of recourse, with recourse

追索權協定(對分期付款的)　recourse agreement

追索權基礎　recourse basis

追逐利潤　profit-seeking, quest for profit

追債　dun for debt, recover debts

追債公司　collecting company

追債代理人　collecting agent

追溯交款　retroactive contributions

追溯既往　［拉］nunc pro tunc

追溯效力　retroactive effect, retrospective application, relation back

追溯法　retroactive method

追溯費率　retrospective rating

追溯調整　retroactive adjustment

追認代理人所訂合同　ratification of

agents' contract

追認的代理　ratification

追償　recovery

追償損失，彌補損失　recover losses

追贓 order the return of stolen money or goods, recover stolen money or goods

逃稅　avoidance of tax, tax evasion, tax dodging

逃稅人　tax dodger

逃稅樂園　tax haven

逃滙　evade foreign exchange

逃債　dodge a creditor

逃避資本　refugee capital

特上品質　superfine quality

特有物權　special property

特快貨櫃/集裝箱列車　container express

特別大減價　giving great bargain

特別支付代理人　special disburser

特別合夥人　special partners

特別折扣　special discount

特別折舊　abnormal depreciation

特別折讓　special allowance

特別法人　special juristic person

特別往來存款　special current account

特別股　special stock

特別股息　special dividend

特別承兌　special acceptance

特別押匯信用證　special documentary credit

特別信貸基金　special credit fund

特別紅利 extra dividend, special bonus

特別背書　special endorsement

特別捐稅公債　special assessment bonds

特別記帳單位　special unit of account

特別海損　particular average

特別海關發票　special customs invoices

特別留置權　particular lien

特別許可證　special license

特別帳戶　special account

特別貨幣安排　special monetary arrangement

特別清算終結委員會(紐約清算委員會為加強 CHIPS 清算的終結性，於 1987 年 1 月 28 日成立的委員會，所有 CHIPS 成員銀行簽字並遵守共同分擔損失的協議) Special Settlement Finality Committee

特別進口　special import

特別裁定　special verdict

特別發行市場(美國術語，指"再購回協議"市場的一個小部份) specific issue market

特別提款權　special drawing right (SDR)

特別意外準備　special contingency reserve

特別審計　special audit

特別艙貯(對危險品) special storage

特別儲備基金　special reserve fund

特別儲藏費率(對貴重貨物)　special storage rate

特例　special case

特性　special characteristics

特性要因分析圖　cause and effect analysis chart

特定生產指數　specific productive index

特定代理商　special agent

特定成本　special cost

特定抵押　special mortgage

特定保單　specific policy

特定保險　specific insurance

特定信用證　special credit

特定財產留置權(對借契上指明之財產)　specific lien

特定貨物運費率 particular commodity transport rate

特定劃線支票 special crossed cheque

特定價格或更優價格(按特定或更優價格交易的一種命令)　at or better

特長期滙(通常指到期日超過12個月的遠期外滙契約)　very long forward exchange

特重特長運費率　heavy & lengthy rates

特重貨物, 超重貨物　heavy cargo

特約商店　appointed store

特約經銷處　special sales agency

特約維修店　special repair shop

特殊包裝　particular package

特殊品　specialty goods

特殊原因收益, 但由收益　but-for income

特殊商品　particular kind of commodity

特殊週期　specific cycle

特殊換算　special conversion

特殊階層　privileged stratum

特許　liberties, franchises

特許公司　chartered company

特許出口商品 goods exported under special license

特許出口證　special permission export

特許會計師　chartered accountant

特許銀行　chartered bank

特許銷售網　franchise distribution network

特許證 special permit, chartered concession

特許權　chartered right

特許權所有人 concessionaire granter

特許權使用費　royalties

特等品質　extra best quality

特惠貨幣(英國貼現銀行提供的一種便利, 使能在每日下午三點從某些銀行借到最後一分鐘的資金)　privilige money

特惠貸款　concessional loan

特惠關稅　preferential duties, preferential tariff

特種收入基金　special revenue fund

特種存款　special deposits

特種信託　special trust

特種基金　special fund

特種商品　special cargo

特種商號　special shop

特種貿易　special commerce

特種運輸費率　special rates

特種銀行帳戶　special bank account

特種關稅減讓　special tariff concession

特價　special price, bargain price

特權　privilege, prerogative

耗用材料成本　cost of raw materials used

耗減費用　depletion expense

耗減優惠　depletion allowance

耗損　deterioration, waste, lose, wear and tear

耗損費用　depletion expense

耗損準備　depletion reserve

耗竭資產　wasting assets

殺空頭(交易所行話)　squeeze the shorts

殺價　force down prices

[ㄱ]

書面申請　written application

書面協定　written agreement

書面契約　written contract

書面許可　written permission

書面報告　written report

書面憑證　written confirmation

書面證明　written document

書信電報　letter telegram

展延有效期　extend the expiration date of ……

展延保險　extended insurance

展延保險批單　extended coverage endorsement

展延保險費　renewal premium

展期　extension

展期合同　renew a contract

展期利率　continuation rate

展期信用證　extended credit

展期費　extension fee

展期貸款　rollover credit

展銷　selling at expositions, sales exhibition

展銷店　show shop

展銷會場　exhibition park

展覽品　displaying items

展覽會　exhibition, [美]exposition

弱性商標　weak trademark

弱幣　less favourable currency, weak currency

除去股息　ex-dividend

除去新股　ex new

除去新股出售　sold ex new

除皮　tare excluded

除皮重量　tare gross

除外責任條款　exclusion clause

除非另有規定　not otherwise provided, not elsewhere specified

除非另定費率　not otherwise rated

除非特別規定　not specially provided for

除淨　ex-all

除權(股票中不附有按一定折扣購新發股票的權利)　ex right

退回支票　returned check

退回股利　rescission of dividend

退回股票　stocks returned

退回保險費　return premium

退回貸款　return loan

退股　retirement, withdraw shares, withdrawal

退押　return a deposit, returning security money

退保金額　cash surrender value

退租　throw a lease

退稅　drawback, tax reimbursement, refund of duty

退稅憑單(海關的)　debenture

退款　refund, drawback

退料單　material credit slip

退貨　goods rejected, goods returned

退貨特約條款　rejection clause

退貨清單　merchandise credit slip

退貨運費　back goods freight, back freight

退貨單據　returned purchase invoice

退滙　reexchange

退夥　withdraw from partnership

退夥人　retiring partner

退賠　pay compensation, restitute

退廢會計　retirement accounting

退廢政策(指折舊)　retirement policy

退還已繳稅款　drawback for duties paid

退還佣金　return commission

退還材料　store returned

退還準備金　deposit released

退關　shut out (S/O)

退關貨物清單　shut out memo

退贓　give up ill-gotten gains, disgorge ill-gotten gains

能量　capabilities, energy

能量代謝率　relative metabolic rate

能量差異　capacity variance

能源成本　energy cost

能源合作　cooperation in the field of energy

能源革命　energy revolution

能源消費　energy use

能源密集的技術　energy-intensive technology

能源資源　energy resources

能源管理　energy control

能源數據系統　energy resources data system

能源貧乏國家　energy poor

能源豐富國家　energy rich

納稅　pay tax, pay duty

納稅人　taxpayer

納稅申報單　tax returns

納稅年度　tax year

納稅的支付能力原則　ability-to-pay principle of taxation

納稅的價值　rateable value

納稅後扣除　after-tax deduction

納稅後利潤　post-taxation profit, after-tax profit

納稅負擔　incidence of taxation

納稅能力　taxable capacity

納稅期限　term of tax

納稅憑證　tax payment receipt

納稅額的減除　tax credit

納稅證明書　certification on tax payment

納稅隱蔽所　tax shelter

紙上利潤（指未平倉合約以一定時間和價格，可實得之利潤） paper profit

紙公司（美國人對熱中於證券和投機企業的一種貶稱） paper company

紙屑　paper scrap

紙袋　paper bag

紙黃金（國際貨幣基金組織特別提款權之別稱） paper gold

紙帶　paper tape

紙帶穿孔機　paper tape punch

紙帶閱讀器　paper tape reader

紙幣　paper currency, paper money

紙幣本位　paper standard

紙幣制度　paper money system

紙幣供給量　money supply

紙幣信用　paper credit

紙幣流通速度　velocity of currency in circulation

紙幣流通量 amount of paper money in circulation

紙幣通貨膨脹 paper money inflation

紙箱，紙盒　carton

紙繞法（包裝）　paper winding

純收入　net income

純成本　flat cost

純交易條件　pure trade terms, barter terms of trade

純利息　pure interest

純利率　pure interest rate

純利潤　pure profit

純金（24 開金）　pure gold, fine gold

純保險費　pure premium

純資本　pure capital, positive capital

純粹動產　pure personalty

純粹競爭　pure competition

紐約可可交易所　New York Cocoa Exchange

紐約皮張交易所　New York Hide Exchange

紐約承兑信用證　New York acceptance letter of credit

紐約咖啡及糖交易所　New York Coffee and Sugar Exchange

紐約股票交換所　New York Stock Clearing House

紐約保險交易所　New York Insurance Exchange

紐約海運協會　New York Shipping Association

紐約商人協會 New York Merchants Association

紐約商品交易所　New York Commodity Exchange

紐約產品交易所　New York Produce Exchange

紐約棉花交易所　New York Cotton Exchange

紐約路邊交易所（1953 年改名為美國證券交易所）　New York Curb Exchange

紐約橡膠交易所　New York Rubber Exchange

紐約證券交易所　New York Stock Exchange［美俗］Big Board

紐約證券交易所普通股票價格指數（以 1965 年 12 月 31 日收盤價格為

50 的所有掛牌普通股票價格的平均數） New York Stock Exchange Common Stock Indexes

娛樂稅　entertainments tax

[丶]

密耳行廣告費率（報紙計算廣告費的單位，即一行 5.5 號鉛字，一欄寬，印 100 份收的廣告費） milline rate

密封　air proof

密封投標　sealed bid, sealed tender

密封貨櫃/集裝箱　sealed container

密封堅固艙　sealed cabin

密集資本　deepening of capital

密語　codewords

密碼　code

寄存單據（指不具備上市條件的證券。為准其進行買賣而設計的一種辦法，發行寄存單據） depositary receipt

寄泊港　port of call

寄託　bailment

寄託信用證（因待條件的成熟而寄託於第三者的信用證） escrow credit

寄售 consignment-out, consignment sales, consignment outward

寄售人　consignor

寄售出口合同　export on consignment sales contract

寄售付款　payment against goods shipped on consignment

寄售品，寄售貨物 consignment goods, goods-out on consignment

寄售契約　agreement on consignment, consignment contract

寄售記錄　consignment records

寄售通知書　consignment note

寄售商店　consignment business, consignment store

寄售費用　consignment expense

寄售貿易　consignment trade

寄售發票　consignment invoice

寄售最低限價 consignment with lowest price limit

寄銷損益　consignment profit and loss

商人　merchant

商人介入（由商人參與某一全國性廣告公司的促銷計劃） dealer tie-in

商人銀行，商業銀行　merchant bank, commercial bank

商人慣常法　law merchant

商法　mercantile law, business law

商事法　business law

商事法院　commercial court

商店櫥窗　shop window

商界　business circles

商約　commercial treaty

商品　merchandise, commodity

商品比價　parity rate of commodity

商品包裝和標簽規定　packing and labelling regulation

商品目錄　catalogue

商品成本　merchandise cost

商品交易　merchandise trade

商品交易所　commodity exchange

商品交易所有限公司(紐約)　Commodity Exchange Inc. (of New York)

商品折扣　merchandise discount

商品個性標誌　trade character

商品展覽會　trade fair

商品票據(指銀行本票和跟單提單)　[美]commodity paper

商品項目　merchandise account

商品期貨交易管理委員會(美)　Commodity Future Trading Commission

商品期貨合營組織(70年代末，80年代初在美國興起的類似互助基金的期貨購買者合夥組織)　Commodity market pool

商品週轉　merchandise turnover

商品與稅率的詳細分類　specialization of commodities and duty rates

商品傾銷　dumping

商品綜合方案　Integrated Programme for Commodities

商品價格　commodity price

商品學　merchandising

商品轉移　merchandise transfer

商務仲裁　commercial arbitration

商務秘書　commercial secretary

商務專員　commercial attacte

商務參贊　commercial counsellor

商務參贊處　commercial counsellor's office

商船　mercantile marine, merchant ship, merchant vessel

商船隊　mercantile marine fleet

商船運輸　merchant shipping

商棧　trade post

商場證券利率　bazaar bill rate

商業　commerce

商業中心　business centre

商業代理合同　commission contract

商業本票　commercial paper

商業代理機構　mercantile agency

商業用語　commercial terms

商業名片　business cards

商業名稱　tradename

商業自由港　commercial free ports

商業回扣　commercial rebate

商業地位，商業信譽　commercial standing

商業交易所(倫敦糖、茶、咖啡等商品交易所)　Commercial Sale Rooms

商業存款　business deposit

商業危機　commercial crisis

商業折扣　trade discounts

商業投資信託公司　commercial investment trust company

商業法　commercial law

商業承兌滙票　trade acceptance draft

商業制度　mercantile system

商業金融公司　commercial finance company

商業信用　commercial credit, mercantile credit, business credit

商業信用保險　commercial credit insurance

商業信用諮詢所　mercantile inquiry agency

商業信用證　commercial letter of credit

商業盈利率　commercial profitability

商業負債　trade liabilities

商業風險　commercial risk

商業家　commercialist

商業條件，商業用語　commercial terms

商業航空業　commercial aviation

商業書信　business correspondence

商業秘密　trade secret

商業通用語言　common business oriented language

商業旅行　commercial traveler

商業陳詞濫調　commercial chestnut

商業符號　commercial symbols

商業習慣　commercial customs, mercantile usages

商業票據　mercantile paper, commercial paper

商業票據託收統一規則(1955年國際商會頒訂) Uniform Rules for the Collection of Commercial Paper

商業票據交易所　commercial paper exchange

商業票據承銷公司，商業證券經紀行 commercial paper houses

商業帳簿　commercial accounts

商業景氣　business boom

商業登記　commercial registration

商業登記證 business registration certificate

商業策略　business strategy

商業貼現　commercial discount

商業發票　commercial invoice

商業貸款　commercial loan

商業貸款利率　commercial loan rate

商業短期押滙票 documentary commercial bill drawn at short sight

商業循環　business cycle

商業循環周期　business cycle

商業滙兌　commercial exchange

商業滙票　commercial draft

商業滙票市場　commercial bill market

商業滙價 merchant rate of exchange

商業資料　business material

商業資料處理 business data processing

商業電報　commercial telegrams

商業電腦　commercial computer

商業道德 commercial character, commercial ethics, commercial morality

商業銀行業務　commercial banking

商業管制　commercial control

商業徵信所 commercial credit agency

商業慣例　commercial usage, commercial practice

商業樣品進口證　ECS carnet

商業銷售 commercial disappearance

商業調節　commercial leverage

商業蕭條，商業不景氣　commercial depression

商業關係　commercial relation

商業環境　business environment

商業總擔保(對商業機構經營人承保僱員不正當行為造成的損失的一種信用擔保)　commercial blanket bond

商業證券　instrument of credit

商業證券經紀行　commercial paper house

商會　chamber of commerce

商標　trademark

商標法　[英]Merchandise Marks Act

商標國際註冊馬德里協定　Madrid Agreement for International Registration of Trademark

商標權　trade mark privileges, ownership of trademark

商戰，經濟戰　commercial struggle, commercial war, trade war

商譽　goodwill

產出，產量　output

產出投入比率　output-input ratio

產生即判力的仲裁裁決　award having the authority of res judicate

產地　origin, locality

產地證明書　certificate of origin

產物　product yield

產供銷關係　production-supply-marketing relation

產品　product

產品工程　product engineering

產品方向　line of production

產品分析　product analysis

產品升級換代　upgrading and up-dating of products

產品生命週期　product life cycle

產品市場　produce market

產品成本　inventoriable costs, product costs

產品安全　product safety

產品收回　product recall

產品交易所　produce exchange

產品合格審查　product qualification

產品技術　product technology

產品系統　product system

產品佈置　product layout

產品定位　product positioning

產品定型化　new design is finalized

產品保險　manufacturer's output insurance

產品返銷　product buy back

產品革新　product innovation

產品高級化　trading up

產品流程圖　product flow process charts

產品展覽　product display

產品混合　product mix

產品研究　product research

產品責任　product liability, product responsibility

產品責任保險　product liability insurance

產品組合　product mix

產品組合的一致性　consistency of product mix

產品組羣分析　product portfolio analysis

產品部門化　product departmentalization

產品設計　product design
產品規格　product specification
產品規劃　product planning
產品普及化(指經營低檔商品以增加
　銷售量)　trading down
產品發展　product development
產品發展管理　management of prod-
　uct development
產品結構　product structure
產品集團　product group
產品試製　trial production
產品線　product line
產品價格　product price
產品選定過程 product-adoption pro-
　cess
產品範圍　product field, range of
　products
產品驗收　product acceptance
產量　output, yield
產量係數　output coefficient
產量法(計提折舊或分配負荷的方法)
　output method
產量定額　output norm
產量單位　output unit
產業合理化 rationalization of industry
產業界　industrial circles, business
　circles
產業稅　property tax
產業結構　setup of production, in-
　dustrial structure
產業循環　business cycle
產額價值　value of output
產權比率　equity ratio
產權契約　title-deed

產權保險　title insurance
產權說明書　abstract of title
產權擔保　warranty of title
產權證明　muniments of title
產權籌資　equity financing
麻紗　yarn of flax & ramie
麻袋　jute bags
部(車輛)　unit
部分付款　partial payment, payment
　in part
部分交付　partial delivery
部分全損險　total loss of part
部分免除責任 partially exempt obli-
　gations
部分均衡　partial-equilibrium
部分或全部艙位　part or whole of
　place
部分承兌　partial acceptance
部分背書　partial endorsement
部分保險　partial insurance
部分效用　partial utility
部分救助成功　partial success
部分現金交易　partial cash trans-
　action
部分規範化決策　partially specified
　decision
部分貨櫃/集裝箱貨船　partial con-
　tainer freighter
部分損失　partial loss
部分賠付　partial coverage
部分審計　partial audit
部分擔保負債 partially-secured liabil-
　ities
部分擔保債權人　partially secured

creditors

部分償付(償付一小部分債，作為承認債務之象徵，又稱象徵性償付) partial payment, token payment

部分繳款債券(購買債券時只需繳付部分款項，餘下部分可在日後一段時期內繳足) partly-paid bond

部門 department

部門化 departmentalization

部門成本 departmental cost

部門經濟學 departmental economics

啟航港 port of embarkation

啟發方法 heuristic method

啟發性規劃 heuristic programming

啟發模式 heuristic model

啟運港碼頭交貨(價) free on board quay

啟運機場交貨(價) FOB airport ……

被拒絕付款的滙票 bill dishonoured by non-payment

被拒絕承兌的滙票 bill dishonoured by non-acceptance

被委託人 mandatary

被受與人 grantee

被保人 assured, insurant

被保險人對賠款方式的選擇權 option

被保證人 warrantee

被封鎖港口 blockaded port

被索賠人 claimee

被排裝或被退關之貨物 shut outs

被通知方 notify party

被控制市場 captive market

被統制帳戶 controlled account

被認可的認繳股份 shares authorized

瓶裝 in bottles, bottling

瓶頸式通貨膨脹(由供給短缺引起的) bottleneck inflation

瓶頸狀態(指生產流程中的阻礙和困難；生產中的薄弱環節；交通或港口的狹隘擁擠等) bottleneck

混入較差品質 inferior quality mixed in

混入較差等級 inferior grade mixed in

混合包紮貨物 mixed consignment

混合市場 marketing mix

混合成本 mixed cost

混合交易 mixed transaction

混合存貨 mixed inventory

混合仲裁法庭 mixed arbitral tribunal

混合股份公司 mixed holding company

混合所有權 mixed ownership

混合協議(許可證貿易中，許可證把專利與技術訣竅訂在一起的協議) mixed agreement

混合型計算機(模擬、數字) hybrid computer

混合信貸 mixed credit

混合保單(指航程與時間的) mixed policy

混合保險 mixed insurance

混合財產 mixed property

混合索賠委員會 mixed claims commission

混合配額 mixed quota

混合帳戶 mixed account

混合動產　mixed pensonalty

混合貨幣　mixed currency

混合税　mixed taxes, mixed duties

混合税率　mixed tariff, compound tariff

混合貸款　mixed loan

混合準備(一項具有兩個以上用途的準備)　hybrid reserve

混合訴訟　mixed action

混合預算　combination budget

混合經濟　mixed economy

混合裝載運輸 consolidated shipment, mixed shipments

混合關税 mixed or compound duties

混合證券　hybrid security

混裝貨物　consolidated cargo

深水港　deepwater harbour, deep-water port

深水泊位　deep-water berths

深凍食品　deep-frozen food

深凍貨物　deep-frozen goods

深艙容積　deep tank capacity

液化天然氣船　liquified natural gas carrier

液化石油氣船　liquified gas carries

液體管道　fluid pipeline

淡水雨淋險　fresh and/or rain water damage

淡水險　risk of fresh water damage

淡水險條款　fresh-water clause

淡友(香港市場對預期價格下跌之人稱淡友)　bear

淡友補倉(淡友買回投機性"空倉"的行為)　bear covering

淡市　bear market

淡季　slack season

清欠　pay off debts

清查　to check, take stock of, investigate

清倉拍賣 clearance sale, clearing stock sale

清除殘損物費用 debris clearing cost

清貨　stock taking

清理, 清算, 清盤　liquidation

清理人掌握的債券或股票　liquidation holdings

清理成本　disposal cost

清理官　official liquidator

清理財產接管人　equity receiver

清理損益　liquidation gain or loss

清理價值, 變現價值 liquidation value, realization, break-up value

清理變產表　liquidation account

清帳 close accounts, square accounts

清帳支付命令　settlement warrant

清帳銀行　reimburse bank

清算人　liquidator, receiver

清算日　settlement day

清算公司　clearing corporation

清算代理人　clearing agent

清算同盟　clearing union

清算式資產負債表, 財產狀況説明書 statement of affairs

清算完結　closure of liquidation

清算所成員　clearing member

清算所成員代表(清算所成員在期權市場上的執行人或場內代表) clearing member's representative

清算美元　clearing dollars
清算協定　clearing agreement
清算制度　clearing house system
清算損失　deficiency account
清算損益　strike a balance, liquidation profit and loss
清算債務　settle a claim
清算銀行　clearing bank
清算價值　liquidation value
清算機構　clearing house
清盤人　liquidator
清盤大拍賣　liquidation sale
清潔大副收據　clean mate's receipt
清潔信用（指授信對象特別可靠，受信人不附任何單據，即可向銀行簽發票據，銀行即予接受）　clean credit
清潔浮動（指政府不加干預的滙率）　clean floating
清潔提單　clean bill of lading
清潔單據　clean document
清關貨場　clearance depot
清繳保費　paid-up insurance premium
清償　satisfaction, settlement, discharge
清償危機　liquidity crisis
清償負債　satisfy the liabilities
清償能力　liquidity
清償能力比率（清償能力與短期債務之比）　liquidity ratio
清償基礎　liquidity basis
清償準備金　liquidation reserve
清償債務　liquidation of debts, fulfilment of a claim

清償債務之要求　liquidated demand
清償債務備忘錄　memorandum of satisfaction
許可方　licensor
許可通商　license to trade
許可轉讓的技術　licensed technology
許可證　license, permit
許可證制度　license system
許可證接受人　licensee
許可證接受方不得違約　licensee estoppel
許可證稅　license tax
許可證費用　licence fee
許可證貿易　licensing trade
許可證貿易協議　licensing agreement
許可證貿易聯盟　licensing pool
許可證價格　licence price
許諾條款　grant clause
訟費　costs
訟費保證金　security for costs
設立公司　incorporation
設施　facility, programmes
設有基金之退休金計劃　funded pension plan
設有基金之準備　funded reserve
設定資本　stated capital
設定價值　stated value
設計不符　different design
設計者　layer, designer
設計計劃預算會計制度　planning-programming-budgeting-accounting system
設計組　design section
設備利用率　capacity utilization rate

設備完好率 proportion of the equipment good condition

設備更新　updating equipment

設備折讓　outfit allowance

設備信託債券 equipment trust bond

設備租用　equipment rental

設備租賃　equipment lease

設備基金　equipment funds

設備債券　equipment bonds

設備運轉率　operation rate

設備維修費　maintenance of equipment

設備變賣損益　gain or loss on sale of equipment

設置基金期間　funded period

設算成本,視同成本　imputed cost

設算利息,視同利息 imputed interest

訣竅(一種可以轉讓和傳授的、公眾所不知道且沒有取得專利權的技術知識，被予以權利化的無形財產) know-how

訣竅市場(技術知識市場) know-how market

訣竅交易　know-how deal

訣竅指導費　know-how fee

烤爐用玻璃器　ovenglassware

粘性價格(指不易變動價格) "sticky" price

粗笨工作　rough work

粗略估計　rough estimate

粗製品　rough wrought, rough quality

粗製濫造　shoddy

粗魯裝卸　rough handle

粗暴操作　rough handling

[一]

票外承兌　extrinsic acceptance

票面　face of an instrument

票面上的　nominal

票面以上　above par

票面利率(指一年的利息佔債券票面金額的比率) coupon rate

票面股本　nominal capital

票面金額　face amount

票面值法　par-value method

票面等級　Aaa-rated

票面價格　face par

票面價值　par value, face value

票面額　face amount, Aaa-rated

票背簽字 indorsement; endorsement

票期未到　bill undue

票滙　demand draft (D/D)

票據　bill, note

票據上的權利　rights arising out of the bill

票據外的證據　evidence outside the instrument

票據市場　bill market

票據付款通知　advice of bill paid

票據收款通知　advice of bill collected

票據交換　clearing

票據交換日期　date of clearance

票據交換所　clearing house

票據交換所黃金證券 clearing house gold certificate

票據交換所清單　clearing house statement

票據交換所貸借決算表　clearing sheet

票據交換所貸款證券　clearing house loan certificate

票據交換所資金(美國術語，指由清算所清算的支票所代表的資金)　clearing house funds

票據交換所銀行相互支付系統 CHIPS —Clearing House Interbank Payment System

票據交換差額　clearing balance

票據交換總額　exchanges

票據再貼現　notes rediscounted

票據法　law of negotiable instrument

票據抵押貸款　loan on bills, loan on notes

票據承兌　bill accepted

票據承兌利率　acceptance rate

票據到期　bill to mature, bill to fall due

票據或證券上的記載事項　statements in the instrument

票據背面　back

票據背後的交易(指票據所根據的交易)　transaction underlying the instrument

票據員　note teller

票據高升水　shaving (a note)

票據處理機　billing machine

票據發行便利　note issurance facilities

票據貼現 notes discount, discounting of bill

票據貼現市場　discount market

票據貼現押金　bill discount deposit

票據經紀人　bill broker

票據轉期　note renewal

票據簿　bills book (register)

區域性經濟結合　regional economic integration

區域網絡系統　local area network system

區間推定　interval estimation

區間清算資金(美國 12 家聯邦儲備銀行所維持的一種黃金證單資金)　interdistrict settlement fund

區間線性規劃　interval linear programming

匿名股東　silent partner, sleeping partner, dormant partner

匿報，隱瞞　concealment

匿報所得額　concealing the amount of income

頂盤　highest quotation

副本　copy, duplicate

副本抄送　carbon copy

副代理人　sub-agent

副合同　subcontract

副承包商　sub-contractor

副保證人　collateral surety

副許可證　sub-licence

副產品　by-product

副產品再加工成本　additional costs assigned to by-product

副產品成本計算　by-product costing

副提單　sub-bill of lading

副業收入　ancillary revenue

副嘜頭　counter mark

副憑單　sub-voucher

現付成本　current-outlay cost, explicit cost

現付利息　explicit interest

現付押匯票　documentary payment bill

現付債額法(攤銷債券折價)　bonds-outstanding method (of amortizing bond discount)

現存公司　existing company

現存特惠(指英聯邦國家間以及歐洲共同市場與其非洲聯繫國之間的特惠關稅待遇)　existing preferential duties

現有存貨　stock inventory, stock on hand

現有的權利　vested in possession

現行市價　current market value

現行通令　standing orders

現行國際交易的支付和轉帳　payments and transfer for current international transaction

現行費率　current rates

現行滙率, 當日滙率　current rate, going rate

現行滙率法　current rate method

現行滙率折算法　current rate translation method

現行價格法　gonig rate pricing

現金　cash, ready money

現金支出　cash disbursement

現金支出日記簿　cash disbursement journal, cash payment journal

現金支出憑單　cash disbursements voucher

現金不足　cash-out

現金日記帳　cash journal

現金日報　daily cash report

現金分錄法　cash journal method

現金付出傳票　cash credit slip

現金付款的最低價格　cash price

現金出納機　cash register

現金市場, 付現市場　cash market

現金存款　cash deposit

現金收入　cash receipt

現金收入日記帳　cash receipts journal

現金收入傳票　cash debit slip

現金收支平衡　balance between cash receipts and payment

現金收支表　cash receipts and disbursements statement

現金收支預算　cash receipts and disbursements budget

現金收付實現制營業收入認定法　cash basis of revenue recognition

現金折扣　cash discount

現金股利　cash dividend

現金押金　cash deposit

現金抵補期權　cash covered options

現金信用證　cash credit

現金紅利　cash bonus, cash dividends

現金枯竭　cash drain

現金流入量　cash inflow

現金流出量　cash outflow

現金流量, 現金流轉　cash flows

現金流動性　cash liquidity

現金流量貼現法　discounted-cash-flow method

現金流量循環　cash flow cycle

現金流轉表　cash-flow statement

現金票據　cash note

現金基礎，現金收付制　cash basis

現金結算　cash settlement

現金循環　cash cycle, operating cycle

現金損失　cash losses

現金運送保險　cash messenger insurance

現金溢缺　cash over and short

現金解約價值(保險)　cash surrender value

現金預測　cash forecast

現金滙款單　cash remittance note

現金預算　cash budget

現金需求　cash requirement

現金對流動負債比率　ratio of cash to current liabilities

現金對銷貨收入比率 cash-to-revenue ratio

現金對總資產比率　cash-to-total assets ratio

現金管理模式　cash management model

現金調撥　cash transfers

現金賠償　reparations in cash

現金餘額　cash balance

現金頭寸　cash position

現金總流量　gross cash flow

現金儲備　cash reserve

現金儲備率　cash reserve ratio

現金虧絀　cash deficit

現金簿　cash book

現狀條件　[拉]tale quale (T.Q.)

現負債券(指未清償的)　bonds outstanding

現值　present value

現值法　present value method

現值美元　current U.S. dollar

現值會計　current value accounting

現值標準　present value standard

現時可達標準　currently attainable standard

現時成本，目前成本　current cost

現時重置成本　current replacement cost

現時貨幣會計　current dollar accounting

現貨　spot cargo, spot goods

現貨日期的次日　spot/next

現貨市場(要立即交收商品或付款的市場)　cash market

現貨交易　spot transaction, over-the-counter trading, spot trading

現貨買家　spot buyer

現貨期權(貨幣期權在執行時將其轉變為一個相應的現貨合約，又稱美式期權)　spot option (American option)

現貨溢價(指現貨價反高於期貨價的部分)　backwardation

現貨樣品　sample of existing goods

現貨賣家　spot seller

現貨價格　spot price

現場(交易所內為買賣期貨合約而設

的活動場所）　pit

現場客（指交易所成員，親自在現場買賣期貨之人）　floor trader

現場研究　field study

現場經紀　floor broker, pit broker

現款，現付現金　spot cash

現款交易　ready money business

現款銷售　sale by real cash

現發股本　capital stock outstanding

現匯交易，即期業務　spot (exchange) transaction

現滙滙率，即期滙率　spot (exchange) rate

現銷　cash sale , sale by real cash

現賣，現貨銷售　spot sale

現實購買力　current purchasing power

現購　cash purchase

現購自運　cash and carry

理事　manager, director

理事會　trustee council, board of directors

理貨　tally

理貨人　tallyman

理貨公司　tally company

理貨單　tally sheet

理想化模型　idealized model

理想的次數分配　ideal frequency distribution

理想值　ideal value

理想標準成本　ideal standard cost

理髮式（用以確定資產符合投資要求之程度，在已知的資產數值中扣除一個百分比）　haircut

理算行，票據交換所　clearing house

理算費用　adjustment cost

理論上的最高責任　maximum theoretical liability

理論成本　theoretical cost

理論折舊　theoretical depreciation

理賠　settlement of claims

理賠代理人　settling agent

理賠代理費　claims settling fee

理賠費用　claims expenses

理賠檢驗代理人　claims surveying agent

理艙費　stowage charges

斑點條款（用於皮革製品運輸的一項條款）　spotting clause

研究成果　research findings

研究和發展成本　research and development cost

研究密集（指研究支出佔淨產值比率高的企業）　research-intensive

研究報告　research report

研究與推廣　research and extension

研究潛能　research potential

規定指標　set quota

規定格式　prescribed form

規定時間內履行合同的選擇權　option

規定價格最低標準　establish a price floor

規定總限額　specified overall limit

規約　covenant

規格　specification

規章，規則　regulation

規章制度　regulatory framework

規費收入　income from the payment of stipulated fees

規模不經濟(企業規模擴大到一定規模時，如再擴大，費用隨之增加，使單位產品成本提高，造成的不經濟)　diseconomy of scale

規模投資比率　size-investment ratio

規模的報酬遞減　decreasing return to scale

規模的報酬遞增　increasing return to scale

規模經濟　economies of scale

規模適宜而獲得的利益　scale merit

規範性決策　normative decision

規範性技術預測　normative technique forecasting

規範法規　"code on standards"

規避送達　avoiding service

規劃功能　planning functions

規劃組織　planning organization

規劃程序　planning process

勘定折舊　observed depreciation

勘探合同(海上石油的)　exploration contract

勘驗　collation

堆　lot

堆棧　pack house, godown, storehouse

堆場　yard

堆場使用費　yardage

堆裝費　stowage

培育關稅　educational tariff

執行人　operator

執行令　writ of execution

執行合夥人　managing partner

執行判決的豁免　immunity from execution of judgement

執行委員會　executive committee

執行契約　execute contract

執行條款　execute treaty

執行程序　executive routine

執行董事　executive director

執行業務股東　active partner, managing partner, working partner

執行權利　enforcement of rights

執票人支票　bearer check

執票人票據　bearer bill

執照　certificate, charter, qualification, licence

執照及許可證　licence & permit bonds

執照稅　licence tax

執業者　practitioner

執業證書　practising certificate

救生艇　life boat

救助作業　salvage operation

救助報酬　salvage award, salvage money

救援船　salvor, salving vessel

救濟方法　remedies

救濟先於權利　remedies precede rights

救濟金　relief payment

救難費　salvage money

救護條款(海上保險)　sue and labour clause

軟件(指成套設備中的技術知識部分或電子計算機的各項程序)　software

軟件工程　software engineering

軟件公司　software firm

軟件交易　soft ware trade

軟度　softness

軟保兌(對信用證有附加條件的保兌)

soft confirmation

軟套利（英國術語，指公共部門票據與私人票據之間的"套利"）　soft arbitrage

軟通貨　soft currency

軟貨物（指不耐用的商品，如紡織品，輕工業品）　soft goods

軟飲料工業（指不含酒精的飲料、果汁等）　soft-drink industry

軟貸款　soft loan

軟貸款窗口（指對發展中國家的優惠貸款業務）　soft-loan window

軟幣國家　soft currency countries

都市化地區　urbanized areas

都會集中觀念　metro-concept

奢侈品稅　tax on luxuries

責任，償付能力　responsibility, obligation

責任支付命令（指未經事前審核的）　accountable warrants

責任成本　responsibility cost

責任保險　liability insurance

責任保險承保人　liability insurer

責任終止條款　cease clause

責任單位會計，核算點會計　segment accounting

責任預算　responsibility budget

責任會計　responsibility accounting

責任審計　responsibility audit

責任範圍　scope of cover

專用分層全貨櫃/集裝箱船　full cellular container vessel

專用決算表　special purpose statement

專用車　special car

專用泊位計劃（新加坡港務局與一些船公司簽署在丹戎巴葛貨櫃碼頭使用專用泊位的合約）　Appropriated Berth Scheme

專用基金　special-purpose fund

專用資本　special capital

專用資本貨物　specialized capital goods

專用銀行借款　special bank loans

專用審計日程表　special-purpose audit programs

專列火車　unit train

專有技術　proprietary technology

專有特權　exclusive privilege

專利　patent, monopoly

專利代理人　patent agent

專利共同使用制　patent pooling

專利共享　patent pool

專利局　patent office

專利法（例）　Patents Act

專利律師　patent attorney

專利特許使用權　patent license

專利許可　patent licensing

專利許可證協定　patent license agreement

專利發明　patented invention

專利期限已滿　patent runs out

專利證書　letter of patent

專利權　patent right

專利權合作條約（1970 年在華盛頓簽訂，至 1978 年底有 15 國參加）　Patent Cooperation Treaty

專利權的分實施權　sub-licence

專利權的交換實施權，相互特許權 cross licence

專利權的侵犯 infringement of patent right

專利權的國際公約 International Convention on Patents

專利權的授與者 patentor

專利權的維持 renewal of licensed patents

專利權的標示 patent marking

專利權所有人 patentee

專利權使用費 patent royalty

專利權持有人 patent holder

專利權登記 registration of patent

專利權期滿 expiration of patent

專利權經常使用費 running royalty

專門分析 ad hoc analysis

專門出口 special export

專門術語 technical terms

專門進口 special import

專門貿易 special trade

專門意義 technical meaning

專享的現行優惠 exclusively preferences in force

專案 project

專案進口簽證 special import licensing

專案管理 project management

專家委員會 expert committee

專家鑑定書 expert statement

專家經營市場制(紐約證券交易所採用的一種制度，規定一項股票的市場經營工作，只能由一個專家掌管) specialist market-making system

專家鑑定書 written expert testimony

專項外滙 special sum of foreign exchange

專項存款 special deposit

專項貸款 special-purpose loan

專買權 exclusive buying right

專賣店 speciality stores

專賣政策 exclusive agency policy

專賣權，包銷權 exclusive selling right

專業 profession

專業化 specialization

專業化協作 specialization and cooperation

專業化協作價格 prices for specialization and cooperation

專業化管理 management specialization

專業商店 single line store

專業會員(紐約證券交易所兼有經紀人及證券自營商雙重身份的會員) specialists

專業經理人 professional manager

專線電報機，用戶電報，電傳 telex (teleprinter exchange 之縮寫)

專營國庫券政策 bills-only policy

專營權，特許權 franchise

專欄日記帳 split column journal

基元 basic dollar

基元統計估值 constant dollar estimates

基元會計 constant dollar accounting

基本存量法(存貨計價)　base-stock method (of valuing inventory)

基本赤字　basic deficit

基本每股收益　primary earnings per share

基本利率　basic rate of interest

基本利率互換交易　basis rate swap

基本的中間變數　basic intermediate variable

基本品級(期貨交易視為準則之品級)　basis grade

基本差異　basic variance

基本差價(見"基差"條)　basis

基本差額　basic balance

基本設施, 基礎結構　infrastructure

基本貨幣　key currency

基本港口　base port, basic service port

基本準備金　basis reserve

基本期權　basic options

基本滙率　basic rate of exchange

基本運費　base freight

基本運費率　base freight rate

基本經濟建設　infrastructure

基本數量分析 basic quantitative analysis

基本數據　benchmark data

基本險　basic insurance

基本點(外滙市場交易員分割一種貨幣所得的最小單位名稱, 即計價貨幣的基本單位的萬分之一)　basis point

基本關稅　basic tariff

基本權利　fundamental rights

基年(指數的)　base year

基金　fund

基金表　statement of fund

基金盈餘　fund surplus

基金帳戶　fund account

基金會計　fund accounting

基金資產　fund assets

基金資產負債表 fund balance sheet

基差(指同一種商品或相關商品的現貨價與指定月份期貨價之間的差額)　basis

基差多倉(香港期貨市場指購入即期商品者, 同時沽出期貨對冲)　long the basis

基期　base period

基準利率互換交易(以一種基準計算的浮息調換成以另一種基準計算的浮息)　basis rate swap

基準貨幣, 基礎貨幣　base money

基欽週期(指物價、生產、就業人數等在40個月的有規律波動, 因約瑟夫・基欽首次詳細研究這種週期而得名)　Kitchin Cycle

基數　cardinal number

基價　base price

基價數　basic

基線預測　base-line projection

基線預算　base-line budget

基線數據　base-line data

基點制, 出貨地加計運費(貨品定價)法　basing-point system (of pricing)

基點訂價　basing-point pricing

基點運費　basing-point freight

基額成本　basic cost

基礎工業　basic industry

基礎工業保護關稅　key industry duty

基礎利息率　prime rate

基礎研究　research in basic science, basic research

基礎協議　basic agreement

黃曲霉素險（海運保險的一種特別附加險）　aflatoxin risk

黃色檢疫旗　yellow flag

黃金本位制　gold standard

黃金存款　gold deposit

黃金危機　gold crisis

黃金券　gold certificate

黃金股票（黃金採礦公司的股票，主要在南非和澳大利亞）gold shares

黃金的符號　token of gold, symbol of gold

黃金的貨幣作用　monetary functions of gold

黃金非貨幣化　demonetization of gold

黃金官價　official gold price

黃金保留條款　gold proviso clause

黃金保值條款　gold guarantee clause

黃金保證　gold guarantee

黃金市場　gold market

黃金平價　gold parity, gold par

黃金外流　gold drain, gold out flow

黃金外滙風潮　gold and foreign exchange turmoil

黃金外滙儲備　gold and foreign exchange reserves

黃金條款（按黃金等值結算的條款）gold clause

黃金部分，黃金份額　gold tranche

黃金部分頭寸　gold tranche position

黃金部分貸款　gold tranche facility

黃金清算基金　gold settlement fund

黃金貼水（指黃金對紙幣的溢價）gold premium

黃金替代帳戶　gold substitution account

黃金期權　option on gold

黃金債券 gold bonds, gold debentures

黃金滙票　gold draft

黃金禁運　gold embargo

黃金價值條款　gold value clause

黃金輸入點　gold import point

黃金輸出點　gold export point

黃金輸送點　gold point

黃金擔保借款　gold collateral loan

黃金總庫　gold pool

黃金雙價制　two-price gold system, two-tier gold price system

黃金證券　gold certificate

黃狗契約（以受僱人不得加入工會為條件的僱傭關係）yellow-dog-contracts

"莫理斯計劃"銀行（指經營一種小型個人放款的金融機構，以創辦人 A. J. Morris 得名）Morris plan banks

荷蘭式拍賣（喊價逐步降低的拍賣）Dutch auction

荷比盧經濟同盟 Benelux Economic Union

荷比盧關稅同盟　Benelux Customs Union

乾船塢　dry dock

乾貨　dry-cargo, dry goods

乾貨船　dry cargo vessel

乾貨櫃/集裝箱　dry container

乾量（容量單位）　dry measure,（重量單位）dry weight

勒索　blackmail

勒索者　blackmailer

逐批結算　load-to-load

逐步激盪術　synectics

逐個商品談判　article-by-article bargaining

逐期一致性　historical consistency

逐期折舊明細表　lapsing schedule

逐項連續取樣　item-by-item sequential sampling plan

逐筆保險單　specific policy

逐月付款的累積購買法　layaway plan

逐年計算折舊　compute depreciation on an annual basis

逐次驗收抽樣法　sequential sampling plan

逐項給予（指按逐項給予的程序給予投資的優惠）　case-by-case

連本帶利　both principal and interest

連保條件　continuation clause

連帶法律關係　joint legal relations

連帶負債　joint and several liabilities

連帶責任　joint responsibility, joint liabilities

連帶費用　joint expense

連帶債務　joint obligation in debt

連帶債權　joint credit

連鎖比例　chain relative

連鎖反應　chain reaction

連鎖合同　chain contract

連鎖折扣　chain discount

連鎖指數　chain index numbers

連鎖倉庫　joint locked warehouse

連鎖效應　chain effect

連鎖商店　chain store, link store

連鎖銀行　chain banking, chain repercussion

連續日（裝卸期條件）　consecutive days

連續成本　running cost

連續式損益表 running form of profit and loss statement

連續契約　continuous contract

連續時（計算裝卸期）　consecutive hours

連續航次　consecutive voyages

連續晴天工作日 consecutive weather working days

連續結轉帳戶　running account

連續裝卸日（風雨和假日均計在內的裝卸期）　running lay days

連續預算　continuous budget

連續償債基金　continual redemption sinking fund

速記打字員　stenotypist

速記員　stenographer

速記機　stenograph

速動資產　quick assets

速運　〔英〕dispatch,〔美〕despatch

速遣費　despatch money, dispatch fee

速遣費按滯期費半數計算　despatch

half demurrage

造冊　tabulation

造船　naval construction

造船工業　shipbuilding industry

造船廠　shipyard

造假市買賣　false market and trading

造假帳　draw up false accounts

造幣廠　mint

捲　roll, coil, reel

控告人　suitor

控告違約　sue for a breach of promise

控制　control

控制式市場試銷　controlled test marketing

控制功能　control function

控制部(電腦)　control unit

控制滙率制度　controlled-exchange system

控制數字　control figure

控制權益, 控制股權　controlling interest

控股公司　controlling company, holding company, parent company

控股公司核數師　principal auditor

控股投資　investment holding

掛失支票　report the loss of check

掛名合夥人　ostensible partner

掛名股東　nominal partner, ostensible partner

掛名董事　nominal director

掛車　trailer

掛帳賒欠　book credit

掛鈎　pegging

掛鈎外滙滙率　pegging exchange rate

掛牌　nominal quotation

掛牌公司(在交易所註冊公開發行股票的公司)　listed company

掛牌利率　nominal rate

掛牌股票總值　total market value of listed shares

掛牌標準　listing standard

掛牌證券　listed security, quoted securities

掛號信　register mail, register letter

掛號郵件　registered mail, registered post

掛號郵件保險　registered mail insurance

授予權責　delegation of authority and responsibility

授權　delegation of authority

授權人員　authorised officer

授權文書　power of attorney, letter of attorney

授權代表　authorized representative

授權代理人　authorized agent

授權付款　authority to pay

授權投資　authorized investment

授權開立滙票　authority to draw

授權證書　certificate of authorization

授權議付, 授權讓購書　authority to negotiate

推定皮重(依當事人間協定推定之重量)　computed tare

推定收入　constructive receipt

推定交貨　constructive delivery, symbolic delivery

推定全損 constructive total loss

推定佔有 constructive possession

推定拒付 constructive dishonour

推定的證據 presumptive evidence

推定結帳 constructive closing

推定價值 constructed value

「推」策略 "push" strategy

推算價格 computed price

推銷費用 marketing expense

推論統計學 inferential statistics

推遲償債期 reschedule the debt

接受外援 receive outside aid

接受佣金 accept a commission

接受低於成本的訂貨 acceptance of an order at below-cost price

接受投資者 investee

接受作證據 admissibility in evidence

接受取樣檢驗 acceptance sampling inspection

接受承付 acceptance and guarantee

接受訂單 accept an order

接受保險 take a risk

接受送達 acceptance of service

接受國 receiving state

接受減價 close with an offer

接受期票 acceptance of promissory notes

接受發盤 accept an offer

接受遠期裝運 accept forward shipment

接到通知即付的股金 callable capital

接後 carried forward

接送貨物服務 pick up and delivery service

接替計劃 under-study plan

接管令 receiving order

接辦企業，兼併 acquisition

接應港 port of recruit

捐客 operator

排水噸位數 displacement tonnage

排他性的管轄條款 exclusive jurisdiction

排他性許可證合同 sole licence contract

排除他人權利 right to exclude all others

掉期 change over

掉期外滙保證 swap exchange guarantee

掉期交易（同時買進和賣出不同期限的同種外幣） swap transaction, swap dealing

探測性技術預測 exploratory forecast

探測性研究 exploratory study

掠奪性要價 predatory pricing

掠奪性傾銷 predatory dumping

掠奪性價格 predatory price

採購 procurement

採購工作週期 procurement cycle

採購方案 procurement scheme

採購成本 procurement cost

採購計劃 procurement program

採購授權書 procurement authorization

採購進程規劃　procurement schedule

採購價格　procurement price

梯式成本　step cost

梯式分攤法　step-ladder method

梯式變動成本　step-variable cost

梯式變動能量成本　step-variable capacity cost

梯形曲線　step curve

桶(容量單位)　barrel

桶號　barrel number

桶塞脫落(提單批語)　bung off

[｜]

國內生產總值　gross domestic product (GDP)

國內市場　home market

國內投資　domestic investment

國內法　municipal law, domestic law

國內消費商品進口報關　consumption entry

國內票據　domestic bill

國內稅　internal taxes

國內發票　inland invoice

國內滙兌　inland exchange, domestic exchange

國內滙兌開發　domestic money order issuing

國外支付　external payment

國外代理人　foreign agent

國外引進項目　projects whose equipment and technology are introduced from abroad

國外付款滙票　bill drawn for payment abroad

國外存款　foreign deposit

國外同業存款　deposit by foreign correspondents

國外合資事業協議　foreign joint venture agreement

國外投資　foreign investment

國外投資淨值　net foreign investment

國外投資氣候　foreign investment climate

國外航空郵件發送時間表　outgoing airmail schedules

國外借款還本付息支出 expenditures for repaying the principal and interest on foreign loans

國外借款餘額　total of outstanding foreign loans

國外發行債券籌資國內使用　out to in external bond

國外發行債券籌資國外使用　out to out external bond

國外發票　foreign invoice

國外貿易　foreign trade

國外期票　foreign promissory note

國外短期資產　foreign short-term assets

國外稅額的減除　foreign tax credit

國外債券　external bond

國外資產淨值　net external assets

國民支出　national expenditure

國民生產力　per capita productivity

國民生產淨值　net national product

(NNP)

國民生產總值　gross national product (GNP)

國民生產總值消除價格波動指數　gross national product deflator

國民生產總值差距　gross national product gap

國民收入　national income

國民收入生產額　amount of national income produced

國民收入會計　national income accounting

國民待遇　national treatment

國民待遇原則　principle of national treatment

國民經濟　national economy

國民總支出　gross national expenditure (GNE)

國民總收入　gross national income

國民總所得　gross national dividend

國民總供給　gross national supply

國民總需求　gross national demand (GND)

國民總儲蓄　gross national savings

國有化　nationalization

國有公司 government-owned corporation

國別風險　country risk

國定及協定稅則　national and conventional tariff

國定關稅　national tariff

國庫 state treasury, exchequer, national purse

國庫支票　treasury check

國庫存款　treasury deposit

國庫收據，國庫存單　treasury deposit receipt

國庫投資累收證(美國無息國庫券之一種，以財政部收據形式的庫券)　treasury investment growth receipts

國庫投資與借款 treasury investment and loan

國庫券 state treasury bonds, national treasury bills

國庫券應收證(美國以財政部收據形式的一種無息庫券，創於 1982 年 8 月) certificates of accrual on treasury securities

國庫定期債券　treasury term bond

國庫盈餘　treasury surplus

國家干預經濟　state intervention in the economy

國家信用　national credit

國家稅　national tax

國家稅率　national tariff

國家資本　national capital

國家預算　national budget

國家預算總支出 total state budgeted expenditure

國家預算總收入　total state budgetary revenues

國家標準　national standards

國貨　native goods

國稅　central tax, national revenue

國債　national debt

國際大石油公司 international major oil companies

國際大米委員會　International Rice Commission

國際小麥協定　International Wheat Agreement

國際工業標準分類　International Standard Industrial Classification

國際化　internationalize

國際分工　international division of labour

國際分保業務　international reinsurance

國際支付　international payment

國際公法　international public law

國際公路　international highway

國際水道　international waterway

國際可比性　international comparability

國際可可協定　International Cocoa Agreement

國際民用航空組織　International Civil Aviation Organization (ICAO)

國際卡特爾　international cartel

國際市場　international market

國際市場萎縮　shrinking international market

國際收支,國際收支平衡表　balance of international payments, balance of payments

國際收支失衡　balance of payments disequilibrium

國際收支危機　balance of payments crisis

國際收支狀況　balance of payment position

國際收支紀律　balance of payments discipline

國際收支逆差　balance of payment deficit, unfavourable balance, passive balance

國際收支順差　balance of payment surplus, favourable balance, active balance

國際收支援助　balance of payment assistance

國際收支資本帳戶　capital account of balance-of-payment

國際收支經常帳戶　current account of balance of payment

國際收支調整　balance of payment adjustment

國際收支調整機制　mechanism of adjustment of balance of payments

國際羊毛事務局　International Wool Secretariat

國際合作　international cooperation

國際仲裁　international arbitration

國際仲裁庭　Court of International Arbitration

國際多種方式聯運　international multimodal transportation

國際多邊貸款　international multilateral loans

國際行銷　international marketing

國際更正權　international right of correction

國際私法　private international law

國際判例法　international case-law

國際辛迪加　international syndicate

國際技術合作　international technical cooperation

國際技術轉讓　international transfer of technology

國際技術轉讓行動守則　international code of conduct for the transfer of technology

國際批發貿易中心　International Centre Wholesale Trade

國際均勢　international equilibrium

國際投資　international investment

國際投資托拉斯　international investment

國際投資糾紛解決中心　International Centre for the Settlement of Investment Disputes

國際投資專業化　international investment specialization

國際投資銀行　International Investment Bank (IIB)

國際法　international law

國際法協會　International Law Association

國際法院　The International Court of Justice

國際性投標　international tender

國際性協調和調整　international harmonization and adjustment

國際性破產　international insolvency

國際空航　international aerial navigation

國際咖啡協定(1962年9月28日)　International Coffee Agreement

國際易貨貿易　international barter

國際爭端　international dispute

國際拍賣　international auction

國際招標　international bidding

國際金融中心　international financial centre

國際金融公司　International Finance Corporation (IFC)

國際金融機構　international financial institution

國際供應承諾　international supply commitment

國際承購應收帳款聯合組織　Factor Chain International

國際定額　international quota

國際信用保險聯會　Union D'Assureurs des Credits Internationanx

國際計量單位　international units of measurement

國際砂糖協定　International Sugar Agreement

國際版權協定　International Copyright Agreement

國際茶葉委員會　International Tea Committee

國際特快專遞郵件　express mail service, courier service

國際特惠關稅　International Preferential Duty

國際海事法　international maritime law

國際海事委員會　International Maritime Committee

國際海域　international waters, international sea area

國際海運商會 International Chamber of Shipping

國際航空 international airways

國際航空運輸協定(1944年12月7日) International Air Transport Agreement

國際航空運輸協會 International Air Transport Association (IATA)

國際航空線 international airlines

國際航運公司 international shipping company

國際航運保險聯合會 International Union of Marine Insurance

國際航運商會 International Chamber of Shipping

國際航線飛機保險 insurance for aircraft on international route

國際流動性 international liquidity

國際借貸 international borrowing

國際借款契約委員會 International Loan Contract Committee

國際租賃 international lease

國際紡織品貿易協議 Arrangement Regarding International Trade in Textiles

國際展覽局 International Exhibition Bureau

國際郵包運輸 international parcel post transport

國際郵政滙票 international postal money order

國際專利合作條約 patent cooperation treaty

國際黃金總庫 international gold pool

國際貨物發運人協會 International Federational of Freight Forwarder Association

國際貨物買賣統一法 Uniform Law on the International Sales of Goods

國際貨運託運書 shippers letter of instruction

國際貨幣 international currency, international money

國際貨幣市場，國際短期資金市場 international money market

國際貨幣改革 international monetary reform

國際貨幣制度 international monetary system

國際貨幣政策 international monetary policy

國際貨幣秩序 international monetary order

國際貨幣基金協定 Articles of Agreement of the International Monetary Fund

國際貨幣基金理事會 Committee of the Board of Governors of the Fund

國際貨幣基金組織 International Monetary Fund (IMF)

國際貨幣基金組織出資份額 International Monetary Fund quota

國際通商 international commerce

國際寄存單據 international depositary receipt [IDR]

國際商品協定 International Commodity Agreement

國際商務管理 international business administration

國際商會(總部設在巴黎) International Chamber of Commerce

國際商會跟單信用證統一慣例 Uniform Customs and Practice for Documentary Credits (ICC)

國際商業 international business

國際商業交易所 International Commercial Exchange

國際商業企業 international business enterprise

國際商業清算所 International Commodities Clearing House

國際開發協會 International Development Association

國際開發署(美國政府設立的直屬國務院的對外援助機構) Agency for International Development

國際清算 international clearing

國際清算銀行 Bank for International Settlements (BIS)

國際清償力,國際清償手段 international liquidity

國際清償單位 international liquidity units

國際票據法 International Law of Bills

國際勞工組織 international labour organization

國際換日線,日界線 international date line

國際援助 international aid

國際貿易 international trade

國際貿易中心 International Trade Centre

國際貿易地區分佈 international trade by regions

國際貿易乘數 international trade multiplier

國際貿易值 value of international trade

國際貿易量 quantum of international trade

國際貿易商品結構 composition of world trade

國際貿易組織 International Trade Organization

《國際貿易組織憲章》 Charter for the International Trade Organization

國際貿易術語解釋通則(1953年) International Rules for the Interpretation of Trade Terms (1953), International Chamber of Commerce Terms

國際貿易標準分類 Standard International Trade Classification (SITC)

國際貿易環境 environment of international trade

國際發展問題獨立委員會 Independent Committee for International Development Problems

國際貸款機構 international lending institutions

國際集裝箱安全公約(1972年12月2日) International Convention for

Safe Container

國際集裝箱局　International Container Bureau

國際復興開發銀行，世界銀行　International Bank for Reconstruction and Development, World Bank

國際復興開發銀行協定　Articles of Agreement of the International Bank for Reconstruction and Development

國際博覽會　international exhibition, international fair

國際資本市場，國際長期資金市場　international capital market

國際資本轉移　international capital movement

國際資金來源　international sources of funds

國際資產管理　international assets management

國際滙兌　international remittance and exchange, international exchange

國際滙兌經營者協會（總會設於巴黎）Association Cambiste Internationale

國際滙票　international bill of exchange

國際債券　international bonds

國際債券商協會（總會設於蘇黎世）Association of International Bond Dealers

國際債務　international obligation (or debt)

國際債務信貸　international debt facility

國際債務差額 balance of international indebtedness

國際會計　international accounting

國際會計專業協調委員會　International Coordination Committee for the Accounting Profession

國際會計標準委員會　International Accounting Standard Committee

國際微型電路卡協會（歐洲金融機構組織的一種關於國際性通用的標準磁卡設計研究的協會）International Association for the Microcircuit Card

國際電信聯盟　International Telecommunication Union (ITU)

國際電報　oversea telegrams

國際電報價目表　rate for overseas telegraph service

國際電傳　oversea telex

國際電話價目表　rates for overseas radiophone service

國際過境　international transit

國際經濟合作　international economic cooperation

國際經濟合作會議　International Economic Cooperation Conference

國際經濟秩序　international economic order

國際經濟發展合作委員會　Council for International Economic Development

國際經濟戰　international economic war

國際經營者服務隊(受國際開發署援助的訓練發展中國家的技術人員的一個非營利機構) International Executive Service Corps

國際需求平衡 equation of international demand

國際銀行便利，國際銀行業務設施 International Banking Facility (IBF)

國際銀行家貿易協會(1921年由美國幾家從事國際業務的銀行組成，現有150家大銀行為正式會員，100家外國銀行為附屬成員) Bankers' Association for Foreign Trade

國際銀團　consortium bank

國際銀團貸款　international syndicate loans

國際慣例 international conventions, international usage

國際價值　international value

國際鋁礬土協會 International Bauxite Association

國際標準　international standards

國際標準工業分類 International Standard Industrial Classification

國際標準化組織 International Organization for Standardization

國際熱線傳真服務 Toll-Free International Fax

國際錫協定 International Tin Agreement

國際機構　international body

國際儲備的創造　international reserve creation

國際儲備貨幣　international reserve currency

國際儲備資產　international reserve assets

國際儲備標準 international reserves criterion

國際環境 international environment

國際聯合運輸 international combined transport

國際雙重課稅　international double taxation

國際禮讓　comity of nations

國際關務手續簡化及一致化公約(即：京都公約) International Convention on the Simplification an Harmonization of Customs Procedures (Kyoto Convention)

國際證券交易所聯會(1961年成立，1987年共有會員33個) The Federation International des Bourse de Valeurs—FIBV

國際競爭規則 rules of international competition

國際鐵路聯運 international railway through transport

國際鐵路聯運單　international through waybill

國境關稅　frontier customs dues

國營公用事業　government utility

累加利息　cumulative interest

累計欠債　accumulated debt

累計折舊　accumulated depreciation

累計表　accumulation schedule

累計消費基金　aggregate consumption funds

累計帳戶　accumulation account

累計資本　accumulated capital

累退稅　regressive tax

累進付款　progressive payment

累進稅　progressive tax

累進償付貸款（規定貸款初期債務本息償付較低，甚至可能是負數，然後逐步增加）　graduate payment loan

累積支出　accumulated outlay

累積分配　accumulated distribution

累積比較　accumulative comparison

累積平均數　progressive average

累積收益 accumulated earnings, accumulated income, accumulated retained earnings, accumulated profits

累積投票制　cumulative voting system

累積投票權（少數股權股東集中投票權選舉的投票方法）　cumulative voting

累積股本　cumulative capital stock

累積股份 cumulative stock, accumulative stock

累積股息　cumulative dividend

累積信用證　cumulative credit

累積紅利　cumulative bonus

累積盈餘　accumulated surplus

累積差誤　cumulative error

累積量　cumulant

累積損失　accumulated loss

累積增長　cumulative growth

累積頻數，累積機率　cumulative frequency

累積頻數分配　cumulative frequency distribution

累積優先股　cumulative preferred stock

累積虧絀　accumulative deficit

累積擴散指數　cumulative diffusion index

累積償債基金　cumulative sinking fund, accumulative sinking fund

累積總需求　aggregate demand

累積總需求函數　aggregate demand function

累積總需求價格　aggregate demand price

累積額　accumulation

略式訂貨單（客戶所持有的在撤銷前仍然有效的買賣訂單）　good till cancelled order

野雞股份公司（指不合格的股票公司）　bogus stock company

常年定期查帳　recurring audit

常規年底盤存　regular end-of-year inventory

常規交割（在紐約證券交易所證券成交後，售方經紀人需在第五個交易日向購方經紀人交付證券並收款）　regular way delivery

常規例外法則　law of exception to routine

常規能源 conventional energy sources

常規檢查 routine inspection

常務董事 managing director, executive director

常態分佈 normal distribution

常態依賴 normal dependency

常態相關 normal correlation

常態相關面 normal correlation surface

常態機率 normal probability

常駐代表 resident representative

常駐採購員 resident buyer

常衡盎司 ounce avoirdupois

帳,帳戶 account

帳戶分類 classification of accounts

帳戶年度 fiscal year, account year

帳戶名稱,會計科目 account title, name of account

帳戶式損益表 account form of income statement

帳戶式資產負債表 account form of balance sheet

帳戶結清借方餘額 closing debit balance in account

帳戶結清餘額 closing balance in account

帳戶滾存餘額結單 running balance statement of account

帳戶編號(法),帳戶代號化 symbolization of accounts

帳冊 account books

帳目不清 accounts are not in order

帳目不實 fale itemization of accounts

帳目分析 account analysis

帳外物資,隱匿資產 hidden assets

帳外負債 liabilities out of book

帳外資產 non-ledger assets, off-the-book property

帳面欠債 book debt

帳面赤字 deficit on the books

帳面利益 paper profit

帳面利潤 book profit

帳面投資報酬率 accounting rate of return, book value rate, unajusted rate of return

帳面信用 book credit

帳面盈餘 book surplus

帳面原值 gross book value

帳面記錄 book entry

帳面結存價值,現存價值,抵押品作價 carrying value

帳面損失 book loss

帳面資產 ledger assets

帳面價值(或成本) book value (or cost)

帳面價值股票 book-value shares

帳面盤存,帳面存貨 book inventory

帳面盤存法 book inventory method

帳頁參考,單據號數參考 folio reference

帳單 bill

帳項 accounting item

帳款 funds on account

帳款結清 account settled

帳簿 account books, accounting books, ledger

帳齡分析表 aging schedule

帳齡分類，帳齡分佈情況　age-dist-ribution

虛市交易　bogus transaction

虛利　nominal profit

虛抬利益，虛抬利潤　inflated profit

虛帳戶，名義帳戶　nominal account

虛假收入　spurious revenues

虛假的陳述　false statement

虛假索賠　false claim

虛假填報（貨物運單）　false billing

虛假需求　fictitious use

虛假聲明　false declaration

虛假購買力　artificial purchasing power

虛假繁榮　false prosperity

虛稅　false tax

虛無假設　null hypothesis

虛牌價　nominal quotation

虛構成本　fictitious cost

虛構帳目　fictitious account

虛構資本，虛擬資本　fictitious capital

虛構價格　fictitious price

虛偽抬頭人　fictitious payee

虛賣　wash sale

虛盤　offer without engagement

虛價　nominal price

虛數　unrealizable figure

虛擬市場　dummy market

虛擬受票人　fictitious payee

虛擬活動　dummy activity

虛擬貨幣　ideal money

虛變數　dummy variables

開（黃金成色單位，一般 5-24 開）　karat

開口合同（即未定數量的合同）　open-end contract

開口式遮蔽甲板船　open shelter-decker

開口抵押權　open end mortgage

開口協議（指無滿期日的協議）　open end agreement

開口訂單　open order, open indent

開口保險單，不定額保險單（大批貨物分批裝運，船名未定的保險單）　open policy

開工不足　operate under capacity

開工率　operating ratio

開支　out-going, expenditure

開支票　write a check

開支減少政策（調整國際收支的政策）　expenditure-reducing policy

開支轉移政策　expenditure-switching policy

開戶存款　initial deposit

開市　open the market

開市訂單（要求在開始交易時在開市價範圍內買或賣出商品合約之定單）　market on opening

開市執行（表明盡可能開市時執行定單）　on opening

開市價　opening quotation

開立信用狀　open a letter of credit

開立帳戶　open an account

開放式商店　free-standing stores

開放式倉庫　open style

開放性系統　open system

開放抵押（指憑原抵押品可再行借貸）　open-end mortgage

開放信託投資　open-end investment trust

開放港口　open port

開放經濟　open economy

開放模型　open model

開明的態度　open-mindedness

開始分錄，開始記錄　opening entry

開始認購比率　opening-to-application ratio

開信用證申請書　application for letter of credit

開除，解僱　dismiss

開除工人　dismiss labourers, fire labourers

開票人　drawer

開設信用證保證金　margin money

開窗包裝　die cut pack

開發　development

開發中國家，發展中國家　developing countries

開發成本　developed cost

開發性行銷　pioneering marketing

開發性項目　exploration projects

開發委員會　Development Committee

開發放款　development loan

開發資金　development capital

開發資源　exploit natural resources

開發銀行　development bank

開單和記帳制　bill and charge system

開源　raise income

開業會計師　public accounting licensed accountant

開蓋貨櫃/集裝箱　open top container

開盤(交易所用語)　opening

開盤行市　opening quotation

開盤叫價　opening call

開盤滙率　opening rate

開盤價　opening prices, opening rate

開標　open tender

開標日　opening date of tender

開價　opening prices, initial price

開辦費，開辦成本　organization costs, preliminary expense

開環系統　open-loop system

開證人　opener

開證申請人　accredited buyer

開證地點承兌信用證　issuing point acceptance credit

開證銀行　opening bank, issuing bank

間接人工　indirect labour

間接人工成本　indirect labour cost

間接分攤法　step-down method, step-ladder method

間接出口　indirect export

間接成本　indirect cost

間接收益　indirect yield

間接交貨　indirect delivery

間接佔有　indirect possession

間接材料　indirect materials

間接投資(指僅買入股票，不參與經營)　indirect investment, portfolio investment

間接負債　indirect liabilities

間接保護　indirect protection

間接效用　indirect utility

間接套利　indirect arbitrage

間接套滙　indirect arbitrage

間接流通　indirect flows

間接稅　indirect tax

間接費用,管理費用,營業開支　overhead

間接測定　proxy measure

間接貿易　indirect trade

間接買賣　indirect business

間接報價法(指以外幣標價的)　indirect quotation of exchange rate

間接損失　consequential damage, indirect loss

間接滙兌率　indirect rate

間接滙票　indirect bill (paper)

間接滙價　indirect quotation

間接需要品　goods of second order

間接管理費　management indirect costs

間接擔保品　indirect securities

間接證據,參考證據　circumstantial evidence, indirect evidence

間斷資料　discrete data

間斷數列　discrete series

間斷變量　discrete variable

閒散資金,游資　idle money

閒散勞動力　idle labour

閒置生產能力　idle capacity

閒置能量成本　idle capacity cost

閒置現金　idle cash

閒置時間,停工時間　idle time

閒置時間補充率　idle time supplementary rate

閒置設備　idle equipment

閒置資金　idle fund, laid-up capital

閒置資源效果　idle resources effect

閒置噸位　laid up tonnage

啤打係數(一種統計數據,用以推測股價對大市升降的敏感程度,又稱"二位係數")　Beta coefficient, β coefficient

啤打函數　Beta function, β function

啣(英制等於:112磅;美制:等於100磅)　hundredweight (cwt)

貶低　debasement

貶值　devaluation, depreciation of value

貶值貨幣　depreciated money

敗訴　losing a suit

販莊　warehouse

販賣商　dealer

販賣術　salesmanship

帶利息　cum interest

帶股息,帶息股價,附有股利　cum dividend, dividend-on

帶息股票　cum coupon

帶權股價(指有購買新股票權利的股價)　cum right

帶電滙條款即期信用證　sight credit with T/T reimbursement clause

帶購買股票權的債券　bonds with stock purchase warrants

情況證據,旁證　circumstantial evidence

情報來源　information source

情報服務　information service

情報處理　information processing

情報貯存　information storage

情報資料　information documents

情報檢索　information retrieval

將來的即期滙率　future spot rate

將來的權利　vested in interest

將來值　future value

將到期負債　maturing liability

將現金或證券存於經紀人做抵押之要求　margin call

將票據權利轉讓他人　indorse over to

[﹚]

"悠悠"股票(指價格像兒童玩具"悠悠"那樣上下波動幅度很大、很不穩定的高價特種股票)　"yo-yo" stocks

售出租回合約　sell-and-leaseback agreement

售出發票　invoice outward

售後服務　service after sale

售貨回扣　sales rebates and allowance

售貨合同　sales contract

售貨員　salesman, sales clerk

售貨單　sales note

售貨確認書　sale confirmation

售貨競爭　sales contest

售短購長的債務調換(指賣出短期債券，買進長期債券的調期交易)　unfunding

售價總數　gross proceeds

側面升遷　lateral promotion

側壁全開式貨櫃/集裝箱　open side container

偏向誤差　biased error

偏於一方　one-sided

偏差, 傾向　bias

偏誤估計　biased estimate

偶生收入　non-recurring income

偶生成本　non-recurring cost

偶生盈利　non-recurring gains

偶生損益　non-recurring profit and loss

偶然交易　casual business

偶然收益　incidental revenue

偶然費用　incidental expense

偶然損益　non-recurring profit and loss

偶然錯誤　accidental slip

偶發性傾銷　sporadic dumping

停工成本　shut-down cost

停工費用　idle time cost

停止支付支票　stop payment on a check, stopping payment of check, stopped check

停止令　order of suppression

停止出售證券　suspension of the sale of securities

停止付款　suspension of payment

停止付款通知書　notice dishonour

停止投資　disinvestment

停止執行　stay of execution

停止發行　stoppage of publication

停止進行訴訟　stay of proceedings

停止營業　suspension of business

《停一走》政策(指在生產過程中，交替採用刺激和抑制的政策)　stop

(-and)-go policy

停泊　anchor, call at a port

停泊日記　port log

停泊在港　laid up in port

停泊退費　laid up return

停泊處　moorings

停泊稅　mooring charge

停泊點　mooring point

停泊權　shore rights

停板定單(交易所用語)　limit order

停板價(升或跌)(交易所每日價格波動限額)　limit (up or down)

停租　off-hire

停租條款　off-hire clause

停租船　suspension of hire

停租證書　off-hire certificate

停留條款　touch and stay clause

停航退費　lay up refund

停業　termination of business, wind up business, close down

停業損失　stop-loss, loss from suspension

停運權(賣方的一種權利，如發現買主無力付款時對已處於運輸中的貨物可停止發貨)　stoppage in transit

停滯　standstill, stagnation

停滯政策　standstill policy

停滯膨脹　stagflation

停靠港，寄泊港　port of call

健康保險　health insurance

健康檢查　health examination

健康證明書　certificate of health

假分紅(指動用資本金分紅)　bogus dividend

假支票　stumer, forged check

假日工資　holiday pay

假扣押　sequestration

假收購　not sales in real sense

假定成本　assumed cost, hypothetical cost

假定利息　hypothetical interest

假定負債，承當負債　assumed liability

假定起息日　focal date

假定發行(指某一證券已授權發行，但並未實際發行，其交易是附帶條件的)　when issued

假冒背書　forged endorsement

假冒簽署　forged signature

假借信用　pledge the credit of

假帳　false account

假設　hypothesis

假設測算法 hypothesis test approach (to audit)

假造支票　[美俚]hang paper

假造的文書單據　forged documents

假造債券　forgery bond

假票據　false bill

假鈔票　forged note, stumer

假想基金　imaginary fund

假擔保　pseudo-guarantee

假證券　straw bond

偷工減料　jerry

偷稅 tax evasion, evade taxes, dodge a tax

偷稅人　tax dodger

偷盜保險　burglary

偷竊及提貨不着險　risk of theft, pilferage and non-delivery (T.P.N.D.)

做多頭投機　speculate on a rise

做投機買賣　speculate

做空頭投機　speculate on a fall

偽造(指簽字，證據等)　forgery

偽造文件　falsification of document

偽造支票　forged check

偽造股票　forged stocks

偽造品　counterfeits

偽造背書　forged endorsement

偽造記錄，假帳　false entry

偽造帳目　falsify accounts

偽造貨幣　counterfeit currency, false coin, queer money

偽造紙幣　counterfeit note, forged paper currency

偽造單據　forged document

偽造簽字　forged signature

偽幣製造者，偽造憑證者　forger

偽證　false testimony

術語，專有名詞　terminology

從"後門"進行公開市場業務活動　"at the back door"

從"前門"進行公開市場業務活動　"at the front"

從量稅　specific duty

從業者　practitioner

從債務　secondary liability

從源課稅(不管納稅人的國籍屬何國，也不管居住何國，只要其收入來源於某一國，該國就有權對其在該國取得的收入賦稅)　tax at source

從價　[拉]ad val, ad valorem

從價法　ad valorem method

從價稅　ad valorem duties

從價稅率　ad valorem tariff

從價等值　ad valorem equivalent

從價運費　ad valorem freight

從屬信用證　ancillary credit, subsidiary credit, secondary credit

從屬費用　incidental charges

從屬條款(債券發行條款，一旦借款人進行清理，股東的權利排列在某些或所有無擔保債權人的權利之後)　subordination clause

船來品　exotic

船上用品稅單　bill of store

船上交貨，離岸價格　free on board (F.O.B.)

船上交貨計價法　FOB pricing

船上交貨提單　on deck bill of lading

船方不負責卸貨費　free out (f.o.)

船方不負責裝卸貨費　free in and out (f.i.o.)

船方不負責裝卸、理艙費　free in, out and stowed (f.i.o.s.)

船方不負責裝貨費　free in (f.i.)

船方不負責駁運費　free into barge

船方責任條款　owner's liability clause

船主，船舶所有人　shipowner

船汗損失　sweat damage

船名錄　register of shipping

船身簸動　pitching

船長不法行為　barratry of the master

船長申報單　captain's declaration

船長海事報告　captain's sea protest

船東保賠協會　Protection and Indemnity Association (P & I Club)

船東保賠協會會員　the member of P & I Club

船東責任限制　limitation shipowner's liability

船的適航性　seaworthiness of ship

船的龍骨　keel

船租　charter hire

船級　ship's class, ship's classification

船級委員會　classification committee

船級條款(不合格貨船要付額外保險費)　classification clause

船級證書副本　copy of class certificate

船員名冊　crew list

船殼　hull

船舷　ship's rail

船舶大修　overhauling

船舶失事　shipwreck

船舶失踪　ship missing

船舶吃水　draught

船舶放空　ship in ballast

船舶免疫證書　clean bill of health

船舶抵押貸款　bottomry

船舶抵押契約　bottomry bond

船舶承租人支付的費用　charterer pays dues

船舶定級社　classification society

船舶長期代理　agency on long-term basis

船舶受載日　laydays date

船舶牲口清單　cattle manifest

船舶重量滿載　down to her marks

船舶建造險　builders risks

船舶保險　hull insurance

船舶航次代理　agency on trip basis

船舶淨註冊噸位　net registered tonnage

船舶排水量　displacement tonnage

船舶商務記錄　carrier statement

船舶深艙　deeptanks

船舶國籍證明書　certificate of registry

船舶註冊港口,船籍港　home port, port of registry

船舶註冊噸位　registered tonnage

船舶解約日　cancelling date

船舶載貨量　cargo carrying capacity

船舶碰撞互有過失條款(英國倫敦保險協會保單一條有關貨物運輸責任條款)　both to blame collision clause

船舶管理人　ship's husband

船舶截載日期　closing date

船舶適航證書　certificate of seaworthiness

船舶積載圖　cargo plan, stowage plan

船舶總註冊噸位　gross register tonnage

船舶檢驗證書　certificate of ship inspection

船舶證件(海商法規定船舶應具有的各種證件)　ship's paper

船貨抵押　respondentia

船貨抵押借款(在一部份貨物安全運到時才償還的借款)　respondentia

船貨配載計劃　cargo planning

船貨容積載運量　cargo cubic capacity

船貨登記簿　cargo book

船期表　sailing schedule

船塢　dock

船樓，上層建築　superstructure

船艙　hold

船艙潮汗　ship's sweat

船邊交貨　shipside delivery, alongside delivery

船邊到船邊 shipside to shipside, alongside to alongside

船齡　age of vessel

船齡折價　age depreciation

船體保險單　hull policy

符合商銷品質　good merchantable quality (g.m.q.)

符號檢定法　sign test

第一手(指商品的最初持有人)　first hands

第一代計算機　first generation computer

第一年100%的資本投資減稅(英國對租賃的一種稅收優惠)　100% first year capital allowances

第一次付郵　by first mail

第一次交割通知日(指期貨市場空頭通知貨物即將交割)　first notice day

第一次股東大會　statutory meeting

第一次繳付　first call

第一危險保險　first loss insurance

第一抵押債券　first mortgage bond

第一抵押權　first mortgage

第一抵押權債券 first mortgage bonds

第一受益人　first beneficiary

第一型誤差　type I error

第一流商行　first class business firm

第一通知日(在期貨市場發生交收實貨商品通知的第一日)　first notice day

第一產業　primary industry

第一稅率　first tariff

第一路　first via

第一期付款　down payment

第一期保費　initial call

第一勢差　first moment

第一逾額　first excess

第一溢額分保 first surplus reinsurance

第一溢額分保合同 first surplus reinsurance treaty

第一優先留置權　first and paramount lien

第二世界銀行(國際發展協會的簡稱)　Second World Bank, International Development Association

第二位的當事人　secondary party

第二位責任，從債務　secondary liability

第二抵押　second mortgage

第二受益人　second beneficiary

第二負債(從負債)　secondary liability

第二型誤差　type II error

第二副本　duplicate

第二產業　secondary industry

第二準備金　second reserves, secondary reserve

第二運貨人　second carrier

第二溢額分保　second surplus reinsurance

第二聯未付（指滙票在第二聯未兌付
時正本才能兌付）　second unpaid,
second of the same tenor and date
unpaid

第二聯滙票　second bill of exchange

第二優先股　second-preferred

第三工作組（經合組織的一個小組，
任務是監視成員國國際收支動向和
一般經濟情況）　Working Parity
Three

第三方權利　［拉］jus tertii

第三世界　Third World

第三代貨櫃/集裝箱船　third gener-
ation container

第三市場（在交易所外按證券行市進
行大量證券交易的市場）　the
third market

第三者保險　third party insurance

第三者條款　third party clause

第三者責任　third party liability

第三者責任法定保險 compulsory third
party insurance

第三者提單　third party B/L

第三託運人　third party shipper

第三副本　triplicate

第三國承運人　third flag carrier

第三國進口　third country import

第三國補貼　third country subsidization

第三產業　tertiary industry

第三債務人（指根據法院扣押令扣押
債務人財產者）　garnishee

第三債務人扣款令　garnishee order

第三聯滙票　third of exchange

第三優先股　third preference share

第四市場（機構投資者和一些巨型公
司以高價購買交易所中席位，專門
從事自己各種股票和債券買賣活動
的市場，又稱"四級市場"。）the
fourth market

第四窗口　fourth window

第四副本　quadruplicate

第四勢差　fourth moment

第五副本　quintuplicate

第六副本　sextuplicate

第七副本　septuplicate

第八副本　octuplicate

第 Q 條規定　Regulation Q

笨重貨物　bulky goods

猛漲、激漲　sharp rise, shot to

貪污盜竊　graft and embezzlement,
graft and theft

貪圖暴利，投機活動　profiteering

夠本分析　break-even analysis

夠本產量　units of product to break
even

夠本圖，營業平衡圖 break-even chart
(or diagram)

脫水　dehydration

脫媒（指大量資金游離金融機構而
去追逐市場的高利率）　disinter-
mediation

脫鈎　shut out

脫價（指期權或期貨合約的證券或商
品的協定價格高於或低於市價）
out-of-the-money

脫離控制的市場　runaway market

途耗　ullage

透支　overdraft, overdraw

透支利息　overdraft interest

透支限額　limit of overdrawn account

透支帳戶　overdraft account

透字簽名,穿孔簽字 perforated signature

袋裝　in bags, bagging

袋鼠船（子母船之俗稱）　kangaroo ship

袋號　bag number

釣餌式廣告　bait advertising

釣餌式推銷法（指登廉價貨廣告，誘顧客上門購買貴貨）bait-and-switch selling

敏感市場　sensitive market

敏感性股票　cyclical stocks

敏感性訓練　sensitivity training

敏感性商品　sensitive goods

敏感性產品　sensitive product

敏感度　sensitiveness

敏感度分析　sensitivity analysis

移動平均成本法 moving average cost method

移動平均數　moving average

移動加權平均法　moving weighted average method

移動均衡　moving equilibrium

移動差距圖　the moving-range chart

移動基期　shifting base period

移動裝配法 moving assembly method

動力　motive power

動力費用　power expenses

動作研究的技術　techniques of motion study

動作研究效果　effects of motion study

動作經濟原則 motion-economy principle

動產　movable property, personal property, ambulatory chattel, personal estate, personality

動產文書　chattel paper

動產和不動產　movable and immovable property

動產抵押　chattel mortgage

動產抵押據　bill of sale

動產抵押權　chattel mortgage

動產租金　rent on movable estate

動產稅　movable property tax

動產訴訟　personal action

動產質權　pledge of movables

動植物檢疫　quarantine of animals and plants

動態分析　dynamic analysis

動態比率　dynamic ratio

動態平衡　dynamic equilibrium

動態規則　dynamic programming

動態結構　dynamic structure

動態經濟　dynamic economy

動態經濟學　dynamic economics

動態需求曲線 dynamic demand curve

動態數列　dynamic series

動態數量管理 dynamic quantity control

動機　motive

動機研究　motivation research
郵包收據　parcel post receipt
郵包保險　parcel post insurance
郵政日戳　post office stamp
郵政信箱　post office box
郵政滙票　postal money order, postal order
郵政截止日　mail day
郵政儲蓄存款　post office savings deposits
郵船, 郵輪　mail steamer, mail boat
郵售　mail order selling
郵售商店　mail house
郵寄樣品　mail sample
郵寄證實書　mail confirmation
郵程利息　transit interest
郵運保險　insurance for postal sendings
郵資總付　postage paid licensee
郵戳　postmark
郵購, 郵售　mail order
郵購部　mail order department
郵購商行, 郵售商行　mail order establishment, mail order house
貨主不明的貨物, 無人提取的貨物 unclaimed goods
貨主負責破損險 owner's risk of breakage
貨主負責損壞險 owner's risk of damage
貨主負責漏損險 owner risk of leakage
貨主負擔風險條款 owner's risk clause
貨主裝載　shipper's load

貨交承運人　free carrier
貨安抵裝運港才有效　subject to safe arrival of goods at port of shipment
貨存關棧(納稅可提)　goods in bond
貨物　cargo, goods
貨物出入口報告書　bill of entry
貨物名稱和規格　name of commodity and specification
貨物收據　articles receipt
貨物吞吐　cargoes loaded and unloaded
貨物所在地法　[拉]lex rei sitae
貨物所有權文據　document of title to goods
貨物承保人　cargo insurer, cargo underwriter
貨物來源證　original certificate
貨物保險　cargo insurance
貨物保險單　cargo insurance policy
貨物保險費　cargo premium
貨物保險費率　cargo insurance rate
貨物留置權　lien on goods
貨物情況(記述)　description of the goods
貨物理賠　cargo claims
貨物稅　excise tax
貨物短缺　short delivery
貨物集散地　entrepot
貨物裝卸　cargo handling
貨物裝船前預付款　advance packing credit
貨物裝運單元化　unitization of cargo
貨物運送人　forwarder

貨物運費　goods freight

貨物運輸保險　cargo transportation insurance

貨物與勞務　goods and services

貨物毀損證書　certificate of breakage

貨物標誌　cargo marking

貨物噸　cargo ton

貨物檢驗　cargo survey

貨物轉口　cargo transhipment

貨物轉運　cargo transportation

貨到付款　payment against arrival, cash on delivery

貨到時淨值　net arrived value

貨倉　godown

貨船　cargo ship, cargo freighter, cargo boat

貨袋破裂　bursting of bags

貨款保收業務(當代流行的新國際貿易方式，由第三者承購單據並保收貨款，又稱貨款保付代理業務或承購應收帳款業務)　factoring

貨款保收商協會(英國1976年成立的)　Association of British Factoring

貨運中途停運權　stoppage in transit

貨運飛機　airfreighter

貨運單　bill of freight

貨運單據　shipping documents

貨損理算　cargo damage adjustment

貨損檢驗　cargo damage survey

貨幣一體化　monetary integration

貨幣升值　currency revaluation, appreciation

貨幣互換交易(以同種利率與異種通貨之互相交換)　currency swap transaction

貨幣互換協定，互惠貸款協定　currency swap agreement

貨幣互換信貸網　network of standing currency swap arrangement

貨幣幻覺　money illusion

貨幣本位　monetary standard

貨幣本位貶值 depreciation of monetary standard

貨幣可得性條款(歐洲市場條款，規定如原先所用貨幣不可得，銀行可改用其他貨幣提供貸款)　currency availability clause

貨幣市場存單 money market certificates

貨幣市場相互基金　money market mutual funds

貨幣市場證券(一般指銀行等金融機構簽發的可轉讓短期票據) money market securities

貨幣主義　monetarism

貨幣主義學說　monetary approach

貨幣平價　monetary parity

貨幣成本　money cost

貨幣同盟　monetary union

貨幣危機　monetary crisis

貨幣利息　monetary interest

貨幣兌換損益 currency exchange loss or gain

貨幣制度　monetary system

貨幣性負債　monetary liability

貨幣性資產　monetary assets

貨幣供應量　money supply

貨幣信託　money trust

貨幣政策　monetary policy

貨幣指標　monetary indexes

貨幣疲軟　currency weakness

貨幣息票互換交易(是一種利率互換和固定利率貨幣互換相結合的交易)　currency coupon swap

貨幣條款　currency clause

貨幣流通　money circulates

貨幣流通量　money in circulation, money stock

貨幣流量分析　money flow analysis

貨幣套頭債券(債券發行與支付利息為一種貨幣,而本金歸還則按預定滙率折合為另一種貨幣)　currency hedge bond

貨幣區　monetary area

貨幣黃金　monetary gold

貨幣貶值　currency devaluation, depreciation

貨幣貶值損失　losses on devaluation

貨幣掉換,貨幣互換　currency swap

貨幣基金(指由貨幣存款構成投資組合的基金)　currency fund

貨幣基礎　monetary base

貨幣單位　monetary unit

貨幣等值　money equivalent

貨幣貸借與股票貸借的比率　ratio of money loans to stock loans

貨幣貸借對股票貸借的差額　balance of money loans over stock loans

貨幣集團　monetary bloc

貨幣期權,貨幣選擇權　currency option

貨幣期權合約　currency option contract

貨幣資本　money capital

貨幣資本比率　money-capital ratio

貨幣債務　money debt

貨幣經濟　monetary economy

貨幣管制　currency control

貨幣增值　appreciation of money

貨幣數量理論　quantity theory of money

貨幣調整　currency realignment

貨幣戰　monetary war

貨幣(調節)機制 monetary mechanism

貨幣矯正(指巴西人對各種交易活動"指數化"以減少通貨膨脹所帶來的不公平或"再分配效應")monetary correction

貨幣購買力　purchasing power of money

貨幣總庫制度 currency pooling system

貨幣總量　monetary aggregates

貨幣儲備　currency reserve

貨輪　cargo vessel

貨價保付(向賣方擔保接受其出售貨物的合格買主的清償能力)　[意] del credere

貨價保付代理商　del credere agent

貨價保付合同　del credere contract

貨價保付佣金 del credere commission

貨價保付協定 del credere agreement

貨艙　cargo hold

貨櫃/集裝箱一般裝卸法　conventional container handling system

貨櫃/集裝箱化 containerization

貨櫃/集裝箱化貨物 containerized cargoes

貨櫃/集裝箱化貨流 containerizable cargo flow

貨櫃/集裝箱化運輸 containerized transportation

貨櫃/集裝箱及部分冷藏船 container/part refrigerated ship

貨櫃/集裝箱互換 container exchange

貨櫃/集裝箱包租 leasing by agreement

貨櫃/集裝箱吊上吊下裝卸法 lift-on/lift-off system

貨櫃/集裝箱吊車(起重機) container crane

貨櫃/集裝箱收貨站 container cargo receiving station

貨櫃/集裝箱服務費 container service charge

貨櫃/集裝箱定程租賃 container leasing by voyage

貨櫃/集裝箱定期租賃 container leasing by time

貨櫃/集裝箱直達列車 direct container unit train

貨櫃/集裝箱租金 container hire

貨櫃/集裝箱租賃公司 container leasing company

貨櫃/集裝箱海陸聯運(尤指海運到洛杉磯長堤經陸運到美國墨西哥灣港口) mini-bridge movement, mini-bridge service

貨櫃/集裝箱浮進浮出裝卸法 float-on/float-off system

貨櫃/集裝箱班輪 container liner

貨櫃/集裝箱船 container ship, container carrier

貨櫃/集裝箱船泊位 container berth

貨櫃/集裝箱區內拆箱 container terminal devanning (TD)

貨櫃/集裝箱區內裝箱 container terminal vanning (TV)

貨櫃/集裝箱區內調運 container terminal transit (TT)

貨櫃/集裝箱專用列車 container unit train

貨櫃/集裝箱基地 container base

貨櫃/集裝箱掛車 container trailer

貨櫃/集裝箱堆場 container pool, container yard

貨櫃/集裝箱貨運站 container freight station

貨櫃/集裝箱貿易 containerized trade

貨櫃/集裝箱提單 container bill of lading

貨櫃/集裝箱進場外地使用 container terminal beyond (TB)

貨櫃/集裝箱當地使用 container terminal arrive (TA)

貨櫃/集裝箱裝卸站 container depot

貨櫃/集裝箱裝卸機 container loader

貨櫃/集裝箱裝箱單 container load plan

貨櫃/集裝箱運清單 container loading list

貨櫃/集裝箱運輸 container transportation

貨櫃/集裝箱滾上滾下裝卸法　roll-on/roll-off system

貨櫃/集裝箱標準規格　container standards

貨櫃/集裝箱碼頭　container terminal

貨櫃/集裝箱碼頭貨站　container terminal depot

貨櫃/集裝箱聯合企業　container consortium

貨櫃/集裝箱翻艙　container rehandling

[一]

通用決算表　general purpose statement (or report)

通用金銀硬幣　current gold and silver coin

通用商用語言 common business oriented language

通用產品代碼 universal product code

通用貨幣　current money

通用稅則　general tariff

通用提貨單　uniform bills of lading

通用資產負債表 all-purpose balance sheet

通行稅　toll

通行證　pass check

通行權　right of way

通知日(買家行使期權的最後一天)　declaration date

通知文句　notification clause

通知付款　advice and pay, notice of

payment

通知公債券還本　call a bond

通知手續費　advising commission

通知存款 call deposit, notice deposits

通知抵押貸款　call loan secured

通知放款　day-to-day loan, call loan

通知放款市場，短期放款市場　call market

通知放款利率　call loan rate

通知信託債券　callable trust bond

通知借款經紀人　call broker

通知期限　notice period

通知損失的義務　obligation of giving claim notice

通知銀行(信用證的) advising bank, notifying bank

通知償還債券，可贖回債券　callable bond

通風車　ventilation car

通風貨物　ventilated cargo

通風貨櫃/集裝箱　ventilated container

通風艙　ventilated compartment

通俗財務報表 layman financial statement

通航水道　navigable waterway

通航護照　passport

通訊網絡　communication network

通商　commercial intercourse

通商自由港　open port

通商保護法　trade safeguarding

通商航海條約　treaty of commerce and navigation

通商港口　open port

通商路線　trade route

通貨　currency, current money

通貨自由兌換　currency convertibility

通貨再膨脹政策　reflationary policy

通貨回籠　recall currency, withdrawal of currency

通貨和銀行鈔票法例　Currency and Bank Notes Act

通貨的實際流通量　effective circulation

通貨券(指外國開出的滙票)　currency bill

通貨貶值　depreciation of currency

通貨票據　currency note

通貨債券(英國：指以本國貨幣償還的債券；美國：泛指以任何國家貨幣償還的債券)　currency bond

通貨緊縮　currency deflation, disinflation, tighten up the money supply

通貨緊縮政策　deflation policy

通貨緊縮缺口　deflationary gap

通貨膨脹　inflation

通貨膨脹扣除率　deflator

通貨膨脹受害者　inflatee

通貨膨脹的國際結構　regime of international inflation

通貨膨脹政策　inflation policy

通貨膨脹缺口　inflationary gap

通貨膨脹恐怖症　[美]inflation phobia

通貨膨脹控制　inflation control

通貨膨脹率　inflation rate

通貨膨脹會計　inflation accounting, accounting for inflation

通貨膨脹壓力　inflationary pressure

通貨膨脹趨勢　inflationary trends

通貨穩定　stabilization of currency

通常破損　ordinary breakage

通常習慣　ordinary practice

通常短缺量　ordinary shortage

通常損失　ordinary loss

通常漏損　ordinary leakage

通達卡(1972年由萬事達集團同英國米蘭、勞合銀行等聯合發行的信用卡)　Access Card

通過金額　amount of vote

通過的議案　resolution passed

通過海關後交貨條件 duty paid terms

通過第三國的滙兌　cross exchange

通過稅，過境稅　transit duties

通運提單　"through" bill of lading

通融　financing, accommodation

通融背書(無關係人亦簽名於背面)　accommodation endorsement

通融票據　accommodation bill (or note), kite

通融票據關係人　accommodation parties

通融貸款　accommodation

通融貸款人　accommodator

通融滙票　accommodation draft

習慣皮重(利用習慣上認定之重量)　customary tare

習慣法　customary law

習慣居所　habitual residence

習慣航線　customary route, customary voyage

習慣做法(國際金融市場的) prac-
tices prevailing

習慣國際法 customary international
law

習慣裝卸速度 customary dispatch

翌日與隔日對做(賣出明天交割的一
種貨幣,同時買進明天以後一天即
交割的該種貨幣,或反之)tom-
next

張(薄鋼板) sheet

張(厚鋼板) plat

陳列品 exposure, display

陳列室 gallery, showroom

陳列櫃 showcase

陳貨 old stock, secondhand goods,
obsolescence

陳報確認書 acknowledgement of
declaration

陳廢率 rate of obsolescence

陳廢資產 dead assets

陳舊設備 obsolete equipment

陸上危險不保條款,水運條款 water-
borne clause

陸上貿易 land-borne trade

陸上運輸線 landline

陸地上碰撞 collision on land

陸地承運人(貨櫃/集裝箱運輸的)
on carrier

陸地橋(指代替傳統海運航路而改用
里程較短的海陸聯運所經過的陸上
通道) landbridge

陸海聯運 joint rail and water transportation

陸運 land transportation, land carriage

陸運共通地點 overland common
point

陸運共通地點優惠運費率 overland
common point rate

陸運保險 insurance for land transportation

陸運條款(指除海運途中以外,承保
裝船前及卸貨後,貨物於碼頭或岸
上其他地方以及在陸上轉運時遭受
約定危險之損失) shore clause,
shore to shore clause

陸運提單 inland bill of lading

陸橋聯運 land-bridge service, land-
bridge movement

組合企業 associated enterprise

組合貨幣債券,綜合貨幣債券(以
SDR 或 ECU 等組合貨幣為面值
的債券) currency cocktail bond

組合價格(幾種商品組合在一起時所
訂的價格) package price

組合概率 combined probability

組合購買 group purchase

組格式貨櫃/集裝箱貨船 cellular
container vessel

組織 organizing

組織化市場(指證券、股票、商品、期
貨、金銀等交易所) organized
market

組織原則 organization principle

組織心理學 organizational psychology

組織行為 organization behaviour

組織行銷　organization marketing

組織章則　constitution

組織革新　organizational changes

組織型態　organizational patterns

組織理論　organization theory

組織發展　organization development

組織職能　organizing function

組裝零件　parts, knock-down parts

組裝零件的購入與供應　purchase and supply of parts

細分　detailed final sorting

細目　item

細則　by-laws, bye-laws, detailed regulations

細帳　itemized account, detailed account

細節　detail

細數　net amount

細頸鋼瓶　flask

終止　termination

終止日期　expiry date

終止協議事件　events of termination

終身年金　life annuity

終身受益人　life tenant

終身保險　insurance for life

終身租賃　life leasehold

終身財產所有權(指非世襲的財產)　life interest

終身就業　lifetime employment

終結股利　final dividend

終結帳簿　book of final entry

終值　final value

終價　final value

參加付款人　payer for honour

參加承兌,榮譽承兌　acceptance for honour

參加承兌支付(滙票付款人拒絕承兌後，第三者為維持出票人信譽而承擔的付款)　payment for honour supraprotest

參加承運人　participating carrier

參加義務履行的第三人　person intervening

參加管理的優先股　participating preference

參考週期　reference cycle

參考羣體　reference group

參考價格　reference price

參考數字　reference number

參考數據　reference data

參債人(可能有一家或多家金融機構作代表的，某一財務事項中的長期出借人)　debt participant

參與,分享　participation

參與分享紅利　participating dividend

參與分紅　participation in the profit

參與分紅股　participating capital stock

參與式民主領導方式　participative-democratic leadership style

參與式管理　management by participation

參與股息　participating dividend

參與盈餘分配　participating

參與率　participation rate

參與費(指參與一筆貸款的費用)　participation fee

參與貸款　participation loan

參與債券(參與盈利分配的公司債)

participating bonds

參與機構 participating agency

參與優先股 participating preferred stock (or share)

參與證單(證明參與辛迪加歐洲信貸的一種證件，一般具有可轉讓性) participation certificate

參與觀察 participant-observation

參照國際市場價格 base on prevailing international market price

參照點，衡量標準 reference point

參數 parameter

參數估計 parameter estimation

參數轉換 parameter transformation

[、]

富商 wealth traders

富國與窮國 "haves" and "havenots"

窗飾帳目 window dressing

窗櫥 window cabin

窗櫥陳列 window display, window dressing

窗櫥廣告 window advertising

游動國庫債券，財政短期證券(在發行日全部承保的英國短期證券) hot treasury bills

游資(湧入套利的短期資金) idle fund, hot money, floating money, unem-

ployed capital, bad money

游資移動 hot money movement

測定值 measurement value

測定誤差 measurement error

測度空間 measure space

測度邊際效用 measuring margin utility

測量 measurement

測量尺度 measurement scale

港口吞吐量 port capacity, volume handled at coastal ports

港口泊位 sea port berths

港口附加費 port surcharge

港口站 port station

港口耽擱日 lay day

港口浮標稅 buoy due

港口設施 port facilities

港口稅 port tax

港口費 port charges, port dues

港口當局 port authority

港口裝卸 port handling

港口運輸 port traffic

港口運輸代理商 port agent

港口慣例 customs of the port

港口險 port risks

港口擠塞 port congestion

港至港提單 port to port bill of lading

港務局 port office, harbor bureau

港務監督 harbor superintendency administration

港規 harbor regulation

港府指數(香港政府統計處每日發表) Effective Exchange Rate Indexes

of Hong Kong Dollar

盜劫保險　robbery insurance

盜竊　rob

減工資　reduce the wage

減少一半　reduce by half

減少外滙風險　reduce foreign exchange risk

減少存貨　inventory liquidating

減少投資　negative investment, disinvestment

減低買價　abatement of purchase-money

減免稅收　reducing or remitting taxes

減股盈餘　surplus from cancellation of stock

減除成本　deductible costs

減除利息和稅款前收益　earnings before interest and tax

減耗資產　wasting assets

減記資產帳面值　write-down

減稅　reduce the duty, abatement of tax

減輕責任　diminished responsibility

減輕債務負擔　reduction or cancellation of debts

減價　reduce the price, mark down

減價平倉單（見限虧止單）　stop loss orders

減價條款　down price clause

減縮指數　deflating index, deflator

減讓　concesion, allowance

訴訟保險　insurance against litigation

訴訟財產（指權利的憑證，如股票、債券、滙票等可向債務人提出權利要求的證據，其價值必要時可通過法律程序予以實現）　choses in action

訴訟時效　limitation of action, prescrition

訴訟假扣押　security for claim

評估損失　assessment of loss (or damages)

評定的優先次序　priority rating

評定等級　rating

評定稅額　assess a tax

評價　appraisement

評價出售的協議　agreement to sell at valuation

評價買賣　sale at a valuation

評價帳戶　qualifying reserve account, valuation account

註冊　registration, incorporation

註冊交易人（在加拿大證交所，起類似於美國專家經紀人作用的場內交易人。在澳大利亞期權市場上指競爭性市場的製造者）　registered trader

註冊法人（負責登記股票轉讓，監督和防止公司發行股票超過授權範圍的信託公司或銀行）　registrar

註冊股本　registered capital

註冊股票　registered certificate of shares

註冊船　registered ship

註冊執照　certificate of registration

註冊商標　registered trade-mark

註冊費　registration fee

註冊港　port of registry
註冊資本　registered capital
註冊會計師　licensed (public) accountant
註冊圖案, 註冊設計　registered design
註冊噸(指船舶容積, 以註冊噸為計算單位, 每一註冊噸等於 100 立方呎或 2.83 立方米)　registered ton
註冊噸位　registered tonnage
註冊證書　certificate of registration
註明運費預付　marked freight prepaid
註銷支票　cancelled check
註銷合同　cancellation of treaty
註銷保險單退費　cancelling returns
註銷遺失的票據　cancellation of a lost instrument
註釋說明, 附註　explanatory notes
詐欺交易(股市用語: 又稱虛拋、虛賣或假像交易)　wash sale, fictitious trading
詐欺取物　obtaining property by deception
詐欺取得金錢利益　obtaining pecuniary advantage by deception
詐欺取得僱用　obtaining employment by deception
詐欺性的不真實說明　fraudulent misrepresentation
詐騙　fraud
詐騙使一切都失效　fraus omnia vitiat
痛苦指數(又稱不安指數)　discomfort index
勞工爭議調解　labour conciliation
勞工卹養保險　workmen's compensation insurance
勞工保險　labour insurance
勞工管理, 勞動管理　labour management
勞工離職率　labour separation rate
勞氏公司 The Corporation of Lloyd's
勞氏公證行　Lloyd's Surveyor
勞氏代理　Lloyd's agent
勞氏承保人　Lloyd's underwriters
勞氏海損契約 Lloyd's Average Bond
勞氏海損契約格式　Lloyd's Form "Average Bond"
勞氏船級　Lloyd's class
勞埃德證書　Lloyd's certificate
勞務　labour service
勞務出口　exporting services
勞務出資　service contribution
勞務收入　service receipts
勞務合作　cooperation in the field of labour service
勞務交換　labour exchange
勞務協議　service agreement
勞務項目　service account
勞務報酬　remuneration of services
勞務購買　purchase of services
勞動力　labour power, manpower, labour force
勞動力市場　labour market
勞動力成本　labour cost
勞動力再生產 reproduction of labour power

勞動力自然更新速度　natural renewal of labour power

勞動力利用率　utilization rate of labour power

勞動力的價值　value of labour power

勞動力流動狀況　degree of mobility within the labour force

勞動力買賣　buying and selling of labour power

勞動力結構　structure of the labour force

勞動力週轉率　labour turnover

勞動力資源　human resources, pool of labour power

勞動人口　labouring population

勞動手段　mean of labour

勞動生產率　labour productivity

勞動收入　labour income, income from work

勞動交換　exchange of labour

勞動者　workman, labouring man, worker

勞動法　labour law

勞動的可用性　labour availability

勞動的貨幣名稱　money-name of labour

勞動的邊際生產率　marginal productivity of labour

勞動定額　work norm

勞動爭議　labour disputes

勞動紀律　labour discipline

勞動政策　labour policy

勞動保險制度　labour insurance system

勞動專業化　labour specialization

勞動密集的　labour-intensive

勞動密集工業　labour-intensive industry

勞動密集生產　labour-intensive production

勞動密集型的產品出口　export of labour-intensive products

勞動強度　intensity involved in the labour, labour intensity

勞動報酬　payment for labour

勞動資本比率　labour-capital ratio

勞動對象　object of labour

勞動熟練程度　skill of labour

勞動積累　accumulation of labour

勞資仲裁　industrial arbitration

勞資糾紛　industrial dispute, labour trouble

勞資糾紛法例　Trade Disputes Act

勞資法庭　Industrial Court

勞資法庭法例　Industrial Court Act

勞資協調　industrial coordination

勞資和諧　industrial harmony

勞資衝突　clash between capital and labour

勞資關係　employee-employer relations, industrial relation, labour management relations

普通及協定關稅 general and conventioned tariff

普通日記帳　general journal

普通支票　open check, ordinary check

普通合夥　general partnership

普通年金　ordinary annuity

普通收據　ordinary receipt

普通利息　ordinary interest

普通投標　ordinary tender

普通法　common law

普通法留置權　common law lien

普通股 ordinary share, common share, ordinary stock, common stock

普通股本　common capital stock

普通股折價帳　discount on common stock account

普通股東　ordinary partner, active partner

普通股與優先股收益差額　yield gap

普通承兌(指不附任何條件的承兌，與特別承兌詞義相對）general acceptance

普通往來款項　open credit

普通事故保險　ordinary accident insurance

普通信用證　ordinary credit

普通盈利　general surplus

普通背書　general endorsement

普通貨　general cargo

普通許可證　common licence

普通許可證合同 simple licence contract, non-exclusive licence contract

普通責任的債務　general-obligation bonds

普通專利　common monopoly

普通基金　general fund

普通現金　general cash

普通商業交易　arm's-length deal

普通稅則　general tariff

普通發票　plain invoice

普通提款權　general drawing rights

普通會計制度　general accounting system

普通劃線支票 general crossed cheque

普通審計　general audit

普通遺贈　general devise, general legacy

普通債務　general debt

普通競賣法　ordinary auction

普遍通貨膨脹　generalized inflation

普遍優惠制　general system of preference

普遍優惠制待遇　general preferential treatment

普遍優惠制產地來源證　generalized system of preferences certificate of origin

善意,真實　[拉]bona fide

善意合約　bona fide contract

善意原告　bona fide claimant

善意第三者　bona fide third party

善意執票人　bona fide holders

善意買方 bona fide purchaser, buyer in good faith

童叟無欺　neither old nor young cheated

牽引車　tractor, traction unit

視同現金支票　check as cash

視覺器材　video equipment

就地審計　site audit

就地檢驗　floor inspection

就買運動(旨在通過增加當前消費者的購買來刺激經濟復蘇的一種計劃）Buy-Now Campaign

就業　employed, obtain employment

就業情況,就業率　employment status

[一]

菲利浦曲線　Phillips Curve

菜單方式(金融術語,指在一個較廣的範圍—"菜單"內採用各種融資手段重新調整債務的方法)　menu approach

焚燒率　burning ratio

焚燬　burnt down by fire

博福特風級(英格蘭銀行對報刊評論貨幣市場活動時,以類似風力等級一詞來表達)　beaufort scale

提出上訴　entry of appeal

提出中止訴訟　enter a nolle prosequi

提出追索　filing a claim for recovery

提成支付(技術貿易的一種支付方式,根據利用技術的效果,按一定百分比提成)　royalty

提取企業基金　retain ...... as enterprise fund

提取債券　drawing of bonds

提取資產　withdrawal of assets

提取積累　accumulation fund draw by

提供技術情報協議　supply of technical information agreement

提供國際投入　delivery of international input

提供銀行信貸　granting bank credit

提供證據　[拉]litis denun ciatio

提前日期提單　pre-date bill of lading

提前成本　anticipated cost

提前利潤　anticipated profit

提前償還　voluntary prepayment

提前轉期　advance refunding

提前贖債溢額　call premium

提高工資　raised wage

提高平價　increase the par value

提高票面價值　increase the par value

提高產品質量　improve the quality of products

提高貨幣價值　raise the value of money

提高貸款利息　marking up loans

提高競爭能力　boosting the competitiveness

提案制度　suggestion system

提倡國貨　encourage native product

提貨不着　non-delivery

提貨不着險　risk of non-delivery

提貨報關代理人　delivery and customs agent

提貨單　delivery order

提貨與付款合同　take-and-pay contract

提現挪用,開空頭支票　kiting

提單　bill of lading

提單日期　B/L date

提單正本　original bill of lading

提單批註　exceptions noted on the bill of lading

提單背書申請書　application for bill of lading endorsement

提單副本　duplicate bill of lading

提款　withdrawal, withdraw deposit

提款卡(向自動櫃員機提款用的)
debit card

提款收據 withdrawal receipt

提款帳 drawing account

提款單 withdrawal ticket, withdrawal slip

提款權 drawing rights

提價 raise price, markup

提價率 markup rate

換文 exchange of notes (or documents)

換月交易(在同一市場了結某月份交易，同時投入另一月份交易，使原來之交易轉入另一月份) switching

換股 exchange of shares (or stock)

換約 exchange treaties

換貨 exchange goods

換貨和付款協定 goods exchange and payments agreement

換滙申請書 application for conversion

換滙成本 costs in terms of foreign exchange

換債操作(指以新公債償還舊公債，調節一般流動性操作方式) funding operation

換算因素 conversion factors

援引條約 invoke a treaty

援外計劃 foreign aid program

援助 aid

援助協定 aid agreement

援助捐款 assistance contribution

援助機構 aid agency

描述統計學 descriptive statistics

揮發險 risk of evaporation

棚車 shed car

棋盤式(帳目)分析表 articulation statement, spread sheet

極大似然法 maximum-likelihood method

極大極大原則 maximax rule

極不公平的合同 unconsionable contract

極不利的價格 penal rate

極限概率 limiting probabilities

棉布袋 sack

棉花交易所 cotton exchange

棉紡錠 cotton textile spindles

棉紡織品協定 Cotton Textile Agreement

棉織品 cotton textiles, cotton fabrics

惡性通貨膨脹 hyperinflation, runaway inflation, malignant inflation

惡味險 risk of bad odour

惡意 mala fide

惡意行為 malicious act

惡意破壞 malicious damage

惡意短量(賣方故意少裝或裝運損壞品，冒充自然短量所發生的缺量) malicious shortage

惡意損害法例 Malicious Damage Act

惡意毀壞物件 malicious injuries to property

喪失能力之股東 incapacitated shareholder

喪失權利 divesting of a right

超大型商場 hypermarket

超支 overexpenditure, overspending

超支挪用 overdrafts and use of money for purposes other than originally budgeted for

超比分配 hypergeometric distribution

超比級數 hypergeometric series

超出法律範圍 ［拉]preter legal

超定值繳入資本 paid-in capital in excess of stated value

超面值繳入資本 paid-in capital in excess of par value, capital contributed in excess of par value, additional paid-in capital, capital surplus, premium on capital stock

超長貨物 lengthy cargo

超重 overweight

超重行李 excess baggage

超限成本 cost overrun

超級 301 條款(美國 1988 年綜合貿易法的部分條款) "super 301" clause

超級公路 super high way

超級市場 supermarket

超級可轉讓提款單帳戶(與 NOW 帳戶同屬支付利息之支票存款，但利率不受管制，故稱超級 NOW 帳戶) super NOW account

超級標準 super-standards

超現值指數 excess present value index

超現值數 excess present value

超速動資產 super liquid asset

超買(指期貨，外滙的) overbought position

超提折舊 over-depreciation

超載，超額運費 overfreight

超過面值 above par

超賣(指對期貨，外滙的) oversold position

超額收入 excess income

超額赤字 excess deficit

超額利潤 excess earnings, exorbitant profit

超額利潤稅 excess profit tax (or duty)

超額供給 excess supply

超額保險 over-insurance

超額盈利稅 excess-profit tax

超額發行 over-issue

超額準備 excess reserves

超額貸款 over loan

超額損失率分保合同 excess of loss ratio reinsurance treaty

超額賠款 excess of loss

超額賠款分保合同 excess of ioss reinsurance treaty

超額賠款保障 excess of loss cover

超齡船 over-age vessel

越權行為 ［拉]ultra vires

越權的 unauthorized

越權者 trespasser

散工，短工 journey work, job work

散裝入船 bulk loading

散裝石油船 bulk oil carrier

散裝界線 bulk line

散裝船 bulk ship

散裝貨物 bulk cargo

散裝貨倉庫 bulk storage warehouse

散裝貨集裝箱 bulk container

硬件 hardware

硬度　hardness

硬貨　hard goods, hardware

硬通貨，硬幣　hard currency, hard money

硬貸款　hard loan

硬幣支付　specie payments

硬幣準備　specie reserve

彭特萊電碼(英人 E.L. Bentley 編的以五個字母為一詞的商用電碼) Bentley's code

彭特萊電碼大全　Bentley's Complete Phases Code

彭特萊第二套電碼　Bentley's Second Phases Code

華沙牛津規則　Warsaw-Oxford Rule

華爾街(紐約股票交易所所在地) Wall Street

華爾街大亨　Wall Streeter

華爾街日報　Wall Street Journal

替代仲裁員，代理仲裁員　substitute arbitrator

替代送達　substituted service

替代效果　substitution effect

替代商品　substitute goods

替代費用　substituted expenses

替代零件　replacement of parts

替代價值會計　replacement value accounting

替代擔保　substituted security

替換　replacement

替換成本　alternative costs

替換帳戶　substitution account

替換率　replacement rate

替換債券(發行新債券替換舊債券)

refunding bonds

替換彈性　elasticity of substitution

項目方案　project alternatives

項目生產(生產的一種類型，通常用於新的和急劇擴展中的業務領域) project production

項目建設進度表　project implementation scheduling

項目指標　project indicators

項目執行　project implementation

項目研究小組　project team

項目設計　project engineering

項目採購　project purchasing

項目報告　project paper

項目評估法　Project Evaluation and Review Technique

項目貸款　project loan

項目資金籌措　project financing

項目經濟估價　project economic evaluation

項目預算　project budget

項目網絡分析 project network analysis

項目網絡法(使用網絡和網絡分析來計劃和管理項目)　project network technique

項目範圍　scope of project

項目擬訂　project formulation

裁決　arbitration award, ruling

裁決人　arbitrator, umpire

裁定　verdict

裁定的救治　cure by verdict

裁定的援助　aider by verdict

裁定書　written verdict

裁定破產 adjudication of bankruptcy

裁判庭　tribunal

裁員　reduce the establishment

"斯特里普斯"證券(即利息和本金分離交易的已登記證券，係美國1985年2月發行的一種國庫券)　"STRIPS"—separate trading of registered interest and principal of securities

斯勒茨基命題(即隨機數列的移動平均數是擺動的)　sluksy's proposition

欺詐侵佔　fraudulent conversion

欺詐授與　fraudulent settlement

欺詐讓與　fraudulent conveyance

欺騙性標記　deceptive mark

期中股利(指決算前預發的股利)　interim dividend

期中報告　interim report

期中報表　interim statement

期中結帳　interim closing

期中審計　interim audit

期末存貨　ending inventory, closing stock

期末報表　end-of-period statement

期末截帳　end-of-period cutoff

期末調整分錄　end-of-period adjusting entry

期末餘額　ending balance, closing balance

期初平均法　beginning average method

期初加重收費　front-end loading

期初存貨　initial inventory, opening inventory

期初盈餘　initial surplus

期初餘額　beginning balance, opening balance

期首年金終值　amount of an annuity due

期待物權合同　catching bargain

期待結果　expected outcome

期待數　expected number

期限延長　renewal

期限條款　duration clause

期值(期權合約與其有效期所剩時間有關的部份價值)　time value

期貨　futures, dealing in future

期貨市場　futures market

期貨外滙，期滙　future exchange

期貨交易　future goods transaction

期貨交易所　futures exchange

期貨交割　futures delivery

期貨合約(用於買賣特定數額外滙的高度標準化的外滙合同)　futures contract

期貨合約有效期　life of contract

期貨合約的期權交易　options on futures contract

期貨式期權　futures-style option

期貨佣金商(指美國芝加哥商人交易所的1300名會員)　futures commission merchants (FCMs)

期貨取消　forward cancelled

期貨保證金　cover cost

期貨指數　futures index

期貨/現貨比率　futures/physical ratio

期貨期權(貨幣期權在執行時將其轉變為一個相應的期貨合約，又稱歐式期權)　forward option (European option)

期貨經紀商 Futures Brokerage House

期貨與現貨差距 forward margin

期貨溢價 contango

期貨溢價交易 engage in contango operations as a taker in

期貨賣方搶購 short squeeze

期貨價格 futures price

期貨銷售 future sales

期票 bill for a term, promissory note term bill, term draft, bill undue

期票附件 additional part of a bill

期票股利(以臨時票據付股利，又稱臨時股利) scrip dividend

期票買價 buying rate for time bill

期票承兌行 acceptance house

期間成本 period cost

期間保單 time policy

期望值 expected values

期望時間 expected time

期望值理論 expectancy-valence theory

期望消費 expected consumption

期望報酬 expected return

期終結帳日 period closing date

期滙淨價 outright rate

期滙業務 forward exchange transaction

期滙滙率 forward exchange rate

期滿兌付 payment in due course

期數 number of periods

期權，選擇權，期券 option

期權交易 option dealing

期權定價模式 option pricing model

期權買入價 option purchase price

期權履約價 option exercise price, option strike price

期權買賣市場 option market

報告，報告書 report

報告式損益表 report form profit and loss statement

報告式資產負債表 report form of balance sheet

報告期 reporting period

報告資料 report data

報表，結單 statement

報表分析，決算表分析 statement analysis

報表名稱 title of statement

報紙上的商業新聞 commercial articles

報紙上的證券發行廣告 tombstone

報消息機(證券及期貨市場術語，指報價格及背景消息之電訊機) broad tape

報帳單 check sheet

報復性關稅 retaliatory traiff (or duties)

報稅單 bill of entry

報酬 reward, returns

報酬率，收益率，盈利率 rate of return

報酬遞減律 law of diminishing returns

報銷 report for deletion

報價 offer, quotation, quoted price

報價採購 quoted purchase

報價單 quotation list

報關 clear the goods through the

customs

報關行　custom house broker

報關海港　port of entry

報關單　entry manifest

報關費　customs cleaning charges

報關經紀人　custom house broker

殘值　residual value, salvage value, scrap value

殘料　junk

殘損率　percentage of damage goods

殘酷競爭　"cut-throat" competition

殘廢險　disability insurance

殘廢償金　disability benefit

場內交易　transaction on exchange

場外　kerbstone, ex-pit

場外市場　kerb market

場外交易 ex-pit transaction, kerb transaction, over-the-counter trading

場外交易市場(店頭市場)　over the counter market

場內經紀人(在期權市場，指期權清算所的僱員，被稱為經紀人之經紀人)　floor broker, board broker

場外交易證券　over-the-counter security, off-board security

場外經紀人　kerbstone broker

[丨]

貼士，小費　tip

貼水　agio, discount

貼水日　marking-up day

貼本　loss money in a business

貼扣現金　discounted cash

貼扣現金流動　discounted cash flow

貼身包裝　wrapping & package

貼現 discount, discount on exchange, discount for cash, time discount

貼現人 applicant for a discount, discount clerk, discount tellers

貼現市場　discount market

貼現行　discount house

貼現回收期 discount payable period

貼現利息　discount interest

貼現系數　discount factor

貼現法　discounting methods

貼現後的現值　discounted present value

貼現政策　discount policy

貼現信貸　discount credit

貼現差額　discount difference

貼現率　discount rate

貼現現金流量　discount cash flow

貼現票據 discount on notes, discounted bill

貼現期限　term of discount

貼現窗口(中央銀行對頭寸吃緊的商業銀行提供短期資金支持所開辦的櫃台業務)　discount window

貼現經紀人　discount broker

貼現滙票，貼現票據 bill discounting

貼現銀行　discount bank

貼現價值　discount value

貼滙水　discount on exchange

貼體包裝　skin packaging

貯存信託公司(紐約證券交易所的子公司，所有參加者將擁有證券存放於該公司，證券交割，通過計算機

控制的清算中心結算）depository trust company

單一方式承運人　unimodal carrier

單一方式運輸　unimodal transport

單一成本制　single cost system

單一交易　single transaction

單一仲裁　single arbitrage

單一物品本位　single commodity standard

單一直接所得稅　single direct income tax

單一品種商店　specialty store

單一倉庫設置模式　single facility models

單一海關單據　single custom document

單一產品制　single product system

單一產品隨機存貨模式　single product stochastic inventory model

單一貨幣掛鈎　single currency peg

單一貨幣貸款　mono-currency loan

單一稅則　single tariff

單一期間均衡　single-period equilibrium

單一匯率　single exchange rate, unitary exchange rate

單一經濟　single-product economy

單一銀行制　unit banking system

單一價格　single price, unitary price

單一標準　single standard

單方不履行債務　unilateral repudiation of a debt

單方行為　unilateral transaction, unilateral juristic act

單方面合同　unilateral contract

單方面承諾　unilateral undertaking

單方面承擔義務的契約　unilateral contract

單方面通訊制度　one-way communication system

單方面廢止（對合同）　unilateral denunciation

單方規定的配額　unilateral quota, unilateral set quota

單方轉移　unilateral transfer

單元化運輸（用大型單一托盤、貨櫃等裝運）　unitized transportation

單元信託，互惠信託基金　[英]unit trust, [美]mutual fund

單元信託投資　unit trust investment

單元信託投資公司股東　[英]unitholder

單元裝運制　unit load system

單向分析　one-way analysis

單向平價套頭（同時購進賣權和買權，或同時賣出賣權和買權，其交易滙價相同時稱"單向平價套頭"，在交易滙價不同時稱"單向差價套頭"）　straddles

單向投機　one-way speculation

單向差價套頭　strangles

單式曲線圖　simple curve chart

單式柱形圖　simple column-diagram

單式條圖　simple bar-chart

單式簿記　single-entry bookkeeping

單因素貿易條件　single factorial terms of trade

單次驗收抽樣法　single sampling plan

單利　single interest, simple interest

單位平均成本　average cost per unit

單位成本　unit cost

單位成本率　cost rate per unit

單位投票制(以一個代表團作為一個
單位進行投票)　unit rule

單位投資額　unit investment quota

單位利潤　unit profit

單位利潤分配　unit profit sharing

單位折舊　unit depreciation

單位容積重量　unit capacity weight

單位產品的物資消耗　consumption
of materials per unit, materials
expended in per unit products

單位產品的原料消耗　consumption
per unit product of raw materials

單位產值能耗　energy consumption
per unit of output value

單位換算價值　unit conversion value

單位價格　unit price

單位價值　unit value

單位價值指數　unit value index

單位積累提供的國民收入增長額
amount of increase in national income provided by the accumulation fund per unit

單步式損益表　single-step income
statement

單到付款　payment upon arrival of
shipping documents

單相關　simple correlation

單純的或要求即付的保函　simple or
first demand guarantee

單純承兌　absolute acceptance

單純的資本變換循環　single capital
conversion cycle

單純背書　absolute endorsement

單純最惠國條款　simple most fav-
oured nation clause

單純債券(即公司發行的不能調換成
股票的債券)　straight bond

單純壟斷價格　simple monopoly price

單峰分佈(統計)　unimodal distribution

單張滙票　sole draft

單程出境簽證護照　single exit visa
in one's passport

單程租船　single voyage charter

單程費　one way fare

單程過境單據　single transit document

單價　unit price

單價偏度　unit value bias

單層袋(提單批語)　single bag

單據　documents

單據已簽　documents signed

單據效力　status of document

單據解付制度(指以單據代現金支付)
chit system

單獨投資　sole investment

單獨法人　corporation sole

單獨保險單　specific policy

單獨海損不賠　free from particular
average

單獨海損全賠　irrespective of percentage

單獨海損理算　adjustment of par-
ticular average

單獨海損險　with particular average

單獨關稅領土 separate customs territory

單邊出口　unilateral exportation

單邊貿易　unilateral trade

單邊進口　unilateral importation

單邊進口配額 unilateral import quota

單邊進口管制 unilateral import control

單證不符 documents not conforming to the provisions of the letter of credit

單證交貨　documentary delivery

單欄稅則　single schedule tariff

黑市　black market, illicit market

黑市交易　black market operations

黑市商人　black-marketeer

黑市滙兌　black market exchange

黑市滙率　black market rate

黑市價格　black market price, black rate

黑白廣告　black and white advertising

黑名單(信譽低劣商行的名單) black list

黑名單證明書(信用證有時要求證明，製造廠商，銀行，保險公司，航運公司或所經航線，停泊港口，不在其來證所規定黑名單之內) Blacklist Certificate

黑貨市場　fence

黑暗的星期四(指 1929.10.24. 紐約股票大跌的日子)　black Thursday

"黑箱原則"(一種用投入和產出的概念說明預測目標的方法)　"black box"

黑箱觀念　black box concept

黑錢　black money, blackhander

跌風　sagging tendency

跌後回升　rally

跌落　recede

跌停板(期貨交易所規定在一交易日內的最低限價)　limit down

跌價　falling price

跌價拍買　dutch auction

跌價總額　gross declination

跑街　drummer, solicitor

跑街經紀人　running broker

喊低價　rule low

喊高價　rule high

喊價(賣家報出賣價)　ask, offer, the price ask

喊價成交　outcry market

喊價拍賣(交易所口頭公開執行定單的活動)　execution by outcry

喊價逐步減低的拍賣，荷蘭式拍賣法 Dutch auction

喊價規則(交易所條例：在交易日結束時正式定出並維持至次日開市有效的現貨商品的價目表)　call rule

喊價棉(指以喊價買入或賣出之棉花) call cotton

喊價權，買權(期權市場術語)　call option

敞車　open car

敞口和有擔保出售期權　naked and covered writing

敞開式購買(指使投資者變成期權購

買地位的交易）opening purchase

敝開式銷售(指使投資者變成期權銷售地位的交易) opening sale

敝篷貨車　open wagon

敝艙船　open ship

買入及持有策略(長期持有一種優質債券直至滿期為止) buy and hold technique

買入及賣出報表(期貨合約套現後,經紀行發給客戶的報表) purchase and sale statement

買入投資證券應付　payable for investment securities purchased

買入套戥,買期保值　buying hedge

買入票據　bill bought

買入滙票　bill purchased

買入滙價,銀行買價　buying rate

買入對冲,買期保值　hedge buying, long hedge

買方　buying part, buyer

買方市場　buyer's market

買方出價　buying offer

買方行為的效果　effect of buyer conduct

買方信貸　buyer's credit

買方信貸合約　buyer's credit agreement

買方倉庫交貨　ex buyer's godown

買方專利　buyers monopoly

買方對貨物檢驗權　rights of buyer as to inspection of goods

買方對賣方的協助　purchaser's co-operation to contractor

買方應準備的現場設施　site facilities to be prepared by purchaser

買方營業處所品質條件 buyer's premises quality terms

買方營業處所數量條件 buyer's premises quantity terms

買方選擇權　buyer's option

買方壟斷　monopsony

買主　customer, buyer, bargainee

買主信用　buyer's credit

買主過多　buyers over

買主意圖　buyer's buying intention

買回,返銷　buy-back

買回價,返銷價　buy-back price

買多市場,多頭市場　long market

買空　buy long, overbuy

買空支票,假票據　fictitious bill (or paper)

買空交割延期費,期貨溢價　contango

買空者,好友,多頭　bulls

買空賣空　cross trade, fictitious bargain, fictitious transactions, bucket

《買美國貨法》 "Buy American" Act

買期貨　forward buying

買進過多(貨物),超買(期貨)買空,多頭　overbuy

買價　purchase price

買價和賣價　purchasing and selling price

買價昂貴　paid dearly for

買賣公平　pay fairly for what you buy, fair in buying and selling

買賣外幣損益　profit and loss on buying and selling foreign coins

買賣合同的要件　the essence of contract of sale

買賣折扣　discount on purchases

買賣股票　agiotage

買賣股票之投機商店　bucket shop

買賣股票通知　contract note

買賣商股票（紐約證券市場專業會員所專業之股票如為冷門股票，市場術語稱為“買賣商股票”）　dealer stock

買賣授權書　power of sale

買賣滙票的專家　cambist

買賣蝕本　on a losing basis

買賣摘要　particulars of sale

買賣贓品　fence

買賣贓品的人　fencer

買權，買入選擇權，看漲期權　call option

貴重貨物　valuable cargo

貴賣　sell dear

晴天工作日　weather working days

晴天工作日假日星期天除外　weather working day holiday and Sunday except

晴雨表股票　barometer stocks

量入為出　measure expenditure by income

量的分析　quantitative analysis

量的限制　quantitative limitation

量的統計　quantitative statistics

量度單位　measure unit

量差　quantity difference

量變　quantitative change

量變項　quantitative variable

景氣　prosperity, boom

景氣年　boom year

最小平方方法，最小二乘法　least square method

最小平方估值　least-square estimation

最小平方線性關係　least-square linear relationship

最小成本網絡流程　minimal-cost network-flow

最小的比較劣勢　least comparative disadvantage

最小最大原則　minimax princip!e

最小費用點　least cost point

最小與最大約定數量　minimum and maximum amount

最大工作面積　maximum working value

最大可接受交貨量　maximum quantity acceptable

最大生產能力　maximum productive capacity

最大地球弧線　great circle line

最大利潤　maximum profit

最大限度　maximatily

最大限價　ceiling price

最大值，峰值　peak value

最大流量算法　maximal-flow algorithm

最大量　maximum

最大期望利潤　maximizing expected profit

最大誠信原則（訂立保險合同必須遵守的基本原則，保險合同雙方當事人必須以誠信為基礎）　principle

of utmost good faith

最大預期損失(在保險市場，指一個特定的危險單位在通常情況下所能預料的最大損失) maximum probable loss

最大載重量　dead weight

最大誤差　maximum error

最大標準差　maximum standard deviation

最大償債能力　ultimate solvency

最少製造量(生產管理用詞，指在生產一項產品上能合算的最少數量) minimum manufacturing quantity

最低成本組合　least cost combination

最低有效位數　least significant digit

最低存量法　minimum stock method

最低自留額　minimum retention

最低利潤　minimum profit

最低波動價位，最低價格變動 minimum price movement, minimum price fluctuation

最低定價法　penetration pricing

最低限度工資　minimum wage

最低限價　lowest price limit, floor price

最低限額價值　floor value

最低訂貨量　minimum quantity per order

最低庫存量，最低存料量 minimum quantity of stores

最低消費量　minimum consumption

最低借款率，最低貸款利率 minimum lending rate

最低黃金準備比率　minimum ratio of gold reserve

最低現金餘額　minimum cash balance

最低清償力　minimum liquidity

最低費用　minimum charge

最低提單費　minimum bill of lading charge

最低準備　minimum reserve

最低報價　lowest quotation

最低預付的保險費　minimum deposit premium

最低預付押金　minimum deposit

最低預期報酬率　minimum desired rate of return

最低運費　minimum freight

最低運費率　minimum freight rate

最低價　rock bottom price, lowest possible price, floor price, reserve price

最低額應繳股本，開業資本　minimum subscription

最佳批量　optimum lot size

最佳股票，藍籌股　bluechip stock

最佳相似法　method of maximum likelihood

最佳商業票據　prime commercial paper

最佳綜合政策　optimal policy mix

最佳證據　best evidence

最近成本　recent cost

最初回收率　primary recovery

最初投資　initial capitalization, initial investment

最初承運人　initial carrier

最初效用　initial utility

最初參數　initial parameters

最宜價格產量政策　price-output policy

最後一筆金額特大的分期付款法（利息不每期支付，而逐期滾轉積累，直至貸款期末連同本金以一筆整數償還）balloon repayment

最後用戶　end user

最後生存年金　last-survivor annuity

最後成本　final cost

最後目的港　final port of destination

最後交易日（指交收月份期最後一個交易日）last trading day

最後交貨日期　end delivery date

最後交割通知日（指期貨市場上，通知手上尚持有未平倉合約應在此日之前平倉，即通知現貨即將交割）last notice day, last trading day

最後估價　final valuation

最後卸貨港　final port of discharge

最後紅利　final dividend

最後負擔　final incidence

最後效用　final utility, terminal utility

最後條款　final provisions, final articles

最後消費者　ultimate consumer

最後消費者市場　ultimate consumer market

最後產品　final goods, final products

最後船運通知　final shipping instruction

最後貸款人　lender of last resort

最後進價法　last invoice price

最後催繳股款　final call

最後實際損失　ultimate net loss

最後償還期　final maturities

最後議定書　final protocol

最高月份價格　peak monthly price

最高生產能量成本，足量成本　capacity cost

最高年產量　peak annual output

最高存量管理法　maximum stock control

最高利潤點　profit maximization

最高法院規程　Rules of the Supreme Court

最高限制　maximum limit

最高限度　ceiling

最高限價（指最高售價）ceiling price

最高紀錄年份　peak year

最高能量　maximum capacity

最高庫存量，最高存料量　maximum quantity of stores

最高率　maximum rate

最高責任　maximum liability

最高產量　peak production, peak output

最高最低稅則　maximum and minimum tariff

最高報價，頂盤　highest quotation

最高資金需要額　maximum financial requirements

最高價　top price, maximum price

最高價訂價法　skimming-the-cream price

最高價競買人　highest bidder

最高點(統計)　peak

最高額　ceiling amount, maximum amount

最高額限制　maximum amount limitations

最高額發行法　maximum issue method

最差收益率　yield to worst

最終用戶　final user

最終股利　final dividend

最終品質證明書　final certificate of quality

最終財務成果　final financial result

最終控股公司　ultimate holding company

最終認購帳(根據認購人對辛迪加經理人發出認購邀請書所作出的書面反應,列出承銷人的最後名單)　final underwriting account

最終購入價格法　method of price of last purchase

最惠國　most favoured nation

最惠國待遇　most favoured nation treatment

最惠國條款　most favoured nation clause

最惠國稅率　most favoured nation tariff

最新成就　last word

最新科學技術成就　most up-to-day science and technology

最新流行品　last cry, last cry first-out

最適宜的政策　optimal policies

最適度的平衡　optimum balance

最適量存貨　optimal inventory

最適量現金餘額　optimal cash balance

最適當生產向量　optimal production vector

最適資本結構　optimum leverage

最適關稅(指一國課徵關稅後,使該國獲得的經濟福利最大的關稅)　optimum tariff

最優化進出口商品結構　optimal structure of imports and exports

最優決策　optimal decision

最優惠利率　prime rate of interest

最優現金結存額　optimal cash balance

最優營業規模　optimal size of business

凱恩斯主義　Keynesianism

凱恩斯效應理論　Keynes-effect theory

凱恩斯經濟學　Keynesian Economics

凱撒式管理,專制管理　Caesar management

閘門價格(歐洲共同市場對進口家禽等規定的最低進口價)　sluice-gate price

圍標(指投標人在投標前阻撓他人報價或串通抬價,俗稱為抬標)　"rigged up" bidding collusion

[ノ]

牌名,牌號　brand

牌名政策,廠牌政策　brand policy

牌名貨　branded goods

牌照稅　license tax

牌價定單或觸及市價定單（指市價移動至指定價位時即成到價定單的定單）　board order or market if touched order

貿易　trade, commercial transaction

貿易中心　trade centre

貿易支付協定　trade and payments agreement

貿易及發展會議　Trade and Development Committee

貿易及關稅總協定　General Agreement on Trade & Tariffs

貿易外滙　trade foreign exchange earnings

貿易用語　trade terms

貿易收支　balance of trade

貿易自由　freedom to trade, liberty of trading, free trade

貿易自由化　liberalization of trade

貿易伙伴，貿易對象　trading partner

貿易合作組織　Organization for Trade Cooperation

貿易交易會　trade fair

貿易年度　trade year

貿易同盟　trade bloc

貿易危險　trade hazard

貿易赤字　trade deficit

貿易往來　trade contacts, commercial intercourse

貿易歧視　trade discrimination

貿易和支付協定　trade and payment agreement

貿易的技術性壁壘　technical barries to trade

貿易協定　trade agreement

貿易信用　trade credits

貿易約束　restraint of trade

貿易限制　trade restriction

貿易政策　trade policy

貿易促進　trade promotion

貿易盈餘　trade surplus

貿易指數　trade index

貿易風險　trade risks

貿易保護主義　protectionism

貿易保護主義者　protectionist

貿易保護法　trade safe-guarding act

貿易保護聯合會　United Association for the Protection of Trade

貿易值　trade value

貿易條件　trade terms

貿易條件效果　terms-of-trade effect

貿易條例　trade regulations

貿易條款　trade clause

貿易格局　pattern of trade

貿易逆差　unfavourable balance of trade, trade deficit

貿易乘數　trade multiplier

貿易差額　trade balance, trade gap

貿易配額協定　trade quota agreement

貿易商　trader, merchant

貿易區　trade zone

貿易帳戶　trade accounts

貿易開拓　trade creation

貿易情報交換所　clearing-house for

trade information

貿易清算帳戶　commercial clearing account

貿易減讓　trade concession

貿易量　trade volume

貿易項目　trade account

貿易順差　active trade balance, favourable balance of trade, trade surplus

貿易渠道　trade channels

貿易循環　trade cycle

貿易資本流動　trade capital movement

貿易滙率　commercial rate

貿易管制　trade control

貿易談判　trade negotiation

貿易慣例　trade usage (or customs)

貿易範圍　trading limit

貿易調整　trade adjustment

貿易餘額效果　real balance effect

貿易機會　trade access

貿易戰　trade war

貿易壁壘　trade barrier, trade wall

貿易優先權　trade preference

貿易擴展　trade expansion

貿易關係　trade relations

貿易環境　trade environment

貿易環境風險指數　Business Environmental Risk Index

貿易總額　total volume of trade

貿易轉向　trade diversion

貿易轉向效果　trade diverting effect

貿易議定書　trade protocol

貿易權利　trade rights

貿易變動　trade fluctuation

貸，貸記，貸項，信用　credit

貸入　borrow

貸方　creditor side, lender, creditor

貸方金額　amount of credit side column

貸方記錄　credit entry

貸方票據　credit note

貸方對銷　contra credit

貸方餘額　credit balance

貸出　lending

貸出能力　banking power

貸差　credit balance

貸借　debit and credit

貸借人　tenant

貸借資金　loan fund

貸借對照表　statement of assets and liabilities, balance sheet

貸項　credit item

貸項憑單　credit memo

貸款，借款　loan

貸款人　accummodator, credit receiver

貸款方向　lending priorities

貸款付息　interest-bearing loan

貸款本金償還額　loan principal repayments

貸款市場　loan market

貸款回收　loan recovery

貸款佣金　loan commission

貸款利用權協議（國際貨幣基金貸款的）　stand-by arrangement

貸款利率　loan interest rate, lending rate, price of money

貸款協定　loan agreement

貸款協會法例　Loan Societies Act

貸款的提取　draw down

貸款限額　basic credit line ceiling

貸款條件　conditions for loans, terms of credit

貸款財團　loan consortium, loan syndicate

貸款帳戶　loan account

貸款通知單　credit note

貸款程序　loan processing

貸款期限　length of maturity

貸款最高限額　loan ceiling

貸款訴訟　moneylender's action

貸款資本　loan capital

貸款損失　loan loss

貸款損失準備金　loan loss provisions, loan loss reserve

貸款與存款比率　loan-deposit ratio

貸款業務　lending programme

貸款銀行　lending bank

貸款對象　prospective borrower

貸款緊縮　credit squeeze

貸款數量　size of the loan

貸款銷售業務（將銀行貸款以證券形式在證券市場上轉讓出售，以收取手續費）　loan sales transaction

貸款擔保品　security for a loan

貸款擔保計劃　loan guarantee programme

貸款總額　loan ceiling

集中分店會計制　centralized branch system

集中決策　concentralization of power in decision making

集中行銷　concentrated marketing

集中率　concentration ratio

集中控制　centralization of control

集中採樣　cluster sampling

集中採購　centralized purchasing, central buying

集中準備　centralized reserve

集中資金　pooling funds, concentrating funds

集中管理　centralized management

集中檢驗　centralized inspection

集合財務報表　conglomerate financial statement

集合體效用極大化　maximum collective utility

集成電路　integrated circuit

集約投資　intensive investment

集散中心市場　terminal market

集散港（指貨櫃/集裝箱的）　feeder port

集資，資本籌措　equity financing

集資成本　fund raising cost

集裝袋　flexible container

集裝箱/貨櫃　container

集裝箱/貨櫃船　container ship

集裝箱/貨櫃海關公約 Customs Convention on Containers

集裝箱/貨櫃運輸　containerized traffic

集團分保　pool reinsurance

集團動態　group dynamics

集團銀行業　group banking

集體支付工資制　group system of

wage payment

集體付款制　group payment system

集體投標　group bidding

集體消費　collective consumption

集體基金　collective fund

集體產品　group product

集體儲備單位（1965 年由法國德斯坦提出，建議將國際儲備的創造同黃金總存量聯繫起來）Collective Reserve Unit

智能卡（國際萬事達卡和 Visa 卡將推出的一種集成電路信用卡，以代替靠磁條記憶的信用卡）Smart Card

智能測驗　intelligence test, aptitude

短少　shortage

短交貨　short delivery

短卸　short-landed

短卸貨　short-landed cargo

短卸證明書　short-land memo

短重　shortage in weight, shortage of weight

短促的人機操作工序 short-cycle man-machine operation

短缺，盤虧，空頭　short

短借長貸　borrowing short to lend long

短距離移動　short move

短途貨運 short-distance freight services

短量　loss of quantity

短量索賠　shortage claim

短量險　risk of shortage in weight

短量險不超過 0.5%　risk of short-age in weight in excess of 0.5%

短量險無免賠率但自然損耗除外 risk of shortage in weight irrespective of percentage but excluding natural loss

短期公債　short-term public loan

短期市場　short-term market

短期外資　short term foreign capital

短期可變賣證券 securities realizable at short notice

短期決策　short-range decision

短期存款　short deposit

短期合夥　joint venture

短期合夥投資　joint venture investment

短期利率　short-term interest rate

短期投資　liquid investment, temporary investment, short-term investment

短期投機買賣　speculation

短期拆借　callable loan, call loan

短期非流動債權　short-term nonliquid claims

短期放款　short-term loan

短期定期儲蓄　short-term time deposits

短期持票人　holder in due course

短期信貸　short-term credit

短期信貸綜合擔保　comprehensive short-term credit guarantee

短期負債　short-term liability

短期計劃　short-term plan

短期限價證券　short tap

短期保險　short term insurance

短期借款　short-term borrowing

短期政府證券　short-term government securities

短期國庫券　short-term treasury bond, treasury bills

短期票據　short-term notes

短期貸放市場　short-term lending market

短期資本　short-term capital

短期資本流動　short-term capital movement

短期資本損益　short-term capital gain and loss

短期資金　short-term fund

短期資金市場　short-term money market

短期資金融通　short-term financing

短期資產　short-term assets

短期債券　short-term bond

短期債務　short-term debt

短期債權　short-term claims

短期滙票　short-dated bills, short-term bills

短期滙率　short quotation, short exchange rate

短期預測　short-term forecasting

短期預測技巧　short-term forecasting technique

短期預算　short-range budget

短期經營計劃　short-range planning

短期墊款　temporary advance

短期趨勢　short swings

短週期，短期循環　short cycle

短裝貨　short-shipped goods

短橋（將集裝箱運輸船隻的航路與陸上鐵路相聯接的橋樑，與"陸地橋"同義）　minibridge

短噸（等於 2000 磅）　short ton

舒適型結構　relaxed and loose structure

舒適纖維（一種平織用的高張力聚酯纖維）　comfort fibre

鈔票　bank note, paper, paper currency

鈔票發行　bank note issue

鈔票發行過多　excessive issuance of bank notes

鈎損險　risk of hook damage

勝訴　winning a suit

象徵性交貨　symbolic delivery

象徵性保費　nominal premium

象徵性償付（償付一小部分債款，作為承認債務的象徵）　token payment

須正本尚未兌付　first unpaid

須副本尚未兌付　second unpaid

須簽字蓋章照付的票據　bill to order

備用成本，休閒維持成本　cost stand-by

備用協定　stand-by arrangement

備用保證（指投資商提供的一種保證）　stand-by commitment

備用信用證　stand-by letter of credit

備用能量　stand-by capacity

備用零件　replacement parts

備用貸款（規定在貸款期限內，借款人根據本身的資金支付與市場利率

情況，可以動用也可以不動用貸款）　stand-by credit

備用貸款安排　stand-by facility arrangement

備用權利（美國術語，指一家公司提供的"購物權力"）　stand-by offering

備件，備用品　spare parts

備忘分錄簿，流水帳，原始帳　blotter

備忘錄　memorandum

備忘錄協議　memorandam agreement

備抵存貨跌價　allowance for reduction of inventory to market

備抵折舊　allowance for depreciation, provision for depreciation, reserve for depreciation

備抵壞帳　allowance for bad debts, allowance for doubtful accounts, allowance for uncollectables, provision for bad debts

備查分錄　memorandum entry

備查分類帳　memorandum ledger

備運提單（船公司已收存貨物，待船舶抵港後再行裝運時，開給託運人的提單）　received for shipment bill of lading, received bill of lading

順序作業　sequential access

順序抽樣　sequential sampling

順序計算　sequencing computation

順序連續記錄　consecutive entries

順序檢驗　sequence checking

順差　favourable balance, surplus

順差國家　surplus country

順滙　favourable exchange

順價，期貨溢價，期貨升水　cantango, normal market

等比尺度　ratio scale

等成本線　isocost line

等同普通股，準普通股　common stock equivalent

等利潤線　isoprof

等級　grade, rate

等級尺度　ordinal scale

等級較差　inferior grade

等級標誌　grade mark

等級證書　grading certificate

等值收入　parity income

等值年成本　equivalent annual cost

等值美元　U.S. dollar equivalent

等值單位，當量　equivalent unit, effective unit

等值貨幣　common dollar

等值貨幣會計　common dollar accounting

等值報酬　parity return

等值債券收益率（美國術語，指計算按折扣出售證券的收益率）　equivalent bond yield

等倍數　equimultiple

等距尺度　interval scale

等距曲線　equidistant curve

等候保險　waiting insurance

等候期間　waiting period

等量曲線　isoquanta curve

等量關稅　equivalent duty

等價交換　equal exchange, equivalent exchange

等價格線　iso-price line

等額分期付款　equal installment

策略計劃　strategic planning

策略管理　strategic management

策略顧問　strategic consultant

策略靈活性　strategic flexibility

進入市場的自由　freedom of entry

進入市場壁壘　barrier to entry

進口代理商　import commission house

進口外滙　import exchange

進口行　import house

進口存款制　import deposit scheme

進口批准單　import permit

進口批發商　importing wholesaler

進口承諾　import commitment

進口附加稅　import surtaxs

進口押金制　advanced deposite, import deposit scheme

進口招標　import tender

進口信用證　import credit

進口限制　import restriction

進口限額　import ban

進口訂貨行　indent house

進口訂貨單　indent

進口值　import value

進口差價稅　variable import levies

進口配額　import quotas

進口配額申請書　application for import quota

進口配額制　import quotas system

進口商　importer, import merchant

進口商報關單　importer's entry of goods

進口貨　imported goods (or commodities)

進口貨物估價表　import valuation list

進口貨臨時報告書　bill of sight

進口許可證　import license

進口許可證制　import license system

進口執照　import certificate

進口量　import volume

進口稅　import duty, import levy

進口稅則　import tariff

進口稅繳納證　import duty memo

進口替代　import substitution

進口程序　import procedure

進口貿易　import trade

進口報關單　import declaration

進口資金融通　import financing

進口匯票　import bill

進口運費及保險費　import freight and insurance

進口運輸　import traffic

進口需求的收入彈性　income elasticity of demand for import

進口需求的價格彈性　price elasticity of demand for import

進口管制　import control

進口價格　import price

進口艙單　import manifest

進口總額　gross imports

進口關稅險　risk of contingent import duty

進口證明　certificate of import

進口簽證更改　imports amendment

進出口交換比價　terms of trade

進出口商同業公會　importers and exporters association

進出口商品結構　import and export by commodities

進出口配額制　import-export quota system

進出口許可證制　import-export license system

進出口連鎖制　import-export link system

進出口價格彈性　price elasticity of import and export

進貨平均價　purchase average cost

進貨合同　purchase contract

進貨利率　interest on payment for purchases

進貨發票　purchasing invoice

進港船舶　ships entered harbor

週末前習慣性平倉（期貨市場用語，指持有多頭或空頭者，通常在假期或週末到來前，都會在收市前想辦法平倉，以避免假後市情變化而受損失）　evening up

週息曲線買賣（根據週息曲線變化之估計買賣利率期貨）　riding the yield curve

週報　weekly reports

週期存貨　cycle inventories

週期性失業　cyclic unemployment

週期性波動　cyclical swing (or fluctuation)

週期性通貨膨脹　cyclical inflation

週期性循環指示數字　cyclical indications

週期性經濟危機　periodic enconomic crises, cyclical economic crises

週期性變動　cyclical variation

週轉　turnover

週轉中貨幣量　amount of money in circulation

週轉金　revolving fund, working fund

週轉性包銷便利（一種新的籌資工具，由一家或多家銀行負責包銷的中期貸款承諾，允許借款人期限內以發行短期票據方式分批動用貸款）　revolving underwriting facility

週轉的週期　cycle turnover

週轉信貸計劃　revolving credit plan

週轉信貸額度　revolving line of credit

週轉基金　circulation fund, working capital fund, revolving fund

週轉率，週轉速度　turnover rate, velocity

週轉現金　working cash

週轉量　volume of the circular flow

週轉稅　turnover tax

週轉資本　working capital

剩餘付款　residual payment

剩餘財產索償權　residual claim

剩餘資本主權　residual equity

剩餘資產　residual assets

剩餘農產品採購授權書　authorization to purchase surplus agricultural commodities

剩餘價值率　surplus value rate

剩餘購買力　discretionary purchasing power

創立公司　establish a company

創立合併　amalgamation

創見管理　creative management

創始投入　initial input

創始費用　initial outlay

創始資金，開辦資金　initial fund

創造行銷　creative marketing

創造價值　creation of value

創構價值（美國反傾銷法中計算非市場經濟國家商品價值的方法）　constructed value

創辦人股份　founder's shares, promotor's stocks

創辦人　organizer, prime mover

創辦成本　initial cost, organization cost

創辦利潤　promoter's profit

創辦時期　initial stage

創辦資本　initial capital

創辦資本投資　initial capital investment

無人工廠　unmaned factory

無人售貨商店　self-service store

無人提取的存款　unclaimed balance

無力償付　insolvency, suspension

無分回業務分保 non-reciprocal reinsurance

無日期　no date

無文據事項　matter in pais

無可異議的推定　conclusive presumptions

無外滙出口　no-draft export

無外滙進口　no-draft import

無用資產　dead assets

無用輸入無用輸出　GIGO (garbage in, garbage out)

無包裝貨物　unpacked goods

無代價的　gratuitous

無母數統計　non-parametric statistics

無母數測驗　non-parametric test

無存款（對空頭支票背批用語）　no effects

無存貨　out of stock

無形出口　invisible export

無形交易　invisible transaction

無形利益　invisible gain

無形股份　invisible stock

無形固定資產　intangible fixed assets

無形供給（指未能準確計算在手的商品存貨）　invisible supply

無形的標準　intangible standard

無形財產　incorporeal property

無形財產權　intangible property rights

無形差額　invisible balance

無形商品　intangible goods

無形開發成本　intangible development cost

無形進口　invisible import

無形項目（用於國際收支表）　invisible items

無形貿易　invisible trade

無形損失　nonphysical loss, nonmaterial loss

無形損耗　moral depreciation

無形資本　immaterial capital, invisible capital

無形資產　intangible assets, invisible

assets

無形資源　intangible resources

無形價值　intangible value

無沒收價值　non-forfeiture value

無利息　ex interest

無投票選舉權的股東　non-voting shareholder

無投票選舉權的股票　non-voting stock (or share)

無免賠率　irrespective of percentage

無拒付抗辯權　no protest for non-acceptance

無抵押擔保之債權人　unsecured creditor

無受益條款（海上貨物保險單上，言明運送人或其他人不得自該保單獲得利益之條款）　not to insure clause

無股息　ex dividend

無股息無分紅無還本也無要求攤派新股的權利　ex all

無股票公司　non-stock corporation

無面值股票　non-par value stock, no par value capital stock

無面額股票　no par stock

無法交付的支票　undeliverable check

無法交付的進口貨　undeliverable import goods

無法收款的支票　uncollectible check

無法控制的　uncontrollable

無法控制的通貨膨脹　run away inflation

無定額保險單　open policy

無抽簽的利益（買賣公債用語）　ex drawing

無相比性資料　non-comparable data

無限公司　unlimited company

無限制的否決權　absolute veto

無限制優惠　non-restricted preference

無限責任　unlimited liability

無限責任合夥企業　unlimited partnership

無限期罷工　strick of indefinite duration

無限擔保　unlimited guarantee

無信用　bad repute, discredited, not trustworthy

無風帆、無動力駁船　dumb barge

無紅股戶　non-dividend shareholder

無訂定的違約賠償金　unlimited damages

無負債　never indebted

無保額保險單　no amount policy

無保證合同（參見"無賠償合同"條）bare contract, nude contract

無保證基金（指無保證最低投資回報率的投資基金）　non-guaranteed fund

無疫證書（指船隻）　clean bill of health

無效　void, null and void

無效工時成本　idle time cost

無效合同　invalid contract

無效投資　make the investment inefficient

無效性，無效力　unavailability

無效果，無報酬(海上救助中被廣泛接受的原則) "no cure, no pay"

無效果，無報酬為條件的救助合同 "no cure, no pay" salvage contract

無息可轉讓提款通知書 non-interest-bearing negotiable order of withdrawal

無息存款　interest-free deposit

無息信貸　interest-free credit

無息票　ex coupon

無息公債　passive bonds

無息票據，不附息票據 non-interest-bearing note

無息債務　passive debt

無息貸款　interest-free loan

無息證券　non-interest-bearing securities

無記名支票　bearer check, bearer cheque

無記名式背書 endorsement in blank

無記名有價證券　bearer instrument

無記名股票　bearer share, bearer stock, bearer stock certificate, unregistered share

無記名信託證券　bearer depositary receipts

無記名票據　bearer paper, bearer instrument, bearer bill

無記名債券 bearer bond, unregistered bond

無記名匯票　bearer draft, bill drawn payable to bearer, bearer bill of exchange

無記名劃線支票 open crossed check

無記名證券　bearer securities

無條件交易 unconditional operations

無條件交貨　free delivery, unconditional delivery

無條件契約(即無擔保契約)　bare contract

無條件限制隨機抽樣　unrestricted random sampling

無條件背書　absolute endorsement

無條件流動能力　unconditional liquidity

無條件接受　clean acceptance

無條件最惠國條款　unrestricted most-favoured nation clause

無條件銷售　absolute sale

無條款信用書(不需有一般所需那類常用單據的一種商業信用證) clean credit, open letter of credit

無差別成本 non-differential cost, common cost, sunk cost

無差別待遇　non-discriminatory

無差異曲線　indifference curve

無差異行銷　undifferentiated marketing

無海岸國家　non-coastal state

無追索資金融通　non-recourse finance

無追索權　without recourse

無追索權信用證　without recourse letter of credit

無追索權背書　endorsement without recourse

無追索權匯票　non-protestable bill

無害通過權(海洋法)　right of innocent passage

無缺點計劃　zero defects programme, ZD programme

無缺點管理　zero defects management

無責任的一方　innocent party

無偏估計　unbiassed estimate

無理的拖延　unreasonable delay

無票面值股票　no par stock, no par value stock

無票面價值　no par value

無票面價值公債　no par certificate of stock

無密押　no test

無商業價值　no commercial value

無清償能力　insolvency

無帳簿會計制度　bookless accounting system

無稅貨物　non-dutiable goods

無稅港口　free port

無期貸款　perpetual loan

無須答辯　no case to answer

無答覆　no reply

無答辯　nihil dicit, nil dicit

無欺騙意圖　without fraudulent intent

無新股息　new share off

無資格的證人　incompetent witness

無牌營業者　interloper

無增支成本　zero incremental cost

無彈性　inelasticity

無彈性供給　inelastic supply

無彈性需求　inelastic demand

無慣例扣減條款(使保險人放棄海損賠付時原有"新換舊"扣減的條款)　no customary deductions clause

無標記　no marks

無賠款折扣　no claim bonus, no claim discount

無賠款退貨　return for no claim

無賠償合同(或稱無保證合同，指雙方雖達成協議，但尚未簽約，不保證履行)　naked contract (或稱 bare contract, nude contract)

無線電傳真費　television fee

無擔保公司債　"naked" debenture

無擔保信用貸款　open credit

無擔保負債　unsecured liability

無擔保帳項　unsecured accounts

無擔保債券，信用債券　unsecured bond

無擔保項目　unsecured accounts, general crossing

無擔保貸款　unsecured loan, signature loan

無擔保融資　accomodation loan

無憑單項目處理系統(一種電子滙款系統)　paperless item processing system

無優先權的債權人　general creditor

無償分發新股票　no-paid allotment

無償出口　unrequited exports

無償使用　use without compensation

無償受讓人　voluntary grantee

無償契約　naked contract

無償援助　nonreimbursable assistance

無償債能力的債務人 insolvent debtor

無償讓與　voluntary conveyance

無競爭的出價　non competitive bids

無競爭力的價格 price not competitive

無體物權　property in action

無權要求新股，無新股息　ex-new

無權認購新股，除權　ex-rights

街市　shopping streets

街招　circulars

街影投射面積　street shadow area

街頭小販　street hawker

復出口　re-export

復貼現，再貼現　rediscounting

復進口　re-import

復業　resume business

復甦 recovery, economic resurgence

循環，週期　cycle

循環式包銷協議　revolving underwriting facilities

循環交換　revolving swaps

循環性支付差額 cyclical disequilibrium

循環性股票(受經濟景氣和蕭條強烈影響的股票，又稱敏感性股票)cycle stock

循環使用貨幣調換服務(交通銀行香港分行向地鐵公司提供的一種資金調換安排) revolving cross-currency swap facilities

循環信用證 revolving letter of credit

循環信貸限額 revolving line of credit

循環指數　cycle index

循環流動　circular flow

循環時間　cycle time

循環效應　cyclical effect

循環基金，週轉性基金　revolving fund

循環開單制，週期開單制　cycle billing system

循環程序　cycle program

循環貸款(借款人在貸款有效期限內，可根據本身對資金的需求和市場的利息水平，提用或償還不確定金額的貸款) revolving credit

稅收　revenue, duty

稅收收入　tax receipts, tax revence

稅收共付票據　tax anticipation bills

稅收印花　revenue stamp

稅收負擔　tax burden

稅收減讓(指對投資的鼓勵)　tax incentive

稅收管理　tax administration

稅收調整　tax adjustment

稅單　duty memo

稅則　tax regulations, customs tariff

稅則的精細分類　refinement of tariff classifications

稅則類別　tariff nomenclature

稅級　tax bracket

稅捐　taxes, duties

稅捐分配　tax allocation

稅捐信貸　tax credit

稅捐貸項　tax-loss credit

稅務功能　tax function

稅務會計　tax accounting

稅務機關　tax authorities

稅率　rate of taxation, tax ratio

稅率表　table of rates

稅率等級　grades of tax rates

稅源　tax fund, source of revenue

稅款　tax payment, taxation

稅款專用　earmarking of taxes

稅款減除數　tax credit

稅種　items of taxation

稀少經濟學(限制產量以保證利潤的一種理論)　scarcity economics

稀缺規律　law of scarcity

稀釋證券(指可調換為普通股, 而導致降低每股盈利的證券)　dilutive securities

程序　procedure

程序化決策　programmed decision

程序分析　procedure analysis

程序交易(一種股票交易方式或策略的統稱, 指利用電子計算機技術在股票現貨與期貨市場上相互配合, 同時進行的一攬子的股票交易)　program trading, computerized trading

程序改變率　rate of change in the process

程序表　process sheet

程序控制　procedure control

程序設計　procedure design

程序設計語言　programming language

程序圖　procedure chart

程序操作　procedure operation

程租船　voyage charter

[一]

費用　expense, charges, fee

費用已付　charges paid

費用比率　expense ratio

費用分配　expense allocations

費用分類　expense classification

費用付現　expense liquidated

費用先付　charges forward

費用成本　expense cost

費用存款　expense fund deposit

費用附加帳戶　expense adjunct account

費用抵銷帳戶　expense contra account

費用常數　expense constant

費用擔保　[拉]cautio pro expensis

費雪效應(愛爾文‧費雪教授提出的一種利率預測理論: 各國的名義利率等於投資者實際回收率與預期通貨膨脹率之和)　Fisher's effect

媒介作用　instrumentality, mediation

媒介效應(指金融中介機構提供大量的金融工具作為資金供求的媒介)　intermediation effect

媒體佣金　media commission

疏忽條款(載於提單上的免除船公司責任的條款)　negligence clause

疏通流通渠道　unclog the channels of circulation, clear circulation channels

登記代表　registered representative

登記合格公司, 列名公司　listed companies

登記合夥營業股東　registered partner

登記股東　stockholder of record

登記費，註冊費　registration fee

登記稅　registration tax

登記債券　registered bond

登記標準　listing standard

登記噸位　registered tonnage

登記證書　certificate of registry

發出訂單　placing an order

發生效力　taking effect, operating upon

發行　float, issue

發行日期　issuing date

發行公債　issue of government bonds, issue of public loans

發行外國債券　foreign bonds issued

發行平價　issue par

發行有價證券　issue of securities

發行地點承兌信用證　issuing point acceptance credit

發行辛迪加　issuer syndicate

發行股票　issuing stock (or shares)

發行股票說明書　prospectus for issuing stock

發行者費用　issuer's cost

發行條件　issue term

發行貨幣　issue of money (or currency)

發行新債券，重新籌資　refinancing

發行新債券取代舊債券　refunding bonds

發行債券　issue bonds (or debentures)

發行債券費用　floatation cost, bond issuance expenses

發行溢價股票　share premium account

發行銀行　issuing bank

發行價格　issue price

發明　invention

發明人證書　inventor's certificate

發明者　inventor

發放貸款　offer loans, extend a loan

發起人股份　founder's shares, promotor's stock (or shares)

發展中公司　growth company

發展中的出口國家　developing exporting countries

發展中國家　developing countries

發展中國家的發展戰略　development strategies of the developing countries

發展成本　development cost

發展民族經濟　national economic development

發展研究　development research

發展基金　development funds

發展稅　development tax

發展貿易　develop trade

發展貸款　development loan

發展貸款基金　development loan fund

發展資金供應　development financing

發展隨機過程　evolutionary stochastic process

發票，發貨單　invoice

發票之核準　invoice approval

發票日後，出票後（票據用語）　after date

發票成本價　invoice cost

發票金額　invoice amount

發票金額錯誤　errors in invoice

發票副本　invoice duplicate

發票價格　invoice price

發票價值　invoice value

發貨　deliver goods, send out goods

發貨人，託運人　consignor, shipper

發貨地價格　free on board in harbor

發貨國　country of dispatch

發貨通知　consignment note

發貨港　port of dispatch

發貨單　dispatch list

發達卡（1981年初由香港南洋商業銀行發行的信用卡）　Federal Card

發達國家　developed nation

發運單　shipping order

發盤，發價　offer

發盤人　offeror

發盤附樣品　offer sample

發還（原法庭）　refer back to

發還令（財物等的）　order of restitution

發霉險　risk of mold

強佔訴訟　trover

強迫公債，強迫債款　forced bonds

強迫付款　forced payment

強迫卸貨　forced discharge

強迫降落　forced landing

強迫借款　forced loan

強迫清算　forced liquidation

強制手段　compulsive means

強制存款　forced deposit

強制仲裁　compulsory arbitration

強制性制裁　compulsory sanction

強制和解　compulsory conciliation

強制保險　compulsory insurance

強制流通　compulsory circulation

強制破產　involuntary bankruptcy

強制執行　compulsory execution

強制解決　compulsive settlement

強制結業（指法院下令公司結束業務）　compulsory winding up

強制履行　compulsory performance

強制購買　compulsory purchase

強制儲蓄　forced saving

強硬措施　strong measures

統一手續費　flat commission

統一市場　uniform market

統一成本會計　uniform cost-accounting

統一責任制　uniform liability system

統一責任標準　uniform level of liability

統一基金　consolidated fund

統一商法典　[美國]Uniform Commercial Code

統一累進稅　consolidated progressive tax

統一費用率　flat rate

統一發票　uniform invoice

統一債券　unified bonds

統一債權（均衡債權）　equalization claim

統一慣例　uniform custom

統一價格　price on a uniform basis, uniform price

統一賠償責任限額規則　uniform monetary limitation of liability rule

統一變數折舊法 depreciation method of uniformity varying amounts

統制分類帳 controlling ledger

統制股權 controlling interest

統制帳戶 control (controlling) account

統計方法 statistical methods

統計分析 statistical analysis

統計分析技術 statistical analysis technique

統計決策 statistical decision

統計序列 statistical series

統計性分類 statistical breakdown

統計表格 statistical table

統計抽樣（法） statistical sampling (methods)

統計的獨立性 statistical independence

統計控制 statistical control

統計推論 statistical inferences

統計常數 statistical constant

統計程序 statistical procedure

統計資料 statistical data

統計預測 statistical forecast

統計圖 statistical chart

統計精度區間 statistical precision interval

統計調查法 method of statistical survey

統計誤差 statistical discrepancy

統計學家 statistician

統計監督 supervision by statistical means

統計變量估計 statistical variable estimation

統保 blanket insurance

統保單 blanket policy

統售價格 flat price

統購統銷 unified purchase and sale

結欠 balance due

結欠清單 account rendered

結出帳戶餘額 balancing account

結存 credit balance

結收外滙 exports proceeds in foreign exchange have been collected

結帳日 day of reckoning

結帳分錄 closing entry

結帳手續，結帳程序 closing procedure

結帳前試算表 pre-closing trial balance, trial balance before closing

結帳後試算表 post-closing trial balance, trial balance after closing, after closing trial balance

結帳整理 closing adjustment

結清債務 settle a debt

結清銀行帳戶 closing the bank account

結清餘額 settlement of balance

結滙 settlement of exchange, convert foreign exchange

結滙實績 exchange record

結滙證 marginal receipt

結算 settling account, closing an account

結算日，交割日 settlement day

結算方式選擇權 settlement option

結算帳戶 clearance account

結算貨幣 currency of settlement

結算貸款　loan for the settlement of accounts

結算單據　document of settlement

結算價格　settlement price

結構分析術　morphological analysis

結構性通貨膨脹　structural inflation

結構性障礙　structural obstacles

結構阻擾(指外國資金、商品、技術、人才進入一國市場起着有形無形、直接、間接、巧妙隱蔽的阻止干擾作用)　structural impediments

結構調整貸款　structural adjustment lending

結轉　carry down, carry-over

結轉下期損失　loss carried forward to the next term

結轉帳戶　continuing account

結轉餘額　balance carried forward

結關, 海關放行　customs clearance

結關貨物　clearance goods

結關貨場　clearance depot

結關費　customs clearance charges

結關港口　port clearance

絕密, 高度機密　strictly confidential

絕對平價　absolute par

絕對成本　absolute cost

絕對全損　absolute total loss

絕對否決權　absolute veto

絕對利益　absolute advantage

絕對所有人　absolute owner

絕對所有權　absolute ownership

絕對所得　absolute income

絕對保險　absolute cover

絕對值　absolute value

絕對效用　absolute utility

絕對差量　absolute dispersion

絕對淨損(保險)　absolute net loss

絕對配額　absolute quota

絕對責任, 絕對賠償責任　absolute liability

絕對無條件付款　absolute promise to pay

絕對需要　absolute demand

絕對禁止令　absolute prohibition

絕對禁運品　absolute contraband

絕對誤差　absolute error

絕對適航保證　absolute warranty of seaworthiness

絕對優勢　absolute advantage

絕對轉讓(指對權益的)　absolute assignment

絕對權　absolute title

給人承包　put out to contract

給予一年寬限　give a year grace

給予折扣　discount granted

給予利息, 佔有權益　vested interest

給予補償　give satisfaction

給予簽證　give visa

給付約定條款　facility of payment clause

[丶]

資力保證　del credere

資力雄厚的銀行　strong bank

資本　capital

資本化　capitalization

資本化成本　capitalized cost

資本化利率　capitalization rate

資本化利潤　capitalized profit

資本化費用　capitalized expenses

資本化價值(指公司發行的各種證券價值總額)　capitalized value

資本化證券(根據普通股持有股份的比例免費提供的新股，亦稱臨時股或紅利股)　capitalization issue

資本支出，耗資　capital outlay, capital expenditure

資本預算　capital budget

資本分擔，資本參與　equity participation

資本公積　contributed surplus

資本未平均化的利潤率　unequalized profit rate of capital

資本外流　capital outflow

資本外逃　capital flights

資本生產率(每單元投入資本的產值)　productivity of capital stock

資本市場　capital market

資本市場管理制度　capital market control system

資本主義　capitalism

資本主義世界貨幣體系　capitalist world monetary system

資本主義市場　capitalism market

資本主義週期　capitalist cycle

資本主權　owners' equity

資本收入　capital receipts, capital income

資本收益　capital gains, capital revenue

資本收益稅　capital gains tax

資本成本(一企業各種資本來源之加權平均成本)　cost of capital

資本交易(指國際間投資與借貸等，或企業營業活動以外的交易)　capital transaction

資本有機構成　organic composition of capital

資本投入　capital input

資本投資　capital investment

資本投資回收年數法　pay-off method for capital investment

資本形成　capital formation

資本形成總值　gross capital formation

資本利息　interest on capital

資本利潤　capital profit

資本利潤率平均化　equalization of profit rates on capital

資本係數　capital coefficient

資本金　capital in cash

資本抽回　revulsion of capital

資本所有權　capital ownership

資本的利得與損失　capital gains and losses

資本性的投資　equity-type investment

資本的國際化　internationalized capital

資本的運用　employment of capital

資本的價值增值　expansion of capital value

資本抵補　replacement of capital

資本要求規則（交易所對成員公司的資本儲備要求）　capital requirement rules

資本信用　capital credit

資本重定　recapitalization

資本紅利　dividend

資本盈利　capital surplus

資本盈利水平　level of capital gains

資本負債　capital liabilities

資本負債比率　ratio of capital to liabilities

資本保險　capital insurance

資本限額　capital rationing, capital optimum

資本財，資本性貨物　capital goods

資本財的生產力　productivity of capital goods

資本財的定義　definition of capital goods

資本財的需求　demand for capital goods

資本流入　capital inflow

資本流動　capital movements

資本流量　capital flow

資本消耗扣除　capital consumption allowance

資本效率　capital efficiency

資本借貸　capital loans

資本耗損　capital destruction

資本租賃　capital lease, financial lease

資本租賃債務　obligations under capital leases

資本配額　capital rationing

資本淨額　net capital

資本比率　capital ratio

資本深化　deepening of capital

資本帳戶，資本項目　capital account

資本產出比率　capital-output ratio

資本貨物　capital goods

資本接受國　capital recipient country

資本密集工業　capital-intensive industry

資本密集度　capital-intensity

資本密集項目　capital-intensive project

資本設備　capital equipment

資本稅　capital levy

資本集中　centralization of capital

資本項目（國際收支一個主要項目）　capital account

資本項目差額　capital balance

資本發展基金　capital development fund

資本結構　capital structure

資本循環　rotation of capital

資本週轉率　capital turnover ratio

資本週轉期　capital turnover period

資本過少　under-capitalization

資本過戶稅　capital transfer tax

資本過剩　surplus of capital, over-capitalization

資本損失　capital loss

資本資產　capital asset

資本資產評價模型　capital asset pricing model

資本槓桿作用（指公司有能力以借入資金為股東謀取額外的收益）　capital leverage

資本與產量比率　capital-output ratio

資本預算　capital budget

資本構成　capital gearing, capital composition

資本需求量　demand of capital

資本對固定負債比率　ratio of capital to fixed liabilities

資本對流動負債比率　ratio of capital to current liabilities

資本增值　increase in capital, capital appreciation

資本增值稅　capital gains tax

資本調整帳戶　capital adjustment account

資本輸出　capital export

資本輸出國　capital export country

資本獨佔　capital monopoly

資本積累　capital accumulation

資本虧空　capital deficit

資本還原成本　capital recovery cost

資本總庫　capital pool

資本總額　total capital, capitalization

資本儲備　capital reserve

資本聯合　capital combination

資本轉化為產品　convert the capital into a product

資本轉移　capital transfer

資本贖回　capital redemption

資金　funds

資金收入率　rate of income from the funds

資金利用效果　effective utilization of funds

資金利潤率　profit rate on funds

資金佔用費　payment for the use of state funds

資金表　fund statement

資金來源　sources of fund

資金來源及運用表　source and application of funds statement

資金"來源去路"表　"where-got where-gone" of funds statement

資金重估　reevaluation of capital

資金流動　cash flow

資金流量分析　flow-of-fund analysis

資金最低標準　minimum funding standard

資金運用表　statement of fund application

資金週轉　turnover of funds

資金週轉率　turnover rate of funds

資金償還　refundment

資金轉形效應(指金融工具的流通與分配，必然影響到財富的生產和所有權關係，從而再影響到實際經濟活動)　asset-transmutation effect

資金籌措　financing, fund raising

資金籌措活動　fund raising activities

資信報告　status report

資信評價(對一機構資信程度的估價)　credit rating

資料，數據　data

資料分析　data analysis

資料庫　data base, data bank

資料處理　data processing

資料儲存　storage of data

資格　qualification

資格股（就任重要職務時的必要股份）qualification stock

資格證明書　qualification certificate

資產市場決定滙率論　asset market approach to exchange rate determination

資產收益比率　asset-income ratio

資產利用情況類比率　asset-utilization ratios

資產折舊年限幅度　asset depreciation range

資產折舊基準期　asset guideline period

資產折舊幅度　asset depreciation range

資產抵減帳戶　asset reduction account

資產持有費用，貯存成本　carrying charge

資產重估價　asset appraisals, revaluation of assets

資產負債比率　equity-debt ratio

資產負債表，平衡表　balance sheet, statement of assets and liabilities

資產負債表日期　date of balance sheet

資產負債表外　off-balance-sheet

資產負債表帳戶　balance sheet account

資產負債表項目外籌資　off-balance-sheet financing

資產負債表項目對沖　balance sheet hedge

資產負債表數據和收益表數據之比率　balance sheet-income statement ratios

資產淨值　equity, net asset value

資產凍結　freezing of assets

資產結構　assets structure

資產報廢　assets retirement

資產週轉率　asset turnover (ratio)

資產置換基金　retirement fund

資產構成　composition of assets

資產對銷帳戶　contra-asset account

資產增值　appreciation in asset value

資產價值對銷貨額比率　ratio of asset value to sales

資產擔保，資產抵償　assets cover

資產購置和退廢預算　asset acquisition and retirement budget

資產總額利潤報酬率　rate of return on total assets

資產變現能力分析　analysis of financial liquidity

資產變價損失　loss on realization of assets

資產廢置損失　loss on property retired

資源　resources

資源分析　resource analysis

資源分配，資源配置　allocation of resources

資源平衡稅　resource equalization tax

資源佔有稅　taxes on the possession of resources

資源轉讓　transfer of resources

意大利船級社　[意]Registro Italiano

意向書　letter of intent

意向協定　intention agreement

意外死亡條款　sudden death clause

意外死亡險 accident death insurance

意外利益　windfall profit

意外事故　accident, contingency

意外事故準備 reserve for accidents, contingent reserve

意外事故頻率　accident frequency

意外保險　accident insurance

意外停泊　unscheduled call

意外費用　unforeseen expenses

意外損失　windfall loss, accidental damage

意外損失基金　contingent fund

意外運費　contingency freight

意外變動　accidental fluctuation

意見交換制度 real-time information system

意見庫　idea bank

意見書　prospectus

意見箱　suggestion box

意思自主(合同法的一項基本原則。) autonomy of the will

意圖條款(歐洲借款活動中的一項條款，說明進行借款的意圖)　purpose clause

誠信(指有誠意，守信用，不隱瞞) good faith

誠信佣金制度(指運費公會對全包託運人)　fidelity commission system

誠信價格　bona fide price

誠實　[拉]bona fide

誠實保證(承保僱員各種不誠實行為的一種信用保證業務)　fidelity bond

詳細內容後告　details to follow

詳細背書　endorsement in full

詳細查帳報告　long-term report

詳細項目單　itemized list

詳細規格書　detailed specifications

詳細概算　detailed estimate

詳細裝箱單　detailed packing list

詳細說明　detailed description

詳細審計　detailed audit

詳情電報(指電告信用證全部內容)　full details cable

試用期　during probation

試查　audit trial

試航航程　trial voyage

試探法　heuristic method

試算表　trial balance

試誤法　trial and error method

試調(檢測定位並排除例行秩序的錯誤，或計算機硬件，製造過程或控制系統的故障)　debug

試銷，試用滿意後付款　sale on approval

試編年度報表　tentative annual report

試編預算　tentative budget

試購　trial order

試驗　trial

試驗工人　experimental labour

試驗方法　experimental method

試驗成本　experimental cost

試驗訂單　trial order

試驗費用　experimental expense

試驗階段　trial and error phase

誇大損失　exaggeration of damage

詢價　enquiry, inquiry

詢價單　inquiry list

補充成本　supplementary cost

補充技術力量　recruit technical forces

補充投資　additional investment

補充協議　complementation agreement

補充信用證　supplementary letter of credit

補充契據　supplemental deed

補充品　complementary goods

補充庫存　replenish the stock

補充港　port of recruit

補交押金通知，補交保證金通知(見 "補倉"條)　margin call, variation call

補助分類帳，明細分類帳　subsidiary ledger

補助分類帳戶，明細分類帳戶　subsidiary account

補助價格　subsidized price

補足保費　restoration premium

補足保額條款　reinstatement clause

補助金　grant-in-aid

補倉(香港市場：①指市勢逆轉轉經紀按客戶手上合約市值而要求增加之按金。②指購入期貨與空倉相抵銷)　①variation call, margin call ②cover

補救的辦法　remedial measure

補救的檢驗　remedial inspection

補稅　revamped tax

補貼　subsidy, premium

補貼出口　subsidized export

補貼價格　subsidized price

補貼辦法　subsidy regulations

補進，補空，拋補，軋平頭寸　buy in, cover the position

補進契約　covering contract

補進短缺　short-covering

補進貨物　covering goods

補進滙款　covering remittance

補遺條款　addendum clause

補償　indemnity

補償交易　compensation transaction

補償金　compensatory amounts

補償性存款　compensatory deposits

補償性財政政策　compensatory fiscal policy

補償性開支　compensatory spending

補償性最低存款額　compensating balance

補償差額　make up a deficiency

補償基金　compensation fund

補償稅　compensatory duty

補償期　payout period

補償項目　offset item

補償費用增加條款(規定借款人必須負擔貸款銀行蒙受因規章制度約束而增加的一切費用)　clause to cover general increases in cost

補償貿易，產品回購　compensation trade, product buyback

補償貿易協定　compensation trade agreement

補償貸款　compensatory financing

補償勞動報酬　compensation for

living labour

補償報酬　compensation payment

補償損失　compensation for loss (or damage)

補償關稅(指進口國對由於出口國補助生產的貨物所徵的關稅，又稱抵銷關稅)　compensation duties

福利　fringe benefit

福利主義　exclusive stress on material benefits, welfarism

福利制度　benefit system

福利政策　welfare policy

福利基金　welfare fund

福利國家　welfare state

福利資本主義　welfare capitalism

塑料工業　plastic industry

塑料伸展包裝　plastic stretch wrapping

塑料信用(具體指以有凸印文字的塑料信用卡和存款銀行發給客戶可以驗證姓名，簽字的塑料支票卡)　plastic credit

塑料貨櫃／集裝箱　plastic container

塑膠袋　plastic bag

塑膠箱　plastic box

義務　duties, obligation

義務年限　obligatory term

義務承擔費　commitment charge

義賣　sale of goods for charity, charity sale

義賣市場　charity bazar

寬限，緩期　grace

寬限日(指滙兌上寬限之時日)　day of grace

寬限期(指票據等到期後的時間)　grace period

塞得爾清算系統(1971年由一批歐洲銀行建立在盧森堡的一家歐洲債券的清算系統)　Cedel. S. A.

新工業區　new industrial district

新公司　new incorporation

新巴塞爾協定　New Basel Agreement

新古典經濟學　neoclassical economics

新立帳戶　new account

新加坡元存單　Singapore Dollar CDs

新加坡國際貨幣交易所　Singapore International Monetary Exchange

新加坡銀行同業拆放利率　Singapore Interbank Offered Rate

新生產方式(日本產業界提出的："多品種而又小量地生產，在短短的交貨期內，製造暢銷商品"的一種方式)　new production system

新年大拍賣　new year sales

新投資　new investment

新投資所得率　rate of return on new investment

新花式　new pattern

新股份，新股票　new share, new stock

新的直接以歐洲美元發行的債券　new straight Euro-dollar bond offerings

新的通貨膨脹差距　new inflationary gap

新的國際經濟秩序　new international economic order

新的最低價位　new low

新的最高價位　new high

新的管理決策科學　new science of management decision

新定單　new order

新金滙本位制　new gold exchange standard system

新便士(英國 1971 年改為十進制後的新輔幣,等於百分之一英鎊)　new penny

新型設計控制　new design control

新政策　New Deal

新杰森條款(適用於海洋運輸合同的一個條款)　new Jason clause

新盈餘(指公司改組後的盈餘)　new surplus

新借款辦法　new technique of borrowing

新船名錄　new register book of shipping

新產品　new product

新產品估價　new product evaluation

新產品發展　new product development

新產品滲透理論(美國艾佛利‧羅渣士提出,認為所有新的產品或概念在被大眾接受前,先經一些地位高、有影響的人使用,然後慢慢引導其他消費者先後試用)　diffusion of innovations

新通貨膨服缺口(指工人平均每小時收入的增加超過每人時產量的增加)　new inflationary gap

新專款授權　new obligation authority

新減債基金　new sinking fund

新國際回合　New International Round

新貨幣主義　New Monetarism

新貨幣借款　new money loans

新發行(紙幣等)　new issue

新發行市場　new issue market

新發行資本股票　new capital issues

新發行債券　new issue bond

新發行熱門股票　hot new issues stock

新發展計劃　new development plan

新換舊　new for old

新換舊條款　new for old clause

新債代舊債　novation

新經理　new manager

新經濟學　new economics

新資源　new resources

新聞廣告　news paper advertising

新興力量　newly emerging forces

新興工業國　newly industrialized country

新興物質生產部門　newly developing material production department

新興科技領域　new scientific and technological undertakings

新增生產能力　new productive capacity for

新增固定資產　newly acquired fixed assets

新增效益　new efficacy

新增消費資金　newly increased consumption fund

新增國民收入　newly-gained national

income

新增價值　newly-increased value

新增積累資金　newly increased accumulation funds

新樣式　new style pattern

新穎性(指專利產品發明)　novelty

廉價　bargain price

廉價中心　bargain centre

廉價出售　sell at a bargain, dispose of at a low price

廉價品　bargain, cheap goods

廉價脫手　bargain away

廉價商店　discount store, [美]cheapie

廉價貨幣政策(目的在擴大信用和降低利率)　cheap money policy

廉價優待　bargain offer

棄船　abandonment of a ship

棄權(期權持有人取消執行期權的行動)　abandon

棄權證　waiver

棄權條款　waiver clause

塗改痕跡　sign of erasure

溢出　overflow

溢卸貨物　overlanded cargo

溢缺額帳戶　over-and-short account

溢開帳款　overcharge an account

溢短裝條款(合同中關於交貨數量可多交或少交多少百分比的規定)　more or less clause

溢價　premium price

溢價債券(指超過票面值的債券或英國政府的有獎債券)　premium bond

溢價儲蓄債券　premium savings bond

溢額　overage

溢額再保險　surplus reinsurance

溢額部分　surplus share

滅失或不滅失條款(海運提單或海上保險單條款)　lost or not lost clause

滅失記錄　loss experience

溝通網絡　communication networks

溝通模式　communication model

滑動平價　gliding parity

滑動條款　escalator clause

滑動稅率　sliding scale duty

滑動滙率體系　sliding parity system

滑動價格　sliding scale price

滑動價格條款　slide clause

滑動關稅　sliding tariff

煙燻損失　smoke damage

道瓊斯三十種工業股票價格平均數　Dow Jones 30 Industrials Averages

道瓊斯平均數　Dow Jones Average

道瓊斯股票價格平均數　Dow Jones Stock Average

道瓊斯股票價格綜合平均數　Dow Jones Composite Average

道瓊斯指數　Dow Jones Index

道瓊斯商品行情指數　Dow Jones Commodity Index

道瓊斯經濟通訊社　Dow Jones

道義上的責任　moral obligation

道義危險(保險)　moral hazard

道德調查　moral survey

滙入滙款　inward remittance

滙水,滙費,貼水　charge for remittance, charges transfer, agio

滙出滙款　outward remittance

滙出額　remitted amount

滙兌平準基金　exchange equalization fund

滙兌平價　par of exchange

滙兌所得　exchange acquisition

滙兌最高限額　superior limit of exchange

滙兌資金　exchange fund

滙兌預約書　exchange contract note

滙兌損益　exchange gain and loss

滙兌銀行　exchange bank

滙兌餘額　balance of exchange

滙返資金　repatriation of fund

滙差年率（指期貨外滙與現貨外滙滙價之間的年差率）　rate differential

滙票　bill of exchange, draft

滙票出票地點　place of drawing

滙票到期　bill to fall due, bill to mature

滙票展期　prolongation of bill

滙票通知書　advice of drawing, letter of advice

滙票樣本　specimen of draft

滙票讓購期限　exchange negotiating date

滙票簿，票據簿　bill book

滙率，滙價 conversion rate, exchange rate

滙率安排　exchange rate arrangement

滙率伸縮性 exchange rate flexibility

滙率制度　exchange rate system

滙率波動幅度 exchange rate margin

滙率波動準備　reserve for fluctuation (in exchange)

滙率的最低限　floor exchange rate

滙率的最高限　ceiling exchange rate

滙率指數　exchange rate index

滙率格局　pattern of exchange rate

滙率差額　exchange rate differential

滙率—產出複合　exchange rate—output complex

滙率調整　exchange rate adjustment

滙率機制　exchange rate mechanism

滙率變動預測　forecasting exchange rate changes

滙率變動儲備金　exchange fluctuation fund

滙款　remittance, remit money

滙款方式　method of remittance

滙款支票　remittance check

滙款收款人　beneficiary of remittance, remittee

滙款單　cash remittance

滙劃銀行　giro bank

滙價下跌，滙率下浮　exchange rate depreciation

滙價上揚，滙率上浮　exchange rate appreciation

滙價風險，滙兌風險　exchange risks

滙總　summary

滙總日（英國銀行業用語，指將各種數字滙總上報英格蘭銀行的那一天。通常指某月的第三個星期三。）　summary date

滙總帳戶　summary account

滙總繳納　　pay on a consolidated

basis

準方案　quasi-project

準不動產(指租借地權等)　chattel real

準失業　quasi-unemployment

準平衡　quasi-equilibrium

準合夥人　quasi-partner

準改組(指對公司的)　quasi-reorganization

準所有權　quasi-proprietary

準兩稅制　partial double tax system

準契約　quasi-contract

準租金　quasi rent

準現金資產　near-cash assets

準現金儲備　secondary cash reserve

準貨物　quasi-goods

準貨幣　near-money

準買賣　quasi-bargain

準資本貨物　quasi-capital goods

準滙率聯盟　Pseudo Exchange Union

準壟斷勢力　quasi monopolistic power

準議付單據　quasi-negotiable document

準備成本　setting up cost

準備出售　for order

準備金　reserve fund

準備金投資　investment of reserves

準備金要求　reserve requirement

準備金恢復使用　desterilization of reserves

準備性負債　reserve liabilities

準備貨幣,儲備貨幣　reserve currency

準備裝卸貨通知書　notice of readiness

準備裝運　ready to be picked up

準備銀行　reserve bank

準據法(雙方當事人在協議中,明示規定的應當適用於其協議的法律。又稱管轄合同的法律)　proper law

[一]

鼓形桶　drum

鼓勵投資　encourage investment

碰損險　risk of clashing

碰撞條款　collision clause

碰撞險　collision insurance

較小利益　inferior advantage

較小滙率波動幅度　narrower fluctuation margin of exchange rate

較大滙率波動幅度　wider fluctuation margin of exchange rate

逼倉(期貨市場,多頭買方預期可交割商品缺乏或將市場現貨收購一空。等交割期到時,空頭被逼以超高價買回,香港稱為"挾倉")　short squeeze, corner

塊　ingot

填早日期,填倒日期　foredate, ante date

填早日期支票(票上日期早於實際出票日)　foredated check, ante date cheque

填早日期票據　foredated bill

填遲日期　post-date

填遲日期支票　post-dated cheque

填遲日期票據　post-dated bill

載重吃水線，載重線　load-line, load waterline

載重吃水線標誌　plimsoll mark

載重表尺　dead weight scale

載重能力　loading capacity

載重量　dead weight capacity

載重噸位　dead weight tonnage

載貨上船　load a ship with cargo

載貨重量噸　deadweight cargo tonnage

載貨容積　cargo capacity

載貨船隻　carrying ship

載貨貨櫃/集裝箱　loaded container

禁止入內　no entrance

禁止出口　prohibition of export

禁止吸煙　no smoking

禁止車輛通行　no thoroughfare for vehicles

禁止直接交易　prohibition of direct transaction

禁止性進口稅　prohibitive import duties

禁止性關稅　prohibitive duty

禁止黃金出口　embargo on the export of gold

禁止停車　no parking

禁止通過　no thoroughfare

禁止船舶出口　embargo on ships

禁止推翻契據　estoppel by deed

禁止推翻租借　lease by estoppel

禁止進口　prohibition of import

禁止進出口　embargo

禁止擺攤　no peddler

禁支基金　nonexpendable funds

禁令　injunction, ban

禁航地區　prohibited area

禁區，禁止航行區域　prohibited area

禁運　embargo

禁運品　prohibited goods

酬金　emolument

電力工業　electric power industry

電力成本　electric power cost

電力機火車　electric locomotive

電子工業　electronics industry

電子元件　electronic components

電子文件歸檔　electronic filing

電子卡片打洞設備　electronic punch-card equipment

電子付款系統（又稱銷售點電子轉帳。見該條）　electronic payment system

電子信號　electronic signal

電子計算器　electric calculator

電子計算機指令編碼　coding of computer instruction

電子計算機會計　computerized accounting

電子郵件　electronic mail

電子現金記錄機　electronic cash register

電子貿易（指以當代最先進的 EDI 技術代替單證來傳遞國際貿易信息、數據，以實現國際貿易的自動化）electronic trade

電子貨幣（應用電腦系統進行結算的一種手段、形式）electronic money

電子資金轉移 electronic fund transfer

電子資金轉帳系統 electronic fund transfer system

電子數據交換(指不同計算機系統之間用電子手段傳遞按約定的電文標準組成的信息數據方法) electronic data interchange—EDI

電子數據處理 electronic data processing

電流中斷保險 power interruption insurance

電氣裝置 electrical device

電梯責任險 elevator liability insurance

電費 electric cost

電報信用證 cable letter of credit

電報訂貨 cable order

電報掛號 telegraphic address

電報費 cable fee

電報確認 confirmation of cable

電報縮略語 cablese

電報議付 cable negotiation

電滙 telegraphic transfer (T/T)

電滙售出 telegraphic transfer sold

電滙買進 telegraphic transfer bought

電滙滙票 telegraphic money order, telegraphic draft

電傳 telex (TLX)

電傳打字電報機 teleprinter, teletypewriter

電傳資料 communication processing

電傳、電訊的縮略語 telexese

電傳機 telex machine

電腦 computer, electronic brain

電腦記帳系統，電腦會計制度 computerized accounting system

電腦記帳服務 computerized accounting service

電腦軟件 computer software

電腦硬件 computer hardware

電腦程序設計 computer programming

電腦傳真 infofax

電腦資料管理 computer resource management

電腦輔助設計 computer-aided design

電話交換機 switch board

電話售貨中心 telephone centre

電熱器 electric heater

零用金 petty cash

零用現金日記帳 petty cash journal

零用現金基金 petty cash fund

零投資供給 zero investment supply

零沽經紀人 odd lot broker

零星批量 job lot

零星股(指股票交易中不足一手交易的零散股) odd lot, broken lot, fractional stock

零星股買賣人 odd lotter

零星股認股權證 fractional stock warrants

零星貨物(少於貿易中常用單位額度) odd lot, unenumerated articles

零星運輸 retail shipment

零相關 zero correlation

零息債券（指沒有定期支付的利息的債券，其最終收益全取決於債券到期時的資本收益） zero coupon bonds

零售　retail selling

零售引力　retail gravitation

零售分配　retail distribution

零售中間商　retailing middleman

零售市場　retail market

零售生意　retail business

零售包裝　retail packing

零售成本　retail cost

零售位置決策　retailing location decision

零售店　retail store

零售物價指數　retail price index

零售信用　retail credit

零售商　retailer

零售商品政策　retailing merchandising policy

零售商業　retail commerce

零售週期　wheel of retailing

零售業會計　retail accounting

零售業標準協會（英國） Retail Trading Standards Association

零售價格　retail price

零售價盤存法　retail method of pricing inventory, retail method of inventory

零售銷售額　retail sales volume

零基法　zero-base approach

零基計劃與預算編制法　zero-base planning and budgeting

零基預算，以零為基礎之預算　zero-base (or based) budget

零基預算法　zero-base budgeting

零階通路　zero-level channel

零線　zero line

零數　fraction

零數驗證　zero proof

零增長，無增長　zero growth

零擔運價　less than car load rate

零點　zero point

落定價　settled price

落後指標，滯後指標　lagging indicator

落後國家　backward country

董事　director

董事會　board of directors

董事長　chairman of board

萬事達卡（1967年開始，由美國3000家銀行通過行際信用卡協會簽發的信用卡） Master Card（原名：Master Charge）

萬能機械手 general-purpose manipulator

萬國郵政公約 Universal Convention of Post

萬國郵政聯盟 Universal Postal Union

萬國勞動協會 International Labour Association

萬國博覽會　World's Fair

募捐　collect contributions

募股書　prospectus

敬請光臨　thanks for your coming

搬家公司　removing company

搬貨許可證　removal permit

搬運工　porter, carrier

搬運公司　removal contractor

搬運費　carriage, stevedorage, cartage

搬運業　cartage undertaking

揭示,企業決算公開　disclosure

揭示主義　disclosure doctrine

損失　loss

損失分攤條款　contribution clause

損失百分比率　percentage of damage

損失所負責任　liability for loss

損失明細表　loss bordereaux

損失率(保險)　loss ratio

損失通知單　notice of loss

損失理算(保險)　adjustment of loss

損失報告書　loss report

損失補償保險　indemnity insurance

損失證明　proof of loss

損失證明書　certificate of damage

損益　profit and loss

損益分配　distribution of profit and loss

損益分配帳戶　profit and loss appropriation account

損益平衡點分析 breakeven point analysis

損益表　profit and loss account, income statement

損益相抵　gains offset the losses

損益帳戶　profit and loss account

損益滙總表　profit and loss summary (account)

損益調整帳戶　profit and loss adjustment account

損益轉帳事項　profit and loss transaction

損害　detriment

損害防止條款，救護條款(海上保險船方的救護條款)　sue and labour clause

損害程度　degree of damage

損害程度的測定　measure of damage

損害賠償　damages

損害賠償估量　measure of damages

損耗　shrinkage, wastage, spoilage

損耗率　attrition rate

損耗費　cost of wear and tear

損耗資產　waste assets

損壞狀態　damaged condition

損壞查定　damage assessment

損壞報告書　damage report

損壞維護　breakdown maintenance

損壞賠償訴訟　damage suit

携款潛逃　run off with money

"搶帽子"(股票市場用語，指靠買空賣空之差額而獲利)　scalp

"搶帽子"交易者　scalper

"搶帽子"行為(投資服務組織壟斷價格的一種犯罪行為。他們購進股票，再勸誘他人尋求服務指導，然後趁高價出售)　scalping practice

搶購　shopping rush

搶購物資　rush for goods, panic buying of goods

搭配　assortment

搭賣　tied sale, tied-in sale

搭賣條款　tied-in clause

瑞士航空公司 Swiss Air

瑞士黃金聯營 Swiss Gold-trading Pool

瑞士國家銀行 Schweizerische National Bank

瑞典中央銀行 Sveriges Riksbank

瑞典學派 Swedish school

[丨]

裝門面措施(指銀行、企業為某一特定日期如年底籌措資金,以示很高的清償力而採取的專門調節措施) window-dressing

裝卸 loading and unloading

裝卸平均品質條件 average or mean shipped and landed quality terms

裝卸作業 loading and unloading operation

裝卸率 rate of loading and discharging

裝卸費用 loading and unloading expenses, terminal charges

裝卸期間 lay days, laytime

裝卸期間損失 loss sustained during loading and unloading

裝卸誤期費 demurrage

裝配 assembly

裝配工業 assembly industry

裝配件 assembly parts

裝配成本 assembly cost

裝配常規 assembly routine

裝配程序 assembling process

裝配線 assembly line

裝貨 loading

裝貨付款 cash on shipment

裝貨次序 loading turn

裝貨收據 shipping receipt

裝貨容量 shipping capacity

裝貨清單 loading list

裝貨港 loading port

裝貨港堆場整裝/卸貨港貨運站分卸 container yard/container freight station

裝貨港堆場整裝/卸貨港堆場整卸 container yard/container yard

裝貨港貨運站拼裝/卸貨港貨運站分卸 container freight station/container freight station

裝貨港貨運站拼裝/卸貨港堆場整卸 container freight station/container yard

裝貨費 loading charge

裝貨經紀人,裝貨代理人 loading broker

裝船地點 shipping point

裝船前不保險 non risk till waterborne

裝船指示 shipping instruction

裝船重量 weight shipped, loading weight

裝船品質 quality shipped, shipping quality

裝船淨重量 net shipping weight

裝船許可證 loading permit

裝船通知 shipment advice, notice of shipment, shipping advice

裝船時間　time of delivery

裝船貨樣　shipping sample

裝船須知　shipping instructions

裝船費　loading charge

裝船期限　date of shipping

裝船提單　shipped bill of lading, on board bill of lading

裝船單據　shipping document

裝運　shipment, load and transport

裝運口岸及目的地　loading port and destination

裝運日價格　day of shipment price

裝運托盤化　palletization

裝運前品質條件　preshipment quality terms

裝運重量, 離岸重量　shipping weight

裝運前資金融通　pre-shipment financing

裝運索賠　shipping claim

裝運港　shipping port, port of shipment

裝載不良　improper stowage

裝載計劃　loading plan

裝載量　loading capacity

裝載超重　overload

裝煤港　port of coaling

裝箱待運　be cased up for transport

裝箱費　crating charge

裝機容量　installed capacity of

裝機費用　installation charge

賊贓　［美俚］hot goods

賄賂行為　corrupt transaction

業主　proprietor

業主資本　proprietary capital, owner's capital

業主權益　proprietary equity, owner's equity

業外收益　non-operating earning

業外費用　non-operating expenses

業外營業　outside ventures

業務中斷保險　business interruption insurance

業務收益　earnings

業務活動　operational action

業務基金　operating fund

業務推廣獎勵折扣　promotional allowance discount

業務經理　office manager, operation manager

業務總裁　chief operating officer

業績評價會計　performance accounting

業權基礎　root of title

業權調查書　requisitions on title

運用財政赤字論(人為地增加財政赤字，創造更大"社會有效需求"以避免經濟衰退，促進經濟增長)　theory of deficit financing

運用資本週轉率　working capital turnover

運用資本準備　working capital reserve

運用資產淨額　net working assets

運作棉包(棉花交易術語，指由軋棉機送出重量不同的棉包數目)　running bales

運行可靠度　operational reliability

運行性因素　operational factor

運行機制　operational mechanism

運河通行費　canal tolls

運河通過稅　canal dues

運送中存貨　inventory in transit

運送成本　shipping and delivery cost

運送合同，租船合同　contract of affreightment

運送單　waybill

運通卡（美國運通公司 1951 年開始發行的信用卡，又稱"捷運卡"）American Express Card, Amexco Card

運貨列車　［英］goods train,［美］freight train

運貨車　delivery truck

運貨飛機　transport plane

運貨噸數　freight tonnage

運單　bill of freight

運費，水腳　carriage, freight, freight charges

運費已付　freight prepaid

運費公會，水腳公會　freight conference

運費分攤　split of lotal freight

運費付至……指定目的地(價) freight or carriage paid to …… (DCP)

運費付訖　freight paid

運費包括延遲費在內　freight and demurrage

運費由提貨人照付　freight forward

運費免付　carriage free

運費延期回扣制度　deferred rebate system

運費到付　freight payable at destination

運費保險　freight insurance

運費保險單　freight policy

運費、保險費付至……指定目的地（價）freight or carriage and insurance paid to …… (CIP)

運費將預付　freight to be prepaid

運費單位　freight unit

運費費率表　freight tariff

運費損失　loss of freight

運費補貼　primage

運輸工具　means of conveyance

運輸方式　means of transportation

運輸代理人　forwarding agent

運輸行　forwarding agent

運輸行提單　forwarder's bill of lading

運輸里程　transport mileage

運輸法例　Carriers Acts

運輸契約　contract of carriage

運輸浪費　misuse of transport facilities

運輸、倉儲及交通業　transportation, storage and communication

運輸途中受損　damage in transit

運輸途中受震　shocks received during transit

運輸途中銷售　sale afloat

運輸部門，送貨部　traffic department

運輸執照　transport certificate

運輸稅　transportation tax

運輸量　freight volume

運輸量增長率　traffic growth rate

運輸費用　forwarding expenses, forwarding charges

運輸單據　transport documents

運輸業　carrying trade

運輸網　transport network

運輸漏損量　transportation leakage

運籌學　operations research

遇難信號　signal of distress

過戶　assign, transfer, transfer of names, transfer ownership

過戶日(英格蘭銀行免費辦理公債等 過戶日,指星期一至星期五) transfer days

過戶冊　transfer register

過戶代理　transfer agent

過戶成本　assigned cost

過戶定期租船　time charter by demise

過戶帳(指股票等的)　transfer book

過失　wrong, default

過失所負責任　liability for fault

過失破產　negligent bankruptcy

過去成本　historical cost

過去的對價　past consideration

過份利得,超額盈利 excess earnings

過多的固定資本投資 overinvestment in fixed assets

過多的流通中的貨幣　excess money in circulation

過多積累　overaccumulation

過低估計　underestimation

過低估價　undervaluation

過低的定價　under-pricing

過度投機　overspeculation

過度供給　oversupply

過度負擔　overburden

過度發行　overissue

過度發展　overdevelop

過度需求　overdemand

過度膨脹　over-expansion

過度繁榮的經濟　overheated economy

過度競爭　over-competition

過高出價　overbid

過高估計　overestimate

過高估價　overvaluation

過時商品　obsolete merchandise

過時產品成本　obsolete stock cost

過帳　posting

過帳依據　posting reference

過帳錯誤　error in posting

過期　overdue

過期支票 overdue check, out-of-date check, stale check

過期未還銀行借款　overdue debts, overdue bank loans

過期利息　overdue interest

過期保險　extended term insurance

過期保險費　insurance expired

過期帳款　past due account

過期票據　overdue bill, past due notes

過期提單(指向開證行提交提單將遲 於貨物抵達目的港的提單) stale bill of lading

過期債務　overdue debt

過期債權　overdue credit

過期應收票據　notes receivable past due

過剩生產能力　surplus capacity

過剩流動性　excess liquidity

過剩現金　excess cash

過剩資本　excess of capital

過渡性貸款（用以解決借款人短期資金週轉需要的銀行貸款）　bridging loan, stopgap loan

過渡性融資　bridging financing

過量現金滾存　accumulation of excess cash balance

過與不足條款（見"溢短條款"）　more or less clause

過載船隻　overloaded vessel

過境手續　transit formalities

過境信用證　transit L/C

過境便利　passage facility

過境國　transit country

過境貨物　transit goods

過境稅　transit duty

過境貿易　transit trade

過境單據　transit document

過境報關單　transit declaration

過境簽證　transit visa

過境權　right of passage

過錯賠償責任　fault liability

過關手續　clearance through custom

過關費　gateway charges

跨月套利，約期套利（買入賣出不同月份的期貨套取差價利潤）　spread, straddle

跨市套利　arbitrage

跨年度　straddle over year

跨行業公司　conglomerate

跨國公司　multinational company, multinational corporation

跨國公司會計　multinational accounting

跨國企業，多國籍企業　multinational firm, multinational enterprise

跨國集團　multinational group

跨國戰略　multinational strategy

跨期分攤（指在兩個會計期間分攤）　interperiod allocation

跟著別人買賣股票的人，跟風買股票者　tailer

跟單承兌　documentary acceptance

跟單信用證　documentary letter of credit

跟單信用證統一慣例（1983年修訂本，簡稱《統一慣例》400）　Uniform Customs and Practice for Documentary Credits—1983 revision

跟單託收　collection by documents

跟單託收滙票　documentary bill for collection

跟單期票　documentary promissory note

跟單滙兌　documentary remittance

跟單滙票　documentary draft, documentary bill of exchange

跟踪系統　servomechanism

跟隨指標（美商務部由失業、停工週數，製造業存貨的銷售比率，製成品人工成本，優惠利率貸款數目，消費者負債升幅與個人收入升幅比率六種指標組成）　lagging indicators

跳樓貨（虧本廉價貨）　distress merchandise

跳躍式發展　development by leaps and bounds

路貨（指裝船在先，而訂約在後的貨物）　floating cargo

路透社商品價格指數　Reuter's Index of Commodity Prices

路線　route

路邊市場（原為紐約交易所外面買賣證券的場所。現指證券交易所和商品交易所正式交易時間以外進行交易的市場）　curb market

路邊交易，場外交易　curb exchange

照市價　at the market

照來樣製成樣品　counter sample

照章納稅　pay taxes according to regulations

照樣出售　sale by sample

照樣品定貨　sample order

照價付款　pay according to the arranged price

照辦或拒受（美國證券市場術語，指必需按固定價值履行某一滙票的全部金額，低於此數則不接受）　all or none

照顧價格　preferential price

暗盤　actual quotation

暗標競投　closed bid

歲入　annual revenue

歲入法案　revenue act

歲入稅　revenue tax

歲入彈性，稅收彈性　revenue elasticity

歲入預算　budget for annual receipts

歲入關稅（為財政收入而徵收的關稅）　revenue tariff

歲出　annual expenditure

歲出預算　budget for annual expenditure

農工聯合企業　agro-industrial complex

農基工業　agro-based industry

農產品　agricultural products

農產品計價法　farm price method

農場交貨價　ex plantation

農業一體化　agricultural integration

農業加工品　processed farm products

農業危機　agricultural crisis

農業保險　agricultural insurance

農業保護主義　agricultural protectionism

農業票據　agricultural paper

農業貸款　agricultural loan

農業資本　agricultural capital

農業資產　farm stock

農業銀行　agricultural bank

農業價格政策　agricultural pricing policy

置信係數　confidence coefficient

置信界限　confidence limit

置信區間　confidence interval

置換分析　replacement analysis

置換產品的創新　product-replacing innovations

勤勉條款　due deligence clause

戥倉（對投機性的約期套利，香港稱為"戥倉"）　straddle

戧倉交易(指購入某一交收月份的期貨，相對沽出同一種商品不同交收月份之期貨)　spread, straddle

歇業　give up a business, close door

圓筒式期權交易(美國花旗銀行推出的一種定頂定底的期權交易，原則是在滙價有利時，客戶放棄一部分應得利益，以換取少付一部分費用而仍得到滙價的保障)　the cylinder option

當日、次日或兩日"可用資金"　zero-day, one-day or two-day availability

當日平倉交易(指同一交易日內買進及賣出同一交割月份及同一數量的期貨)　jobber trade

當日交易人(指在同一交易日內以保證金信用方式多次買賣一種證券的人)　day trader

當日訂單　day order

當日報價　known price

當天指令(僅當天交易期間內有效的指令。如當天未成交，指令作廢)　day orders

當年價格　current year's price, the price of the respective year

當年還本付息　repay principal and interest within the current year

當地，當場　[拉]loco

當地交貨條件　loco terms

當地交貨價(指原產地)　loco price

當地拆箱(指貨櫃/集裝箱)　local devanning

當地信用證　local letter of credit

當地律師　local lawyer

當地費用豁免　local cost waiver

當地提單　local bill of lading

當地訴訟　local actions

當地裝箱(指貨櫃/集裝箱)local (vanning)

當地運價　local rate

當地價格　local price

當押　pawn

當押商　pawnbroker

當押舖　pawn shop

當事人　party, part concerned

當事人自主　party autonomy

當事人職責　responsibility and function

當負利息,應歸利息　imputed interest

當票　pawnticket

當量　equivalent weight

當場付款　prompt cash

當場交貨　spot delivery

當期成本　period cost

當期費用　period charges

當期債務利息　interest on current debt

當然違法　[拉]per se illegal

[丿]

與另一種貨幣掛鈎的債券(世界銀行發行的一種購與還均用美元結算，但規定美元與瑞士法郎滙率掛鈎的債券)　currency linked bonds

與他物接觸受損　damage through

contact with other cargo

與合同規定不符　different from contract

與訂單不符　discrepancies in an order

與高關稅的降價值相等的減讓　a concession equivalent in value to the reduction of high duties

與債權入和解　compound with creditors

亂行(價格術語，指商品市場及證券市場價格移動混亂，全無規則)　random walk

亂收費用　collect fees arbitrarily

亂拉資金　misuse of specified fund

亂攤成本　unjustified additions to production costs

會計比率　accounting rate

會計分錄　accounting entry

會計年度　accounting year, fiscal year

會計長，主計長　controller

會計法　accounting law

會計制度　accounting system

會計事項　accounting event

會計(帳面)所得　accounting income

會計科目　account titles

會計科目卡　card of accounts

會計科目表　chart of accounts

會計信息系統　accounting information system

會計政策　accounting policy

會計恒等　accounting identity

會計恒等式　accounting equation,

accounting formula

會計師　accountant

會計師事務所，會計公司　accounting firm, public accounting firm

會計師意見書　opinion of independent accountant

會計原則，會計原理　principles of accounting

會計原則委員會　Accounting Principles Board

會計矩陣　accounting matrix

會計哲理　accounting philosophy

會計記錄　accounting records

會計個體　accounting entity

會計個體慣例　entity convention

會計責任　accountability

會計專家　expert accountant

會計處理　accounting process

會計期間　accounting period, fiscal period

會計規程　accounting manual

會計基礎　basis of accounting

會計報告　accounting reports

會計程序　accounting procedure

會計報表　accounting statement

會計假定　accounting assumption

會計循環　accounting cycle

會計滙率　accounting rate

會計慣例　accounting convention

會計實務　accounting practice

會計標準　accounting standard

會計暴露　accounting exposure

會計憑證　accounting document

會計總報告　general accounting report

會計職能　accounting function

會計職業組織 accounting profes-
sional organization

會計變通辦法 accounting alternatives

會員運費率(運費同盟、海運公會的)
member rate

會員銀行　member bank

會談紀要　memorandum of meeting

會議錄　conference proceedings

解決國家與其他國家國民間投資爭端
公約(又稱"華盛頓公約"，1965 年
世界銀行通過) Convention on
the Settlement of Investment
Disputes between States and
Nationals of Others States

解決投資爭端的國際中心 Inter-
national Centre for the Settlement
of Investment Dispute

解決爭議　settle dispute

解決索賠　settle a claim

解約　break off an agreement, cancel a contract

解約書　letter of cancellation

解約條款　cancelling clause

解約權　right of rescission

解除　discharge

解除上市資格(對違反交易所制定的
基本標準的公司，解除其股票上市
資格) delist, detisting

解除出口禁令　removal of export
ban

解除合同日期　cancelling date

解除合同的補償費 compensation for
concellation of contract

解除扣押　release of distress

解除抵押　release of a mortgage

解除契約　discharge a contract

解除負債　exoneration

解除破產命令　order of discharge

解除貨幣管制　desterilization

解除債務　release from liability

解凍銀行存款　release of bank account

解款　pay in, pay into

解款單　cash remittance note

解僱　discharge

解僱費　severance pay

解釋規則　interpretative rule

解釋權　right to interpret

催收貸款　call in a loan

催告　interpellation

催繳股本(包括已收及催繳未收的股
本) call-up capital

催繳股款通知書　notice of call

催繳股款簿　call book

債主　creditor

債主權益　creditor's equity

債台高築　debts are rolling up, deep
in debt, heavily involved in debts

債券　issues, bond certificate, debenture certificate, instrumen-
talities

債券平均期限收益率　yield to aver-
age life

債券付息日 pay date of bond interest

債券市場　bond market

債券市場利息率　bond yields

債券包銷　bond underwriting

債券收回溢價　premium on bonds, redeemed

債券式票據, 保稅倉庫單 bond notes

債券自營商　bond dealer

債券回顧交易(Gen-Saki 指債券以再贖回為條件的出售。在日本由證券機構經管的, 根據回顧協定在中級市場銷售債券的市場)　Gen Saki market

債券兌回, 債券償還　bond redemption

債券兌換　bond conversion

債券利息　bond interest

債券投資　bond investment

債券投資信託 bond investment trust

債券估價　bond valuation

債券折價　discount on bonds, bond discount

債券折價累積　bond discount accumulation

債券表　bond tables

債券股利　bond dividends

債券抵押貸款　bond collateral loans

債券受託人　bond trustee

債券持有人　bond holder

債券信託契約　bond indentures

債券負債(指以發行公司債的形式而負擔的債務)　bonded debt

債券負債淨額　net bonded debt

債券負債總額　gross bonded debt

債券計價　bond pricing

債券息票　bond coupons

債券基金　bond funds

債券掉期(將一種債券賣掉而同時買入另一種債券)　bond swaps

債券費用　bond expenses

債券發行 bond issue, bond floatation

債券發行人　floaters

債券發行市場　bond floatation market

債券發行成本　bond issue cost

債券發行費用 bond issuing expense

債券登記簿　bond register

債券換新, 債券替代(指發行新債以償還舊債)　bond refunding

債券買賣的現金盈差(美國術語, 指由於一筆大宗債券出售, 並以較低的成本購入另一筆大宗債券而引起的現金增加)　take-out

債券買賣提高收益率(美國術語, 指出售一批債券又買進一批收益率更高的債券後, 在收益率上取得的收益)　pick-up

債券資本　debenture capital

債券債務(見"債券負債"條) bonded debts

債券債務準備　reserve for bonded debts

債券債務證書(指由金融機構出具擔保某項債券債務契約履行的文書)　bond

債券認購書　bond subscription

債券價值　bond value

債券溢價　bond premium

債券溢價的攤銷　bond premium amortization

債券擔保人 bond underwriter

債券償債基金 bond retirement fund, bond sinking fund

債務 debt, liabilities, indebtedness

債務人 debtor, loanee

債務人的期票 promissory note

債務人破產申請書 debtor's petition

債務人傳票 debtor summons

債務人與債權人之和解方案 deed of arrangement

債務人認為無誤的確定清單 account stated

債務公司 debtor corporation

債務支出 repayment of loan

債務扣押 attachment of debts

債務折扣 debt discount

債務免除 debt relief

債務更新 novation

債務係數(指債務總額對資產總額的比率) debt factor

債務表 debt tables

債務的承諾 acknowledgement of debt

債務的優先考慮(根據不同情況,優先考慮一種或多種債務的償還) prioritization of debt

債務到期日 date on which the claim becomes due, date of exigibility of the obligation

債務到期結構 maturity structure of debt

債務抵補率(實際年淨收入同年還本付息額之比率) debt coverage ratio

債務重訂,債務調整 debt restructuring

債務重新編網(在倫敦正在試行的一種國際銀行間結算外滙交易合同的新方法,兩個銀行間一天所作的全部交易,可改用一個總合同來代替) netting by novation

債務重議 rescheduling of debt

債務限額 debt ceiling, debt limit

債務保證 security for debt

債務國 debtor nation

債務資本化(把外幣表示的債務轉換成以債務國貨幣表示的債務:債權銀行把債務國的帳面債務折價出售給投資者,投資者則按債務原值折為債務國貨幣進行投資) debt capitalisation

債務與自然掉換(前西德對解決債務國外債負擔的一種做法:工業國豁免、減免發展中國家債務或提供新的財政援助信貸,必須以保護環境和關心生態平衡為前提) debt-for-nature swap

債務與股本交換 debt-equity swap

債務陷阱 debt trap

債務週轉信貸 debt financing

債務履行地法 [拉]lex loci solutionis

債務憑證期權 option on debt instruments

債務簡易訴訟 default summons

債務償付義務 debt-service obligation

債務償還比率 debt-service ratio

債務償還佔國民生產總值的 % debt service as a % of GNP

債務償還佔貨物和勞務出口額的 % debt service as a % of exports of

goods and service

債務償還的開支　debt service payments

債務償還數字　debt-service figures

債務還本付息　debt service

債務證券　debt instrument

債務籌資　debt financing

債務權益比率　debt-equity ratio

債務讓渡（指企業把已發行的外債應付的本利債務讓渡給銀行）　debt assumption

債票　bill of debt

債權　creditor's rights, financial claim

債權人，債主 creditor, loaner, debtee

債權人分戶帳　creditor's ledger

債權人的債權人　creditor's creditor

債權人破產申請書　creditor's petition

債權投資人　creditor investor

債權抵押　pledge of obligation

債權受益人　credit beneficiary

債權國　creditor country, creditor nation

債權銀行　creditor bank

債權轉讓　subrogation, cession of claim

債權轉讓書　subrogation form

債權證書債券　schuldschein-backed straight bond

傾銷　dumping

傾銷市場 dumping grounds, dumping market

傾銷地　dumping field

傾銷政策　dumping policy

傾銷差額　margin of dumping

傾銷稅　dumping exchange duty

傾銷價格　dumping price

傳票 [會計]voucher,[法律]summons

傳訊令更新　renewal of writs

傳統會計，慣例會計 conventional accounting

微利　meager profit

微波通訊 short-wave communication, micro-wave communication

微型　micro

微型化　micro-scale technology

微型產品　microminiaturization

微型電子計算機　microcomputer

微型膠卷　micro-film

微動作研究　micromotion study

微動計時器　microchronometer

微動裝置　micromotion unit

微陸橋運輸（貨櫃/集裝箱海陸聯運）micro-land bridge transport

微量調整　micro-adjustment

"微調"（用於經濟政策）　"fine turning"

微觀分析　micro-analysis

微觀效益　microeconomic returns

微觀會計　microaccounting

微觀經濟　microeconomy

微觀經濟政策　microeconomic policy

鉛皮胎箱　tinlined case

鼠咬損　damaged by rats

愛皮西世界商業密碼　ABC Universal commercial telegraphic code

毀壞信用　injury of credit

逾期　past due

逾期未公佈股利　passed dividend

逾期未付年金　annuity in arrears

逾期未付帳款　overdue account

逾期未收帳款　delinquent accounts receivable

逾期未遷出之承租人　tenant on sufferance

逾期貸款加息制度　system of charging a higher interest rate on overdue loans

躲債　run away from one's creditor

詹森條款（運輸提單中有關共同海損分攤的一個條款）　Janson clause

節約支出　curtail expenditures

節約資本發明　capital-saving invention

節約運費　save on transport costs

節省投資　reduce investment outlay

節省開銷　pare down expenses

節減費用　reduce expenses

〔一〕

經紀人　broker

經紀人自己提供資金　financing from broker's own capital

經紀人在場外直接進行的交易　transaction on dealers' basis

經紀人行業　brokerage business, broking

經紀人佣金　brokerage commission

經紀人的買賣　agency marketing

經紀人約書　broker's contract note

經紀人訂單　broker's order

經紀人留置權　broker's lien

經紀人貸款，墊頭貸款　broker's credit, broker's loan

經紀人傳票　broker's slip

經紀費　brokerage charges

經商　do business

經理　manager

經理制投資公司　management-investment company

經理基金　managerial fund

經常性支付　current payments

經常性支出　ordinary expenditure, recurrent expenditure

經常性失業　chronic unemployment

經常性收入　regular income

經常性投入　current input

經常性股息　regular dividend

經常性損益　recurrent profit and loss

經常國際交易（即經常項目交易）　current international transaction

經常項目（國際收支的主要項目）　current account

經常項目交易　current transactions

經常項目同國內生產總值比率　ratio of the current account to GDP

經常項目和長期資本往來的平衡　balance on current account and long-term capital

經常項目差額　balance of current account, current balance

經常費用　overhead charges, current

expenditure

經常預算支出 above-the-line expenditure

經常補助費 permanent subsidy, current subsidies

經常審計 continuous audit

經過票據所的票據交換總額 inclearing

經過證明的副本 certified copy

經銷協議 distributorship agreement

經銷商 distributor

經銷業 distributive trade

經濟一體化 economic integration

經濟力量 economic force

經濟中心 economic center

經濟互助委員會 Council for Mutual Economic Assistance

經濟分析 economic analysis

經濟手段 economic means

經濟比較 economic comparison

經濟不穩定 economic instability

經濟外交 economic diplomacy

經濟生存能力 economic viability

經濟立法 economic legislation

經濟司法 economic judicature

經濟目標 economic target, economic objective

經濟失調 economic ailment, economic disproportion

經濟失衡 economic unequality

經濟平衡 economic equilibrium

經濟主體 economic entity, economic body

經濟自由 economic freedom

經濟自由化 liberalization of the economy

經濟自由主義 economic liberalism

經濟成本 economic cost

經濟成果 economic fruit

經濟成長,經濟增長 economic growth

經濟成長率,經濟增長率 economic growth rate

經濟成效 economic effects, economic performance

經濟合同 business contract

經濟合同法 economic contract law

經濟合作 economic cooperation

經濟合作和發展組織 Organization for Economic Cooperation and Development

經濟合作署(美國) Economic Cooperation Administration

經濟共同體 economic community

經濟地位 economic status

經濟決定論 economic determinism

經濟有效原則 principle of economic efficiency

經濟行為 economic performance

經濟同盟 economic union

經濟危機 economic crisis

經濟作物 cash crops, industrial crops

經濟改革 economic reform

經濟利益 economic interests

經濟技術指標 economic and technical norms

經濟批量 economic lot size, economic batch quantity

經濟形勢 economic situation

經濟攻勢　economic offensive

經濟困難　economic difficulty,〔美俚〕up against it

經濟狀況　pecuniary condition, economics

經濟性投資（即直接投資，能促進社會資本財富增加，提高生產力）economic investment

經濟法典　economic code

經濟法則　economic law

經濟法庭　economic tribunal, economic courts

經濟法規　economic statutes, economic legislation, economic laws and decrees

經濟的黑暗大陸（指經濟未開發的非洲）economy's dark continent

經濟法實體　sustance of economic law

經濟物品　economic goods

經濟命脈　economic lifeline

經濟制度　economic system

經濟制裁　economic sanction

經濟波動　economic fluctuation

經濟事態　economic events

經濟依賴　economic dependence

經濟奇蹟　economic wonder

經濟界　economic world

經濟界限　economic boundaries

經濟限制　economic limit

經濟信息　economic information

經濟活動　economic activity

經濟活動機制　mechanism of economic activities

經濟恢復　economic recovery

經濟政策　economic policy

經濟計量預測法　econometric forecasting method

經濟計量模型　econometric model

經濟計量模型分析　econometric model analysis

經濟計量學　econometrics

經濟計劃　economic planning

經濟指標　economic indicator

經濟指數　economic index

經濟風險，經濟暴露　economic exposure

經濟負擔　economic burden

經濟科學　economic science

經濟刺激　economic stimulus (or incentive)

經濟訂購量　economic order quantity

經濟封鎖　economic blockade

經濟客體　economic object

經濟時（即夏令時）daylight saving time

經濟效用　economic utility

經濟效益　economic benefit, economic efficiency

經濟效率　economic efficiency

經濟秩序　economic order

經濟特使　economic mission

經濟特區　special economic zone

經濟特點　economic traits

經濟原則　economic principle, economic doctrine

經濟起飛　economic takeoff

經濟衰退　economic recession

經濟流通　economic circulation

經濟差距　economic gap

經濟時間數列　economic time series

經濟恐慌 economic panic, economic crisis

經濟核算　economic accounting (or calculation)

經濟問題　economic problem

經濟區　economic region

經濟參事　economic counselor

經濟密度　economic density

經濟規律　economic law, canon of economics

經濟現象　economic phenomenon

經濟停滯　economic stagnation

經濟動態　economic dynamics

經濟動機　economic motivation

經濟崩潰　economic breakdown (or bust)

經濟實體　economic entity

經濟組識　economic orgainization

經濟基礎　economic base, economic foundation

經濟單位　economic institution

經濟援助　economic aid

經濟援助協定　agreement on economic aid

經濟統計　economic statistics

經濟發展　economic development

經濟週期　economic cycle

經濟復甦　economic resurgence

經濟集團　economic bloc

經濟結構　economic structure

經濟割據　economic separation

經濟萎縮　economic contraction

經濟循環,經濟週期 economic cycle, circular flow of economic system

經濟落後國家　backward country

經濟資料　economic data

經濟資源　economic resources

經濟運動　motion of economic

經濟與貨幣聯盟 economic and monetary union

經濟預測 economic projection, economic forecasting

經濟零增長　zero-growth

經濟對抗　economic confrontation

經濟槓桿　economic levers

經濟滲透 economic penetration, economic infiltration

經濟網絡　economic network

經濟綜合體　economic complex

經濟潛力　economic potential

經濟增長　economic growth

經濟增長率 rate of economic growth

經濟價值　economic value

經濟調整　economic readjustment

經濟摩擦　economic friction

經濟數學模型　mathematical economic model

經濟戰　economic war (or warfare)

經濟戰略　economic strategy

經濟獨立　economic independence

經濟蕭條　economic depression

經濟職能　economic function

經濟優勢 economic advantage, favourable economic condition

經濟趨勢　economic trend

經濟繁榮　economic prosperity

經濟環境　economic environment

經濟競爭　economic competition

經濟變革　economic change

經濟變數　economic variable

經濟觀測指標　economic barometer

經營分析　operations analysis

經營內部化(指資金、技術和零部件的流動和轉讓大部分在公司內部經營)　operation internalization

經營成本　operational cost

經營成果　business performance

經營決策　operating decision

經營租賃　operating lease

經營效率　operating efficiency

經營資本利益率　operating earnings rate

經營管理　operating management

經營管理水平　managerial and administrative expertise

經營管理會計　administrative accounting

經營管理審計　administrative audit

經簽字蓋印之契據　specialty

經驗眾數　empirical mode

經驗認定法　judgemental identification

經驗管理學派　experience school of management thought

經驗調查　experience survey

隔日交割　overnight delivery

隔日借貸，隔夜借貸　overnight loan

隔離熱源(包裝外表標誌)　keep away from heat

預支信用證　anticipatory letter of credit

預支條款　red clause

預支票據(船員在航行中因預支薪水交給船主的票據)　advance note

預付　prepay, advance payment

預付工資　advance wages

預付年金　annuity in advance

預付佣金投資基金(互助基金的一種)　front-end loan fund

預付押金　advanced deposit(s)

預付定金　advance money on a contract, down payment

預付所得稅　provision for income tax

預付保險費　advance payment of premium, deposit premium

預付帳戶　account of advances

預付部分貨款　partial cash in advance

預付現金　cash in advance

預付貨款　payment in advance

預付票款(指預付遠期票據)　anticipated payment

預付款　imprest, advanced payment

預付款不足　insufficiently prepaid

預付費用　advanced charges

預付項目　prepayment item

預付資本　advanced capital

預付經費　advance fund

預付運費　advance freight

預付滙款　advance remittance

預付廣告費　advertising expense prepaid

預收　receive in advance

預收(付)合同款　advance on contract

預收利息　interest received in advance

預收利潤　unearned profit

預收貨款　advance on sales

預收款　advance received, advance collection

預收款帳戶　advances received account

預收項目　items received in advance

預收催繳股款　calls in advance

預先安排的交易(期貨市場，經紀之間根據原有合約或非正式議定而進行之交易)　prearranged trading

預先承兌　anticipated acceptance

預先期望的資料　anticipations data

預先違背契約　anticipatory breach of contract

預扣稅　withholding tax

預扣認購的股份　own as you earn

預估　prediction, estimate

預估保費　estimated premium

預估負債　estimated liabilities

預估損失　estimated initial loss

預定日期付款的滙票　bill payable at a definite time

預定日期後若干日付款的滙票　bill payable at a fixed period after date

預定的最低報酬率　minimum reserved rate of return

預定保證金　margin money

預定起航時間　expect to sail, expect to depart

預定採購　scheduled purchasing

預定基差(於指定期間內，用雙方預先同意之基差，報出當時的期貨價)　booking the basis

預定違約金　estimated penalty, liquidated damages

預防性保養　preventive maintenance

預防性檢驗　preventive check

預防事故　prevention of accidents

預防費用　prevention costs

預防損失措施　loss prevention

預計收益　projected income

預計成本　anticipated cost, projected cost

預計年限總數折舊法　depreciation-sum of expected life method

預計折扣　anticipated discount

預計利潤　anticipation of profit

預計開始和完成日期　predicted starting and finishing dates

預計費用　projected expenditure

預計資金運用　estimated application of funds

預計資產負債表　projected balance sheet

預計裝卸完成時間　expected end of landing

預計銷售損失　estimated loss from sales

預計營業收入，歲入預計數　anticipated revenue

預計應付支付命令　anticipation warrants payable

預計變數　projected variables

預約分保 facultative obligatory reinsurance

預約保險單　open cover

預訂費　subscription

預料風險　anticipating risk

預託證券　depository receipt

預得利益　pre-acquisition profit

預期　expectancy

預期心理　psychological expectation

預期成本　anticipated cost

預期收益 prospective earnings, prospective yield

預期存貨　anticipation inventory

預期行動　anticipatory action

預期利益保險　insurance on imaginary profit

預期利益點　desired profit point

預期利潤　anticipated profit

預期利潤率　expected rate of profit, enticipated rate of profit

預期值（指從有限的或無限的範圍內反復抽樣而得的單項觀察資料的平均值）　expected value

預期售貨報告　pro forma account sales

預期報酬　prospective returns

預期損失　expected loss

預期價格　anticipated price

預期購買　anticipated buying

預測　forecast

預測成本　predicted costs

預測的可靠性 forecasting reliability

預測風險　forecasting risk

預測指數　predictive index

預測資產負債表　forecast balance sheet

預測模型　predictive model

預測價格　forecast price

預備支付人，預備付款人（指出票人和背書人可指定在付款地的第三人作預備付款人）　referee in case of need

預備數據　preliminary data

預算　budget

預算方案　budget program

預算支出冲回　appropriation refund

預算外收入　receipts not covered in the state budget

預算外投資　extrabudgetary investment

預算外資金　extrabudgetary fund

預算收入　budget revenue

預算赤字　budget deficit

預算明細表　budget schedule

預算盈餘　budget surplus

預算草案　drafted budget

預算差異分析 analysis of budget variances

預算執行　budget enforcement

預算控制制度 budgetary control system

預算基數　budget base

預算項目　budget item

預算準備　budget allowance

預算準備金　budget reserve

預算會計　budgetary accounting

預算資產負債表　budgeted balance

sheet, pro forma balance sheet

預算經費　budgetary resources

預算管理，預算控制　budget control

預算編制　budget-making, budgeting

預算編制過程　budgeting process

預算總收入　total budgetary revenue

預編損益表　pro forma income statement

預編資產負債表　pro forma balance sheet

預購合同　forward purchasing contract

預購定金　advance payment for future purchase

預繳出口外匯　advance surrender of export exchange

預繳外匯　advance settlement of foreign exchange

預繳進口保證金（亦稱"進口存款預交制"）　prior import deposit, advance import deposit

羣組技術　group technology

羣叠代法　group internation

十四畫

[、]

認人支票　check to order

認付，承兌　accept

認付費，承兌費　acceptance fee

認付滙票，承兌滙票　bill for acceptance

認付滙票人，承兌滙票人　accepter

認可股份，額定股本　authorized stock

認可抽樣檢驗　lot-acceptance sampling

認可資本，法定資本　authorized capital

認可資產，可稅資產　admissible assets

認股，認繳股款，認購債券　subscription, subscription for shares

認股人，債券認購人　subscriber

認股分戶帳　subscription ledger

認股日期　subscription date

認股冊　subscription list

認股合同　subscription agreement

認股書　application for shares

認股記錄　subscription records

認股選擇權　stock option

認股簿，認購債券簿　subscription book

認股權（指股東以低於市價購買增資股票的權利）　right, right to shares

認股權證　subscription warrant, stock warrant

認定份額　subscription quota

認定股利　consent dividend

認票不認人（支票用語）　pay to self, pay to bearer

認債　admission of liability

認賠書，賠償保證書　letter of indemnity

認購　subscription

認購人　subscriber

認購人收益　yield to subscribers

認購人選擇權　underwriter's option

認購分配數　allotment

認購分期付款債券　subscription instalment book

認購公債　subscribe government bond

認購股本　subscribe capital stock

認購股票　subscribe for shares

認購期限　subscription period

認購權，認股權　subscription right

認繳　subscribe, paid in

認繳分期支付股款　subscription instalment book

認繳份額　subscription quota

認繳股本　capital stock subscription

認繳普通股本　subscription to common capital stock

認繳債券　bond subscription

認繳價值　subscription price

認證，驗證　authentication

說明書(對物品的)　description, instruction, program

說明理由令　order to show cause

說明項　descriptive item

誤工　loss of working time

誤付　payment by mistake of fact

誤卸　mislanding

誤記　misdescription

誤記日期　misdate

誤報　misdeclaration, misrepresentation

誤期表　overdue list

誤期船舶　overdue vessel

誤解事物　mistake of facts

誤算　miscalculation, miscount

誘因　inducement

誘致投資　induced investment

誘致系數　inducement coefficient

誘致流動　induced flow

誘勸消費　induced consumption

榮譽付款，參加付款(在因拒絕付款而退票並已作成拒付證書情況下，非滙票債務人可參加支付滙票票款)　payment of honour

榮譽付款人，參加付款人　payer for honour

榮譽承兌(出票人拒絕承兌時，由第三方代為承兌，又稱參加承兌或代兌退票)　acceptance for honour

榮譽承兌人，參加承兌人　accepter for honour

裸裝貨　nude cargo

裸麥條件(倫敦市場規定穀物交易運輸途中穀物變質的損失由賣方負全部責任)　rye terms (R.T.)

敲竹槓，詐取　fleece

敲詐　blackmail

敲詐錢財　levy blackmail upon

敲詐錢財的人　blackmailer

豪商　merchant prince

精工　fine workmanship

精明商人　sharp trader

精品店(多售名牌商品並特別注重與顧客維繫的商店)　boutique

精益求精(商標用語)　excelsior

精算師(保險)　actuary

精確利息　exact interest

精確計量　accurate measurement

精確指數　index of precision

精選品　selected quality

精選品質　choicest quality

寡頭統治　oligarchy

寡頭統銷價格　oligopoly price

寡頭統購價格　oligopsony price

寡頭獨佔　oligopoly

滯延指數　lagging index

滯卸費　congestion surcharge

滯後經濟指標(指在總的經濟活動趨勢已改變之後一段時間才上升或下降的指標)　lagging indicator

滯後經濟指標綜合指數　composite index of lagging indicators

滯納利息　defaulted interest, arrear of interest

滯納金　fine for paying late, overdue fine

滯納稅款　overdue tax payment, delinquent tax

滯留(產品在銷售過程的一種現象，發生在產品成熟之後，衰退之前)　stagnation

滯留期，滯期費　demurrage

滯脹(指經濟停滯的通貨膨脹)　stagflation

滯期天數　demurrage days

滯港費　demurrage charge

滯銷股票　inactive stock

滯銷商品　unsalable goods

滿足需要　satisfaction of wants

滿期　maturity

滿期前都附利息　interest to maturity

滿載　full and down

滿載貨物　full and complete cargo

滲透　infiltrating

滲漏　leakage, seepage

滲漏險　risk of leakage

漲風　upward trend of price

漲停板(指由交易所訂出的一個交易日內上漲的最大幅度，其起算水平，一般由前一天的收盤價為基準)　limit up

漲價　rise in prices, inflation of prices, hike in prices

漲價盈餘，增值準備　appreciation surplus

漲價準備　reserve for appreciation

漲價趨勢　upward price trend

漲價總額　gross appreciation

滾存利益　accumulated profit

滾存盈餘　accumulated surplus

滾存帳款　surplus account

滾存費用　deferred charge

滾存資金　deferred assets

滾存數，轉歸後期數　carryover

滾存餘額　balance forward

滾利作本　capitalization of interests

滾動預算　budget rollover

滾裝　ro-ro (roll-on roll-off)

滾裝法(貨車直接開上開下的裝運法)　ro-ro system, roll-on roll-off system

滾裝船　ro-ro ship, ro-ro vessel

滾裝泊位　ro-ro berth, roll-on roll-off berth

滚裝貨　ro-ro cargo, roll-on roll-off cargo

滚裝貨櫃　集裝箱船 ro-ro container ship, roll-on roll-off container ship

滚裝碼頭　ro-ro dock, roll-on roll-off dock

漏斗貨櫃　集裝箱(底部裝有漏斗設備，用於裝運粉粒狀貨物的專用貨櫃)　hopper container

漏帳錯誤　errors of omission

漏稅　evade taxation, tax dodging

漏報應稅貨品　evade declaration of dutiable goods

漏損　leakage, ullage

漫天要價，失去市場　price oneself out of the market

漢堡條款(1978 年關於海上貨物運輸的聯合國公約)　Hamburg Rules

[一]

遠洋班輪　ocean liner

遠洋航線　ocean-going shipping line

遠洋貨輪　ocean-going vessel

遠洋貿易　ocean trade

遠洋運輸　ocean carriage, ocean shipping

遠洋運輸保險　ocean shipping insurance

遠洋運輸費率　ocean freight rate

遠期付款　payable at usance

遠期外滙　forward exchange

遠期外滙干預(指中央銀行在遠期市場買賣貨幣以影響"即期市場"的貨幣行為)　forward exchange intervention

遠期外滙升水　forward exchange premium

遠期外滙市場　forward exchange market

遠期外滙市場保值，遠期市場對冲　forward exchange market hedge

遠期外滙平價　forward exchange parity

遠期外滙合約　forward exchange contract

遠期外滙抵補　forward cover

遠期外滙買入價　a bid forward quotation

遠期外滙貼水　forward exchange discount

遠期外滙報價　forward exchange quotations

遠期外滙報點報價法　forward exchange point quotations

遠期外滙對做(賣出或買進一種貨幣的遠期，同時買進或賣出這種貨幣期限更長的遠期，又稱複合遠期交易)　forward forward

遠期外滙賣出價　an ask forward quotation

遠期外幣借款票據　long bill issued in the operation of lending foreign money

遠期平價(指期權交易價等於遠期滙率)　forward par

遠期合同　forward contract

遠期交易　forward transaction

遠期交貨　forward delivery, future delivery

遠期美元報價　forward dollar quotations

遠期抵補　forward cover

遠期拍賣　forward sales

遠期信用證　usance letter of credit

遠期保值(在未來特定日期，按商定價格，購入或售出一定數額的某種外滙的協議)　forward cover

遠期票據　long note, long-dated bill, long paper

遠期援助計劃　forward aid programme

遠期滙兌　forward exchange

遠期滙率　forward exchange rate

遠期滙票　usance draft, usance bill

遠期滙票期限，償付期限　usance

遠期滙票價，期票貼現率　usance bill rate

遠期債券(二十年以上的)　long bond

遠期裝運　forward shipment

遠期價格　forward price

遠程終端服務設施　Accounts Accessible through Remote Service Units

遠程運輸　long hauls

遠離鍋爐　stow away from boiler

酸性測驗(把流動資產負債與流動資產作比較，以確定其償債信用)　acid test

酸性測驗比率(指借款人償債能力的流動比率，即流動資產對流動負債的比率)　acid test ratio, quick ratio

駁船　craft, barge, lighter

駁船上交貨(價)　free on lighter

駁船費　lighterage

駁船險，駁運險　craft risk

駁覆書　counter-statement

截止日期　cut-off date

截止限制　cut-off limiting

截止時間　cut-off time

截止過戶日期　date of record

截面分析　cross-section analysis

墊本　advance capital for

墊款　advance in cash

墊料，墊充　padding

墊頭(用於股票購買的保證金)　margin

墊頭借支　margin borrowing

墊頭貸款(指銀行對證券經紀人提供以一定數量證券作抵押的貸款)　margin credit

墊頭貸款的保證比率(指證券經紀人借款數額佔所提供證券價格的比率)　margin requirement

墊縮單位包裝　pallet shrink

壽命週期成本　life cycle costing

壽命週期價格　life cycle costing

壽限折舊法，餘壽——總壽推算折舊法　depreciation-age-life method

需求下降　recession in demand

需求因素　demand factor

需求分析　demand analysis

需求引起的通貨膨脹　demand-pull inflation

需求曲線　demand curve

需求的特性　demand characteristics

需求的價格彈性　price elasticity of

demand

需求函數　demand function

需求律　law of demand

需求差異訂價法　demand differential pricing

需求結構　demand structure

需求與供給　demand and supply

需求遞減法則　law of diminishing demand

需求模式　demand model

需求增長　demand growth

需求彈性　demand elasticity

需求價格　demand price

需求膨脹　demand inflation

需求點　demand point

需求壓力　demand pull

磁心　magnetic core

磁性墨水識別碼的通用機器語言（美國銀行家協會同美國聯儲在 1956 年制定的磁性墨水編碼系統，可反映出一張支票屬何銀行、何聯儲區等情況）MICR-magnetic ink character recognition

磁帶　magnetic tape

磁帶文件　magnetic tape file

磁盤　magnetic disk

輕工業　light industry

輕型重油油輪　handy-size dirty carrier

輕型散裝貨輪　handy-size bulk carrier

輕型輕油油輪　handy-size clean carrier

輕率的行為　reckless conduct

輕率的訴訟　reckless litigation

輕率造成的損失　recklessness caused loss

輕量貨品　light cargo

輔助生產成本　manufacturing service cost

輔助部門　auxiliary department

輔助商業交易　subsidiary commercial transaction

輔助帳簿　subsidiary book

輔幣　auxiliary coin, subsidiary money

蒲式耳（英、美使用的容量單位）bushel

蒲席袋　matting bale

蓋子鬆落（提單批語）　top off

蓋面貨　topper

蒸汽成本　steam cost

蒸汽機火車　steam engine locomotive

蓄意行為　wilful act

蓄意的違法行為　wilful misconduct

蓄意造成的損失　wilfully caused loss

"墓碑"廣告（指宣布安排一筆信貸或發行債券的廣告，因這種廣告常框以黑色而得名）〔俚語〕tombstone

蒙受損失　incur losses, sustain losses

槓桿比率（有價證券對市場風險受影響的程度，一家公司可通過發行債券和股票來增加其資本，這兩者的風險關係稱槓桿比率）　leverage

槓桿因素　leverage factor

槓桿收購（1987 年股災後最常見的收購企業方式。指利用銀行借款和發行高息債券籌資收購，然後把收購企業的資產分拆或變賣，並利用其

流動資金來償債，香港市場稱之為
"拆骨"） leveraged buyout

槓桿作用合約（通常稱保證金戶口，
槓桿戶口，要求交收商品時，全部
費用分期付清） leverage contract

槓桿作用利益（公司年終獲利，先付
公司債利息，次付優先股紅利，有
餘才付普通股紅利，對普通股說，
叫做槓桿作用利益） leverage

槓桿租賃（出租人提供設備價款 20-
30%，餘由金融機構提供。貸款人
只能依靠出租設備租金償還其貸款
的一種租賃） leverage lease

槓桿率（最初支出增量和由此而產生
國民所得的附加量之間的關係的係
數） leverage ratio

槓桿貨幣存款（大通銀行最新推出的
一種讓客戶在存款開戶之後，可以
借回相等於存款額五倍的貸款）
leveraged currency deposit

槓桿程度（指銷貨增加某一百分比而
引起利潤增加的百分率） degree
of leverage

槓桿經紀（槓桿交易的主要人物，常
隨意決定交易活動，製造市價上
升） leverage dealer

摘由 reference, excerpts

摘要 summary, digest

摘要欄 remarks

摘錄 an excerpt

摻假 adulterate

摻假貨 adulterated goods

摻雜物 adulterant

境內帳戶 internal account

境內機構 domestic institution

境外帳戶 external account

境外機構 external institution

[丨]

獎金 bonus, incentive pay, incentive compensation

獎金制度 incentive system; incentive plan

獎勵工業 incentive industry

獎勵分紅基金 bonus and dividend
fund

獎勵及福利基金 bonus and welfare
fund

獎勵出口制 incentive export system

獎勵投資條例 Investment Incen-
tive Law

獎勵建議制度 incentive suggestion
system

對方 opposite party

對比廣告 comparison advertising

對付款地點加以限制的承兌 ac-
ceptance qualified as to place

對付款時期加以限制的承兌 ac-
ceptance qualified as to time

對出口補貼的附加規定（關貿總協
的） additional provisions on export subsidies

對外出口 export abroad

對外支付差額 balance of external
payments

對外收支不平衡 external imbalance

對外成交　do business with foreign firms

對外兌換性　external convertibility

對外投資利潤　income on investment abroad

對外承包工程　contract foreign projects

對外協調　external coordination

對外信貸保險協會(美國)　Foreign Credit Insurance Association (U.S.A.)

對外借入能力　ability to borrow overseas

對方借方餘額　foreign debit balance

對外國人的短期負債　short-term claims on foreigners

對外責任的否認　disclaimer

對外商品交換　exchange of commodities in foreign trade

對外清償力　external liquidity

對外貿易　foreign trade

對外貿易仲裁委員會　Foreign Trade Arbitration Commission

對外貿易利益　benefit from trade; gain from trade

對外貿易的國際結算　international settlements in connection with foreign trade

對外貿易逆差，外貿赤字，入超　foreign trade deficit

對外貿易政策　foreign trade policy

對外貿易乘數(指由於外貿出口增加，導致國民收入增加的比率)　foreign trade multiplier

對外貿易區　foreign trade zone

對外貿易理事會(美)　National Foreign Trade Council (U.S.)

對外貿易商　foreign trader

對外貿易商品結構　foreign trade structure

對外貿易國家專營制　foreign trade under state monopoly

對外貿易量　physical volume of foreign trade

對外貿易順差，出超　favourable balance of trade export duties, foreign trade surplus

對外貿易資金融通　foreign trade financing

對外貿易銀行　foreign trade bank

對外貿易管制　foreign trade control

對外貿易額　value of foreign trade

對外貸方餘額　foreign credit balance

對外短期負債　external short-term liabilities

對生意外行　ignorance of business

對沖　hedging

對外償付能力　external solvency

對抗關稅　counter tariff

對於不付款的法律救助　remedies for non-payment

對於交貨日期的法律救助　remedies as regards the date of delivery

對於交貨地的法律救助　remedies as regards the place of delivery

對於延遲交貨的法律救助　remedies

as regards delay of delivery

對於貨物不符合同的法律救助 remedies for lack of conforming

對於違約的法律救助 remedies for breach of contract

對於賣方不履行合同義務的法律救助 remedies for the seller's failure to perform his obligations

對所有權之誹謗 slander of title

對物權 ［拉］jus in rem

對開信用證 reciprocal credit, counter letter of credit

對帳單 statement of account

對等貨樣 counter sample

對等查核,奇偶校驗 parity check

對等償付的債權,反索賠 counter claim

對新發行股票無認購特權 ex rights

對價 consideration

對銷分錄 contra entry

對銷帳戶,抵銷帳戶 contra account, offset account

對銷貿易 counter trade

對銷購買 counter purchase

對應支出 counterpart expenditure

對應捐助 counterpart contribution

對應資金,對等基金 counter fund, counterpart fund

對轉售價格的控制 resale price maintenance

幣制 currency system

幣制改革 monetary reform, currency reform

幣值不變的假定 stability of monet-

ary unit assumption

幣值升降 currency depreciation and appreciation

幣值 currency value

幣值波動 currency fluctuation

幣值後進先出法 dollar-value LIFO method

幣值堅挺 currency value is firm

幣值調整 currency realignment

幣值調整因素 currency adjustment factor

幣值調整附加費 currency adjustment surcharge

幣值穩定 currency stabilization

緊急附加費 emergency surcharge

緊急情形下代理人 agent of necessity

緊急進口稅 emergency import duties

緊急關稅 emergency tariff

緊缺商品 commodities in short supply

緊縮性財政政策 tight financing policy

緊縮信用 contraction of credit, tight credit

緊縮政策 deflation policy, retrenchment policy

緊縮開支 retrench expenditure

緊縮貨幣投放 tighten up the money supply

緊縮銀根 tight money

緊縮銀根時期 tight money period

緊縮經濟 tighten the economy

團體人壽險 group life insurance

團體保險 group insurance

團體殘廢險　group disability insurance

團體標準　group standard

圖示目錄，圖解目錄　illustrated catalogue

圖形報表　pictorial statement

圖表研究（指利用圖表對市場進行技術分析，追查價格走勢，價格移動的平均數）　charting

圖表管理　management through figures

圖解網絡評核法　GERT network method

賒欠免言　no credit charges

賒欠清單　charge list

賒帳　on account, give credit

賒帳交易　credit transaction

賒帳條件，信用條件　terms of credit

賒銷，信用銷售　credit sale, charge sale, sale on open account

賒銷法　tally system

賒銷貿易　tally trade

賒銷發票　credit sale invoice

賒銷價格　credit price

賒購，信用購貨　credit purchase, give tick, buy on tally

賒購商店　tally shop

罰款，違約罰金　penalty, fine, amercement

罰款收入　fines, forfeits and penalty receipt

罰款總額　penal sum

遣散費　release pay, compensation for termination

嘜頭　mark

監事會　board of supervisors

監視　surveillance

監管的留置權　charge lien

監護人　guardian

監護權　guardianship

暢銷　sell like wild fire, sell well, good market

暢銷品　best seller, fast seller

暢銷證券　marketable securities

慘跌　sharp drop, sharp fall

慘淡經營　careful and thorough operation

[ノ]

管制市場　controlled market

管制股　controlled stock

管制貨物出口申請書　application for exportation of controlled commodities

管制貨物進口申請書　application for importation of controlled commodities

管制商品　controlled commodity

管制對外貿易　control of foreign trade

管制價格　controlled price

管倉收據　warehouse keepers certificate

管理才能　management talent

管理工程　control engineering

管理水平　control level

管理功能　management function

管理主義　managerialism

管理成本　handling cost

管理成效　management performance

管理決策　managerial decision

管理決策程序　managerial decision-making process

管理作風　managerial style

管理技術　managerial technique

管理系統　management system

管理制度　managerial system

管理的革命　managerial revolution

管理的責任　managerial responsibility

管理的控制　managerial control

管理的領導　managerial leadership

管理狀態　controlled state

管理界限　control limit

管理信息系統　management information system

管理要素　elements of management

管理型態　managerial style

管理指數　management index

管理科學　management science

管理哲學　managerial philosophy

管理原則　principles of management

管理效率　managerial efficiency

管理浮動(滙率制)　managed floating

管理浮動滙率制度　managed floating rate system

管理財產　administration of property

管理動力　dynamics of management

管理措施　control measures

管理通貨政策　managed currency policy

管理專業化　professionalization of management

管理貨幣　managed currency

管理貨幣制度　managed currency system

管理費　management fee, management expenses

管理程序　managerial process, administrative procedure

管理集團　managerial body

管理階層　management echelon, managerial hierarchy

管理循環　management cycle

管理會計　management accounting, managerial accounting

管理會計師　management accountant, managerial accountant

管理業務　management's business

管理滙率　managed exchange rate

管理經濟學　managerial economics

管理網　managerial grid

管理實務　management practice

管理價值　managerial value

管理價格　administered price

管理學　management science, management study

管理戰略　management strategy

管理機構　setup for economic administration

管理藝術　managerial art

管理權分散(在一個組織結構中分散決策權的管理辦法)　decentralization

管理權威　managerial authority

管道運輸(對石油、煤氣等運送）pipe-line transportation

管轄幅度 span of control

管轄權爭議 jurisdictional dispute

算法語言 60(一種高水平的用於科學計算機程序設計語言） algol 60

算帳 do accounts, work out accounts, reckoning

算術平均數 arithmetic average (or mean)

算術平均數指數 arithmetic average index

算盤 abacus

算錯 wrongly calculated, miscount

遞延毛利 deferred gross profit

遞延收入 deferred income

遞延回扣支付制 deferred rebate system

遞延股息 deferred dividends

遞延負債 deferred liability

遞延借項 deferred debit

遞延帳戶 deferred account

遞延費用 deferred charge, deferred expense

遞延貸項 deferred credit

遞延債券 deferred bond

遞延資產 deferred assets

遞延營業收入 deferred revenue

遞耗資產 diminishing assets, wasting assets

遞減成本 decreasing cost

遞減折舊法 decreasing-charge method

遞減訂價 market skimming price

遞減累進稅 degressive tax, regress-ive tax

遞減費用折舊法 depreciation-reduc-ing-charge method

遞減餘額定率折舊法 depreciation-declining-balance method

遞增付款 progressive payment

遞增成本 increasing cost

遞增費用 progressive charges

領水 inland waters, territorial waters

領水員 navigator, pilot

領事發票 consular invoice

領事簽證費 consulage, consular fee

領海 territorial sea

領海寬度 extent of territorial sea

領航 pilot, navigate

領航入港費 pilotage inwards

領航費價目表 pilotage tariff

領航圖 pilotage chart

領料單 material requisition

領港 pilot a ship into or out of a harbor

領港費，領航費 pilotage

領頭定價 price leadership

領頭定價者 price leader

種植場交貨 ex plantation

種類 description

僱工 hire labour, hire man

僱工薪工稅 employer's payroll taxes

僱用掮客 floor broker

僱主責任險 employer's liability in-surance

僱主聯合會 employer's association

僱員保證服務合同 servant's secur-ity agreement

僱員報酬　compensation of employees

僱船契約　contract of affreightment

僱傭合同　employment contract

僱傭率　hiring rate

僱傭關係　employer-employee relationship

銘謝光顧　thanks for patronage

銀行支付單據(一家銀行開出對另一家銀行付款的滙票或票據) banker's payment

銀行支票　〔美〕bank check, 〔英〕bank cheque

銀行支票員　〔美〕bank teller

銀行支票帳戶　bank checking account

銀行水單,兌換單　bank slip

銀行用比率(指銀行家用於分析企業支付能力的比率,即企業的流動比率)　banker's ratio

銀行公會　bankers' association

銀行手續費　bank charges, bank commission

銀行本票　cashier's check, banker's orders, officer's check

銀行可接受作擔保的證券,合格票據　eligible papers

銀行可貼現性　bankability

銀行可擔保的項目　bankable project

銀行代碼手冊(美國銀行家協會出版的手冊,每家銀行給予一個代碼,用以識別票據的付款行)　Key Book

銀行合併　bank merge

銀行年金(政府向銀行收取的年金)　bank annuity

銀行年度　bank year

銀行收益　bank return

銀行存款　bank deposit

銀行存款保證額　banker's margin

銀行存款創造　creation of bank deposit

銀行存款解凍　release of bank accounts

銀行存款證　bank deposit certificate

銀行存摺　bank book

銀行再貼現率　bank rate of rediscount

銀行同業外滙交易　interbank exchange dealing

銀行同業存款　interbank deposit

銀行同業往來　dealing between banks

銀行同業拆放市場　interbank market

銀行同業拆息率　interbank offer rate

銀行自動清算服務(英國清算系統之一,辦理電子滙兌的服務)　Banker's Authomated Clearing Service

銀行有價證券　bank portfolios

銀行危機　bank crisis

銀行利率　bank interest rate

銀行兌現準備金,銀行儲備金　banking reserve

銀行投資　bank financing, bank investment

銀行投資能力　banking power

銀行券,鈔票,銀行兌換券　bank note

銀行承兌　bank acceptance

銀行承兌市場　bankers' acceptance market

銀行承兌信用證　banker's acceptance credit

銀行承兌率　banker's acceptance rate

銀行承兌滙票　bank acceptance, banker's acceptance bill, bank acceptance bill

銀行往來帳　bank account

銀行往來帳餘額　bank balance

銀行往來調節表　bank reconciliation

銀行抵押業務　mortgage banking

銀行制度　banking system

銀行股票，銀行資本　bank stock

銀行直接轉帳制　bank giro

銀行取款　bank debits

銀行取款單　counter check

銀行長期票據　bank long bill

銀行的銀行（即中央銀行）　banker's bank (central bank)

銀行信用卡　bank card

銀行信用過戶　bank credit transfer

銀行信用證　banker's letter of credit

銀行信用證轉讓　bank credit transfer

銀行信託公司　bankers' trust company

銀行信貸　bank credit and loan, banker's credit

銀行信貸收支　bank credit receipts and payments

銀行信貸估計（指對商業銀行的貸款和投資活動每日所作的粗略估計）　bank credit proxy

銀行信貸資金　bank credit capital

銀行信貸管理　supervision of banks over credits

銀行持股公司　bank holding company

銀行限制債券　bank restricted bonds

銀行計息存款　interest-bearing bank deposit

銀行保密責任　banker's duty of secrecy

銀行保險庫　bank safe custody

銀行保險箱　safe deposit box

銀行保證書　bank guarantee

銀行家　banker

銀行條例　bank act

銀行倒閉　bank failure

銀行流動比率　bank liquidity ratio

銀行恐慌　banking panic

銀行財閥　bankocrat

銀行留置權　bank lien

銀行帳目核對　reconciliation of bank accounts

銀行規則　bank regulations

銀行郵滙　bank post remittance

銀行間滙率　interbank exchange rate

銀行通貨　bank currency

銀行票據　banker's bill, bank paper

銀行票據交換所　banker's clearing house

銀行清償能力　bank liquidity

銀行買入滙率　bank's buying rate

銀行透支　bank overdraft

銀行貸出能力　banking power

銀行發票　bank invoice

銀行貼現　bank discount (B/D)

銀行貼現率，銀行利率 banker's rate

銀行貼現費(息)　bank discount

銀行貸款　bank loan

銀行集團　bank group

銀行業　banking, banking business

銀行資本　banking capital

銀行資信證明書　banker's reference

銀行資產負債表　balance sheet of banks

銀行資產流動性　bank liquidity

銀行資產流動能力　bank liquidity position

銀行意見(對調查資信的)　bank opinion

銀行債券　bank debenture

銀行債務　bank debt

銀行滙票 bank bill, bank draft, banker's bill, bank money order, [德]bankanweisung

銀行滙款單　bank money order

銀行電滙　bank telegraphic transfer

銀行管理　banking management

銀行監督　bank inspection, banking supervision

銀行劃撥　bank transference

銀行賣出滙率　bank's selling rate

銀行徵信　bank reference

銀行撥款單　bank money order

銀行擔保　bank guarantee

銀行機密　banking secrecy

銀行學派　banking school

銀行融通　bank accommodation

銀行償付信用　bankers' reimbursement credit, bankers' disposal credit

銀行償付保證書　bank refundment guarantee

銀行擠兌　run on a bank

銀行豁免(指銀行對滙票付款後發行的一種文件，准許貨物的買方提貨)　bank release

銀行儲備金　bank reserve

銀行簿記　bank bookkeeping

銀條，銀錠　silver bar, silver ingot

銀根緊　pressure in money market, tight money, stringent cash

銀根鬆　easy money

銀貨兩訖 cash on delivery, both sides clear

銀團　bank consortium

銀團貸款，辛迪加貸款　syndicated loan

飽和，市場供應充足　saturation

飽和曲線　saturation curve

飽和係數　saturation coefficient

飽和度　saturation ratio

飽和重量　saturated weight

飽和單位重量　saturated unit weight

飽和量　saturation capacity

飽和價格　satiety price

飽和點　saturation point

製成品 manufactured goods, finished goods, finished products

製成品成本　cost of goods manufactured

製成品成本對固定資產比率　ratio of cost of goods manufactured to

fixed assets

製成品週轉率　turnover of finished goods

製成品盤存　finished products inventory

製成拒絕證書的滙票　bill duly protested

製作過程　manufacturing process

製造成本　manufacturing cost

製造成本表　manufacturing statement

製造成本單　factory cost sheet

製造成本預算　manufacturing cost budget

製造者市場　mill market

製造商的新訂貨　manufacturer's new orders

製造商品質證明書　manufacturer's certificate of quality

製造商廠牌　manufacturer's brand

製造商數量證明書　manufacturer's certificate of quantity

製造商檢驗證明書　manufacturer's inspection certificate

製造費用　burden, manufacturing burden

製造費用分配　manufacturing expense distribution

製造費用分配基礎　basis for application of overhead

製造費用分類帳　factory expense ledger

製造費用效能差異　manufacturing overhead efficiency variance

製造費用耗費差異　manufacturing overhead spending variance

製造費用數量差異　manufacturing overhead volume variance

製造業會計，工業會計　manufacturing accounting

製造預算　manufacturing budget

製銷成本　cost to make and sell

[一]

熊市, 淡市, 空頭市場　bear market

熊市策略　bear-market strategies

劃紅線提單　red bill of lading

劃帳　remit account

劃線支票　cross check

劃線結平帳戶　ruling and balancing account

維修成本　maintenance cost

維修折舊法　depreciation-maintenance method

維持你方報價　keep your quotation

維持性行銷　maintenance marketing

維持性價格　support price

維持原狀, 按原樣　[拉]in statu quo

維持帳戶　maintaining account, servicing account

維持轉賣價格　resale price maintenance

維持證券的最低價格(通過大量買進)　stabilize a security

維護費　sum of maintenance

綜合分析　aggregate analysis, comprehensive analysis

綜合比率　composite ratio

綜合平均年限折舊法　depreciation-composite life method

綜合平均數　compound average

綜合平衡　overall balance

綜合年限　composite life

綜合收益　composite income

綜合折舊　composite depreciation

綜合折舊率　composite depreciation rate

綜合制度　combine system

綜合物價指數　composite price index, synthetic price index

綜合盈利率　comprehensive profit rate

綜合契約　general contract

綜合計劃　comprehensive planning

綜合指標　aggregative indicator, overall target

綜合指數　composite index number

綜合保險　comprehensive insurance

綜合保險單　comprehensive policy

綜合商品指數　composite merchandise index number

綜合貨船　composite vessel

綜合週轉率　composite turnover

綜合資產負債表　composite balance sheet

綜合模式　aggregative model

綜合價格　composite price

綜合價格換算係數　implicit price deflator

綜合儲蓄　package saving

綜合償債保障率　overall coverage ratio

綠皮書（英意等國政府的）green book

綠色英鎊（英國加入歐洲共同體後，在共同農業政策下用於對歐洲貨幣單位換算的高滙率英鎊）green pound

綠色革命（指農業生產的革命）green revolution

綠色條款（信用證預支條款的一種，規定出口商有義務將預支後所採購之貨物，以開證行名義存入倉庫）green clause

綠色條款信用證　green clause credit

綠色貨幣（歐洲共市執行共同農業政策所使用的本國貨幣兌換率）green currency

綠色魔力，金錢力量　green power

綠河條例（環境保護）green river ordinance

綠背紙幣（美鈔俗稱）green back

網狀提單　network bill of lading

網狀賠償責任制　network liability system

網絡分析，系統分析　network analysis

網絡結構　network configuration

違反分期付款的義務　breach of obligation to pay an instalment

違反有代理權的保證　breach of warranty of authority

違反合同要件　breach of condition

違反明示的擔保　breach of an express guarantee

違反信託　breach of trust

違反保結　breach of recognizance

違反航行範圍的保證　breach of trading warranty

違反特約條款（水險單上附加的條款）
　breach of warranty

違反條件　breach of condition

違反諾言　breach of promise

違反擔保　breach of warrant

違約成本　penalty cost

違約者　defaulter

違約當事人　delinquent party

違背契約　breach of contract, default

違背信託　breach of trust

違章　breach of regulation

違禁品，走私貨　contraband goods

違禁貿易　illicit trade, contraband of trade

十五畫

［、］

摩托車保險　motor cycle insurance

摩登式樣　modern style

窮國　poor country

寬限日，延付日　days of grace

寬限期　grace period

寬容條款（指容許的數量差額）　allowance

寬容貨損率　allowance for damage rate

實支成本　outlay cost

實收股本　paid-up capital

實收保險費　earned premium

實收資本　issued capital stock, paid-in capital

實地盤存制　physical inventory system

實物工資　natural wages, wages in kind

實物支付　payment in kind

實物交易，物物交換　barter

實物股息　dividend in kind, property dividend

實物信用　real credit

實物品質　actual quality

實物稅　real tax

實物資產　physical assets

實物賠償　reparations in kind

實物擔保，不動產擔保　real guarantees

實效　actual effect, practical results, substantial results

實時信息系統（能在數據發生的同時，快速處理數據的電子計算機系統）　real-time information system

實時處理　real-time processing

實值資產　real-value assets

實得工資　take-home pay

實得率法，實際報酬率法　effective yield method

實得增值　realized appreciation

實得還款數目　liquidated sum

實帳戶（即資產帳戶、負債帳戶及資本帳戶）　permanent account, real account

實際工資　real wage

實際工資率　real wage rate

實際皮重　actual tare, real tare, actual gross weight

實際市場滙率　market rates of exchange in effect

實際收入　real income

實際成本　actual cost

實際成本計算　actual costing

實際成本慣例　historical-cost rules (for revenue recognition)

實際有效滙率(剔除通貨膨脹因素後的滙率)　real effective exchange rate

實際交貨　actual delivery

實際全損　actual total loss

實際全損理算　adjustment of actual total loss

實際完成情況,實績 actual performance

實際投資　real investment

實際利息收益　actual interest income

實際利息法　effective interest method

實際利率　effective rate of interest

實際利潤　realized revenue, realized profit

實際拒付　actual dishonour

實際所得　real income

實際供給　actual supply

實際承運人　actual carrier

實際負債　real liabilities

實際盈餘　realized surplus

實際效用　actual utility

實際淨利潤　real net profit

實際時間　material time

實際國民生產總值　real gross national product

實際國民收入　national income in real terms

實際現金價值　actual cash value

實際產量　real output

實際參數　actual parameter

實際損失　actual loss

實際損耗率與廢棄率　actual rate of wastage and obsolescence

實際與估計損益比較表　comparative statement of actual and estimate profit and loss

實際與標準製造費用比較表　comparative schedule of actual and standard overhead costs

實際滙率　actual exchange rate

實際債款　actual debts

實際裝載量　actual weight of load

實際需求　actual demand, physical demand

實際需要量　actual requirement

實際增長率　real growth rate, actual rate of growth

實際價值　actual value, real value, realistic value

實際價格　realized price

實際餘額效應論　real-balanceeffect theory

實際獲利　yield

實際獲利率　yield rate

實際總重量　actual gross weight

實際儲蓄　real saving

實際儲蓄總額　aggregate realized

savings

實業界巨頭，大亨 tycoon

實價 real price

實數 real quantity, real number

實數分析法 actual number analysis

實質上的損害 essential quality of damages

實質因素 physical causes

實質收益 economic income

實質折舊 economic depreciation

實盤交易 firm bargain

實繳 paid in

實繳部分 paid-in portion

實繳股本 paid-in capital

實體法 substantive law

實體分配 physical distribution

實體分配管理 physical distribution management

審計，查帳 audit

審計法 audit law

審計的統計估算法 statistical estimation approach to audit

審計客戶表白書 letter of representation

審計客戶律師表白書 legal representation letter

審計準則聲明 statement on audit standards

審計解釋部分 explanatory paragraph

審計學 auditing

審查範圍 scope of examination

審核通知書 advice of audit

審理通知書 notice of hearing

審理貨幣條款（歐洲信貸、歐洲債券協定中的條款，保護貸款人避免因用一種貨幣貸款而法院用另一種貨幣審理而引起的損失） judgment currency clause

審慎投資 prudent investment

養老金 pension, annuity

養老保險單 endowment policy

養殖業 fish breeding and poultry raising

鄭重方式 solemn mode

複本位 multiple standard

複合分錄，多項式分錄 compound entry

複合成本 multiple cost

複合企業 business conglomerate

複合供給 composite supply

複合信託 complex trust

複合貨幣 compound currency

複合稅 compound duty

複合期權頭寸（通過期權交易把盈利限定在一事先確定的幅度內，使虧損限定在一可接受的幅度內的頭寸組合） complex option positions

複合資本結構 complex capital structure

複合需求 composite demand, joint demand

複合遠期交易（期貨市場上按不到期日同時買進或賣出一種貨幣） forward forward

複合增長率 compound growth rate

複合頻率分佈 compound frequency distribution

複合總量因素 compound amount factor

複式稅則 complex tariff

複式期權(指對客戶已買的期權，再提供一個期權，即客戶有權再以預定的滙價和固定的遠期買進第二個特定的期權) compound option

複式運費率 multiple freight

複式管理 multiple management

複式簿記 double entry bookkeeping

複利 compound interest

複利本利和，複利終值 compound sum, compound amount

複利公式 compound interest formula

複利年金 compound interest annuity

複利法 compound interest method

複利折舊法 compound interest depreciation-method

複利律 compound interest law

複利率 compound rate

複利期 compounding period

複利期間 conversion interval

複利攤銷法 compound-interest method (of amortization)

複相關 multiple correlation

複相關係數 multiple correlation coefficient

複稅制 double taxation

複貼現 compound discount

複發電報 multiple telegram

複發電傳 multiple telex

複滙率 multiple exchange rate

複製成本 reproduction cost

複製價值 reproduction value

複製樣 duplicate sample

複製簽名 facsimile signature

課稅年度 taxable year

課稅扣除 tax credit

課稅估價 assessment valuation

課稅所得 taxable income

課稅所得額之扣除 tax deduction

課稅品 object of taxation

課稅後收益 earnings after tax

課稅前帳面收益 pretax accounting income

課稅財產留置權 tax lien

課稅根據 evidence at assessment

課稅準則 basis of assessment

課稅價值 value of assessment

談判 negotiation

談判失敗 fail in one's negotiation

談判合約條件 negotiation of contract term

談判者 negotiator

調入(指紡織品配額的) swing-in

調出(指紡織品配額的) swing-out

調用定限(指紡織品配額) swing margin

調用權(指紡織品配額) swing right

調和中項(統計) harmonic mean

調和平均指數(統計) harmonic average index

調和級數 harmonic progression

調和關稅 compromise tariff

調查性研究 survey study

調查損害 sounding in damages

調查範圍　scope of survey

調停，調解　mediation

調停人　adjuster

調期（指取消一種單手期貨合約，重做距離交收期較遠的另一月份的合約）　roll-over

調換（以舊票據或債券換取新票據或債券）　refunding

調換債券　refunding bonds

調換價格（公司債券調換普通股票的價格）　conversion price

調節表　reconciliation statement

調節性交易　accommodating transaction

調節性援助　adjustment assistance

調節國際收支　balance of payment adjustment

調節稅　regulatory tax

調節經濟　regulating economy

調節餘缺　regulate supply and demand

調頭寸　make up deficit

調整比價　adjust the price ratios

調整分錄　adjusted entry

調整外滙滙率　exchange rate adjustment

調整投資使用方向　redirecting the use of investment

調整投資結構　changing the distribution of investment

調整供求關係　adjust supply to a current demand, regulate supply and demand

調整後成本基礎　adjusted cost basis

調整後所得　adjusted income

調整後試算表　adjusted trial balance

調整後最早到期日收益率　yield to adjusted minimum maturity

調整前試算表　unadjusted trial balance

調整風險後貼現率　risk-adjusted discount rate

調整記錄　adjusting entries

調整帳戶　adjusting account

調整國民收入　adjustment of national income

調整產品方向　reorienting production

調整售價法　adjusted selling price method

調整期　adjustment period

調整資本　recapitalization

調整需要量　"backing out" requirements

調整價格　readjust prices

調整憑單　adjustment memo

調整變數　adjusting variables

請求人　petitioner, applicant

請求書　petition, application

請求擔保　application for bail

請告（支票）命運（收票銀行向開票銀行查詢支票帳戶能否兌現）　"advise fate"

請君一試　try it yourself

請帖　letter of invitation

請查問出票人　refer to drawer

請索賠款　claim for indemnity, claim

compensation

請閱後頁　please turn over

請願，請願書　petition

請購單　purchase requisition form

潮口　tide port

潮水　tide

潛水作業　diving operation

潛在市場　potential market

潛在失業　potential unemployment

潛在交通流量（可能達到的最大交通強度）　potential traffic flow

潛在危險　potential hazard

潛在利益　potential income

潛在拒付（指對票據）　latent dishonour

潛在的借款方　potential borrower

潛在的國民總產值　potential gross national product

潛在的貸款方　potential lender

潛在的資源　potential resources

潛在供給　potential supply

潛在效用　potential utility

潛在財富　potential wealth

潛在缺陷　latent defect

潛在資本　latent capital

潛在需求　potential demand

潛在價值（香港市場指期權行使價與現市價的差價）　intrinsic value

潛在影響　potential impact

潛在競爭　potential competition

澳大利亞1928穀物租船合同代號　Austral

澳大利亞1956穀物租船合同　Austwheat

澳大利亞金融投資銀行　Australian Finance and Investment Corp

澳洲羊毛協會　Australian Wool Corporation

澳洲國民銀行快捷貿易諮詢服務系統　National Australia Bank Express Trade Enquiry Services

廢約（指聲明契約無效）　denunciation

廢品率　rate of spoiled products, reject rate

廢品損失　loss due to spoiled work

廢料　waste material

廢除命令　annulment of order

廢棉　waste cotton wool

廢棄成本　obsolescence cost

廢棄費用　abandonment charge

廢棄條款　denunciation clause

廢棄損失　abandonment loss

廣告　advertisement, advertising

廣告公司，廣告商　advertising agent (or firm)

廣告合同　advertising contract

廣告津貼　advertising allowance

廣告計劃　advertising project

廣告效果　advertising effectiveness

廣告郵件　advertisement matter, advertising post

廣告設計　advertising design

廣告費　advertisement charge or fee

廣告媒介　advertising media

廣告策略　advertising strategy

廣告傳真　adfax

廣告經理　advertising manager

廣告溝通效果　advertising communication effect

廣告預算　advertising budget

廣告調查　advertising research

廣告價格　advertising rates

廣告銷售效果研究　advertising sales-
effect research

廣告戰　advertising war

廣義的貨幣供給量　broadened money
supply

廣義貨幣　broad money

廠房與設備　plant and equipment

廠商　manufacturer

廠商出口代理　manufacturer's ex-
port agent

廠商發票　factory invoice

廠牌，商品製造牌　manufacturer's
brand

廠牌政策　brand policy

廠牌戰　the battle of the brands

廠價　price at factory

廠場估價　plant appraisal

廠場設備分類帳　plant ledger

廠場資產漲價　plant appreciation

遮蔽甲板船　shelterdeck vessels

適用法律　applicable law

適合人類的食用　for human consumption

適合性　fitness

適合商銷　in merchantable condition

適宜交收情形　deliverable state

適於航行　navigability

適度管理　moderate management

適當的公共機關　appropriate public
authority

適當的委付通知(保險)　reasonable
notice of abandonment

適當單據　proper documents

適當擔保　justifying bail

適航包裝　seaworthy packing

適航能力　seaworthiness

適應市場經濟的計劃　plan-oriented
market economy

適應性　adaptability

適應的技術　appropriate technology

適應控制　adaptive control

[一]

麵包牛油股票(紐約證券交易所專業
會員其所專業之股票為熱門股票,
市場術語稱為"麵包牛油股票")
bread and butter stock

撥付憑單　invoice of transfer

撥用期限　appropriation period

撥定利潤　appropriated profit

撥定盈餘　appropriated surplus

撥款，歲出預算　appropriation, allotment

撥款分類帳　allotment ledger

撥款申請書　appropriation request

撥款法案　appropriation act

撥款退回，歲出沖回數　appropriation
refund

撥款帳戶，盈餘分撥帳，盈虧撥補帳
appropriation account

撥款補還數　appropriation reimbursement

撤回支付　countermand of payment

撤回前有效　good till countermanded

撤回要求　withdrawal of claim

撤回要約　withdrawal of an offer

撤回起訴　［拉］nolle prosequi

撤銷要約　revocation of an offer

撤銷訴訟　discontinuance

標印　stamping

標低貸款利息　marking down loans

標金　standard gold

標明定價　stated price

標明轉讓　marked transfer

標高貸款利息　marking up loans

標售　selling tender

標準（貨幣和外滙市場上，把一定數量和一定到期日說成是標準數量或標準到期日）　standard

標準工資率　standard wage rate

標準化　standardization

標準化商品　standardized commodities

標準化會計　standardized accounting

標準尺寸　standard size

標準尺度　standard scale

標準分批成本單　standard job cost sheet

標準式，標準格式　standard form

標準交收點（指期貨交易交收商品之標準質素）　par

標準年金　standard annuity

標準年率　standard annual rate

標準成本　standard cost, target cost

標準成本差異　standard cost variance

標準成本差異之處理　disposition of standard cost variances

標準成本制度　standard cost system

標準成本會計　standard cost accounting

標準成本與實際成本雙重記帳法　dual plan for standard costs

標準合同　standard contract

標準合同格式　standard contract form

標準合同規定　standard contract provisions

標準材料　standard material

標準批量　standard-run quantity

標準批運　standard shipment

標準作業程序　standard operation procedure

標準利潤　standard profit

標準法定價格　standard legal price

標準股票　standard stock

標準保單條件　standard policy condition

標準保溫貨櫃/集裝箱　normally insulated container

標準品質　standard quality

標準值　standard value

標準差　standard deviation

標準條件　standard condition

標準條款　standard clause

標準時間　standard time

標準海運契約　type charter party

標準減除額　standard deduction

標準設備　standard equipment

標準國際貿易分類　Standard International Trade Classification

標準貨櫃/集裝箱　standard container

標準貨櫃/集裝箱配件　standard container fittings

標準費用　standard fee

標準貿易條件　standard trade terms

標準統保單　standard blanket policy

標準提單　standard bill of lading

標準買賣　sell goods by sample

標準與普爾500種股票價格指數 Standard & Poor's 500 Stock Price Indexes

標準與普爾500種股票指數期貨 Standard & Poor's 500 Stock Indexes Futures

標準與普爾混合指數　Standard & Poor's Composite Index

標準經濟定貨量　standard economic ordering quantity

標準誤差　standard error, standard deviation

標準樣品　standard sample, type sample

標準價格　standard price

標準操作業時間　standard working time

標準操作業規程　standard practice instructions

標價　posted price, bid price

標購(指通過招標購買商品)　buying tender

標籤,附加標誌　countermark

標籤　label

標籤條例(海上貨物保險特約條款之一)　labelling regulation

標籤費(指在貨物包裝之外，加貼標籤之費用)　labelling

標籤數據寄存器　label data register

標籤險　labels insurance

概不賒帳　no credit given

概念　concept

概念分析　conceptual analysis

概念分類　conceptual category

概括損失　general damages

概值　probable value

概率　probability

概率比例　probability proportion

概率比例抽樣法　probability proportional sampling

概率預算　probabilistic budget

概率誤差　probable error

概算　rough estimate, financial estimates, budget estimate, rough calculation

概算書　prospectus, book of estimates

概算填補法　estimate system

樣本　sample book, pattern

樣本空間　sample space

樣本郵件　sample post

樣品中位數　sample median

樣品出口　sample export

樣品平均數　sample mean

樣品平均數差　difference of sample means

樣品間　sample room

樣品等級(指商品的最低等級，不能作交收期貨合約之用)　sample

grade

樣品買賣的默認條件　implied warranties in sale by sample

樣品數量, 樣品規模　sample size

樣品檢驗　sample survey

橫向合併　horizontal merger, horizontal consolidation, horizontal amalgamation

橫向貿易(經濟水平相近國家之間的貿易)　horizontal trade

橫向聯合　horizontal integration

橫向聯繫　horizontal ties

橫向擴散　horizontal proliferation

橫向轉移　horizontal transfer

橫式查帳　horizontal audit

橫線支票, 劃線支票　crossed check

槽形貨櫃/集裝箱　tank container

模擬抽樣　simulated sampling

模擬計算機　analog computer

模擬值　value of simulation

模擬實驗　simulation

確定收入實現之原則　realization rule for revenue recognition

確定成色, 分析, 化驗　assay

確定年金　fixed annuity

確定性決策　certainty decision

確定的要約　firm offer

確定的賠償金　liquidated damages

確定的權利　established right

確定訂貨　firm order

確定買賣, 實盤交易　firm bargain

確定銷售契約　firm sale contract

確認信用狀　confirmed letter of credit

確認重量　ascertained weight

確認損失　ascertainment of damage

確認債務　acknowledgement of debt

確認銀行　confirming bank

確認樣本　confirmed sample, confirmatory sample

確證　conclusive evidence

鞍點　saddle point

鞍點定理　saddle point theorem

磅(一般指常衡磅, 等於 0.454 公斤)　pound

磅秤　pound scale

磅碼單　weight note, weight memo

輪船　steamer, steamship

輪班工作　shift work

輪流投標　by-turn bidding

輪翻提價　price spiral

熱門股票, 藍籌股　fancy stocks, "blue chip" share

熱封塑膜包裝　heat-wrapping

熱效率　heat efficiency

熱錢(為獲高利或保值在國際間頻繁流動的短期資金), 游資　hot money

碼頭工人　docker

碼頭交貨　EX Quay (EXQ)

碼頭交貨價　free on quay

碼頭收據　dock receipt

碼頭到戶　pier-to-door

碼頭到倉庫　pier-to-house

碼頭到碼頭運輸　quay-to-quay transportation

碼頭倉庫　dock warehouse

碼頭稅　dock dues, pierage, pier dues

碼頭費　wharfage, dockage

碼頭棧單　dock warrant

歐式期權，歐洲期權　European option

歐亞大陸橋路綫　Europe-Asia land bridge line

歐非共同體　Eurafrica

歐洲一體法案　Single Europe Act 1985

歐洲大陸寄存單據（由幾家荷蘭銀行以不記名形式發行的）　continental depository receipt

歐洲支付同盟　European Payments Union

歐洲支付協定　European Payments Agreement

歐洲支票卡（在西歐幾國使用的一種購買貨物用的信用卡）　Eurocheck Card

歐洲內部支付協定　Intra-European Payments Agreement

歐洲日圓　Euroyen

歐洲日圓債券　Euroyen bonds

歐洲卡（美國萬事達集團同歐洲信用卡組織聯繫，在歐洲大陸發行的信用卡，又稱歐羅卡）　Euro Card

歐洲主要港口　European main port

歐洲市場　Euromarket

歐洲自由貿易區　European Free Trade Area

歐洲自由貿易聯盟　European Free Trade Association

歐洲共市基金　European Fund

歐洲共市開發基金　European Development Fund

歐洲共同市場（歐洲共同體之通稱）　European Common Market

歐洲共同浮動幅度安排　European common margins arrangement

歐洲式旅館開帳法（指膳費另開）　European plan

歐洲辛廸加股票指數　Euro-syndicate General Share Index

歐洲投資銀行（歐洲共同市場的金融機構）　European Investment Bank

歐洲法郎　Eurofranc

歐洲股票（指一種不同於按交易國貨幣計價的股票）　Eurostock

歐洲美元　Eurodollar

歐洲美元市場　Eurodollar market

歐洲美元浮動利率票據　Eurodollar floating rate note

歐洲美元債券　Euro-dollar bond

歐洲美元銀行信貸　Eurodollar bank loan, Eurodollar credit

歐洲信貸（指一切用歐洲貨幣提供的貸款）　Eurocredit

歐洲英鎊　Eurosterling

歐洲馬克　Euromark

歐洲寄存單據（在歐洲進行交易並證明非歐洲證券所有權的一種寄存單據）　European depositary receipt

歐洲通貨（指各國金融機構所接受本國通貨之外的一切外幣存款）　Eurocurrency

歐洲商業票據　Eurocommercial paper

歐洲貨幣　Eurocurrency

歐洲貨幣市場　Eurocurrency market

歐洲貨幣合作基金　European Monetary Cooperation Fund

歐洲貨幣存款　Eurocurrency deposit

歐洲貨幣辛迪加貸款利息　interest on syndicate Eurocurrency credit

歐洲貨幣單位(由一定量的歐洲貨幣體系成員國貨幣組成的綜合貨幣單位)　European Currency Unit

歐洲貨幣貸款市場　Eurocurrency credit market

歐洲貨幣綜合單位(根據歐洲共同體成員國貨幣而建立的一種非官方的記帳單位)　European Composite Unit

歐洲貨幣體系　European Monetary System

歐洲專利權　Europatent

歐洲國際銀行　European Banks of International Company

歐洲商業票據　Euro commercial paper

歐洲票據　Euronote

歐洲清算系統(由摩根信託保證公司於1968年在布魯塞爾建立並經營至今的歐洲債券清算系統)　Euroclear System

歐洲港口　European port

歐洲最惠國條款政策　European Most Favoured Nation Policy

歐洲復興方案　European Recovery Program

歐洲預託證券(即"歐洲寄存單據")　European depositary receipt

歐洲經濟合作組織　Organization for European Economic Cooperation

歐洲經濟共同體　European Econ-omic Communities

歐洲經濟共同體部長理事會　Council of Ministers of European Economic Community

歐洲經濟與貨幣同盟　European Economic and Monetary Union

歐洲債券　Eurobond

歐洲債券市場　Eurobond market

歐洲債券清算儲存系統(一種為歐洲債券的安全監護、交割和支付的電子計算機清算儲存設備)　Euroclear

歐洲煤鋼聯營　European Coal and Steel Community

歐洲選擇權交易所　European Option Exchange

歐洲聯合浮動協定　European Joint Float Agreement

歐洲議會　European Parliament

歐陸交易所　continental house

歐陸兌現支票(英國銀行發行的)　Eurocheque

歐陸的通貨,大陸幣　continental currency

賣方市場　seller's market

賣方自發報價　unsolicited offer

賣方信貸　seller's credit

賣方慣例　seller's usance

賣主　vendor, seller

賣主留置權　vendor's lien

賣主績效指數(美國企業採購部門對供應者遲交貨的報告編製的指數)　vendor performance index

賣出套戥,賣期保值　selling hedge

賣出期貨,賣空　sell short

賣出滙率,賣出價　selling rate

賣出遠期(外滙)　selling forward

賣出舊船再租回　charter back

賣外滙　selling exchange

賣回溢價　call premium

賣空　sell short, over sold, bear

賣空合約　short contract

賣空行為　bear operation

賣空者　short interest, bears

賣空浪潮　bear raid

賣家套頭保值　seller's hedging

賣期保值(香港市場稱"賣出套戥")
hedge selling

賣價　selling rate

賣權,賣出選擇權,看跌期權　put
option

賣據　conveyance on sale

穀物交易所　corn exchange

穀物條例　corn law

穀物貿易條款　corn trade clause

穀物經紀人　corn broker

穀物關稅　corn duty

增大增長速度　growthmanship

增支成本,邊際成本　incremental cost,
marginal cost

增加生產　increase of production

增加危險　increase of risk

增加供給　increase of supply

增加保費　increase of premium

增加庫存　increase of stocks

增加流通渠道　multiply the channels
of circulation

增加貿易作用　trade creation effect

增加需求　increase of demand

增加總股本,普遍增資　general
capital increase

增加額　increase in amounts

增長的百分數　percentage increase

增長的限度　limit to growth

增長的絕對數　increase in absolute
figures

增長股票　growth stock

增長率　rate of increase, growth
rate

增長速度　increment speed

增長潛力　growth potential

增股籌資　equity financing

增值　increase of value, increment,
added value

增值成本,增量成本　incremental
cost

增值成本分析　incremental cost analysis

增值的生產能力　productivity of added
value

增值保險　increased value insurance

增值通貨　appreciated currency

增值稅　added value tax, value added
tax, increment value duty

增值資本　appraisal capital

增益控制　gain control

增益餘量　gain margin

增高標價,加價　mark-up

增強出口計劃　export enhancement
programme

增減條款　increase or decrease clause

增量　increment

增量比　incremental ratio

增量分析　incremental analysis

增量成本　incremental cost

增量利潤　incremental benefit

增量預算法　increment budgeting

增強產品的競爭能力　make its goods more competitive

增載　increment of load

暫付款帳戶　suspense payment account

暫付款項　temporary payment, suspense debit

暫付關如的條款　open terms

暫行條例　interim regulations, provisional regulations

暫行辦法　interim procedure, temporal method

暫收款　suspense credit

暫收款帳戶　suspense receipt account

暫定股利(公司在一定經營期確定的利潤分配，即期中股息)　interim dividend

暫定的發貨單　pro forma invoice

暫定按金　indicated deposit, initial margin

暫定船位　tentative booking

暫保收據　binding receipt

暫時出口　temporary export

暫時平價　temporary par of exchange

暫時收入　transitory income

暫時存款　sundry credit, temporary deposit

暫時合夥　temporary partnership

暫時均衡　temporary equilibrium

暫時逆差　temporary deficit

暫時借款　temporary loan

暫時進口　temporary import

暫時貿易　temporary trade

暫時貸款，活期信用放款　cash credit

暫時解僱　lay off

暫時解僱率　lay off rate

暫時價格　interim price

暫記欠款　temporary advance and sundry debtor

暫記待結轉帳戶　clearing account

暫記借項，暫付款　suspense debit

暫記帳戶，暫記帳　suspense account

暫記貸項，暫收款　suspense credit

暫記預支，短期墊款　temporary advance

暫記資本帳戶　temporary proprietorship account

暫停支付　suspend payment

暫停交易　trading suspended

暫停營業　temporary cessation of business

遷延的答辯　dilatory plea

[丨]

罷工　strike, to go on strike

罷工附加費(運費)　strike surcharge

罷工保險　strike insurance

罷工追加費用保險　strike expenses insurance

罷工條款　strike clause

罷工、暴動和國內騷動風險 strike, riot and civil commotion risk

罷市 shopkeeper's strike, close up shop

暴利 sudden huge profits

暴風雨保險 storm and tempest insurance

暴動 riot

暴動及民眾騷亂保險 riot and civil commotion insurance

暴跌 slump, bust

暴發戶 jumped up people

暴露(指產品、人、企業通過出版物、電台等在公眾面前出現的程度,指資金或保險額暴露在有遭受損失的情況下) exposure

暴露危險 exposure hazard

暴露滙兌風險 exposure to exchange risk

影子價格,推算價格 shadow price

影印本 photostat copy

影印副本 photocopy

影射商標 imitation brand, counterfeit trademark

影像剖視儀 photographic image

劇烈競爭,殘酷競爭 cut-throat competition

賞金 reward

數目順序 numerical order

數字 figure

數字倒置 transposition

數字控制 numerical control

數字電腦 digital computer

數字標記 numerical symbol

數字錄音帶 digital audio tape

數字總和法(美國租賃業一種折舊法) sum-of-the-year-digits

數百萬 multimillion

數值 numerical value

數值分析 numeric analysis

數值碼 numeric code

數理規劃,線性規劃 mathematical programming

數理統計學 mathematical statistics

數理經濟學 mathematical economics

數量成本 volume cost

數量折扣 quantity discount

數量差異 quantity variance

數量索賠 quantity claim

數量管制 quantitative restriction

數量證明書 certificate of quantity

數量覆驗 check weight

數據文件(將可通過計算機存取的按一定方式組織的有關數據,記錄滙集在一起,即可構成一個數據文件) data file

數據代理終端 data agent

數據庫 data base, data bank

數據消減(由於一不可逆轉的過程而造成的信息或數據損失) data degradation

數據記錄(用一種形式簡單的計算機來記錄設備性能) data logging

數據處理(把大量數據轉換為有用的、有條理的或簡化的信息形式) data reduction, data processing

數據處理系統(指能接受信息按規定

進程處理信息並產生所需結果的一系列裝置）data-processing system

數據處理活動 data processing activity

數據集分配 data set allocation

數據集存取 data set access

數據集信息 data set information

數據集結構 data set organization

數據集識別 data set identification

數據集輸出入 data set I/O (in/out)

數據傳輸 data transfer

數據轉換器 data converter

數學法 mathematical method

數學的或然律 mathematical law of probability

數學的期望值 mathematical expectation

數學推論 mathematical inference

數學模型 mathematical model

賤買貴賣 buy cheap and sell dear

賤賣, 虧本出售 sacrifice

賤價拋售 go for a song

賠本 sustain losses in business, get less than the capital invested

賠付損失 settlement of loss

賠款 make compensation, pay reparations

賠款成本（指"再保險"損失的比例, 導致"分保公司"的"從屬保險費"）burning cost

賠款保函 repayment guarantee

賠款後保險金額復原條款 loss reinstatement clause

賠款率, 損失率 loss ratio

賠款準備金 loss reserves

賠款選擇（保險） settlement option

賠償 compensate, reparation, indemnity

賠償人 compensator

賠償支付命令 loss indemnity payment order

賠償名譽 indemnity for defamation

賠償金 compensation

賠償的義務 obligation of compensation for losses

賠償協議 indemnity agreement

賠償限度 measure of indemnity

賠償保證書 letter of indemnity

賠償責任的免責事項 exception from liability

賠償損失 indemnity for damages and losses

賠償實物 indemnity in kind

噚（等於 1.829 米） fathom

[ノ]

價目表 price list, quotations table

價目單, 產品目錄 catalogue

價值工程 value engineering

價值分析 value analysis

價值平均化運動 movement towards equalization of value

價值決定 determination of value

價值形成過程 process of producing value

價值的外在表現 external expression of value

價值的貨幣表現　expression of value in money

價值重量比率　value-weight ratio

價值規律　law of value

價值規律自發地起調節作用　law of value spontaneously plays a regulatory role

價值規範　criteria of value

價值量　magnitude of value

價值構成　value composition

價值增值過程　process of creating surplus value

價值線綜合指數(指股票中所有公司的股票進行幾何平均)　value line composite index

價值觀　values

價格　price

價格已下降　price has dipped, price has sagged

價格已上漲　price has hiked

價格下限,最低價　price floor

價格下降　sink in price, price ruled lower

價格下降準備　reserve against decline in prices

價格上限,最高價　price ceiling

價格上漲　advance in price, price hikes

價格水平,物價水平　price level

價格尺度　price measure

價格支持,價格補貼　price support

價格支持方案(指政府為防止市場價格跌到某一最低水平以下而設計的

方案)　price support program

價格比值,單價比　price proportion

價格公道　at fair price, reasonable price

價格可比性　price comparability

價格卡特爾,價格同盟　price cartel

價格平衡,價格均衡　price equilibrium

價格決定的共同因素　codeterminants of price

價格收益比率,市盈率　price-earnings ratio

價格行情　price quotations

價格向量　price vector

價格折扣　price mark-down

價格形成,定價　pricing

價格形成的成本　cost in price formation

價格系統　price system

價格歧視,價格上的區別對待　price discrimination

價格伸縮性　price flexibility

價格表示　price indication

價格協定　price cartel, price agreement

價格保持　price maintenance

價格政策　price policy

價格限幅　price limit

價格突然下降　price has tobogganed

價格突然高漲　spurt

價格相當高　price is rather stiff

價格信號　price signal

價格指標　price target

價格指數　price index number

價格指數化　price indexation

價格條件　price terms

價格條件比較表　comparative list

價格差距，價差　price spread

價格差別，物價分等　price discrimination

價格差異　price variance

價格凍結　price freeze

價格剪刀差　price scissors

價格動向　price movement trend

價格偏低　price is on low side

價格偏高　price is on high side

價格移動限額(指同一交易日內容許價格高於或低於上日收市價的最大限度)　price movement limit

價格—產量的決定　price-output determination

價格敏感性　price-sensitive

價格猛漲　spurt in prices, price has skyrocketed

價格幅度　range of price

價格普遍偏低　prices ruled low

價格普遍偏高　prices ruled high

價格結構，價格機制　price mechanism

價格循環　price cycle

價格欺騙　price-gouging

價格意見　price idea

價格補貼　price bonification

價格預測　price expectation

價格傾銷　price dumping

價格漲落，價格波動　price fluctuations

價格漲落條款　rise and fall clause

價格彈性　price elasticity

價格管制　price control

價格監視線(交易所為保持價格的相對穩定而設置的一種價格限度監管體系)　on-line price surveillance

價格暴跌　price has plummeted

價格暴漲　flare-up in price, big bulge in price

價格調整　price adjustment

價格調整條款　price adjustment clause

價格適應　price adaptation

價格戰(價格上一再削價的商業競爭)　price war

價格積數　price-aggregate

價格趨漲　price tend upwards

價格穩定　price steadiness

價格穩定性　price rigidity

價格競爭　price competition, price-stabilizing

價格體系　pricing structure

價格變動法　price change approach

價格變動保證金(指交易所由於價格變動對期貨買賣增收的保證金)　variation margin

價格變動條款　price change clause

價高無銷路，高於市價　price out of the market

僵局　deadlock

僻地港，次要港，外港(指遠離主要海關或貿易中心的港口)　outport

僻地港附加費　outport surcharge

衝突　conflict

衝突法律　conflict rules

衝動性購買(指不問價錢、質量、用

途，一時興起的購買）impulse buying

衝動性顧客　impulse buyer

衝動性購買　impulse buying

衝擊效果　impact effect

衝擊性貸款（日本公司籌資之重要方法，指一家外國銀行用外幣對一家日本公司提供的一種中期貸款）impact loan

德國無記名證券 German bearer certificate

德爾菲法（技術預測法）Delphi method

德爾菲技術　Delphi technique

徵用　expropriation, requisition, take over for use

徵用財產　requisitioning of goods

徵用權（國家的）　eminent domain

徵收　levy, assess, collect, impose

徵收罰款　levying of fines

徵信書　character book, questionnaire

徵信機構　credit information service, inquiry agency

徵稅　tax collection, levy tax

徵稅參考價格　tax reference price

徵稅貨物　dutiable goods

徵稅管理　management of taxation

徵稅標的　tax base

徵購土地　purchase the land

徵稅權　right of taxation

徵詢要求　request for references

箱形托盤　box pallet

箱裝　in cases

箱號　case number

靠岸停泊，使船靠岸　touch and stay

靠港　touch at a port

稻草，無價值的東西　straw

稻草編製品　straw product

盤　tray

盤存，盤點　stock taking, inventory taking

盤存折舊法　depreciation-inventory method

盤存缺溢　inventory short and over

盤存記錄　inventory record

盤存貨物　goods on hand

盤存損益　inventory profit and loss

盤帳，查帳　check accounts, audit accounts

質次價高　inferior quality-high price

質押　pledge

質押品　collateral security

質押書　letter of hypothecation

質的因素　qualitative factor

質的限制　qualitative limitation

質的規定性　qualitative prescription of

質的觀察　qualitative observation

質量分析　quality analysis

質量成本　quality cost

質量因素　quality factor

質量低劣　inferiority of quality, inferior quality

質量要求　quality requirements

質量指標　quality target

質量指數　quality index number

質量保證　quality assurance

質量差價　quality price differentials

質量第一　quality first

質量控制　quality control

質量幅度(指品質的機動幅度) quality latitude

質量管理　quality management

質量標準　quality specification, quality standard

質量檢查　quality inspection

質量鑒定　quality determination

質量靈敏值　mass-sensitive quantity

質詢　interpellation

質變　change in quality

質變項　qualitative variable

銷後租回　sale-and-leaseback

銷後買回　sale-and-repurchase

銷除　elimination

銷除法　writing-off process

銷帳　charge-off

銷售力量　sales potential

銷售工程　sales engineering

銷售公司　sales company

銷售毛利　gross trading profit

銷售分析　sales analysis

銷售代表　sales representative

銷售代理商　sales agent

銷售代理業務　sales commission

銷售成本預算　selling cost budget

銷售合同　sale contract

銷售合同應收帳款　sales contract receivable

銷售危機　selling crisis

銷售折扣　sales discount

銷售佣金　selling commission

銷售技術　sale technique

銷售利潤邊際　margin-profit on sale

銷售定單　sales order

銷售性租賃(美國規定出租人不能享受投資減稅和加速折舊優惠的租賃)　conditional sale

銷售刺激因素　sales stimulation factor

銷售後市場　after market

銷售後技術服務　after-sale service

銷售促進, 促銷　sales promotion

銷售政策　sales policy

銷售計劃　sales planning

銷售保證　sales warrant

銷售能力　sales force

銷售條件　condition of sales

銷售效果研究　sales-effect research

銷售記錄　sales record

銷售淨額　net sales

銷售配額　sales quota

銷售組合計劃　marketing-mix program

銷售情況　sales status

銷售部門　sales department

銷售現金　sales dollar

銷售淡季　period of slack sales

銷售產品　sell goods, market products

銷售區域　sales territory

銷售量　sales volume

銷售稅　sales tax

銷售最大化　sales maximization

銷售費用　selling expense, marking expense

銷售發票　sales invoice

銷售貸款公司　sales finance company

銷售渠道長度　the length of distribution channel

銷售週轉　sales turnover

銷售與固定資產比率　sales to fixed assets ratio

銷售與淨值比率　sales to net worth ratio

銷售與商品盤存比率　sales to merchandise inventory ratio

銷售與應收帳款比率　sales to receivable ratio

銷售損益　sales profit and loss

銷售經理　sales manager

銷售預測　sales forecasting

銷售預算　sales budget

銷售管理　sales management

銷售網點　commercial network

銷售潛力　sales potential

銷售實力　sales strength

銷售調查　marketing research

銷售價格　sales price

銷售價值　sales value

銷售確認書　sales confirmation

銷售點終端機　point-of-sale terminals

銷售點電子轉帳（一種通過商店、銀行聯接的電腦系統，自動轉帳購物的辦法）　electronic funds transfer at point-of-sale

銷售總額　gross sales

銷售競爭　sales contest

銷售體系　marketing system

銷貨毛利　gross profit on sales, gross margin

銷貨毛利分析　gross profit analysis

銷貨毛利與銷貨比率　ratio of margin on sales to net sales

銷貨收入　sales revenue

銷貨成本　cost of sales

銷貨回佣　sales rebate

銷貨折扣　sales discount

銷貨折讓　allowance on sales

銷貨車費　cartage-out

銷貨知識　sales knowledge

銷貨退回　sales return

銷貨退回折扣　discount on returned sales

銷貨退回通知單　credit memo for sales return

銷貨淨利　net profit on sales

銷貨淨額對資產總額比率　ratio of net sales to total assets

銷貨預算　sales budget

銷貨與管理費用　selling and administrative expenses

銷貨會談　sales convention

銷貨總成本　gross cost of merchandise sold

銷貨憑證　sales voucher

銷路　consumption

銷路不佳　lack of a market, poor sales

銷路好　salability, in good demand, good market

銷燬（貨幣等）　melt down

銷燬證明書　cremation certificate

鋁製乾貨櫃/集裝箱　aluminium dry cargo container

蝕本　loss capital

蝕本出售　selling at less than cost, sell at a loss

蝕本生意　lossmaker, lose money in a business

舞弊行為　corrupt transaction

[一]

線(再保險術語，將分保分出人的自留額稱為"一線"。分保額就以"線"計算)　line

線上項目支出　above-the-line expenditure

線性不等式　linear inequality

線性方差　linear equation

線性成本　linear cost

線性成本功能　linear cost function

線性決策律　linear decision rule

線性回歸分析　linear-regression analysis

線性消費函數　linear consumption function

線性組合　linear combination

線性規劃(在滿足用線性不等式表示的約束條件的情況下，使線性目標函數最優化的一種數學方法，用來從幾種行動方案中選擇一種最有可能達到理想目標的行動方案)　linear programming

線性規劃分配法　distribution method of linear programming

線性趨勢　linear trend

線性關稅減讓法　linear reduction of tariffs

線性體系　linear system

緩期交易(多用於證券交易所)　carriage over

緩期與否決定日(英國交易所用語)　carriage over day

緩衝存貨　buffer stock

緩衝庫存基金　buffer stock fund

緩衝庫存貸款　buffer stock financing

緩衝基金，平準基金　buffer fund

緩衝器，緩衝體　buffer

編表設備　tabulating equipment

編報表　prepare statement

編製分錄　journalizing

編製側重投入的預算　input-oriented budgeting

編製程序　program composition

編製資本支出預算　capital budgeting

編製預算　budget presentation, prepare budget

編號會計科目表　accounts code list, chart of accounts

編碼　coding

編碼指令　coded order

編碼機　code machine

履行日期　date for performance

履行合同風險　performance risk

履行合同保證人　performance guarantee

履行合同保證書　performance bond

履行合同義務　performance obligation of contract

履行法律協議　execute one's obligations under the pertinent law

履行部分　operative part

履行義務地法律　［拉］lex loci solutionis

履行償付債務的義務　performance obligations

履約　performance

履約保函　performance guarantee

履約保證信用證　performance credit

彈性（一變量對另一變量微小的百分比變化所作的反應）　elasticity

彈性工時制　elastic work schedule system, flexible work hours system

彈性因素　elasticity factor

彈性係數　elasticity coefficient

彈性供應　elastic supply

彈性貨幣供應　elastic money supply

彈性滙率　flexible exchange rate

彈性預算　flexible budget

彈性需求　elastic demand

彈性製造系統　flexible manufacturing system

彈性關稅　elastic tariff

彈性限度　elastic limit

層次隨機取樣　stratified random sampling

層格式貨櫃/集裝箱船　cellular container ship

層級制　hierarchy

層級組織　hierarchical organization

十六畫

［丶］

褪色　discoloration

辦公室自動化　office automation

辦公室費用　office expense, office overhead

辦事員　office clerk

辦事章程　by-law

辦貨代理人　buying agent

辦理保險　underwrite insurance for, handle insurance for

辦理貸款手續　process a loan, handle procedures for a loan

親自申請　apply in person

親收送達　personal service

親筆簽字　handwritten signature

親筆證書　holograph

謀生手段　means of livelihood, means of life

謀生活　earn one's bread (or living)

謀職　seek employment, apply for a job

諮詢公司　consultant firm

諮詢文件　consultant paper

諮詢代理　consulting agent

諮詢服務　consultancy service

諮詢委員會　consultative committee

諮詢專家　consultancy expert

諮詢費　consulting fee

激光卡（利用特殊電腦終端機發射的激光，在卡上燒出黑色微點來記錄、閱讀的一種信用卡）　Laser Card

激跌　sharp fall

激漲　sharp rise

激增　jump from, shoot up, increase sharply

激勵　motivation

激勵因素　motivator

激勵因素研究　motivator research

激勵期望模型　expectancy model of motivation

燃料附加費　bunker surcharge

燃料調整因素　bunker adjustment factor

燒光，燒燬　gutted by fire

遵守合同　keep a contract

憑收條付款信用證　payment on receipt credit

憑收據付款　payment on a receipt

憑抵押品貸款　lend money on security

憑信用借款　draw on one's credit

憑信用證交貨　delivery against letter of credit

憑型號售貨　sale by type

憑時效取得財產權　usucaption

憑票即付持票人　note order payable to bearer

憑規格售貨　sale by specification

憑商標售貨　sale by trade mark

憑單支票　voucher check

憑單付款　payment against document

憑單證付現金，交單付現　cash against documents

憑單證付款信用證　payment against document credit

憑買方樣品質量交貨　quality as per buyer's sample

憑提單交貨　delivery against bill of lading

憑跟單信用證付款　payment against documentary letter of credit

憑跟單滙票付款　payment against documentary draft

憑滙票付款信用證　payment against draft credit

憑運單付款　payment against presentation of shipping document

憑說明售貨　sale by description

憑賣方樣品質量交貨　quality as per seller's sample

憑標準買賣　sale by standard

憑樣買賣　sale by sample

憑證　receipt, voucher

[一]

頭寸，持有額　position

頭寸單（銀行及交易所對滙兌買賣日計表的俗稱）　position sheet

頭寸寬裕　easy position

頭寸緊缺　tight position

頭寸鬆　loose money

頭等貨　first-class quality

頭等艙　first-class cabin

頭等證券 blue chip shares, first-class paper

擔保 guaranty

擔保一切險 against all risks

擔保人 surety, bondsman, guarantee voucher

擔保代理人 del credere agent

擔保公司債券 guaranteed debentures

擔保充分之負債 fully secured liabilities

擔保交易的完善化 perfection of secured transaction

擔保企業 guarantor enterprise

擔保系統 guarantee chain

擔保股利 guaranteed dividend

擔保承兌 acceptance on security

擔保協定 guarantee agreement

擔保品 security, hypothecated goods

擔保信用證，備用信用證 stand-by L/C

擔保信託公司 guaranty trust company

擔保契約 hypothecation

擔保負債 secured liabilities

擔保書 warranty

擔保借款 loan on security

擔保帳款 secured accounts

擔保票據 guaranteed bill

擔保期 period of guarantee

擔保提貨申請書 application for issuance of letter of guarantee

擔保提貨保證書 indemnity and guarantee delivery without bill of lading

擔保短期籌資 secured short-term financing

擔保解除抵押證書 release of mortgage

擔保債券 guarantee bond, surety bond

擔保債權 secured debt, secured claim

擔保債權人 secured creditor

擔保實物 security in kind

擔保還錢 money-back guarantee, del credere

擔保證券總額 omnium

擔保權 security right

擔保權益 secured interest

擔當罪名 bear the guilt

據報(提單批語) said to be

據報內裝……(提單批語) said to contain

據報重量……(提單批語) said to weigh

"據稱"條款，"據報"條款 "said to be" clause

擱淺 grounding, stranding

擱置保險 deferred insurance

擇期 to select a good time

擇機代價，選擇成本，替換成本 alternative cost

擇優選購 purchase goods on a selective basis

操作分析 operation analysis

操作規程 operation standard, operational procedure

操作順序分析 operation sequence analysis

操作程序圖 operation process chart

操作數據 operation data

操作運轉的保證　operation guarantee

操縱，囤積　rig

操縱市場　operate, rigging the market, play the market

操縱者（操縱股市的人）　manipulator

操縱外滙價格　manipulate the rates of exchange between the currencies

操縱供應　manipulation of supply

操縱價格　administered price

擁有出口優勢　hold the trump-card in the export of

擁有半數以上股權　majority holding

擁有過半數股權之附屬機構　majority-owned subsidiary

機帆船　motor junk

機車　locomotive

機車載重量　hauling capacity of a locomotive

機制　mechanism

機師　airpilot

機師險　airpilot risks

機能失調　dysfunction

機率　probability

機率曲線　probability curve

機率事件　probability of events

機率函數　probability function

機率律　probability law

機率密度　probability density

機械工業　machine-building industry

機械手　manipulator

機械化，自動化　mechanization

機械技術　modern mechanical know-how

機械性組織結構　mechanistic organization structure

機械動力　machine power

機械控制　machine control

機械產品　engineering goods

機械理倉　mechanized stowage

機械單體　machinery and equipment without assembling and installation

機械裝備　mechanized equipment

機械銷售　mechanical sales

機械選擇　mechanical selection

機組功率　power of the assembling unit

機組容量　capacity of generator sets of hydroelectric power station

機場交貨　ex aerodrome

機動預算　flexible budget

機動滙率　flexible exchange rate

機動償付計劃　flexible payment plan

機會成本　opportunity cost

機會成本值　opportunity cost of value

機會均等　equality of opportunity, equal opportunity for all

機會替換成本　opportunity alternation cost

機會損失　opportunity loss

機構交易網（亦稱第四市場，是一私營的計算機交易體系，主要協助大宗股票交易）　institutional network

機構仲裁　institutional arbitration

機構投資（指各種投資公司，年金基金、保險公司、互助儲金協會等專業金融機構大量購買和持有證券）

institutional investment

機構投資者　institutional investor

機器人，自動裝置　robot

機器大工業　modern industry, mechanized big industry, large-scale mechanized industry

機器小時法（指分攤製造費用的標準）machine hour method

機器小時率　machine hour rate

機器及工具　machinery and tools

機器及設備　machinery and equipment

機器打包　machine press-packing

機器成本　machine cost

機器安裝保險　erection insurance

機器定額　rating of machine

機器負荷　machine burden

機器計算　machinery account

機器能讀之記錄　machine-readable records

機器能讀之數據　machine-readable data, machine script

機器能讀出的信息　machine-sensible information

機器率法　machine rate method

機器過帳　machine posting

機器損壞保險　machinery breakdown insurance

機器緊壓包　machine press-packed bale

機器操作包裝場　mechanized packing yard

融通支票　accommodation cheque

融通性的金融交易　accommodating financial transaction

融通背書（無關係人亦簽名於背面，以增加一重保障）accommodation endorsement

融通票據　accommodation paper (or note)

融通票據關係人　accommodation party

融通資金安排　financing arrangement

融通業務　accommodation line

融通滙票　accommodation bill

融通額度　line of credit

融資成本　financing cost

融資性租賃　financial lease

輸入口岸　port of entry

輸入外資　introduce foreign capital, incoming of foreign capital

輸入法規　law of import

輸入限額　import quota

輸入配額制　import quota system

輸入許可　import admission

輸入許可證　import licence

輸入就業　import employment

輸入稅　import duty

輸入稅率，輸入稅則　import tariff

輸入港水上船邊交貨　overside delivery

輸入為先的對開信用證　back to back credit import first

輸入獎勵金　import bounty

輸入價值　import value

輸入簽證制　import licencing system

輸出入相抵協定　import export offset agreement

輸出入貨物指數　index number of imports and exports

輸出入連鎖制　import export link system

輸出比例　export ratio

輸出失業　exporting unemployment

輸出目標制　export target

輸出地點　export point

輸出空運港機上交貨價　ex plane

輸出信用保險　export credit insurance

輸出限制　export restriction

輸出保險　export insurance

輸出限額　export quota

輸出許可證　export permit, export licence

輸出港　delivery port, outport

輸出為先的對開信用證　back to back credit export first

輸出勞動力　export labour power

輸出貸款　export loan

輸出結構　export structure

輸出傾銷　export dumping

輸出獎勵金　export bounty

輸油輸氣管道　oil and gas pipeline

輸金點　gold point

輸送帶　coveyor

霓虹招牌　neon sign

靜力試驗　static test

靜止率　statics rate

靜坐罷工　stay-down strike

靜態比率　static ratio

靜態分析　static analysis

靜態報表　static statement

靜態統計　static statistics

靜態結構　static structure

靜態預算　static budget

靜態經濟學　static economics

輻射損害　radiation damage

賴債，拒付欠款　repudiate a debt

賴債者　repudiator

整元會計　whole-dollar accounting, cents-less accounting

整合效果，協同作用　synergy

整件提貨不着　non-delivery of entire package

整件遺失　loss of package

整批出售　sell by wholesale, sell wholesale

整批成本計算法　batch costing

整批交易　package deal

整批定價法　batch pricing

整批保險　wholesale insurance, package insurance

整批購買　basket purchase

整車　car load

整車貨　car load lot

整車運價　car load rate

整版廣告　full page ad

整套部件分析　complete component analysis

整套提貨單據　full set of bills of lading

整套購買　basket purchase, lump-sum purchase

整理後重量　dressed weight

整理帳　adjusting entries

整理費　reconditioning fee

整筆付清費用　lump-sum fee

整筆運費租船，包乾租船　lump-sum charter

整筆撥款　lump-sum allotment, bloc allocation

整筆總付辦法　lump-sum basis

整買零賣　buy wholesale and sell retail

整裝貨櫃/整裝集裝箱　full container, load container

整裝/整拆，貨櫃場至貨櫃場　container yard to container yard

整廠輸出　package plant export

整數　integer

整數股（股票交易通常 100 股為一整數批量，少於 100 股為零星股）round lot

整數界限　integral boundary

整數計算機　integral computer

整數規劃　integer programming

整數預算　lump sum budget

整數線性規劃　integer linear programming

整機進口　import of complete machines

整櫃交，拆櫃接　FCL/LCL (full container load/less container load)

整櫃交/整櫃接，整裝/整卸　FCL/FCL (full container load/full container load)

整櫃折扣，整車折扣　full container load discount (FCL discount)

整櫃裝（指貨櫃/集裝箱的整櫃/整箱裝卸）　full container load (FCL)

整櫃裝貨物　full container load cargo (FCL cargo)

整體化管理計劃　integrated management planning

整體結構管理　configurative management

蕭條　depression, slump, sluggishness

蕭條市面　sluggish market

蕭條地區　depressed area

蕭條期　slack time

霍桑試驗（美國西方電器公司 1927-32 年在芝加哥的霍恩廠所作的人羣關係試驗，是以從前作過的車間照明強度對勞動效率影響為基礎所作的一系列當勞動條件改變時對繼動器裝配效率影響的試驗）　Hawthorns experiment

霍桑效應（見"霍桑試驗"條）　Hawthorns effect

歷史成本（即取得成本或原始成本。一項資產在購置時的成本，對以後價值的變化未作任何調整）　historical costs

歷史成本基礎　historical cost basis

歷史成本假設　historical cost assumption

歷史成本會計　historical cost accounting

歷史成本與可變現淨值熟低　lower of historical cost or net realizable value

歷史法　historical method

歷史統計　historical statistics

歷史最高水平　all-time high

歷史數列（統計）　historical series

歷史觀點　historical viewpoint

歷年資料外推法　historical data extrapolation

[丨]

噸　ton

噸位　tonnage

噸稅(按進港船舶註冊噸徵稅)　tonnage due

噸稅單　tonnage slip

噪音　noise

噪音控制　noise control

戰爭條款　war clause

戰爭賠款　war indemnity

戰爭險　war risk

戰爭險水面協定　water-borne agreement

戰爭險保險單　war risk policy

戰爭險費率　war risk rate

戰爭險註銷條款　war cancellation clause

戰爭繞航條款　war deviation clause

戰時公債　war bond

戰時信貸　war credit

戰時產物(指因戰時需要而發展的工業、產品、證券等)　war baby

戰時經濟　war time economy

戰時緊急撥款　war emergency grant

戰術性計劃　tactical planning

戰略性農產品庫存　stockpile of strategic agricultural materials

戰債　war debt

遺失支票　lost check

遺失後補繳全部保險費　full premium if lost

遺失貨物　missing goods, missing cargo

遺產本金,基金本金　corpus

遺產本值　estate corpus

遺產收益　estate income

遺產稅　estate duty, death duty, estate tax

遺產會計　estate accounting

遺產繼承人　legatee of inheritance

遺產繼承稅　inheritance tax

遺族保險　survivor's insurance

遺族恤金　survivor's benefit

遺傳工程　genetic engineering

遺傳物質　genetic material

遺傳密碼　genetic code

遺傳資源,生成資源　genetic resources

遺囑人　estator

遺囑更改　codicil

遺囑裁判庭　probate court

遺囑認證稅　probate duty

頻率,次數(統計上,在同一組距裏出現的事例)　frequency

頻率分佈(統計上,表明某一事件在某一數值或範圍發生的次數)　frequency distribution

頻率曲線　frequency curve

頻率曲線圖　frequency curve chart

頻率表　frequency table

頻率面　frequency surface

頻率函數(表明一個隨機變量的概率分佈的數學函數)　frequency function

頻率理論(按照歸納法求得的在與某

一事件相似情況下，同類事件發生的比率） frequency theory

頻數數列 frequency series

頻數圖 frequency chart

默示批准 implied ratification

默示的承認 implied recognition

默示的條款 implied terms

默示的授權 implied authority

默示條件 implied condition

默示義務 implied undertaking

默契的接受 tacit acceptance

默契的轉期 tacit renewal

默許信託，默許賒帳 implied trust

默認合夥 implied partnership

默認作廢 repeal by implication

默認契約 implied contract

默認保證，默示保證 implied warranty

〔丿〕

興趣測驗（人事管理用詞） interest test

學徒式訓練 apprentice training

學徒制，學徒身份 apprenticeship

學徒條例 apprenticeship act

舉債 borrow, float a loan

舉債籌資（以發行債券或期票籌集資金） debt financing

舉證 testification

舉證事實 factum probantia

舉證責任 onus of proof, burden of proof, [拉]onus probandi

儘快（租船合同用語，指船方有責任盡量按船隻所能裝、卸的速度接貨和交貨） as fast as can

儘快裝船 shipment as soon as possible

衛生工程學 health engineering

衛生檢疫 health quarantine

衛生檢疫規定 Health and Sanitary Regulation

衛生證明書 bill of health, health certificate

衛星工業 satellite industry

衛星城市 satellite town

衛星通訊技術 satellite communication technology

衡平利益 equitable interest

衡平法 law of equity

衡平法留置權 equitable lien

衡平法律師 equity lawer

衡平租賃（見"槓桿租賃"條） leverage lease

衡平規則 rule of equity

衡平轉讓（普通法不予承認的某種財產的轉讓，而衡平法可以承認的轉讓） equitable transfer

衡平權比率，產權率 equity ratio

衡量償債保障的尺度（用以衡量企業能如期償付某些定期帳目的能力） measures of coverage

獨立公證行 independent surveyor

獨立公證證明書 independent inspection certificate

獨立投資 autonomous investment

獨立的經濟實體 independent economic entity

獨立的擔保人 independent guarantee

獨立拼箱經營人 independent group-age operator

獨立責任 independent liability

獨立商店 independent store

獨立國庫 independent treasury

獨立經紀人（紐約證券交易所交易廳內會員，為其他經紀人或交易廳內無會員的其他公司執行指令。原稱：美元經紀人）independent broker

獨立經營承包商 independent contractor

獨立經濟 independent economy

獨立需要 independent demand

獨立審計 independent audit

獨立辯護 independent defence

獨立驗貨證明書 independent inspection certificate

獨任仲裁員 sole arbitrator

獨佔市場 monopolistic market

獨佔主義 monopolism

獨佔包銷協議 exclusive sale agreement

獨佔者 monopolist

獨佔性競爭市場 monopolist competition market

獨佔許可證 exclusive licence

獨佔許可證合同 exclusive licence contract

獨佔區域 exclusive territory

獨佔經營權 exclusive right

獨家代理 sole agency

獨家代理人，包銷人 sole agent

獨家排斥式經銷 exclusive dealing

獨家專利權 exclusive patent right

獨家區域代理權 exclusive territorial distributorship

獨家貿易商，專營商 sole trader

獨家發盤 sole offer

獨家資本 monopoly capital

獨家經銷商 sole distributor

獨家經銷權 exclusive selling rights

獨家談判權 exclusive bargaining right, sole bargaining right

獨家銷售代理人 exclusive selling agent

獨家購買，壟斷性購買 monopsony

獨家購買代理人 exclusive buying agent

獨裁主義 authoritarianism

獨裁管理 autocracy

獨資 sole proprietorship, individual proprietorship

獨資公司 sole corporation

獨資經營 single proprietorship, sole proprietorship

獨資經營空運聯合公司（美國）Independent Aviation Operators

獨資銀行家協會（英國）Independent Banker's Association

積下欠帳 run an account

積欠股息 dividend in arrears

積累方式 accumulative means

積累的新增國民收入 accumulation of newly gained national income

積累率 rate of accummulation

積累基金 accummulation fund

積累規模 size of accummulation

積累擴散指數　cumulative diffusion index

積極平衡　positive equilibrium, active balance

積極所得效果　positive income effect

積極的管理　aggressive management

積極限制　positive check

積載因素(表示一長噸貨物在裝船時實際佔據若干米的空間，包括因空艙所浪費之容積)　stowage factor

積載排水量　load displacement

積載圖(以不同顏色表明已裝載各批貨物位於船上哪一部分的圖紙)　stowage plan

積蓄　make saving, hoarding

積壓未交貨　backlog

積壓物資　arrear of stock, overstocking of goods

穆迪氏投資者服務公司(美國一家評定證券等的公司，從 Aaa 級，Baa 級，一直排到 C 級)　Moody's

餘利　dividend

餘值　residual value

餘款　residue

餘額　excesses of earnings, residual, balance of clearing

餘額，差額，平衡　balance

餘額承前　balance brought forward

餘額倍減折舊法　double-declining balance method

餘額移後　balance carried down

餘額試算表　trial balance of balances

餘額遞減折舊法　declining-balance method

餘額遞減式損益表　reducing-balance form of profit and loss statement, report form of profit and loss statement

餘額調整　adjustment of balance

餘額轉入新帳　balance transferred to new account

餘額欄式分類帳　balancing ledger

錢　money, [美俚]dough, mint drops

錢莊　money house, native bank, exchange shop

錢袋，荷包　pouch

錢幣兌換器　money changer

錯交貨物　misdelivery

錯判　miscarriage of justice

錯算　miscalculation

錯誤百出　full of mistakes

錯誤更正　error correction

錯誤和遺漏　errors and omissions

錯誤和遺漏除外　errors and omissions excepted

錯誤敍述　misdescription

錯誤記錄　error logging

錯搭浮動利率票據　mis-match floater

錄音郵件　phonopost service

鋼瓶，鋼筒　cylinder

鋼條捆紮(包裝)　steel strapping

鋼製品　steel

鋼製乾貨貨櫃/集裝箱　steel dry cargo container

鋼鐵工程，鋼結構　steel work

鋼鐵工業　steel industry

艙口　hatchway

艙口檢視　hatch survey

艙內條款　under-deck clause

艙內貨　under-deck cargo

艙內噸位　under-deck tonnage

艙位　shipping space

艙面條款　on deck clause

艙面貨物　deck cargo

艙面貨物由貨主擔風險　deck cargo shipper's account

艙面運費率　deck rate

艙面險　on deck risk

艙單　manifest, inward manifest

[一]

隨市發行的債券(根據"隨市需要"所發行的如存款證之類的有價證券) tap securities, tap stocks

隨定單支付現金　cash with order

隨附債務　contiguous obligation

隨附屬性　subsidiary attribute

隨時可收回的貸款　money on call

隨開存單(指銀行願意根據投資者要求的金額和條件籌進資金所發行的存單) tap certificate of deposit (Tap C/D)

隨船送達郵件　captain's mail

隨意消費　optional consumption

隨意過帳　random posting

隨意漲價　wilful inflation of prices

隨機，隨意，偶然　random

隨機方法　random method

隨機化行動　act of randomization

隨機分組法　randomized block

隨機分散(投資)策略　random diversification strategies

隨機存取(電子數據處理用詞。在不先掃視其他數據情況下，檢索存入存儲器裏的任何數據) random access

隨機決策樹分析　stockastic decision tree analysis

隨機走向(有時用於證券和外滙市場方面的一種理論，指在一種情況下，看到一種事物向前或向後走幾步，在每走一步時，下一步可能是向前或向後走，而不考慮一切過去的事件) random walk

隨機事件　random event

隨機抽查　random check

隨機抽樣　random sampling

隨機過程　random process, stochastic process

隨機誤差　random error

隨機數　random number

隨機獨立　stockastic independence

隨機整數　random integer

隨機變異　random variation

隨機變動　random fluctuation

隨機變數(統計上，表示事件發生前數值不定的變量) random variable

隨機觀察(在工作抽樣中所作的隨機觀察) random observation

選擇人才　select good persons

選擇成本　alternative cost

選擇性分配　selective distribution

選擇性存貨控制　selective inventory control

選擇性招標　selective tender

選擇性法律條款　choice of law clause

選擇性信用管理　selective credit control

選擇性信息　selective information

選擇性保留　selective retention

選擇性資本　optional capital

選擇性債務　alternative obligation

選擇使用　alternative use

選擇卸貨港和附加費　optional destination and option fees

選擇供貨單位　choice sources of supply

選擇條款　optional clause

選擇參數　selection parameter

選擇貨幣貸款　optional currencies loan

選擇稅　alternative duty

選擇港　optional port

選擇港交貨　optional delivery

選擇港貨物　optional cargo

選擇港提單　optional bill of lading

選擇程序　selection process

選擇運銷通路　selection of channel

選擇關稅　selectionary tariff

選擇權交易　option dealing

選擇權協議　option agreement

選樣認可　acceptance sampling

選購品　shopping goods, free choice of goods

遲付即期信用證　deferred sight credit

遲付放款　doubtful loan

遲付款　delay in payment

遲延交貨的補救　remedy of delay shipment

遲延收入　deferred income

遲延利息　delay interest

遲延清償債務者　defaulter

遲延提示（指信用證受益人，在規定期限後始提示單據請求銀行押滙）late presentation

遲延裝運　delay in shipment, delayed shipment

遲到的承諾　late acceptance

遲索的賠款　belated claims

遲期付款信用證　deferred payment credit

十七畫

[、]

講價，討價還價　haggle over prices, haggle over a bargain

謝絕來賓　visitors not admitted, no visitors allowed

謝絕訂貨　decline an order

謝爾曼反托拉斯法（美國在 1890 年通過的一個法案）　Sherman Anti-Trust Act

瀆職　malversation

瀆職罪　malfeasance

濫支　lavish expenditure

濫用　misuser

濫用訴訟　vexatious action

濫用壟斷權　abuse of monopoly

濫收　receive too much

濫開帳目　overcharge an account

濫發（鈔票，支票等）　over issue

濫發紙幣　inflate the paper money, issue banknotes recklessly

濫發獎金　over issue of bonuses

營業比率　operating ratio

營業日調整　trading day adjustment

營業中斷收益損失保險，利潤損失保險　loss of profit insurance

營業外收入　nonbusiness income

營業收入，收入，歲入　revenue

營業收支預算　operating budget

營業收入債券　income bond

營業收款憑證　voucher for business receipts

營業成本　operating cost

營業成果　operating results

營業年度　business year

營業地原則　principle of business premises

營業地點　place of business

營業自動化　business automation

營業利得稅　business profit tax

營業利潤　operating profit

營業股權公司　operating holding company

營業股權總帳，營業分類帳　operating ledger

營業盈餘　earning surplus

營業盈餘表　retained earnings statement

營業信譽　business reputation

營業租賃　operating lease

營業帳戶　operating account

營業現金流動　cash flow from operation

營業控股公司　operating holding company

營業稅　business tax

營業項目　item of business

營業報告　operating report

營業報表　operating statement

營業晴雨表　business barometer

營業循環，營業週期　operating cycle

營業資本　operating capital

營業資本收益率　operating earning rate

營業資金　operating funds

營業資產週轉率　operating assets turnover

營業損失　operating loss

營業槓桿率，營業挺率　operating leverage

營業實績　operating performance

營業實績比率　operating performance ratio, operating ratio

營業實績收益表　operating performance income statement

營業範圍　business scope

營業邊際　operating margin

營業虧損　operating deficit

營運資本　working capital

營運資金　circulating capital, working capital

營運資金週轉率　working capital turnover

營運資產　working assets

豁免，免稅額　exemption

豁免捐稅　exemption of tax

豁免條款，免責條款　escape clause, exemption clause

豁免債務　remit a debt

襄理，助理　assist in management

罋　jar

應升值資產　appreciable assets

應付，欠人　due to

應付工資　wage payable

應付支付命令　warrants payable

應付未付票據　bills payable

應付合夥人票據　partner's notes payable

應付利息　interest in red, interest payable

應付利息準備　interest payable reserve

應付承兌票據　acceptance payable

應付抵押款　mortgage payable

應付抵押債券　mortgage bonds payable

應付所得稅　income tax payable

應付長期票據　long-term notes payable

應付持票人　payable to bearer

應付借款　loan payable

應付票據　note payable, bill payable

應付帳款　payable account

應付帳款清單　statement from creditors

應付款　accrue payable, money dues, amount dues

應付貿易帳款　trade payable

應付貿易貨款週轉期　trade payable turnover period

應付稅捐　tax payable

應付債券　bonds payable

應付債券折價　discount on bonds payable

應付債券息票　coupon payable

應付債券溢價　premium on bonds payable

應付債款　debt payable

應付滙價　giving quotation

應付憑單　voucher payable

應付憑單制　voucher system

應用成本比例計算期末存貨　applying cost ratio to ending inventory

應用科學　applied science

應用計量學　applied metrology

應用研究　applied research

應用統計　applied statistics

應用會計　applied accounting

應用概率　applied probability

應收，人欠　due from

應收入金額　amount receivable

應收分期帳款　instalment accounts receivable

應收未收利息　interest receivable

應收未收票據　bill(s) receivable

應收收益　accrued revenues

應收利息　interest in black, interest receivable

應收股利　dividends receivable

應收股東票據　notes receivable from stockholder

應收股款　subscription receivable

應收承兌票據　acceptance receivable

應收抵押票據　mortgage notes receivable

應收抵押款　mortgage receivable

應收定額補貼　quoted government subsidies receivable

應收帳款　accounts receivable

應收帳款之挪後補前　leading and lading

應收帳款分類帳　accounts receivable ledger

應收帳款平均收現日數　number of days' sales in receivables

應收帳款平均收帳期　average collection period of receivables

應收帳款平均帳齡　average age of receivables

應收帳款的分期　aging accounts receivable

應收帳款貼現　accounts receivable discounted

應收帳款貼現佣金支出　commission paid on discounted accounts

應收帳款週轉率　accounts receivable turnover

應收帳款轉讓　accounts receivable assigned

應收寄銷人款　due from consignor

應收票據　bill receivable, note receivable

應收票據貼現，已貼現的應收票據　notes receivable discounted

應收款作擔保的借款　loan secured by account receivable

應收款讓售　factoring of receivables

應收貸款　loan receivable

應收滙價　receiving quotation

應收銀行到期存款　deposit due from bank account

應收銀行款　due from banks

應收認繳股款　due from subscribers

應收應付制　accrual basis, accounting on the accrual basis

應收籌資帳款　accounts receivable financing

應交折舊基金　depreciation funds payable

應扣代付運費　freight to be deducted

應折舊成本　depreciable cost

應折舊年限　depreciable life

應折舊值變率折舊法　depreciation-changing percentage of cost less scrap method

應折舊資產，要折舊資產　depreciable assets

應計不動產稅　accrued real estate taxes

應計未付利息　accrued interest payable

應計未收利息　accrued interest receivable

應計未收股利　accrued cumulative dividends

應計收益　accrued income, accrued revenue

應計利息　accrued interest

應計利潤　accrued profit

應計折舊　accrued depreciation

應計股利　accrued dividend

應計開支　accrued expenditure

應計費用　accrued expenses, accrued charges

應計項目　accrued items

應計稅捐　accrued taxes

應計期票利息　accrued interest on notes payable

應計債券利息　accrued interest on bonds

應計債務,應計負債　accrued liabilities

應計資產　accrued assets

應計營業收入　accrued revenue

應急帳戶　contingency account

應急基金　contingent fund

應急準備金　contingent reserve

應保險　insurable

應納稅的入息　chargeable income

應納稅的利潤　taxable profit

應納稅的純入息　net chargeable income

應納稅財產　ratable property

應得價款的請求　claim for proceeds

應評稅之收入　assessable income

應稅金額的扣除　tax deduction

應稅貨品　dutiable goods

應稅船舶用品　dutiable store

應募人(公司債的)　subscriber

應募公司債簿　subscription book

應募股票人　applicant for shares

應解滙款　drafts and telegraphic transfers payable

應罰款的違法行為　pecuniary offence

應歸成本,應負成本,假設成本　imputed cost

應歸利息,應負利息　imputed interest

應償債務　debt repayable

應變規劃(指為今後預計不會出現但也可能出現的商業條件進行規劃)　contingency planning

應變聯合貸款人(指在英國外幣出口信貸,如不能從歐洲市場獲得資金,通常安排一項"違約條款",允許銀行要求賠償。英國"出口信貸保證局"就變成"應變聯合貸款人")　contingent co-lender

應變關稅　contingent duty

[一]

"戴茨"證券(一種每日調整利率的免稅證券) "DATES"—daily adjusted tax-exempt securities

擠兌(指向銀行擠提存款)　run on a bank

擠進　forced entrance

擠壓型經濟結構　tightly-pressed structure

擬派股利　proposed dividend

擊碎　shatter

聲稱之侵權行為　alleged tort

薪工,薪工表　payroll

薪工成本　payroll cost

薪工帳戶　payroll account

薪工稅　payroll tax

薪工會計　payroll accounting

薪工審計　payroll audit

薪水，薪金　earning, salary, pay, wages, [美]compensation

薪水支票　pay check

薪俸稅　salaries tax

薪給報酬所得稅　income tax on salaries and remuneration

薪金結構　salary structure

薪金標準　wage level

薪資曲線　wage curve

檢定力　power of test

檢查　rummage, jerque

檢查人　rummager

檢查報告　inspection report

檢查錯誤　detection of error

檢疫申請書　quarantine declaration

檢疫法　quarantine law

檢疫浮筒　quarantine buoy

檢疫船　quarantine boat

檢疫規定　quarantine regulations

檢疫處理　quarantine treatment

檢疫港　quarantine harbour

檢疫對象　quarantine object

檢疫範圍　quarantine range

檢疫機構　quarantine office

檢疫、衛生及燻蒸消毒　quarantine, sanitation and fumigation

檢疫錨地　quarantine anchorage

檢疫證書　quarantine certificate

檢控　indictment

檢控書　bill of indictment

檢驗　inspection

檢驗公司　inspection and testing company

檢驗報告單　inspection report

檢驗證明書　inspection certificate

環比指數　chain index

環形聯合　circular integration

環境失調，公害　environment disruption

環境生態學　environment ecology

環境污染　environmental pollution

環境保護　environment protection

環境參數　environmental parameter

環境經濟　environment economy

環球銀行間金融電訊協會(1973年5月由西歐、北美的200多家銀行聯合發起組織)　Society for World Wide Interbank Financial Telecommunication (SWIFT)

環球會計(即多國公司會計)　global accounting, multinational accounting

環境風險指數(一些跨國公司對投資的環境風險編製的指數)　index of environment risk

環境管理　environment management

環境調查　environment inquiry

環境質量管理　environmental quality control

環境證據　circumstantial evidence

環境變遷　change of circumstances

聯行，往來客戶　correspondent

聯行往來(指銀行各分行與總行之間的存放款關係)　intra-bank account

聯行往來利息　interest on inter-branches accounts

聯行往來帳戶　inter-branch account

聯合大企業　conglomerate company

聯合戶口（兩名期貨經紀商共用之戶口）　Omnibus Account

聯合公司發行的證券　securities issued by affiliated companies

聯合分配　joint distribution

聯合出口部　joint export department

聯合代理人　joint agent

聯合生產成本　joint cost of production

聯合平穩隨機過程　joint stationary random process

聯合成本　joint cost

聯合次數函數　joint frequency function

聯合決議草案　joint draft resolution

聯合投資　joint investment

聯合股東　joint holders

聯合抵制　boycott

聯合抵制外國貨　boycott foreign goods

聯合供給　joint supply

聯合依變數　jointly dependent variable

聯合招標　joint invitation to tender

聯合信貸　joint credit

聯合要價　joint bid

聯合浮動,共同浮動　joint float

聯合配額　combination quota

聯合國工業發展組織　United Nations Industrial Development Organization

聯合國世界知識產權組織　United Nations World Intellectual Property Organization

聯合國海上貨物運輸公約（1978 年）　United Nations Convention on the Carrier of Goods by Sea, 1978 年

聯合國開發計劃署　United Nations Development Programme

聯合國國際貨物多式聯運公約　U. N. Convention on International Multimodel Transport of Goods

聯合國國際貨物買賣時效期限公約　U.N. Convention on the Limitation Period in the International Sale of Goods

聯合國國際貿易法委員會　United Nations Commission on International Trade Law

聯合國國際貿易標準分類　United Nations "Standard International Trade Classification"

聯合國國際銷售貨物合同公約　United Nations Convention on Contract for the International Sale of Goods

聯合國貿易和發展會議　United Nations Conference on Trade and Development

聯合國貿易單據固定格式　United Nations Layout Key for Trade Documents

聯合國資本開發基金　United Nations Capital Development Fund

聯合國跨國公司委員會　United Nations Commission Transnational Corporations

聯合國經濟及社會理事會　United Nations Economic and Social

Council

聯合國經濟發展特別基金 Special United Nations Fund for Economic Development

聯合國標準協調委員會 United Nations Standard Coordinating Committee

聯合國關於行政、貿易和運輸部門電子數據交換準則（1988 年國際標準化組織將該準則命名為 ISO 9735 國際標準） United Nations Electronic Data Interchange Fact

聯合貨船 combination carrier

聯合貨運制 joint cargo system

聯合商標 associated trade mark, united brand

聯合商議 joint consultation

聯合最大化 joint maximization

聯合訴訟人 joinder of persons

聯合集裝箱班輪公司 Associated Container Line

聯合集裝箱運輸公司 Associated Container Transportation Ltd.

聯合債務 consolidation of debt

聯合經理人（指在歐洲信貸中，僅次於牽頭經理的貸款人。在美國通常指任何一個不經管辛迪加帳簿而發行債券的經理） co-manager

聯合預算 combination budget

聯合運輸 combined transport

聯合運輸費用 joint charges

聯合運輸提單 combined transport bill of lading (CT B/L)

聯合運輸單證 combined transport

document (CTD)

聯合運輸經營人 combined transport operator

聯合銀行（由一組其他銀行入股組成的銀行） consortium bank

聯合廣告 collective advertising

聯合概率 joint probability

聯合擔保 joint mortgage

聯合融資，聯合提供資金 joint financing

聯合雙邊援助 associated bilateral aid

聯合簽署 joint signature

聯名帳戶（銀行的） joint account

聯名票據 joint note

聯邦存款保險公司（美國） Federal Deposit Insurance Corporation

聯邦食品、藥品及化妝品法（美國） Federal Food, Drug and Cosmetic Act

聯邦貿易委員會（美國） Federal Trade Commission

聯邦資金利率（美國） Federal Fund Rate

聯邦儲備委員會（美國） Federal Reserve Board

聯邦儲備基金（美國） Federal Funds

聯邦儲備銀行（美國） Federal Reserve Bank

聯產品 joint product

聯產品成本計算 joint products costing

聯產品法 joint product method

聯單滙票（正副雙聯式或三聯的） set of exchange

聯運 combined transport, through

traffic, through transport, multi-modal transport

聯運協會　through-transit club

聯運提單　through bill of lading

聯運運費率　through rate, combination rate

聯絡，聯營　affiliation

聯絡公司，附屬公司　affiliated company

聯絡股權，聯營股權　affiliated interests

聯絡處　liaison office

聯號(業務經營上的聯繫)，聯營公司　associated company, allied company

聯號往來帳　inter-branch accounts

聯機，聯線(電子數據處理用詞)　on line

聯機存貯器　on-line storage

聯營　affiliation, pooling

聯營公司　affiliated company, related company

聯營公司往來帳　inter-company accounts

聯營公司間內部盈利　inter-company profit

聯營公司間內部帳目之抵銷　inter-company elimination

聯營公司間會計事項　inter-company transactions

聯營方案，分攤方案　pool scheme

聯營出口公司　allied export selling company

聯營法，權益聯營法　pooling of interest method

聯營協定　pooling agreement

聯營股權　affiliated interests

壓抑通貨膨脹　depressed inflation

壓低基數　lower base figure

壓指標　forcing up the target

壓價　force price down

壓艙物　ballast

壓艙貨物　ballast cargo

壓艙費　ballastage

壓艙櫃　ballast tank

壓縮庫存　reduce stocks

壓縮國內要求　depress domestic demand

[丨]

臨時工　jobber

臨時支出　non-recurrent expenditure

臨時分保　facultative reinsurance

臨時分保合同　facultative treaty

臨時合同　provisional contract

臨時收入　incidental income

臨時收據　interim receipt, temporary receipt

臨時利息　interim interest

臨時投資　temporary investments

臨時股份或股票分割　temporary share or stock fraction

臨時股票，股票臨時收據　scrip

臨時股票持有者　scrip holder

臨時股票發行　scrip issue

臨時協定　provisional agreement

臨時性帳戶　temporary account

臨時的禁止令　temporary prohibition

臨時指數　interim index

臨時條款　provisional treaty

臨時措施　provisional measure

臨時執照　provisional charter

臨時進口證, 臨時過境證　ATA carnet

臨時透支　temporary overdraft

臨時報告　provisional report

臨時貸款　bridging loan, temporary loan, interim credit

臨時發票　provisional invoice

臨時預算　temporary budget

臨時價格　provisional price

臨時證件　provisional certificate

賺大錢　〔美〕killing, make a killing

賺得收益　earned income

賺得利息　earned interest

賺得利潤　realize a profit

賺得盈餘　earned surplus

賺得能力　earning power

賺得率, 收益率　earning rate

賺得資本　earned capital

賺頭　jobber's turn

賺錢　earning

賺錢計劃　money-making proposition

賺錢買賣　good bargain

賺錢賣出　sell at a profit, job off

賺錢機會　earning chance

購入原價　buying cost

購入債券折價　discount on bonds purchased

購回　repurchase

購回協定(在公開市場中從交易商買入債券，及在指定日期及價格由交易商購回)　repurchase agreement

購回註銷(由發行人從市場上購回債券予以註銷)　purchase in the market

購回債券　repurchase of obligations

購光票　clean bill bought

購物中心　shopping centre

購物袋　〔美〕shopping bag, 〔英〕carrier bag

購物袋信用證(以開證申請人的代理人為受益人的可轉讓循環信用證，可"分割"給不同的供貨人)　shopping-bag credit

購物籃信用(即"一般用途信用限額")　shopping basket credit

購股單　stock purchase

購貨日記帳　purchase journal, bought day book

購貨分類帳　purchase ledger

購貨成本, 進貨成本　purchase cost, cost of goods purchased

購貨合同　purchase contract

購貨折扣　purchase discount, discount received

購貨折讓　purchase allowance

購貨退出　purchase returns, returns outwards

購貨退出通知單　credit memo for purchase returns

購貨運費　carriage inward, freight-in

購貨價格　purchase price

購貨發票　purchase invoice

購貨債務　trade liabilities

購貨確認書　purchase confirmation

購貨簡約　purchase note
購貨轉口　buying for re-export
購貨轉銷　buying for resale
購票銀行　negotiating bank
購買力　purchasing power
購買力平價　purchasing power parity
購買力平價論　purchasing power parity doctrine
購買力價值　purchasing power value
購買力轉移　transfer of purchasing power
購買方式　buying pattern
購買本票的貸款　note purchase facility
購買曲線　purchase curve
購買合併　consolidation by purchase
購買折扣　discount on purchase
購買狂熱　buying spree
購買者行為　buyer behaviour
購買者傾向　buyer's trend
購買承諾　purchase commitments
購買政策　buying policy
購買配額　buying quota
購買基金　purchase fund
購買習慣　buying habit
購買動機　buying motive
購買稅　purchase tax
購買貸款者　purchaser of loans
購買集團　purchase group
購買資本性貨物　capitalized purchase
購買價　purchase price
購買頻率　purchase frequency
購買選擇權(交易所術語)　call option

購買證券　security purchase
購買證券成本　securities cost
購買證券費用　securities charge
購買權　purchasing right
購銷盈餘　trading surplus
購銷損益表　trading and profit and loss account
虧欠　have a deficit, be in arrears
虧本　loss capital, lose money in business
虧本出售的商品　distress merchandise
虧本生意　lossmaker, lossing proposition, sell at a loss
虧空，虧絀　be in debt, be in the red, deficit
虧損　deficiency, incur a loss
虧損總額　total loss
虧蝕企業　losing proposition
虧蝕部門　loss centre
虧艙(艙內裝貨不規則造成的艙位損失)　broken stowage
虧艙位　broken space
虧艙運費　shortfall freight
點(表示商品、外滙、證券交易所價格漲跌的最小單位,如滙率指 1 單位的 0.0001;證券則指每 100 鎊中的一鎊)　point, pip
點交　check and hand over
點收　check and receive
點貨　tally the cargo, tallying
點貨員,理貨員　cargo checker, tally man
點綴品　ornament, decoration

點數　tally, check the number

點數目　check the number

點數結餘(期貨經紀商發出的報表，根據官方收市價計算出各種未平倉合約的盈虧)　point balance

嚇人的價格，抑制購買的價格　prohibitive price

還本付息　pay principal and interest, repay capital with interest

還本付息支出　interest and amortization charges

還本股息　liquidating dividends

還款式銷售稅扣稅制度　refundable sales tax credit system

還押　remand

還清債務　extinction of debt

還款契約　contract of repayment

還債　pay one's debt, pay off a debt

還債協議　scheme of arrangement

還債期限　term of redemption

還價　counter offer, abate a price

[丿]

獲利　at a profit, yielding

獲利比率　profitability ratio

獲利回吐　profit-taking

獲利年度　profit-making year

獲利的潛力　potential earning power

獲利指數　profitability index

獲利效率　profit earning efficiency

獲利能力　profitability

獲利能力會計　profitability accounting

獲利倍數比率　times earned ratio

獲利額對固定利息的倍數比率　times-fixed charge earned ratio

獲得公積　acquired surplus

獲得折扣　discount taken, discount obtained

獲得利潤　profit making

獲得淨利　net profit

獲得資財　acquisition of property

獲得專利　get a patent, take out a patent

薄膜套膠包裝　lamipacking

鍋爐保險　boiler insurance

鍋爐艙　boiler room

鍋爐爆炸保險　boiler explosion insurance

邀請投標人做交易　invitation to treat

邀請捐款　invitation for subscription

邀請發盤　invitation for offer

邀請認購(由牽頭人向可能參與在初級市場特別是在歐洲市場發行債券的人，發送電傳，列出條件並徵詢是否願意參加認購)　invitation to subscribe

簡式提單　short-form bill of lading

簡易人身保險　simple life insurance

簡易支票(只有一人簽名的)　one-name paper

簡易仲裁　arbitration by summary procedure

簡明性　simplicity

簡明損益表　condensed income statement

簡明資產負債表　condensed balance

sheet

簡單分錄　simple entry

簡單平均　simple average

簡單再生產　simple reproduction

簡單收益率(指投資項目達到全部生產能力情況下，正常年份中利率與投資額的比率)　rate of investment

簡單回歸分析(只有一個自變量的回歸分析)　simple regression analysis

簡單協作　simple coordination

簡單套利　simple arbitrage

簡單商品經濟　simple commodity economy

簡單國際技術轉移　mere international technological transfer

簡單貨幣流通　simple money circulation

簡單幾何平均指數　simple geometric index number

簡單資本結構　simple capital structure

簡單數字制　simple numerical system

簡單算術平均　simple arithmetic mean

簡單算術平均指數　simple arithmetic index number

簡單概率曲線　simple probability curve

簡單隨機抽樣　simple random sampling

簡捷分析　short-cut analysis

簡捷法　short-cut method

優先出口　preferential export

優先付給　preferential payment

優先合夥人　predominant partner

優先股，優先股票　preference share, preferred stock

優先股本　capital stock-preferred

優先股回收基金　preferred stock sinking fund

優先股東　preference stock shareholder

優先股息　preferred dividend

優先抵押權　preferred mortgage

優先取償　preferential claim

優先使用國庫券政策　bills-preferable policy

優先負債　preferred liabilities

優先留置權　paramount lien, first lien

優先期貨交易　option dealing

優先清償的債務　preferential debt

優先進口　preferential import

優先普通股票　preferred ordinary share

優先債務　preferred debt

優先債權　privileged debts

優先債權人　preferential creditor, [美]preferred creditor

優先認購權　pre-emptive right

優先調用權(紡織品配額的)　preferential swing right

優先靠碼頭(租船用語)　free stem

優先擔保　senior security

優先償付　preferential payment

優先購買權　preemption, privilege

優先證券　senior security

優先權　right of priority, preferential, preemptive right

優利存款,優惠存款 preferential interest deposit

優良品質 fine quality

優良票據 gilt-edged bill, fine bill

優惠戶口(香港滙豐銀行近年開辦的一種把活期儲蓄與銀行信用卡聯成一體的戶口) prime account

優惠利率,最低利率 prime rate, prime rate of interest

優惠利率貸款 prime-based loan

優惠放款利率 prime lending rate

優惠股權發行 right issue

優惠區域 preferential area

優惠待遇 preferential treatment

優惠條款 preferential clause

優惠差額 margin of preference

優惠減稅額 preferential tariff cut

優惠幅度 margin of preference

優惠稅則 preferential tariff

優惠稅率 preferential rate of duty

優惠貼現率 fine rate

優惠關稅 preferential duty

優惠關稅產地證明書 generalized system of preference certificate of origin

優越所有權 superior title

優等,高級品 superior quality

優等證券 fine paper

優等證券市場的長期證券交易 long-end of the market

優質便宜貨 good cheap

優勢 superiority

儲戶 depositor

儲存 storage

儲存倉庫 warehousing storage

儲存費用 warehousing expense

儲備比率 reserve ratio

儲備交易 reserve transaction

儲備存量 reserve stock

儲備有關信貸 reserve-related credit

儲備金比率標準 reserve ratio test

儲備政策 reserve policy

儲備流動 reserve movement

儲備情況 reserve position

儲備基金 reserve fund

儲備貨幣 reserve currency

儲備貨幣國家 reserve currency country

儲備貨幣債務人 reserve currency debtor

儲備貨幣債權人 reserve currency creditor

儲蓄過度理論 oversaving theory

儲備資產 reserve assets

儲備銀行 reserve bank

儲備餘額 reserve margin

儲備頭寸 reserve position

儲蓄比率 saving ratio

儲蓄公債 savings bond

儲蓄存款 savings deposit

儲備存款制度 reserve deposit requirement system

儲蓄存摺 savings pass-book

儲蓄放款 loans by savings department

儲蓄帳戶 savings account

儲蓄基金 saving fund

儲蓄傾向　propensity to save

儲蓄會社　saving society

儲蓄銀行　savings bank

儲蓄總量　aggregate saving

儲蓄總額　total savings deposit

償付力比率　liquidity ratio

償付能力　solvency, ability to pay

償付債務開支　meet expense, debt service payment

償付銀行　reimbursing bank

償清國債　liquidate the national debt

償清債務　clear off debt, liquidate a debt

償債　debt service

償債支付　payment of debts

償債收益　redemption yield

償債收據　acquittance

償債能力　debt paying ability

償債基金　sinking fund, redemption fund

償債基金公司債券　sinking fund bonds

償債基金收入　sinking fund income

償債基金投資　sinking fund investment

償債基金折舊　depreciation-sinking fund

償債基金委託人　sinking fund trustee

償債基金按期攤款　sinking fund installment

償債基金盈餘　sinking fund surplus

償債基金現金　sinking fund cash

償債基金費用　sinking fund expense

償債基金準備　sinking fund reserve, reserve for bond redemption, reserve for debt assets

償債溢付，贖回溢價　redemption premium

償債價值　redemption value

償還，贖回　redemption, liquidate

償還比率　rate of redemption

償還日期　date of repayment

償還性援助　refundable assistance

償還信貸　reimbursement credit

償還時毛收益率　gross yield redemption

償還時淨收益率　net yield redemption

償還借款　loan repayment

償還基金　redemption fund, recourse fund

償還期　maturity

償還貸款本息　pay the principal and interest on the loans

償還資本準備基金　capital redemption reserve fund

償還債務　acquittal, service a debt, redemption of debt, repayment of debt

償還債務的開支　debt service payment

償還匯票　reimbursement draft

簍　basket

簍費（裝箱簍費）　crating charge

[ㄅ]

避風港規則　safe harbor rules

避稅投資　tax avoidance investment

避稅港，低稅國　tax haven

避難港，遇難港　port of distress, port of refuge

臂挽臂（商業交易中滲入了個人關係，在很大程度上由於這種關係而達成交易）　arm-in-arm

隱名股東　dormant partner

隱含同意　implied consent

隱含利息　implicit interest

隱含的契約　implied contract

隱含的條件　implied condition

隱蔽失業　disguised unemployment

隱蔽的通貨膨脹　hidden inflation

隱蔽財產　hidden wealth

隱蔽稅，間接稅　hidden tax

隱蔽準備，間接準備　hidden reserve

隱蔽傾銷　hidden dumping

隱藏成本　hidden cost

隱藏商譽　implied goodwill

隱藏資產　hidden asset

縱向一體化（指跨國公司的垂直型經營）　vertical integration

縱向分析，垂直分析　vertical analysis

縱向合併　vertical consolidating, vertical merger

縱向多樣化　vertical diversification

縱向結合　vertical integration

縱向調查　longitudinal study

縱向轉移　vertical transfer

縱式貿易（指先進國與落後國之間的貿易）　vertical trade

縱式聯合　vertical combination merger

縱坐標　vertical axis

縱的一致性　vertical consistency

縱的競爭　vertical competition

縱條圖　vertical bar-chart

縱斷面　vertical section

績效分析與管理制度　performance analysis and control system

績效股份　performance share

績效考核　performance appraisal

績效考核制度，考績制度　merit system

績效指數（用預先擬定的一指數去考察管理人員的績效）　performance index

績效容限（對工人工作容許出錯和缺乏效率的限度）　performance tolerance

績效評價　performance evaluation

績效與工薪聯繫制（指按工作成績付酬的工薪制）　performance-linked pay

績優提工薪　merit increase

總支出　aggregate expenditure

總支付協定　overall payment agreement

總公司　head office

總日程表　master scheduling

總分類帳　general ledger accounts

總出口　general export

總出納　general casher

總平均　overall average

總付息保障率（參見"付息保障倍數"）　total interest coverage ratio

總代理　general agency

總代理人　general agent

總代理商　universal agency

總生產能力　total productive capacity

總生產量預測　total-products forecast

總生產額　aggregate output

總目標　general objective

總收入，所得毛額　gross revenue, gross income, gross receipt

總收入提成折舊法　gross earning depreciation method

總成本　total cost

總成本與總市價孰低　lower of total cost or total market

總合折扣　aggregate discount

總合有效需求　aggregate effective demand

總合價值　aggregate value

總危機　general crisis

總決算　general final accounts

總批量　total lot amount

總批發　wholesale

總投資　gross investment

總投資率　rate of gross investment

總投資對國民總產值的比率　ratio of gross investment to gross national product

總利潤　gross profit

總和　sum

總和年數折舊法　sum-of-the-years digits depreciation

總和指數　summary index

總和符號　summation sign

總和數字法　sum-of-digits method

總的外滙頭寸，總的外滙持有額，總的外滙地位　overall position of exchange

總承包合同　general contract

總承包者　general contractor

總股本　general capital

總法律顧問　General Counsel

總所得稅　gross income tax

總供給　aggregate supply

總供給函數，總供給量　aggregate supply function

總供給價格　aggregate supply price

總物價水平的變動　general price level change

總物價指數　general price index

總則　general provisions

總計　grand total, total, gross total, total amount

總計劃　general plan, master plan

總括式損益表　all-inclusive income statement

總括法　lump sum method

總括保險(美國保險市場慣用術語)　blanket insurance

總括保險單　blanket policy

總括保證保險　blanket bond

總括訂貨　blanket order

總重量　gross weight

總信貸　overall credit

總負債　total liability

總指數　combined index

總限額(配額的)　aggregate limit

總相關係數　coefficient of total correlation

總值 total value, gross value, aggregate value

總值加權法 aggregate-value method of weighting

總效率 general efficiency

總租船契約 gross charter

總留置權 general lien

總差額(國際收支的) overall balance

總量分析 macroanalysis

總量生產函數 aggregate production function

總量模型 aggregative model

總許可證 blanket license

總產值 total output value, gross output value

總容許限度 total tolerance

總清單 master list

總商會 general chamber of commerce

總開銷 overhead charges

總崩潰(指市場) crash

總進口 general import

總註冊噸位 gross registered tonnage

總貿易 general trade

總稱,通稱 generic terms

總資本 general capital

總資本利潤率 total capital profit ratio

總資本構成對國民總產值比率 ratio of gross capital formation to gross national product

總資產 total assets

總資產負債表 general balance sheet

總資產報酬率 rate of return on total assets

總資產週轉率 turnover of total assets

總損益 consolidated profit and loss

總經理 general manager

總經銷 general agency

總經銷人 wholesale distributor

總預算 general budget

總需求 aggregate demand

總需求函數,總需要量 aggregate demand function

總價 total price

總價入帳法 gross price method

總罷工 general strike

總增益 overall gain

總概算 general estimate

總營業收入 gross operating income

總營運資金 gross working capital

總體分析,宏觀分析 aggregate analysis, macro-analysis

總體方案 overall plan

總體市場 aggregate market

總體決定 aggregate decision

總體企業 macrobusiness

總體預測,宏觀預測 macroforecast

總體經濟,宏觀經濟 macroeconomy

總體經濟不平衡 macrodisequilibrium

總體經濟政策,宏觀經濟政策 macroeconomic policy

總體經濟學,宏觀經濟學 macroeconomics

總體銷售 macromarketing

彌補損失　make up a loss
彌補虧空　cover deficit

十八畫

[、]

謹防假冒　beware of imitations
燻船　fumigation
雜股　miscellaneous share
雜貨　fancy goods, general merchandise, sundry goods
雜貨市集　fancy fair
雜貨形式　break-bulk form
雜貨批發商　general merchandise wholesaler
"雜貨"班輪　break-bulk liner
雜貨泊位　break-bulk berth
雜貨貨櫃/集裝箱船　break-bulk container ship
雜貨運費率　general-cargo rate
雜稅　sundry tax, miscellaneous taxes
雜費　petty expenditures, sundry charges
雜費已付　charges paid
雜項支付　miscellaneous payments
雜項收益　miscellaneous income
雜項存款　sundry deposit
雜項帳戶　sundry account
雜項費用,雜費　miscellaneous expenses, sundry expenses
雜項損失　miscellaneous loss

雜項資產　miscellaneous assets
雜項債務人　sundry debtor
雜項債權人　sundry creditor
雜險　miscellaneous risks
竄改帳目　manipulation of accounts
額外收入　extraneous income, extraordinary receipt
額外危險　extraordinary risk
額外投入資本　additional paid-in capital
額外折扣　extra discount
額外利潤　extraordinary profit, surplus profit
額外折舊　extra depreciation
額外股利　extra dividend, [美俚] melon
額外津貼　extra allowance
額外保險費　extra premium
額外停留期　extra period of detention
額外費用　extra expenses, extra charge
額外發行　extra-limit issue, excess issue
額外損失　extraordinary loss, extraneous loss
額外運費　extra freight
額外補貼　perquisite
額外賺得　extraneous earnings
額外營業收入　extraneous earnings
額定公債　bond authorized
額定股本　capital stock authorized
額定股數　authorized shares
額定抵押債券　authorized mortgage bonds

額定資本　authorized capital
額定價值　authorized value
禮品包裝　gift packaging
禮品店　gift shop
禮券，贈與支票　gift cheque
禮券兌付　gift coupons cashing
顏色搭配　colour assortment
顏色樣品　sample of colour

[一]

覆核　recheck, double check
覆蓋率　coverage rate
覆評訟費　review of taxation
擴大再生產　expand reproduction
擴大企業　enlarging enterprise
擴大抽樣　extension sampling
擴大風險保險　extended risk guarantees
擴大風險保證　extended risk guarantees
擴大就業面　expand employment
擴大資本　widening of capital
擴大滙率波動幅度　widening of margin in exchange rate fluctuations
擴展市場　expansion of market
擴展保險範圍　extended coverage
擴展責任(保險)　extended cover
擴展責任條款　extended cover clause
擴展貿易　expansion of trade
擴張營業　expansion of business
擴散指數　diffusion index
擺動信貸，互許差額　swing credit
擺動帳戶　swing account

擺動額(指支付協定中對兩國間清算結果的支付差額預先規定的最高限度)　swing limit
櫃台　counter
櫃台交易(指交易所場外的直接交易)　over-the-counter
櫃台交易市場，場外交易市場　over-the-counter market
櫃台售貨員　over-the-counter sales person
舊文據　ancient writings
舊包裝　second hand packing
舊股份　old share
舊例　old terms
舊盈餘　old surplus
舊帳，老帳　old account
舊貨　second hand goods
舊貨市場　second hand market
舊貨店，舊貨攤　junk shop, junk store
舊貨廉賣　[英]jumble sale
舊償債基金　old sinking fund
藐視法庭　contempt of court
藍天立法(美國各州政府為防止欺詐性憑空發行股票證券而立的各種法律，又稱"青天法")　blue-sky legislation, blue-sky law
藍皮書(任何政府公佈的文件，具體指英國中央統計局每年公佈的關於國民收入和支出的文件)　blue book
藍信用卡(法國使用較廣的一種信用卡)　Carte Bleu
"藍鈕扣"(指交易所的低級職員)　blue button
藍牌職員(倫敦證券交易所成員公司

在交易廳內的非授權僱員的別稱）
blue button

藍領工人　blue-collar worker

藍圖，規劃　blueprint

藍籌股，大公司股票，熱門股票　blue chip share

藍籌股投資，穩健投資　blue chip investment

轉入次頁　carried forward

轉口　transit

轉口貨物　transit goods

轉口商品　merchandise in transit

轉口稅　entrepot duty

轉口貿易　carrying trade, entrepot trade

轉分保　retrocede

轉分保分出公司　retroceding company

轉分保合同　retrocession treaty

轉分保接受人　retrocessionaire

轉分配　sub-allotment

轉手交易　switch operations

轉手貨物　switch cargo

轉手貿易　switch trade

轉手滙率　switch rate

轉名（指股票的）　transfer of names

轉名日，過戶日　transfer day

轉交　care of (c/o)

轉回分錄，還原分錄　reversing entry

轉向信貸（經互會國家規定年度借貸，以資助兩國間貿易的制度）　swing credit

轉求市場（美國聯儲局進行公開干預業務時，向美國政府證券主要經營

人發出通知政府準備買進或賣出的意圖，然後尋求他們的還價或報價）　go around

轉助記錄　auxiliary record

轉助帳簿　auxiliary book, subsidiary book

轉租　sublease, sublet

轉租人　sublessor

轉租人所付租金　subrent

轉租承受人　sublessee

轉租船舶　subchartering

轉售，再出售，倒賣　resale, resell

轉船　transhipment

轉帳　transfer of account

轉帳支票　transfer check

轉帳付款制度　giro system

轉帳性支付　transfer payment, giro-cheque

轉帳傳票　transfer slip

轉帳價格　transfer price

轉帳憑單　transfer voucher

轉帳機構　transfer mechanism

轉移人工　transferred labor

轉移信用　transferred credit

轉移責任之約定　hold-harmless agreement

轉移貿易作用　trade diversion effect

轉移貿易關稅　trade diverting tariff

轉移資金　transfer of financial resources

轉移價值　transfer value

轉開信用證　back-to-back credit

轉現貨交易　exchange for physical

轉買　subpurchase

轉買人　subpurchaser
轉換分銷商　distributor switching
轉換曲線　transformation curve
轉換合約（以指定期貨價為基礎，買入或賣出即期棉花的合約）　conversion contract
轉換定位機　transfer posting machine
轉換抵押　pass-through security
轉換保險　convertible insurance
轉換牌子　brand switching
轉換程序　tranformation process
轉換貸款　conversion loan
轉換權利　conversion privilege
轉期存單（美國摩根保證公司 1976 年發行的一種一攬子存單）　Rollover CD, Roll-poly CD
轉期信貸技術　revolving credit technique
轉期票據　note renewals
轉運，轉船　transhipment
轉運口岸　entrepot
轉運公司　transfer company, transit company
轉運站　transfer point
轉運許可證　transhipment permit
轉運途中　in transit
轉運貨物　transhipment cargo
轉運港　port of transhipment
轉運報單　transhipment entry
轉運提單　transhipment B/L
轉運艙單　transhipment manifest
轉運證明書　diversion certificate
轉嫁經濟危機　transfer of economic crisis

轉讓　transference
轉讓一攬子　transfer package
轉讓人　transferor, assignor
轉讓手續費　transfer commission
轉讓代理人　transfer agent
轉讓交易，過戶業務　transfer transaction
轉讓危險　assigned risk
轉讓利益　assignment of interests
轉讓性付款　transfer payment
轉讓條款　assignment clause
轉讓書　letter of assignment, transfer form
轉讓租船合同　demise charter party
轉讓條款　assignment clause
轉讓配額　transfer of quota
轉讓產權　assignment of property
轉讓稅　transfer tax
轉讓費　transfer fee
轉讓權利　assignment privilege
職工代表大會　congress of workers and staff, workers' congress
職工升調　promotion and transferring of employee
職工平均收入　average income of non-agricultural workers
職工股票購買權　employee stock option
職工退休基金　employee's pension fund
職工週轉率　employee turnover ratio
職工福利基金準備　benefit fund reserve
職工聯合會　employee association

職位　position, post, job
職位分類　position classification
職位空缺　job vacancy
職位輪調　job rotation
職別　level of position
職前指導　job orientation
職前訓練　vestibule training
職務工資　pay according to one's post
職務工資率(一具體職務的最低工資率)　job rate
職務津貼　duty allowance
職務執行令　mandamus
職務等級工資制　post-rank salary system
職能化(按職能主義設置機構的政策和程序)　functionalization
職能式分權制　functional decentralization
職能合併　functional consolidation
職能訓練　functional training
職能部門　functional department
職能組織　functional organization
職能資本家　entrepreneurial capitalist, industrialist and businessman
職能會計　functional accounting
職能權限　functional authority
職責　responsibility
職稱　positional title, professional rank and titles
職稱等級　professional qualification
職業介紹所　employment agency
職業安全　occupational safety

職業性意外事故　occupational accident
職業前程發展管理　career management
職業前程輔導　career counseling
職業健康　occupational health
職業查帳員，會計師　professional auditor
職業病　employment disease, occupational disease
職業流動性　occupational mobility
職業責任保險　professional liability insurance
職業結構　occupational structure
職業會計師，開業會計師　professional accountant, public accountant
職業道德　professional ethics
職權　authority
醫院管理　hospital management
醫療服務　medical service
醫療保險基金　medical benefits fund

[丨]

豐田式生產制度　Toyota Production System
蟲蛀　worm-eaten, damaged by vermins

[丿]

翻船　overturning of vessel
"翻轉"權(指沒有期限的票據可以重

新換回永久性票據或有期限、低收入票據的權利） flip flop option

雙方同意　by mutual consent

雙方過失碰撞條款　both to blame collision clause

雙列，二數列　bi-serial

雙列相關比率　bi-serial ratio of correlation

雙列相關係數　bi-serial coefficient of correlation

雙向交流信息　two-way flow of message

雙向差額套頭（指買入一個買權，再賣出一個買權；或買進一個賣權，再賣出一個賣權） spreads

雙向報價　two-way price quotation

雙向溝通　two-way communication

雙向溝通渠道　two-way communication channel

雙因素理論　two-factor theory

雙因貿易條件　double-factorial terms of trade

雙名票據　double-name paper

雙名滙票　two party draft

雙次驗收抽樣法　double sampling plan

雙重上市（除在一個交易所上市外，還在另一個或幾個交易所掛牌的股票） dual listing

雙重分配通路　dual system

雙重代表權　dual representation

雙重用途包裝　dual-use packaging

雙重外滙市場　dual exchange market, two-tier foreign exchange market

雙重利潤　double profit

雙重金價制　two-tier gold price system

雙重背書　double endorsement

雙重負債　double liabilities

雙重保險　double insurance

雙重保險單　double insurance policy

雙重黃金市場　two-tier gold market

雙重貨幣債券（以一國貨幣付息，以另一國貨幣償還的債券） dual currency bond

雙重基點制　dual basing-point system

雙重國籍　dual nationality

雙重稅　double taxation

雙重稅協定　double-tax treaty

雙重稅率制　double tariff system

雙重滙率　dual exchange rate

雙重運費制（運費同盟的兩價運費制） dual rate system

雙重經濟結構　dual structure of economy

雙重對冲，雙重套期交易　double hedging

雙重價格　double price, two-tier price

雙重價格條款　dual valuation clause

雙重價格基礎　double price basis

雙重選擇權，雙重期權　double option

雙重關稅　double tariff, dual tariff

雙軌貿易　two-way trade

雙軌銷售　dual distribution

雙倍收費　double charge

雙倍賠償　double indemnity

雙倍賠償條款　double indemnity clause

雙帳式資產負債表　double account form of balance sheet

雙帳制　double account system

雙麻袋　double jute bag

雙程出入境簽證　two-way exit-entry visa

雙層甲板船　tweendeck ship

雙層市場　two-tier market

雙頭壟斷(即市場某一商品由兩家賣主壟斷)　duopoly

雙頭壟斷市場　duopsony

雙聯合同(表明證券發行者義務或證券持有者權益的合法合同)　indenture

雙聯訂單　indent

雙聯滙票　draft in duplicate

雙邊支付協定　bilateral payments agreement

雙邊中期貸款　bilateral midterms loan

雙邊合夥　bilateral partners

雙邊有價證券投資　bilateral porfolio investment

雙邊性投資　bilateral commitments of capital

雙邊和多邊經濟合作　bilateral and multilateral economic cooperation

雙邊協定　bilateral agreement

雙邊法律關係　bilateral legal relations

雙邊信貸互惠協定　bilateral swap agreement

雙邊套利　bilateral arbitrage

雙邊配額　bilateral quota

雙邊專約　bilateral convention

雙邊清算　bilateral clearing

雙邊貨幣進出國境協定　bilateral agreement on the movement of currencies into and out of each other's territory

雙邊進口配額　bilateral import quotas

雙邊稅收抵免協定　bilateral agreement on tax credit

雙邊援助　bilateral aid

雙邊貿易　bilateral trade

雙邊貿易及支付協定　bilateral trade and payments agreement

雙邊貸款　bilateral loans

雙邊滙率價格指數(亦稱有效滙率)　price index of bilateral foreign exchange rate

雙邊經濟援助　bilateral economic aid

雙邊對流　bilateral flow

雙邊談判和協定　bilateral negotiation and agreement

雙邊壟斷　bilateral monopoly

雙欄式分類帳帳戶　double-column ledger account

雙欄稅則　double-column tariff

歸收滙票　bill for collection

歸復(指事物回歸到其舊主人)　result

歸復信託　resulting trust

歸還　restitution

鎢生產商協會　Association of Tungsten Producers

[ㄱ]

"斷折的"需求曲線 "kinked" demand curve
斷定抽樣法 judgement sampling
斷絕貿易關係 sever trade relation
斷熱貨櫃/集裝箱(即保溫貨櫃/集裝箱) insulated container
斷續服務 intermittent service
斷續運轉 intermittent working
斷續製造程序 intermittent process

[㇔]

爆竹 fire-cracker
爆炸物品 explosive
爆炸保險 explosion insurance
瀝青紙 tar paper
離岸市場 offshore market
離岸股票,歐洲股票 Eurostock
離岸物業投資 offshore property investment
離岸金融中心 offshore financial centre
離岸控股保險公司(一種只從擁有它的公司集團收取保險金的為有限顧客服務的保險公司) offshore cap-

tive insurance company
離岸債券,歐洲債券 Eurobond
離岸銀行單位 off-shore banking unit
離岸銀行業務 off-shore banking transaction
離岸價,船上交貨價 free on board (F.O.B.)
離差,離中趨勢 dispersion
離散係數 coefficient of dispersion
離散度,差異量 measure of dispersion
離港船 outgoing steamer
離港證明書 certificate of departure port
離職率 separation rate
離職培訓 off-the-job training
壟斷 monopoly
壟斷市場 hold the market, engross the market, monopolize the market
壟斷主義 monopolism
壟斷企業,壟斷康采恩 monopoly enterprise, monopolistic concern
壟斷利潤 monopoly profit
壟斷者 monopolist
壟斷性力量 monopoly power
壟斷性購買,買主壟斷 monopsony
壟斷性競爭 monopolistic competition
壟斷產品,哄抬市價 engrossment
壟斷貿易權 monopolistic trading right
壟斷集團 monopoly
壟斷資本,獨佔資本 monopoly capit-

al

壟斷資本集團　monopoly-capital group

壟斷銷售，專賣　monopoly sale

壟斷價格　monopolistic price

證言規則(英美法解釋合同的一項規則，不允許以口頭協議改變書面合同的內容)　Parol Evidence Rule

證明已納稅印花　denoting stamp

證券　security, instrument

證券化(指金融市場上所出現的傳統的銀行資產，主要是貸款或住房抵押貸款變換成可轉讓證券的趨勢)　securitization

證券公司　securities company

證券分析　securities analysis

證券分析家　securities analyst

證券及投資　securities and investments

證券及投資損益　profit and loss on securities and investment

證券出售　offering of bonds

證券市場　securities market, stock market

證券包銷集團　underwriting syndicate

證券在市場確立的時間　seasoning

證券交易　securities trading

證券交易法　Securities Exchange Act

證券交易所　securities exchange, stock exchange, bourse(歐洲，尤指法國的證券交易所)

證券交易所委員會　stock-exchange committee

證券交易所委員會財務報表規則　re-

gulation S-X

證券交易所牌價　stock exchange list

證券交易清算　stock exchange settlement

證券交易稅　securities transfer tax

證券交易管理委員會　Securities and Exchange Commission

證券收益及費用　security income and expense

證券存款　certificate deposit

證券批發商(在英國以證券經紀人為買賣對象的)　[英]stock jobber

證券兌換　exchange of securities

證券投資　portfolio investment

證券投資分析　securities analysis

證券投資信託　securities investment trust

證券投資風險　portfolio risk

證券投機　speculation in securities

證券抵押　lombard rate

證券抵押信託債券　security collateral trust bond

證券抵押借款　security collateral loans

證券的承包費用　underwriting fees

證券金融公司　securities finance company

證券持有人　security holder

證券停止交易通知書　stop order

證券組合風險　portfolio risk

證券組合效應　portfolio effect

證券組合理論　portfolio theory

證券組合期望收益　expected return of a portfolio

證券組合選擇　portfolio selection

證券兜售書，募股書 prospectus

證券推銷所 boiler room

證券發行公告 tombstone advertisement

證券發行成本 cost of flotation

證券發行價格 issurance price

證券等級 securities ratings

證券買賣商 securities dealer

證券買賣商協會 association of securities dealers

證券評價線 security-valuation line

證券跌價損失 market loss on security

證券搶先成交 beating the gun

證券業自動化公司（紐約證券交易所和美國證券交易所聯合建的附屬機構）Securities Industry Automation Corporation

證券經紀人 ［美］stock jobber

證券經紀人公會 Open Board of Stock Brokers

證券電腦活動中心（對歐洲債券等進行安全保管、交割、清算活動的電腦系統，管理處設在盧森堡）［法］Centrale de Livraision de Valeurs Mobilieres

證券意識 stock-minded

證券銀行 merchant bank

證券價格 security price

證券價格平均數 stock price average

證券賣價 asked price

證券銷售書，投股說明書 prospectus

證券銷售集團承銷部分（指證券銷售集團留出一定百分比的證券）selling group pot

證券擔保信託公司債 collateral trust bond

證券擔保債款 loan(s) on collateral

證券優惠售價 selling concession

證券鎊 security sterling

證券轉帳成交制度（德國術語，指不同實物證券用記帳形式進行證券交割的一種成交制度）［德］effektengiro

證券蘭德（表示南非出售投資的收入，倫敦有證券蘭德交易的大規模市場。自 1979 年 1 月以來，改稱"金融蘭德"）securities Rand

證實 substantiate, confirmation, verify

證實書 letter of confirmation

證據 evidence, testimony

寶石 precious stone

寶石商 jeweller

寶庫 treasure house

寶號 your esteemed company

類比方式 analogical pattern

類比電腦 analog computer

類別 category, specification

類別尺度 nominal scale

類別量數 categorical measure

類別數列 categorical series

類別產品損益表 product-line profit and loss statement

類型 type

類壟斷 quasi monopoly

[一]

壞票（指無法收現的票據）uncollectible notes

壞帳　bad debt, uncollectible debt, bad account, uncollectible account, dead account

壞帳收回　bad debt recoveries

壞帳沖銷　bad debt write-off

壞帳準備　reserve for bad debts, allowance for uncollectibles

壞帳損失　bad debt losses, loss on bad debts

壞資產　bad assets

藥水擦改　eradicator erase

藥衡盎司（等於 1/12 磅）ounce, apothecaries' measure

藝術品　work of art

藝術設計　art layout

藝術陶瓷　art pottery

難船救助人員　salvor

難銷貨物　drug

騙人金錢　financier a person out of his money

騙人貨　duffer

騙子　cheater, faker

騙取　defraud

騙取信用　obtaining credit by fraud

騙買　kiting transaction

[丨]

關卡　customs barrier

關於利息的合同規定　stipulation for (of) interest

關係企業　affiliated enterprise

關係性研究　interrelationship study

關係導向　relationship-oriented

關稅　customs duty, tariff

關稅已付　duty paid

關稅水平，關稅比率　tariff level

關稅升級　tariff escalation

關稅及貿易總協定　General Agreement on Tariff and Trade

關稅未付　duty unpaid

關稅自主　tariff autonomy

關稅合作理事會　Customs Co-operation Council

關稅同盟　customs union

關稅改革　tariff reform

關稅的初高點　initial height of the tariff

關稅制度　tariff system

關稅政策　tariff policy

關稅保險　duty insurance

關稅保護　tariff protection

關稅條約　tariff treaty

關稅退稅　duty drawback

關稅配額　tariff quota, duty quota

關稅率　tariff rate

關稅率表，稅則　tariff schedule

關稅減讓　tariff diminution, tariff concession

關稅稅則　customs tariff, tariff schedule

關稅報復　tariff retaliation

關稅最高限額　tariff ceiling

關稅結構彈性 flexibility in tariff structure

關稅領域 customs area

關稅談判 tariff bargaining

關稅戰 tariff war

關稅壁壘 tariff barriers, tariff wall

關稅優惠 tariff preference

關稅聯盟的組成領土(關貿總協定術語) constituent territories of the custom union

關棧交貨 ex bond

關棧費 bonding fee

關棧價格 in bond price

關境 customs frontier, customs boundary

關鍵人物 key man

關鍵工業 key industry

關鍵用語定義 definition of keywords

關鍵字句 key word

關鍵部門 key sector

關鍵通貨,基本貨幣 key currency

贈券 gift coupons

贈股盈餘 surplus from donated stock

贈品 extra gift

贈與稅 gift tax, donation tax

羅(計量單位,等於十二打) gross

羅巨戴爾原則(關於合作經營) [英] Rochdale principles

曠工 neglect business

曠職 delinquency

[ノ]

穩妥的股票 seasoned securities

穩妥價值,合理價值 sound value

穩定一種證券(通過大量買進以維持其最低價格) stabilize a security

穩定市場 stabilize the market

穩定平衡 stable equilibrium

穩定但可調整的平價 stable but adjustable par value

穩定性出價(歐洲證券及美國證券市場術語,指證券發行經理人對所發行的證券開出的價格) stabilising bid

穩定股票市場價格的業務活動 operations for stabilizing the stock-market price

穩定物價 stabilize the prices of commodities

穩定的價格 stable price

穩定借款 stabilization loan

穩定基金 stabilization fund

穩定貨幣 stable currency

穩定滙率 stable exchange rate

穩定幣值會計(指會計報表按物價指數作了調整) stabilized accounting

穩值債券(參見"指數化債券"條) stabilized bond

穩健原則 conservatism

邊註(指會計報表上的邊註) marginal note

邊列條款(保險人為排除其擔保責任而印在保險單正面主文左下邊的特別條款,又稱"欄外條款") marginal clause

邊際支出傾向 marginal propensity

to spend

邊際分析(觀察一個變量每增加一個單位和另一個變數增量的關係) marginal analysis

邊際付款 marginal payment

邊際出口傾向 marginal propensity to export

邊際生產力 marginal productivity

邊際生產商 marginal producer

邊際代替比例 marginal rate of substitution

邊際成本(指增加一單位額外產量所相應增加的成本) marginal cost

邊際收益(指邊際收入大於邊際成本的差額) marginal income

邊際收益率 marginal income ratio

邊際存貸率 marginal deposit-loan ratio

邊際投資效率 marginal efficiency of investment

邊際投資傾向 marginal propensity to invest

邊際利潤 marginal profit

邊際利潤率 marginal profit ratio

邊際所得總額 marginal revenue

邊際供給價格 marginal supply price

邊際信用,信用限度 marginal credit

邊際負效用(指每額外生產一件產品所產生的負效用) marginal disutility

邊際要素成本 marginal factory cost

邊際風險(有關"遠期合同"的外滙術語。指客戶在簽訂遠期合同後破產了，銀行必須結束其承擔的義務，

從而承擔在此期間滙率不利變化所帶來的風險) marginal risk

邊際效用 marginal utility

邊際效用本位 marginal utility standard

邊際效用遞減法則 law of marginal decreasing utility

邊際財務收益 marginal financial return

邊際消費者 marginal consumer

邊際消費函數 marginal consumption function

邊際消費傾向 marginal propensity to consume

邊際貢獻，邊際收益 contribution margin, marginal contribution

邊際貢獻法 contribution margin approach

邊際貢獻率 contribution ratio, profit volume ratio

邊際產出 marginal output

邊際產品 marginal product

邊際現儲備 marginal cash reserve

邊際進口傾向 marginal propensity to import

邊際買方 marginal buyer

邊際貿易 marginal trading

邊際稅率 marginal rate of tax

邊際資本成本 marginal cost of capital

邊際資本系數 marginal capital coefficient

邊際資本產出比率 marginal capital-output ratio

邊際需求 marginal demand

邊際需求價格 marginal demand price

邊際價格　marginal price
邊際價值　marginal value
邊際實質產量　marginal physical product
邊際購買　marginal purchase
邊際營業　marginal business
邊際儲蓄傾向　marginal propensity to save
邊境交貨　delivered at frontier (D.A.F.)
邊境兌換　exchange at frontier
邊境貿易　frontier trade
邊緣海，陸緣海　marginal sea
邊緣銀行(指在英國經營某項銀行業務的公司)　fringe bank
邊緣機率　marginal probability
簿記　bookkeeping
簿記交易　bookkeeping transaction
簿記事項　bookkeeping items
簿記員　book-keeper
簿記費用　bookkeeping fee
懲罰性附加稅　punitive surtax
懲罰性損害賠償　vindictive damages
懲罰稅　penalty duty
懲罰稅率　penalty rate
鏡像規則(普通法關於承諾的規則，認為承諾必須像鏡子一樣照出要約的內容。)　mirror image rule
簽名　subscribe, sign
簽名蓋章　signed and sealed
簽字　signature
簽字樣本　specimen signature
簽字蠟封合同　signed and sealed contract

簽字蠟封式的要約　offer under seal
簽約，簽署合同　sign a contract
簽約日期　date of contract
簽條，標簽　label
簽發票據　issuance of a note
簽發滙票　issue of bill of exchange
簽署發票　signed invoice
簽證卡(1966年由美洲銀行和30個國家的銀行聯合發行的信用卡。原稱美洲銀行卡，1977年改為現名)　Visa Card 又稱: Bank Americard
簽證條款　attestation clause
簽證費　licencing fee
簽證發票　certified invoice
簽證機關　signatory authorities
辭職　resignation

[ㄅ]

繳入盈餘　contributed surplus, additional paid-in capital, paid-in surplus
繳入資本，實收資本　contributed capital, paid-in capital
繳足股本　paid-up share, fully-paid capital stock
繳庫　pay into the treasury
繳納使用費　pay for the use of
繳納稅款　tax payment
繳納罰款　pay the penalty
繳款(給銀行)　paid in
繳款通知　payment notice
繳稅通知書　notice of tax payment
繳銷營業執照　hand in business li-

cence for cancellation

[、]

議付正本　negotiable original copy

議付外國滙票　negotiation of foreign bills

議付手續費　negotiation commission

議付金額　negotiated amount

議付信用證　negotiation credit

議付票據　negotiated bills

議付期限　negotiating date

議付業務　negotiating transaction

議付銀行　negotiating bank

議決分派的股利　dividend declared

議定文本　agreed text

議定再出售而買入的證券　securities purchased under agreement to resell

議定金價（由倫敦五大黃金商行一天兩次在自由市場議定的黃金價格，包括要價與開價）　gold fix

議定書　protocol

議定貿易量　agreed quantity of trade

議價採購　negotiated purchase

議銷價格　sale at negotiated price

議購價格　purchase at negotiated price

譯電費　coding fee

譯解密碼　decode

譯碼指令　translation instruction

譯碼機　code translator

贏利　profit, gain, get out of the red

贏利股，紅利股　bonus dividend, bonus stock

贏餘　abundance, surplus

贏餘毛利　gross profit

競爭　compete, competition, rivalry

競爭力　competitive power

競爭公司　rival firms

競爭市場　competitive market

競爭地位　competitive position

競爭地帶　zone of competition

競爭交易人（係交易所成員，為取得利潤在交易所進行股票交易，亦稱"註冊交易人"）competitive trader

競爭者　competitor, rival

競爭性　competitiveness

競爭性工資　competitive wage

競爭性投資　competitive investment

競爭性的非升值　competitive nonrevaluation

競爭性貶值　competitive depreciation, competitive devaluation

競爭性報價　competitive bidding

競爭性補貼　competitive subsidization

競爭性運價表　competitive tariff

競爭性廣告　competitive advertising

競爭性輸入　competitive import

競爭的合作　competitive cooperation

競爭信息　competitive information

競爭政策　competition policy

競爭船（運費公會用於競爭的）fighting ship

競爭規則 rules of competition

競爭商品 rival commodities

競爭產品 competing product

競爭策略 competitive strategy

競爭對手 competitor

競爭需求 competitive demand

競爭價格 competitive price

競爭導向的價格政策 competitive-oriented pricing

競爭優勢 competitive edge

競買人 bidder

競買的最低價(指投標的) lowest bid

競買的最高價(指投標的) highest bid

競標,公開招標 competitive bidding, competitive tender

競銷 competitive sale, auction

競賽 emulation

競賽理論 game theory

[一]

攙水(超過實際資產 的估價或股額) water, water down

攙水股(指價值不實的股份,俗稱"空氣股") watering of stock

攙水股票 watering stock, watered stock

攙水資本(指虛假資本) watered capital

蘇伊士運河航線 via Suez Canal shipping line

躉批 sell wholesale

躉售 corner the market combination sale, package deal

躉售價值 wholesale price

躉船交貨條件 ex lighter terms

礦山開發 mine development, mine exploitation

礦物儲量 mineral deposit

礦砂船 ore carrier

礦砂散裝貨兼用船 ore and bulk carrier

礦砂/散裝貨/石油三用船 ore/bulk/oil ship

礦產品 mineral

礦產稅 mine tax

礦產業 mining industry

礦產資源 mineral resources

[丨]

嚴守秘密 strictly confidential

嚴重失業地區 substantial unemployment area

嚴重過失 gross negligence

嚴重虧損 heavy loss

嚴封堅固艙 sealed cabin

嚴格賠償責任 strict liability

嚴格遵守合同條款 strict performance of contract

嚴格檢查 close inspection, meticulous inspection

[丿]

觸及外物致污 contact with external substances soiled by

觸及其他貨物 contact with other car-

go
觸動價格　trigger price
觸碰損壞　contact damage
觸感　feeling
籌集貸款, 舉債　float a loan
籌集資金, 籌款　raise money, raising fund, raise the wind, financing
籌備支出　preliminary expenditure
籌備費　organization cost, start-up cost
籌備期間保險　preliminary term insurance
籌款債券　funding bond
籌資方法, 賦稅方法　ways and means
籌資安排　financing arrangement
籌資協定　replenishment agreement
籌資性租賃　financing lease
籌資費用　financing expense
籌資業務　financing operation
籌資機構　financing body
籌碼　counter, dough
犧牲血本拋售　sacrifice
犧牲財產　sacrifice property
犧牲船舶　sacrifice of ship

[一]

繼承人　inheritor, successor
繼承稅　inheritance tax
繼承權　right of succession
繼續成本, 繼續結轉成本　continuing cost
繼續交易　standing business
繼續交易市場　continuing market

繼續年金　continuous annuity
繼續保險　continued insurance
繼續條款　continuation clause
繼續結轉帳戶　continuing account
繼續經營　continuity of life, going concern
繼續經營假設　continuity of life assumption, going concern assumption
繼續審計　continuous audit

[、]

顧客定金　customer's deposit
顧客服務　customer service
顧客情況檔案　customer information file
顧客理想　customer's image
顧客銀行通訊終端　customer bank communication terminal
顧客需要　in demand by the customer
顧問, 諮詢人員　consultant
顧問公司　consultant firm
顧問團　consultant mission
辯方證人　defence witness
辯護人　advocate
辯護費　defence cost
襯墊物　padding
襯鐵皮箱　tin-lined case

[一]

攜帶包裝　carrier pack

[丨]

蠟燭競賣法（到蠟燭點完為止，決定
　成交）　auction by candle

[丿]

鐵皮條打包　iron strapping
鐵皮鬆開　iron-strap loosened
鐵桶　iron drum
鐵路　〔英〕railway，〔美〕railroad
鐵路平車運輸　piggyback service
鐵路交貨　free on rail (F.O.R.)
鐵路事故　railway accident
鐵路股票　rails
鐵路承運人　rail carrier
鐵路稅　railway duty
鐵路等級　classification of rail
鐵路提單　Railway B/L
鐵路債券　Railroad bond
鐵路運費　Railage, Railway freight
鐵路運單副本　duplicate of way bill
鐵路運輸　railway transportation
鐵路綜合運價　freight of all kinds
鐵路聯運　railroad through trans-
　port
鐵道郵遞信件　railway letter
鐵箍　iron hoop
鐵櫃條款　iron safe clause

鐵礦砂出口國協會　Association of
　Iron-Ore Export Countries
鐵罐　iron flask
鷄尾酒式貨幣（日語用詞，指一種"記
　帳貨幣"，由一些貨幣組成）　cur-
　rency cocktail
鷄尾酒貨幣債券（指債券以多種貨幣
　混合標價、混合計息，以分散投資
　者風險的債券）　currency cocktail
　bond

[ㄱ]

續生成本，經常成本　recurring cost
續生收益　recurring income
續生利益　recurring gains
續生損益　recurring profit and loss
續保　renew, renewal of insurance
續保收據　renewal receipt
續保費　renew premium
續訂貨　renew order
續航　continuation of the journey
續運合同（貨櫃/集裝箱運輸）　con-
　tract of on-carriage

二十二 畫

[、]

彎曲和凹陷條款（指對桶裝貨的）　bend-
　ing and denting clause

[一]

權利, 認股權　right
權利人　obligee
權利代位, 代位求償權　subrogation
權利代位書　subrogation form
權利的消滅時效　prescription of rights
權利終止期　cesser
權利債券（投資者可在預定時間內，
　根據事先規定條件，優先購買公司
　發行的其他債券或股票）　bonds
　with warrants
權利與義務的平衡　balance of right
　and obligations
權利擔保　warranty of title
權利轉讓　subrogate, subrogation of
　rights
權利轉讓證書　subrogation form
權利證明要約書　abstract of title
權益　interest, equity
權益入股法　pooling of interests method
權益比率, 產權率　equity ratio
權益法, 權益計價法　equity method
權益投資者　equity investor
權責應計制　accrual basis
權責應計制會計　accrual (basis) ac-
　counting
權責應制慣例　accrual convention
權責應計制營業收入認定法　accrual
　method of revenue recognition
權變理論　contingency theory
攤派稅捐, 攤派權, 派繳額外股款
　assessment

攤派稅捐收入　assessment receipt
攤派費用　assessed cost
攤派稅捐基金　assessment fund
攤派預算　assessed budget
攤提固定資產　amortization of fixed
　assets
攤銷　amortization
攤銷表　amortization schedule
攤銷準備　reserve for amortization
攤銷短期投資　amortization short-
　term investment
攤餘成本　amortized cost
攤餘債券折價　unextinguished dis-
　count on funded debt
攤還　dividend, amortization
攤還股本　capital returned to stock-
　holders in dividends
攤還借款　amortization loan
攤還期　amortization period
攤償債款　amortization
聽, 鐵罐　tin
聽差　commissionaire

[丨]

贖回　call, redemption, redeem, re-
　tirement
贖回抵押權　equity of redemption
贖回典契　redemption of mortgage
贖回票據　bills retired
贖回債券溢價　call premium on bonds
贖回溢價　call premium, redemption
　premium
贖回價格　call price

贖回價值　redemption value

贖金　ransom

贖票　retiring a bill, take up a bill

贖票申請書　application for retiring bill

贖票率　retirement rate

贖單　retire shipping document

贖換代理(專門辦理債券的損壞、被盜和遺失等的贖換工作機構)　replacement agent

贖債基金，償債基金　redemption fund

[ﾉ]

籠　cage

罎　demijohn

鑑定人　appraiser, connaisseur

鑑定行報告　surveyor's report

鑑定法　survey method

鑑定重量證書　surveyor's weight certificate

鑑定品質證書　surveyor's quality certificate

鑑定售價　justified selling price

鑑定商標　certification mark

鑑定費　surveyor's fee, appraisal cost

鑑定報告　survey report

鑑定證明書　survey certificate

鑑證，驗證　verification

鑑證程序　procedure of verification

鑄幣　coin money

鑄幣回收　coin withdrawal

鑄幣費　brassage

[、]

變更卸貨港條款　diversion clause

變更卸貨港貨物　diversion cargo

變更卸貨港費用　diversion charge, alteration of destination fee

變更商業登記　amendment of registration

變更啟運港　alteration of port of departure

變更註冊事項　alteration on entries in the register

變更資本　capital amendment

變約　alter an agreement

變相失業　disguised unemployment

變相貿易壁壘　covert trade barrier

變相漲價　disguised price increase

變相讓與　disguised cession

變產　realize property

變產盈溢，變產利得　gain on realization of assets

變產清算表　statement of realization and liquidation

變產損益　realization gain and loss

變產損益帳戶　profit and loss on realization account

變產與清理　realization and liquidation

變現，變產 realization

變現能力，流動性 liquidity

變現帳戶，變產帳戶 realization account

變現溢價 liquidity premium

變現價值 realization value, cash realizable value

變異，方差 variant

變異系數 coefficient of variation

變異度（控制論中，一個系統或一個系統的一個成份的可能狀態的總數） variety

變異指數 variable indicant

變異指標 variable indicator

變異數 variance

變異數據分析 analysis of variance

變動百分率 variable per cent

變動成本 variable cost

變動成本比率 variable cost ratio

變動成本法 variable costing

變動年金 variable annuity

變動利益 variable profit

變動係數 coefficient of variation

變動供給 variable supply

變動按金，價格變動押金 variation margin

變動要素投入量 variable input

變動率 rate of change

變動減除數 variable deduction

變動進口稅徵收額，進口差額稅 variable import levy

變動費用 variable expense

變動資本 variable capital

變動損益平衡點定價 flexible break-even pricing

變動預算 sliding budget, variable budget

變動價格 flexible price, variable price

變動價格政策 variable price policy

變動標準 variable standard

變動權數 variable weight

變量 variation

變量比，方差比 variant ratio

變量抽樣 variable sampling

變量差分法 variate-difference method

變量測試 variable test

變量誤差 variable error

變量數列 variable series

變質 deterioration

變質險 risk of inherent or vice proper

變賣所得 proceeds

變賣財產 realization of property

[一]

驗付條款 payment after inspection clause

驗收 acceptance of goods, examine and receive

驗收人 accepter, receiver, payee

驗收合格證 acceptance certificate

驗收抽樣 acceptance sampling

驗收報告 receiving report

驗明支票的取款人 identification of the payee of a check

驗後放行 release if in order after examination

驗貨，檢查員 examiner

驗貨後付款　payment after inspection

驗貨單　particular paper

驗關　customs examination, customs inspection

驗關地點　sites of customs inspection

驗簽條款　attestation clause

驗簽副本　attested copy

[|]

顯示牌價銀幕或螢光屏(交易所) teleregister

顯著水平　level of significance

顯著的疏忽　gross negligence

體積　volume

體積貨物　measurement goods

體積噸　measurement ton

[乛]

纖維長度　staple

纖維板箱　fibre-board box

[、]

讓股, 股票過戶　transfer of shares

讓股人　transferor

讓受, 取得　acquisition

讓受人　releasee, assignee, grantee

讓渡財產　execute an estate

讓與人　assignor, releasor, grantor

讓與所有權　yield possession

讓與證書　grant certificate, transfer certificate

讓購(轉讓給第三者付款)　negotiate

讓購信用證, 議付信用證　negotiation credit

讓購匯票銀行　negotiating bank

[一]

靈活凍結(美國總統布希推出凍結預算的辦法：只凍結支出總額, 具體的支出項目則可以調整)　flexible freeze

靈活運用關稅保護　flexible use of tariff protection

靈活預算　flexible

靈活關稅　flexible tariff.

[丿]

罐　jar

罐車　tank car

罐狀貨櫃/集裝箱, 液體貨櫃/集裝箱　tank container

罐裝　canning, in tins

罐頭　[英]tin, [美]can

罐頭食品　canned food

罐頭貨品　canned goods

罐頭蔬菜　canned vegetables

〔一〕

觀光旅行　tour

觀光團　tourist group, tourist party

觀察，檢查　observation

觀察比率研究　observation ratio study

觀察法　observational method

觀察員身份　observer status

觀察組　observation group

觀察對象　observation object

觀察數據　observed data

覊押（金錢或文據等物，由法院或其他合法當局保管）　custody

A 規則（規定新發行證券的價值不超過 150 萬美元的公司，只需向證券交易委員會準備一簡短的註冊報告）　Regulation A

C. 礦 7 式租約（地中海國家礦運租船合同）　C. Ore 7 (ore charter party for use in Medit erranean)

C. 礦 8 式租約（自比斯開灣裝運的礦運租船合同）　C. Ore 8 (ore char-

ter party from Bay of Biscay)

DIY 商品（即“自己動手商品”，指供人們組裝、拼配成日常適用物品的成套部件，以及供自己加工製作的工藝品的配套原材料）　do it yourself

ECU 銀行聯盟（1985 年 9 月由西歐 18 家有以 ECU 為籌碼業務的銀行組成，至 1987 年成員銀行增至 80 家）　ECU Banking Association

J 曲線（貨幣貶值後收支平衡表所遵循的曲線形狀）　J-curve

Q 規則（美國對商業銀行支付定期存款利率予以限制的一項規則）　Regulation Q

T 規則（美國用以管理經紀人或自營商貸款給客戶購買證券的規則）　Regulation T

U 形曲線（統計上表示一個頻率分佈在兩端發生的事例最多的曲線）　U-curve

U 規則（美國用以管理銀行給客戶購買證券的貸款的規則）　Regulation U

X 光違禁品檢查器　inspectoscope

X–效率（資源分配上的效率）　X-efficiency

X 理論（X 理論與 Y 理論係美國道格拉斯·麥格雷戈教授所提出。X 理論指對執行者要經常進行管理和監督的觀點）　theory X

χ^2 檢驗（查看兩次調查研究結果之間的差別有無重要意義之統計檢驗法）　chi-square test

Y 理論(假設沒有必要規定嚴格的監
督，因執行者就其本性言，具有創
造的才能) theory Y

Z 字圖(統計圖上有三條線以便於比
較，三條線所形成 Z 狀) Z chart

Z 證單(英格蘭銀行發給貼現行的用
以代替債券證單的一種憑證) Z
certificate

附錄一
國際經濟貿易縮略語表

（按英語字母排列）

A

a.	account 帳目，帳戶
	audit 稽核
	accepted 承受，承兌
	acre 英畝
@	at 每
A1.	first-class 第一流
	denoting first quality 表示一等品質
a.a.	always afloat 船恒漂浮
AAOEC	Afro-Asian Organization for Economic Coorperation 亞非經濟合作組織
a.a.r.	against all risk 全險
A/B	air bill 空運提單
	air borne 空運的，飛機上的
abs.	abstract 摘要，節略
abs. sta.	abstract statement 摘要說明書
ABS	American Bureau of Shipping 美國驗船局
abt.	about 大約
ac	acre 英畝
AC	automatic control 自動控制
a/c	alternating current 交流電
	account, account current 帳目，流水帳
A/C	absolute ceiling 絕對升限
acc	acceptance, accepted 受領，接受；承兌，已承兌
acc/o, a/o	account of 記入某人帳內
acct	account, accountant 帳，會計；會計人員
acct. & aud.	accountant and auditor 會計兼審計

acct. gen	accountant general　會計長
ACCY	accessory　附件
ACD	Asian Clearing Dollar　亞洲決算貨幣
ace.	automatic computing engine　自動計算機
ACH	automated clearing house　自動清算所
ackgt.	acknowledgement　承認：收帖，回單
ACN	air consignment note　空運託運單
acrg.	acreage　土地面積
A/cs. Pay	Accounts Payable　應付帳款
A/cs. Rec.	Accounts Receivable　應收帳款
actg.	acting　代理
AD	Anno Domini = since the birth of Christ　公元，紀元
a.d., a/d	after date　期後(票據用語)，出發票後定期付款，⋯⋯日後
ad., advt.	advertisement　廣告
ADB	Asian Development Bank　亞洲開發銀行
add.	address　地址
ADF	Asian Development Fund　亞洲開發基金
ad int.	adinterim (in the meantime)　休會期間
admr.	administrator　財產管理人
ADMS	Advanced Data Management System　高級數據管理系統
ADPS	Automatic Data Processing System　自動數據處理系統
AF	Advance Freight　預付運費
AFAS	Automatic Fund Allocation System　自動資金分配系統
AFB	Air Freight Bill　空運提單
afft.	affidavit　具結書
aftn.	afternoon　下午
agg., aggr.	aggregate　共計，總數
Agr.	agriculture　農業
agt.	agent　代理人
a.i.	accident indemnity　意外保險
AI	Approval of Import　進口許可
AID	Agency for International Development　美國國際開發署
AIQ	automatic import quota　自動進口配額
AJE	adjusting journal entry　調整分錄
altho.	although　雖然
Amb.	ambassador　大使

amp.	ampere 安培
amt.	amount 總數, 金額
ann.	annals, annual, annuity 年表, 每年, 年金
anon.	anonymous 隱名, 不記名
ans.	answer, answered 答覆
a/or	and/or 與/或
a/p	account paid 帳款付清, 付訖
	additional premium 追加保險費
	additional payment 追加付款
A/P	Advise and Pay 通知付款
	authority to purchase 採購授權書
APB	Accounting Principles Board 會計原則委員會
APC	Automatic Programme Control 自動程序控制
Apl. Apr.	April 四月
app.	appendix 附錄
appl.	application 申請書
approx.	approximately 大約, 近似
APSAC	Authorization to Purchase Surplus Agricultural Commodities 剩餘農產品採購授權書
a.r.	against risk 防備危險
	all risks 一切險, 全險
a/r	all-round 共計
arr.	arrivals, arrived 到貨, 到船
arrt.	arrangement 整理, 籌備
art	article 物品, 條款, 貨號
a.s.	at sight 即期
A.S.	account sales 賒銷
a/s	after sight 見票後即付
AS.	as stated 如上所述
asap	as soon as possible 盡快
ASE	American Stock Exchange 美國股票交易所
ASP	American Selling Price 美國銷售價格
ass	assessed 估價, 定稅
	assessment 估價, 徵稅
assn	association 會, 公司, 社團
assoc	associated, association 聯營, 會

asst.	assorted　分類，花色配搭
	assistant　助手，助理
asst. sec.	assistant secretary　助理秘書
A/T	American terms　美國條款（穀物等級）
	Air Transportation　航空運輸
ATS	Automatic Transfer Service Account　自動撥款帳戶，自動轉帳存款
att., att'n	attention　請注意
att., atty	attorney　代理人，律師［美］
AUC	average unit cost　平均單價，平均單位成本
auct.	auction　拍賣
Aud.	audit　審計
Aug.	August　八月
A/V	according to value　按值
a.v.	ad valorem　從價，從值計算
av, A/V	average　平均數
av. eff.	average efficiency　平均生產率，平均效率
avg.	average　平均的，海損
avoir.	avoirdupois　常衡，重量
AVW	Average Width　平均寬度
AW	all-weather　全天候
a.w	all wool　純毛
A/W	actual weight　實際重量，淨重

B

B	bond　契約，債券
	budget　預算
B/	second class　二等（船）
B1	B one　二級
BA	Bank Acceptance　銀行承兌票據
back.	backwardation　（證券）交割延期費
bal.	balance　餘數，平均
bal. b/d	balance brought down　餘額轉下
bal. b/f	balance brought forward　餘額承前
bal. c/f	balance carried forward　餘額結轉

bal. trans	balance transferred　餘額過入
banky.	bankruptcy　破產，倒閉
bar., brl.	barrel　桶
BB	bankbook　銀行存摺
	branch bill　分行票據
	bill book　票據簿，出納簿，支票簿
	buy back　回購
	back-to-back account　對開帳戶，背對背帳戶
BC	Before Christ　公元前
	Beneficial Cost　受益成本
	bulk cargo　散裝貨
	bill of collection　託收票據
BD	bill discounted　貼現期票
B/D	bank draft　銀行滙票
b/d, b.d.	brought down　過下頁，轉下
bd.	bond　票
	bound　訂立
	board　部
bdl.	bundle　捆，束
BDR	bearer depositary receipts　無記名受託管票據
bdth.	breadth　寬闊
B/E, b.e, b.ex	bill of exchange　滙票
BEP	Break Even Point　損益兩平點
B/F	brought forward　承前頁
b.f.	[拉]bona fide　善意，真實
B/G	Bonded Goods　保稅貨物
bg.	bag　袋
BHN	Basic Human Needs　人類基本需要
BIS	Bank for International Settlement　國際清算銀行
BK.	Bank　銀行
Bkg.	Banking　銀行業
bkt,bsk	basket　籃子
B/L	bill of lading　提單
bl	bale　包
blading	bill of lading　（電報用字）
bldg.	building　大廈，建築物

B/N, b.n.	bank note 鈔票，紙幣
b/o	brought over 過入
BO	Buyer's option 買方選擇權
	Branch Office 分店
	Blanket Order 總括定貨單
BOC	Bank of China 中國銀行
bom	beginning of month 月初
bott	bottle 瓶，壜
B/P, b.p.	bills payable 應付票據
B/P	bill purchased 出口押滙，帳單
	Balance of Payment 國際收支
BP	British Patent 英國專利
BPB	Bank Post Bill 銀行郵寄滙票
BPC	book prices current 現行帳面價格
br.	brand 商標
BR	bank rate 銀行利率
B/R, b.r.	bills receivable 應收票據，收款單
Brit	British, Britain 英國的，英國
brkge.	brokerage 佣金
brt.fwd.	brought forward 承前
B/S, b.s.	Balance Sheet 清單，平衡表，資產負債表
	bill of sale 出貨單，銷貨單
bsh., bu.	bushel 蒲式耳（容量＝8 加侖）
b/st	bill at sight 見票即付滙票
BT	British Ton 英噸
	before tax 稅前
bt	bought 購入
BTT	bank telegraphic transfer 銀行電滙
BTN	Brussels' Tariff Nomenclature 布魯塞爾關稅則目錄
BV	Book Value 帳面價值
bx.	box 箱
bxs.	boxes 箱

Ⓒ

C/., c.	cent 分（美國貨幣）

centi– 百分之一

centime 生丁（法國貨幣的分）

currency 貨幣

cubic 立方

coupon 息票

case 箱

cargo 貨物

c.a.	capital assets 固定資產
	credit advice 貸項通知單
	current assets 流動資產
CA	Chartered Accountant （註冊）會計師
	cash advance 預付現金
	cost account 成本會計，成本帳
	Controller of Accounts 會計主任
C/A	capital account 資本帳
	credit account 貸方帳戶，賒購帳
	current account 現金帳，活期存款
	commercial agent 商業代理
ca.	centare 一平方公尺
C.A.D.	Cash against documents 付款交單
C.A.F.	cost, assurance, freight 即 CIF，到岸價格
C & D	collection & delivery 收款發貨
C & F	cost and freight 成本與運費（價格）
Canc.	cancel, cancelled, cancellation 註銷
Canclg.	cancelling 註銷
cap.	capacity 容量
	capital 資本
caps.	capital letters 大寫
capt., cpt.	captain 船長
car.	carat 克拉
carr.	carriage 運費，車費
carr. fwd.	carriage forward 運費已付
carr. pd.	carriage paid 運費付訖
cash.	cashier 出納員，司庫
CAT	Civil Air Transport 民用航空公司
cat.	catalogue 目錄

CB., C/A	cash book	現金出納帳
CB	Commercial Bank	商業銀行
c/b	clean bill	信用票據, 光票
cb. ft., cbft.	cubic feet	立方英尺
CBD	cash before delivery	提貨前付款
cbm.	cubic metre	立方公尺
CBS	cash before shipment	裝運前付款
CBT	commercial benefit tax	商業利潤稅
c.c.	carbon copy	複寫紙, 複寫副本, 副本抄送
	cash credit	現金貸款
	cashier's check	(美銀行)本票
	currency clause	貨幣條款
	current cost	時價, 市價
	country cheque	英國地方銀行支票
c.c., ccm.	cubic centimetres	立方公分
CC	Chamber of Commerce	商會
	Control Center	控制中心
CCA	Centre for Commercial Arbitration	商業仲裁中心
CCT	Common Customs Tariff	共同關稅率(歐洲共同體)
c.d.	cash discount	現金折扣
	cum dividend	附股息
C/D	Certificate of Deposit	存款證(可轉讓)
	Certificate of Delivery	交貨單, 交貨證明書
	Creditor and Debtor	債權國與債務國
	cash against documents	憑單據付款
	Customs Declaration	海關申明
	Bookkeeping carried down	帳簿上的結轉下頁
C & D	collection and delivery	收款發貨
CDA	[法]Comraissement Direct aller (= Through bill of lading) 直運提單(貨物需中途轉船但可向目的港取貨而不需更換的提單)	
CDR	Cargo Delivery Receipt	交貨收據
CEA	Counterpart Expenditure Authorization	相對基金支用授權書
Cent., Ct.	centum, hundred	一百, 百
cert.	certificate	證書, 憑單, 執照

CET	common external tariff　共同對外關稅
CF	Common Fund　共同基金
	Counterpart Fund　對等基金
cf.	confer, compare　比較, 協商
C & F	cost and freight　離岸價加運費, 成本加運費價
c.f. & c.	cost, freight and commission　貨價、運費、佣金在內價, 離岸價加佣金
c.f. & i.	cost, freight and insurance　貨價、運費、保險費在內, 離岸價加保險費
CFS	container freight station　貨櫃　集裝箱集散站
cgo	contango　[英]交易延期費, 延期日息
c.g.t.	capital gains tax　資本利潤稅
C.H.	Customs House　海關
	Clearing House　票據交換所
ch.	charge(s)　費用
	chapter　章, 節
cheq., chq.	cheque　支票
ch. fwd.	charges forward　費用先付
ch. pd.	charges prepaid　費用預付
CHIPS	Cleaning House Interbank Payment System　清算付款系統（紐約地區的銀行劃撥清算系統）
cht.	chest　箱, 金庫
C.I.	Consular invoice　領事發票
C/I	Certificate of Insurance　保險單
C & I	cost and insurance　離岸價加保險費
C.I.A.	cash in advance　預付現金
CIC	China Insurance clause　中國保險條款
Cie.	Compagnie (Company)　公司
CIF	Cost, Insurance and Freight　到岸價格
CIF & C	cost, insurance, freight and commission　到岸價加佣金
CIF & E	cost, insurance, freight and exchange　到岸價加滙費
CIFC & I	cost, insurance, freight commission and interest　到岸價加佣金和利息
CIF & I	cost, insurance, freight and interest　到岸價加利息
CIF net	cost, insurance and freight net　到岸價格淨價
CIF plane	cost, insurance and freight by plane　空運費、保險費在內的

機上交貨價

CIF inland water way	cost, insurance, freight inland water way 到岸價加內河運費價	
CIF landed	cost, insurance, freight landed terms 到岸價加卸貨價	
CIF liner	cost, insurance, freight liner terms 到岸價加班輪費用	
CIFW	cost, insurance, freight and war risk 到岸價加戰爭險在內價	
C.I.O.	cash in order, cash with order 訂貨時付款	
CKs., ck.	casks 桶	
	checks 支票	
	check 核對	
CL	clause 條款	
	class 等級	
	clerk 書記	
	claim 索賠	
	centiliter 厘升(= 1/100 升)	
cld	cleared (goods, shipping) 清關(從海關提取貨物)	
	cost laid down 成本支出	
cm.	centimeter 公分, 厘米	
CM	Common Market 公共市場	
C/M	credit memo 貸項帳單	
	Certificate of Manufacture 製造證明	
cml.	commercial 商務的	
C/N, c.n.	credit note 收款帳單, 貸記通知書	
	contract note 契約書	
	circular note 託運單, 通知單	
CNITB	China National Inspection & Testing Bureau 中國商品檢驗局	
c/o	carried over 轉期(證券交易用語)	
	care of 代收, 轉交	
	certificate of origin 原產地證明書	
C/O	cash order 即期票, 現金滙票	
Co., Coy.	company 公司, 商行	
COBOL	common business oriented language 商業通用語言	
C.O.D.	cash on delivery 貨到付款, 現金提貨	
	collection on delivery 貨到收款, 交貨託收	

collr.	collector　收帳人，收款員
com.	commercial　商業的
	commission　佣金，手續費
	committee　委員會
comp.	composition　債款折償
	compilation　收集
consgt.	consignment　委託銷售，寄售：發貨
Con. Inv.	Consular invoice　領事發票
cont., contr.	contract　合約
coo	chief operating officer　業務總裁
co-op.	cooperation　合作經營
	cooperative　合作社
co-part	copartner　合夥人
corp., corpn.	corporation　公司，法人
COS, c.o.s.	cash on shipment　現款載貨，裝貨時付款
CP	commercial paper　商業票據，短期期票
	compare　比較
c.p.	charges paid　費用已付
C/P	custom of the ports　港口習慣
C/P, c.py	charter party　租船契約
C.P.A.	certified public accountant　會計師
CPI	consumer's price index　消費者物價指數
C.Q.D.	customary quick despatch　習慣速遣，迅速遣送
Cr.	credit　信用
	creditor　債權人
cred.	credit　貸方
C.R.	current rate　現行利率或滙率
	company's risk　公司的風險
CRm	cash by return mail　回信付款
	cash on receipt of merchandise　收到貨物付款，憑貨物收據付款
C.R.S.	cash by return steamer　回船付款
CTA	communicate to all address　不保密(分送電)
CTD	combined transport documents　聯合運輸單據
ctge., ctg.	cartage　搬運費
C.T.L.	Constructive Total Loss　推定全損

CTO	combined transport operator　聯合運輸經紀人
cur.	currency　幣制，貨幣
cum. pref	cumulative preference (share)　累積優先（股）
C.W.	commercial weight　商業的重量，原量，純重
C.W.O.	cash with order　定貨時付現
Cwt.	Hundredweight　英啝（在英國等於 112 磅：在美國等於 100 磅）
CXT	Common External Tariff　對外統一運費（歐洲共同體）
cy	currency　通貨，貨幣
	crop year　作物年度
CY/CY	container yard to container yard　整裝/整拆，貨櫃場至貨櫃場
CZ	canal zone　運河地帶

D

D.	degree　度
	draft　滙票
D.A.	debit advice　借項通知單
D/A	days after acceptance　承兌後天數，承兌後若干日交款
	documents against acceptance　承兌交單
	discharge afloat (chartering)　船上卸貨或浮卸貨（租船）
	deposit account　存款帳戶，存款簿
	document attached　附單據
d/a, D/A	days against acceptance　幾天內承兌
D.A.D	documents against discretion of collection bank　隨收款銀行的意見交單
DAF	delivered at Frontier — named place of destination　指定邊境交貨價
D/B	daybook　日記簿
dbk	drawback　退稅，退款
dbl	double　一倍，加倍
dbt	debt, debit　欠款，債，應收帳
d.c.	direct current　直流電
D.C.,/ D/C	deviation clause (Insurance)　繞道條款（保險）
D/C	discount　折扣，貼現

	detention clause　阻留條款 (租船)
DCP	freight or carriage paid to — named point of destination inland transport only　運費付至……內陸指定目的地價
D.D.	direct debit　直接借方
	double draft　聯單
	differential duties　差別關稅
D/D, D.D.	documentary draft　跟單滙票
	demand draft　即期滙票
d/d, d.d.	delivered　已交付
	days after date　立字據後若干日
DDP	delivered duty paid — named place of destination in the country of importation　進口國指定地點交貨價
dd/s	delivered sound　已妥當交付
de, DE	deferred　延期, 遞延帳項
deb.	debenture　債券, 海關退稅憑單
debt.	debtor　借方, 債務人
def.	deferred　延期
deft.	defendant　被告
del.	delegate　代表; 授權
dem.	demurrage　滯期費, 裝卸誤期費
dep.	deposit　存款
	deputy　代理人
d.f.	dead freight　空艙費
dft	draft　滙票
dg.	decigram　分克, 公釐
dia.	diameter　直徑
diff	difference　差額, 餘數
dir.	director　董事
dish'd	dishonoured　拒付; 不名譽
divd.	dividend　股息, 紅利
D.K, dk	dock　船塢, 碼頭
DLF	Development Loan Fund　開發貸款基金
DLT	day letter telegram　日間遞送電報, 書信電
D/N	Debit Note　欠單, 欠貨單, 借款項通知單
D/O	Delivery Order　提貨單, 貨物出倉憑單
do., dto.	ditto (= the same)　同上

Doc	document 文件，單據
doc. att	document attached 附證件，單據附上
DOF	Delivery On Field 就地交貨
d.p.	direct port 直航港
D/P	deferred payment 遲付貨款
	documents against payment 付款交單
D/P after sight	document against payment-after sight 遠期付款交單
D/P sight	document against payment-sight 即期付款交單
D/P. T/R	document against payment, trust receipt 付款交單，憑信託收據供貨
dpth.	depth 深度
Dr.	Debit 借方
	Debtor 債務人，欠戶
	Drawer 出票人
D/R	deposit receipt 存款收據
D.R.	discount rate 貼現率
D/S, d.s.	day's sight, days after sight 見票後若干天
Ds	debt service 債務清償（業務）
d.s.t.	daylight saving time 經濟時（即夏令時）
Dup., Dupl	Duplicate 副本，抄件
D/W	Dock Warrent Delivered Weight 碼頭倉單
d.w.	deadweight 按重量計

E

EA	Economic Adviser 經濟顧問
e. & o.e.	errors and omissions excepted 錯誤必改：如有錯漏，有權更正：錯漏除外
E.B.	export bounties 出口津貼
EC	error correction 錯誤更正
	ex coupon 除息票
Ec	exempli causa = for example 例如
ECU	European Currency Unit 歐洲貨幣單位
ECM	European Common Market 歐洲共同市場
ED, e.d.	ex dividend 除息：無紅利；股息除外
	estate duty 財產稅

EDP	electronic data processing　電子數據處理
EDPS	electronic data processing system　電子數據處理系統
E.E., e.e.	errors excepted　錯誤除外；錯誤不在此限
EEC	European Economic Community　歐洲經濟共同體
EIB	European Investment Bank　歐洲投資銀行
emb	embargo　禁運
EMF	European Monetary Fund　歐洲貨幣基金
enc. encl.	enclosure　同函附件；附件
encd.	enclosed　函內附件
END	endorsement　背書
EO	examining officer　檢查員
e.o.d., eod.	every other day　隔日
EOM	end of month　月底
EOQ	economic order quantity　經濟定貨量
EOY	end-of-year　年終
EPL	excess profit levy　超額利潤稅
EPS	earnings per share　每股收益
EPU	European Payment Union　歐洲支付同盟
eq.	equal　相等
	equivalent　等量，等值
EURIT	European Investment Trust　歐洲投資信託證券
ex, exch.	exchange　滙兌
exd.	examined　已檢查
ex int.	ex interest　無利息
exp.	export　輸出
	exit pemit　出境許可證
	express　快運
	expenses　費用
EXPO	World Exposition　世界博覽會
EXQ	Ex Quay-duty paid (named port)　買方碼頭交貨價(指定港口)
Ex R	ex right　無權購新股，除權
ext.	extract, extention　摘錄，延期

F

F. fc., fr.	franc 法郎（法國貨幣單位）
FA	Free Alongside 船邊交貨
FAA	Foreign Assistance Act 援外法（美國）
FAA, f.a.a.	free of all average 全損賠償（水險用語）
FAO	Foreign Affairs Office 外交部
FAQ, f.a.q.	Fair Average Quality 平均良好品質，大路貨
FAS, f.a.s.	free alongside ship 船邊交付價
FB	freight bill 運貨單
FBE	foreign bill of exchanges 外國滙票
FBH	Free on Board in Harbor 發貨地價格
FCBP	foreign currency bills payable 可付外幣
FCC	First Class Certificate 一級品證明書
FCIS	Foreign Collective Investment Securities 外國集體投資證券
FCL	full container load 整箱裝（貨櫃/集裝箱）
FCS	Fair Cost System 合理運費制度
f.c.s.	free of capture and seizure 虜獲奪取不賠
F/D, f/d.	free docks 碼頭交貨，船塢交貨
	free dispatch 免費發送
	forward delivery 定期交貨
F & D	freight and demurrage 運費和滯期費
FDPC	Federal Data Processing Center 美國聯邦數據處理中心
f.e.	for example 例如
FEOF	Foreign Exchange Operation Fund 外滙週轉基金
FEFC	Far Eastern Freight Conference 遠東運費協會, 俗稱¨遠東運費同盟¨
FF, fc.	French Franc 法國法郎
f.f.a	free from alongside 船邊交貨
F.F.A	Foreign Freight Agency 國外貨運代理人
f.f.d.	free from damage 損害不賠償
	free from duty 免稅
f.g.	franc gare ［法文］鐵路交貨
F.G.A., f.g.a.	free of general average 共同海損不賠

	foreign general average　外國共同海損
fha	fechado　［西班牙語］日期(= date)
F.I., f.i	for instance　舉例
	free in　船方不負擔裝貨費(租船用語)
f.i.a.	full interest admitted　允許全部權益
f.i.b., fib	free into barge　駁船上交貨價格
fifo.	first in first out　先入先出法
F.I.O., f.i.o.	free in and out　船方不負擔裝卸費用(租船用語)
f.i.o.s.	free in and out and stowed　船方不負擔裝卸費用及積載費
f.i.o.s.t.	free in and out and stowed and trimmed　船方不負擔裝卸費用、積載費及平艙費
fin. stat.	financial statement　財務報表
fin. standg.	financial standing　財務狀況
fin.yr.	financial year　會計年度
f.i.t.	free of income tax　免除所得稅
f.i.w.	free in waggon　裝入貨車
fltr.	floater　債券發行人
F.O., F/O	free out 亦稱 free discharge　船方不負擔卸貨費用
	free overside　船邊交貨(到港價格)
	firm offer　確定報價
	firm order　實盤
	for order　準備出售
	forward order　定貨
	in favour of　抬頭人，受益人
FOB, f.o.b.	free on board　船上交貨價，離岸價格
f.o.b & c	free on board and commission　船上交貨加佣金價
FOB destination	free on board destination　目的地交貨
FOB port	free on board of shipment　裝貨港離岸價
FOB plane, FOP	free on board plane　飛機上交貨價
FOB quay, FOQ	free on board quay　碼頭上交貨價
FOB train	free on board train　火車上交貨價
FOBST	free on board stowed and trimmed　包括積載費及平艙費在內的離岸價格
f.o.c.	free of charge　免費
f.o.i.	free of interest　免息
fol.	folio　頁數

f.o.r., FOR	free on rail	火車上交貨價
f.o.s., FOS	free on steamer	船上交貨
f.o.t., FOT	free on trucks	卡車上交貨價
fo.vo.	folio verso (turn the page)	翻次頁，轉下頁
f.o.w.	first open water	（解凍後)初次開航，首航
	free on wagons	車上交貨
FOX	Forward with Option Exit	可轉期權的遠期外滙買賣
F.P.	fully paid	全部付款，付清
F/P	fire policy	火險單
	floating policy	船名不詳的保險單
	fine paper	有信用的票據
FP	floor price	最低價格
	French Patent	法國專利
FPA, f.p.a.	free from particular average	單獨海損不賠，平安險
FRA	Forward Rate Agreement	遠期利率合同
frt.	freight	運費，水腳
frt. pd.	freight paid	運費已付
frt. ppd.	freight prepaid	運費已預付
F.S.	[法文] faire suivre	追蹤電報
F.W.D., f.w.d.	fresh water damage	淡水損害，淡水險
F.Y.	fiscal year	會計年度
FZ	Franc Zone	法郎區

G

g., gm.	gram	克
GA., g/a	general average	共同海損，總平均
gal.	gallon	加侖
GATT	General Agreement on Trade & Tariffs	貿易及關稅總協定
g.b.o.	goods in bad order	故障貨物，貨物損壞
G.C.	general cargo	雜貨，一般貨物
	general catalogue	總目錄
GDP	gross domestic product	國內生產總值，國內總產值
GDS	gross domestic storage	國內總儲備
GEMS	Global Enviromental Monitoring System	全球監測系統

GIP	General Insurance Policy 總括保險單
G.M.B.	good merchantable brand 優良品
G.M.Q.	good merchantable quality 品質優良，上等可銷品質
GMT, Gmt.	Greenwich mean time 格林威治時間
G/N	gross for net 以毛作淨
	guarantee of notes 承諾保險
GND	Gross National Demand 國民總需求
GNE	Gross National Expenditure 國民總支出
GNI	Gross National Income 國民總收入
GNP	Gross National Product 國民生產總值
GNS	Gross National Supply 國民總供給
GNW	Gross National Welfare 國民總福利
G.P.	Grace Period 寬限期
GPLA	general price-level adjustments 按一般物價水平調準
gr.	grain 喱(最小重量單位 = 0.0648 gram)
gro.	gross 羅(= 12 打)
GRT	Gross Registered Tonnage 註冊總噸位
GRWT	Gross Weight 總重量, 毛重
GSP	Generalized System of Preferences 普遍優惠制
	Gross Social Product 社會總產值
g.s.w.	gross shipping weight 裝船毛重, 總載貨量
G.T.C., g.t.c.	good till cancelled 取消前有效
G.T.M.	good this month 限當月有效
G.T.T.	Give and Take Trade 互讓貿易
G.T.W.	good this week 本週內有效
g.v.	fast goods train 快速貨車

H

HAC	Hague Arbitration Convention 海牙仲裁公約
H.A. or D.	Hamburg, Antwerp or Dunkerque 穀類交易所指定的歐洲卸貨港: 漢堡, 安特衛普或敦刻爾克
H.B.	Brinell Hardness 布氏硬度
HCLO	Holding Company Liquidation Committee 控股公司清理委員會
HD, hhd	hogshead 大桶(= 52½ 英制加侖或 63 美制加侖)

H.E.	High Efficiency　高效率
	Human Engineering　人類工程學
H/H	house to house　出口商倉庫裝櫃/進口商倉庫拆櫃(貨櫃運輸方式)
HIBOR	Hong Kong inter bank offered rate　香港銀行同業拆放利率
HIFO	highest-in first-out method　高入先出法
HM	[拉] hoc mense　本月內
	Hot Money　熱錢, 國際游資
H.O.	head office　總行, 總公司
Hon'd	Honoured　承兌
Hp, h.p.	horsepower　馬力
H.P.	hire purchase　英國以分期付款方式購買貨品
H/P	house to pier　出口商倉庫至進口商碼頭(貨櫃運輸方式)
hp.-hr.	horsepower-hour　馬力小時
HSAN	High-Speed Accounting Machine　高速記帳機
H.T.	High Tide　高潮
h.w.	high water　漲潮

I

i. int.	interest　利息
Ia.	[拉] prima　第一的, 最上的
IAS	International Accounting Standard　國際會計準則
IATA	International air Transport Association　國際航空運輸協會
I.B.	in bond　保稅倉庫交貨
	invoic book　發票簿
ib., ibid.	[拉] ibidem (= in the same place)　在同一場所
IBO	Interbank Offered Rate　銀行同業拆息率
IBP, IBOP	International Balance of Payment　國際收支
IBRD	International Bank for Reconstruction and Development　國際復興開發銀行
I/C	inward collection　代收款項
ICA	International Co-operation Administration　國際合作總署
	International Coffee Agreement　國際咖啡協定
ICAO	International Civil Aviation Organization　國際民用航空組

織

ICC, I.C.C.	International Chamber of Commerce	國際商會
ICCO	International Cocoa Organization	國際可可組織
ICF	International Compensation Fund	國際賠償基金
I.C.U.	International Code Used	國際使用的密碼
id.	[拉] idem = the same	同前，同上，同書
IDA	International Development Association	國際開發協會
	Import Duties Act	進口稅法
IDB	Inter-American Development Bank	泛美開發銀行
IDC	Ill Developing Countries	不發達國家
I.D.L.	International date line	國際日期轉換線
IDP	integrated data processing	集成電路數據
i.e.	[拉] id est = that is	即，就是
IFC	International Finance Corporation	國際金融公司
I/L	Import licence	輸入許可證
IMF	International Monetary Fund	國際貨幣基金組織
IGA	International Grain Agreement	國際穀物協定
imit.	imitation	倣造品
Inc.	incorporated	法人組織的，有限責任，股份有限公司
INCOTERMS	International Chamber of Commerce Terms, 1936	國際商會貿易條件(1936 年)
	International Rules for the Interpretation of Trade Terms, 1953	關於國際貿易條件之解釋通則(1953 年)
INTLX	international telex	國際電報交換
I/O, i.o.	inspecting order	檢驗單
I.O.P.	irrespective of percentage	不計免賠率(海上保險)
I.O.U.	I owe you	我欠你，借據
I/P	insurance policy	保險單
I.P.A.	including particular average	包括單獨海損
i.q.	idem quod (= the same as)	同，與……相同
I.Q.	import quota system	輸入配額制
IQC	International Quality Centre	國際質量中心
I/R	inward remittance	滙入款項
ISA	International Sugar Agreement	國際砂糖協定
I.S.A.	International Standards Association	國際標準協會
ISIC	International Standard Industrial Classification	國際工業

標準分類

I.T.	Immediate Transportation　立即轉運
	in transit　在運途中
ITA	International Tin Agreement　國際錫協定
I.T.O.	International Trade Organization　國際貿易組織
I.V.	Increased Value　增值
	Invoice Value　發票價值
IWA	International Wheat Agreement　國際小麥協定
IWS	International Wool Secretariat　國際羊毛事務局

J

J/A, j/a	joint account　共同帳戶
JES	Japanese Engineering Standards　日本技術標準規格
JIS	Japanese Industrial Standard　日本工業規格
JV	Joint Venture　聯合企業，合資企業
JVC	Joint Venture Corporation　合資公司
JWOB	jettison/washing overboard　投棄或波浪掃落

K

K	karat　開(黃金成色單位)
KD	knocked down　拆卸裝運
KG	[德語] kommanditgesellschaft　兩合公司
KID	Key Industry Duty　基礎工業保護關稅
K.W.	kilowatt　千瓦
KYD	kiloyard　千碼

L

L.A.	Loan Agreement　貸款協定
L/A	Landing Account　起貨單
	Letter of Authority　授權書
	Letter of Authorization　委託書
L & D	loss and damage　損失與損壞
	loans and discount　放款及貼現

L.B.C.	London bar silver　倫敦銀條
L/C	Letter of Credit　信用證
LC	Leased Channel　租用線路
LCGTOG	Letter of Credit of Government to Government　政府間信用證
LCL	less than container load　併櫃裝，併裝，未滿載貨櫃
L.C.L.	less-than-car-load lot　零擔貨運
LDP	London Daily Price　倫敦每日行情
L.E.	Liberalization of Exchange　滙兌自由化
LFQS	License Fee Quota System　特許權使用費配額制
L/G	letter of guarantee　信用保證函
L/H, L.H.	letter of hypothecation　質權書，抵押證書
L/I	letter of indemnity　賠償保證書
LIBOR	London Interbank Offered Rate　倫敦銀行同業拆息
LIP	life insurance policy　人壽保險單
Lifo	Last in first out method　後入先出法
LLT	London Landed Terms　倫敦起貨條件
LME	London Metal Exchange　倫敦五金交易所
LNWT	legal net weight　法定淨重
LOA	Letter of Agreement　契約書，議定書
LOI	Letter of Instructions　指令書
L.P.	linear programming　線性規劃
	London price　倫敦價格
LR	Lombard Rate　金融市場利率
L/T	Letter of Trust　信託書
LT	letter telegram　書信電
LT, l.tn	long ton　長噸
Ltd., Ld.	limited　有限公司
L/U	letter of undertaking　承諾書
L.W.M., l.w.m.	low water mark　低水線

m/a, M. Acct.	my account　本人帳戶
m/a/c	money on account　帳上貨幣，計算貨幣
MAP	maximum average price　最高平均價格

MARC	Monitoring and Research Assessment Centre 檢查及研究估價中心（聯合國）
MBO	management by objectives 目標管理
M/C	marginal credit 信用放款限度
MCA	monetary compensatory amount 貨幣補償總額
	Mutual Currency Account 共同通貨帳戶
MCI	Marketing Cost Index 銷售價格指數
MCX	minimum cost estimating 估計最低成本
M/D	Memorandum of Deposit 存款單，存款傳票
	month after date 到期後一月，發票後一月
m/d	months day 自立約日起後若干月
memo.	memorandum 備忘錄，便箋
mfd.	manufactured 製造
mfg.	manufacturing 製造中
MFN	most favoured nation 最惠國
MFNC	Most Favoured Nation Clause 最惠國條款
mfr.	manufacturer 製造者
mgr.	manager 經理
MI	marine insurance 水上保險
min, B/L	minimum bill of lading 最少提單
MIP	Marine Insurance Policy 水險保險單
	Monthly Investment Plan 月投資計劃
MIS	Management Information System 經營情報系統
M.I.T.	Market-if-Touched 到價定單
mk	mark 商標，嘜頭
mkt.	market 市場
M/L clause	more or less clause 過與不足條款
MLR	Minimum Lending Rate 最低貸款利率
M.M.	merchant marine 商船
M.O.	money order 郵政滙票，郵滙
	mail order 郵購
Moti	more-out-than-in method 出多入少法
M.P.	market price 市場價格
M/P	months after payment 付款後月數
M.R.	money remittance 滙款
M/R	mate's receipt 大副收據，收貨單

M/S, m.s.	manuscript 稿本
	mail steamer 郵船
	motor ship 輪船
	months after sight 見票後月數
MSA	Merchant Shipping Act 商人船務條例
MSP	Minimum Safeguard Price 最低保護價格
M.T.	Memorandum Trade 備忘錄貿易
M/T., m.t.	mail transfer 信滙
MT	multimodal transport 多式聯運
mtg.	mortgage 抵押
MTO	multimodal transport operator 多式聯運人
M.U.	million units 百萬單位
	Monetary Unit 貨幣單位

N

N.A.	no account 無此帳戶, 無往來關係
	not applicable 不適用
	non-available 無資料, 不詳; 無效的
N/A, n/a	no acceptance 拒絕承兌
	new account 新開銀行帳戶
	non acceptance 不承兌
	no advice 未通知
N.B.	[拉] nota bene = take notice 注意, 留心
	New Bond 新公債
	Nothing Between 無往來, 無交易
NC	no circuit 無路線 (telex 用語)
	net capital 淨資本額
	no change 無變化
	no correction 無更正
	noncommital 不表明態度, 不承擔義務
	Numerical Control 數字控制
N/C	no charge 不計費, 免費
NCC	Non-Convertible Currencies 非兌換貨幣
NCD	Negotiable Certificate of Deposit 不記名可轉讓定期存單
NCV	no commercial value 無商業價值

N.D.	National Debt	國債
	no date	無日期
	non delivery	未交貨
N/D	not dated	未註明日期
N.E., n/e	no effects	無存款，無財產
	not enough	數量不足
n.e.i.	not elsewhere included	不包括
neg.	negotiable	可轉讓的，可議付的
n.e.m.	not elsewhere mentioned	如無其他記載時
net p.	net proceeds	純利淨收
NEW	net economic welfare	經濟福利淨額
n.f., N/F	no funds	無資金，無款項(一般指銀行存戶存款不足)
NFTC	National Foreign Trade Council	美國對外貿易委員會
NFT	no fixed time	無固定時間
N.G., n.g.	net gains	純收益
	no good	無價值，不良(品)
N.I.	National Income	國民收入
	National Insurance	國民保險
NIC	Newly Independent Countries	新獨立國家
	Newly Industrializing Countries	新興工業國
Nifo	Next in first out method	次入先出法
NIS	not in stock	無庫存
N.L.	Net Loss	純損
NLT	Night Lettergram	夜信電
	not later than	不遲於……
N/M, N.M.	No mark	無裝運標誌，無商標
NMP	Net Material Product	物質生產淨值
N.N.	no name	無簽名(票據退票理由之一)
N/N	non-negotiable, not negotiable	不可轉讓
NNE	Net National Expenditure	國民純支出
NNI	Net National Income	國民純收入
NNP	net national product	國民生產淨值
NNW	net national welfare	國民福利淨額
N/O	no order	不指定人(銀行用語)，無抬頭人
NOP	not otherwise provided	無其他規定
N/P	no payment	拒絕付款

	net proceeds 淨收入
	net profit 純利
	No protest 無拒付證書，免除拒付證書
N.P.	National Price 國內價格
	Notary Public 公證人
NPQ	Negotiated Price Quota 談判價格限額
NQ	New Quota 新分配額
NR	New Round 新回合
	No Risk 無危險，無須保險
N/R clause	not responsible clause 免責條款
NRT	Net Registered Tonnage 淨註冊噸位
N.S.	new style 新型
	not specified 無指定
	not sufficient 存款不足（銀行退票理由之一）
N/S	none in stock 存貨不足
NSF, n.s.f.	not sufficient fund 存款不足
n.s.p.f.	not specially provided for 未特別規定
N.T.	New Terms 新條件
NTB	Non-Tariff Barrier 非關稅壁壘
N.T.O.	not taken out 禁止帶出
N.U.	name unknown 船名不詳
N.V.O.	Non-Vessel Owner 非船主
NVS	Non Voting Stock 無表決權股
N.wt., Nt.wt.	net weight 淨重

O/	to the order of 交付，某某之指定人
O.A., o.a.	on acceptance 於承兌時
	on account 賒帳，先付
	outstanding account 未清帳目
O/A, o/a	Open Account 來往帳戶
	Our account 我方帳戶
	on account of 記入某帳
OAPEC	Organization of Arab Petroleum Exporting Countries 阿拉伯石油輸出國組織

O.B.	opening of book　開戶
	Order Book　定貨簿
O/B	opening bank　開信用證銀行
O.B/L	order bill of lading　指示式提單
Oc.B/L	ocean bill of lading　海運提單
O/C	Open Charter　預約租船合同，貨港未定租船
	Outward Collection　輸出代收款，出口託收
	overcharge　超載貨物；超收費
OCC	Oil Consuming Countries　石油消費國
O.C.L.	Overseas Containers Ltd.　英國海外貨櫃運輸公司
O.C.P.	Overland Common Points　共同卸貨點，任意港到達後交貨地點
O/D, od.	on demand　即期（見票即付）
	overdraft　滙票超過金額，透支
	on deck　裝在甲板上
OECD	Organization for Economic Cooperation and Development　經濟合作與發展組織
OEEC	Organization for European Economic Cooperation　歐洲經濟合作組織
OEL	Open End Licence　開放式進口許可證
O.F.	ocean freight　海運運費
O.M.	Orderly Marketing　有秩序的市場銷售
On Cons.	on consignment　寄售
o/n	on/net　淨計
O/O	Order of　定單，定貨
	Our Order　我們的定單
O.P., o.p.	open policy　預約保險單
op. opt.	option　選擇權，期權
OPA	Overall Payment Agreement　總括支付協定
O.pa.	all paid　全部付清
OPC	Oil Producing Countries　石油生產國
OPEC	Organization of Petroleum Exporting Countries　石油輸出國組織
OPM	Other People's Money　借入款，別人存款
	output per man　每人產量
OPO	one price only　只有一個價，不二價

OR, O/R	outward remittance　滙出滙款
	owner's risk　貨主擔當風險
O.R.B.	owner's risk of breakage　破碎險由貨主承擔
O.R.C.	owner's risk of chafing　擦破險由貨主承擔
O.R.D.	owner's risk of damage　損壞險由貨主承擔
	owner's risk of deterioration　變質險由貨主承擔
O.R.F.	owner's risk of fire　火險由貨主承擔
O.R.L.	owner's risk leakage　漏損險由貨主承擔
O/S, o.s.	old style　老式樣
	out of stock　缺貨，無存貨
	on spot　現場交易
	on sale　出售
	oversight　失察
O/T	old term (grain trade)　舊條件(穀物交易)
O.T., O/T	on truck　在卡車上
O.W.	[德語]ohne wert = without value　無價值
oz.	ounce　盎斯，英兩
oz. ap.	ounce apothecaries　藥量盎斯
oz. av.	ounce avoirdupois　常衡盎斯
oz. t.	ounce troy　金衡盎斯

P.	per　每
	priority　優先
	page　頁
	port　港口
p.a.	[拉]per annum (per year)　每年，按年期算
P/A	Particular Average　單獨海損
	Private Account　私人帳戶
	power of attorney　委託書，委任書，代理權
	procurement authorization　採購授權書
P.A.	Payment Agreement　支付協定
P and L, P. & L.	Profit and Loss　損益，盈虧
Pat.	patent, patented　專利權
PAYE	Pay As You Earn　付現款

payt.	Payment　付款
P.B.	Private Brand　私人商標
PC	payment Committee (OECD)　支付委員會
	Program-control　程序控制
	［拉］per centum = by the hundred　每百
pc.	piece　件，片，個，塊
p/c. P/C	price current　市價表
	per cent　每百(%)，百分比
	petty cash　零用現金
	port charge　港口費用
pd, p'd	paid　付訖
P.D.	Preferential Duties　特惠關稅
P.D., p.d.	Port Dues　港口捐，港口向船方收的費用
	Post-dated　郵局日期
	property damage　財產損失
p.d.	［拉］per diem = by the day　每日
P.D.D.	past due date　過期
PEC	Petroleum Exporting Countries　石油輸出國
per an., per ann.	［拉］per annum = by the year　每年
per m.	by the thousand　千份之(幾)
per pro	［拉］per procurationem = by proxy　委任代理
P.F.	Private Flow　私人投資來源
	Private Fund　私人資金
P.F., p.f.	［拉］Pro Forma　估計的，假定的，形式的
PFU	prepared for use　備用
p.h.	per hour　每小時
P & I	Protection & Indemnity　船東責任保險
P & I Club	Protection and Indemnity Club　保障賠償互助會(英國)
PICC	Provisional International Computation Center　臨時國際計算中心
PIK	payment in kind　實物支付
PK	peck　配克(英量名，等於 9.092 公升)
pkgs.	packages　包，包裝，件貨
p.l.	partial loss　部份損失
PLR	Prime Lending Rate　優惠貸款利率
Pm.	premium　保險費

p.m.	[拉] post meridiem = afternoon	下午
P.M.O.	postal money order	郵政滙票，郵滙
Pmt., payt.	payment	支付
P/N, P.N.	Promissory Note	本票，期票
P.O.	post office	郵局
	Postal Order	郵政滙票
	Private Offering	交易所外證券交易
P/O	payment order	付款通知
P.O.B.	post office box	郵箱
P.O.C.	port of call	停泊港
P.O.D.	pay on delivery	貨到付款
	Port of Debarkation	卸貨港
P.O.E.	Port of Embarkation	裝貨港，發航港
	Port of Entry	通關港，進口港
P.O.O.	post office order	郵政滙票
P.O.R.	payable on receipt	收貨付款
P.P.	Please Pay	請付款
	Particular Port	特定港
	per procuration	委任代理
	Personal Property	動產
	post paid	郵資已付
	Posted Price	標價
	Producer's Price	生產價格
	Public Property	公共財產
	Purchasing Power	購買力
P.P., pp.	picked ports (chartering)	挑選港口（租船業務）
ppd.	prepaid	預付
p.p.i.	policy proof of interest	保險單證明書權益
PPPs	purchasing power parities	購買力平價理論
Ppt.	Prompt	付款日期，交割日期
	Prompt Loading	快裝
P.Q.S.	Percentage Quantity System	（出口配額）比例分配制
Pres.	President	總統，行長，會長，總經理
prox.	[拉] proximo = next month	下月
P.S.	Pre-set System	半自動化控制系統
	post script	附言，再啟

	Production sharing　產品分享
	Profit Sharing　利潤分享
P/S	Public Sale　拍賣
PSI	paid service indication　納費業務標誌
P.T., pt.	pint　品脱(英美乾量或液量名 = 1/2 夸脱)
	Part payment　部份付款
PT	Purchase Tax　購置税
PTO	Place, Time and Object　地點、時間和目的
P.T.O.	please turn over　請轉下頁，請閲背面
PTY, Pty	proprietary　控股公司；企業公司(澳洲的公司名稱多含有 Pty. Ltd 字樣)
p.u.	paid-up　已付
P.X.	Please Exchange　請交換

Q

Q., qt., quty.	quantity　數量
Q.A.	Quality Assurance　質量保證
QC	Quality Certificates　質量檢查證
	Quality Control　質量控制，質量管理
	Quality Check　質量檢查
qlty.	quality　品質
QR	Quantity Restriction　數量限制
qr.	quarter　四份之一，一刻
qto.	quarto　四開
quotn.	quotation　行情表，估價單
q.v.	[拉]quod vide = which see　請查閲，參照
qy.	query　查核
	quay　碼頭

R

R	Registered　之簡寫，標明於商標旁邊，表示為註冊商標
R/A	Refer to accepter　請與承兑人聯繫
R. & a.	Rail and air　鐵路和空運
R. & o.	Rail and ocean　鐵路和海運

R. & t.	Rail and truck　鐵路和卡車運輸
R. & w.	Rail and water　鐵路和水運
RBP	Restrictive Business Practice　限制性商業慣例
rbo	[西班牙語]recibo　收據
R.C.	Red Cross　紅十字會
	Release Clause　豁免條款
	Revolving Credit　循環信用證
RCE	Remote-Control Equipment　遙控設備
rd.	road　路
	rod　杆
R/D, RD	refer to drawer　請與出票人接洽（銀行用語）
	Running-down clause　船隻碰撞條款（保險）
R/E	refer to endorser　請與背書人接洽
R.E.	Royal Exchange　倫敦交易所
RE, re.	with reference to　關於，參照
rec.	receipt　收據
	received　收訖
	record　記錄，錄音
recr.	receiver　收款人
redn.	reduction　減價
"red" B/L	red bill of lading　劃"紅線"提單
re-ex	re-export　再輸出，復出口
ref.	referee　公正人
	reference　參照
reg.	registered　掛號，登記
rem.	ream　令（量紙單位）
rem, RM	remittance　滙款
REOURTEL	refer to our telegram　參照我方電報
REURTEL, RYT	re your telegram　關於你方電報
Rev. A/C	revenue account　出納帳
RF	Reserve Fund　準備金
R.I., r.i	re-insurance　再保險
RO	remittance order　滙款委託書
R.O.	Receiving Office　收入行（處）
ROC	re our cable　關於我方電報
R.O.D.	Refused on delivery　拒絕交貨

R.O.E.	rate of exchange	滙率
R.O.G.	Receipt of Goods	貨物收據，貨已收到
ROI	return on investment	投資報酬率
ROL	re our letter	關於我方信函
ROP	record of production	生產紀錄
R/P	Return of post	請即回信
RP	Real Property	不動產，房地產
	Reference Price	參考價格
	Retail Price	零售價格
	Rule and Practice	規則和慣例
	Reply Paid	回電費已付
RQ	Reserved Quota	保留份額
RR	Rediscount Rate	重貼現率
R.S.D.	receiving, storage and delivery	收儲及交貨費用
RSVP	［法］repondez s'il vous plait (= reply, if you please) 請答覆
RTA	Reciprocal Trade Agreement	互惠貿易協定
RUF	Revolving Underwriting Facility	自動展期包銷信貸
RVSVP	［法］repondez vite s'il vous plait (= please reply at once) 請即刻答覆
RYT	replying to your telegram	敬覆貴電

S

S.A.	Subject to approval	以批准為條件
	Society Anonymous	不記名股票公司，有限公司
	System analysis	系統分析
s.a.	［拉］sine anns = without year or date 無日期
S/A	special authority	特別代理商
S. &. H.ex.	sundays & holidays excepted	星期日及假日除外
S. & L.C.	sue and labour clause 損害防止條款，施救條款（海上保險）
S.B.	Small Bond	小額債券
	Sales Book	售貨簿
	Savings Bank	儲蓄銀行
S.C., s.c.	salvage charges	救助費用
	see copy	請閱副本

	Suez Canal 蘇伊士運河
	supreme court 最高法院
	same case 同案，同樣情況
	service contract 業務合同
SC., s.c.	service charge 服務費，勞務費
Scp.	scrip 股單(臨時股款憑證或收據)準股票
S.D., S/D	sea damaged 海水損害(穀物交易)
	sight draft 即期滙票
	[拉]sine die = indefinitely 不定地，無期限
	short delivery 交貨不足
	same day 同一天
	Security Deposit 押金，保證金
SDN	Semi-Developed Nations 半發達國家
SDR	Saving Deposit Rate 儲蓄存款利率[美]
	Special Drawing Rights 特別提款權
SDT	short dry ton 短乾噸
Sdy.	sundry 雜貨，雜項
S.E.	System Engineering 系統工程
se.	securities 證券，債券
SE	Stock Exchange 證券交易所[英]
SEC	Securities and Exchange Commission 證券交易(管理)委員會[英]、[美]
S.E. ou O.	[法]Sauf erreurs ou omissions = E. & O.E. 錯誤遺漏除外
S.E.Y.O.	[西班牙]Salvo error Y omision = E. & O.E. 錯誤遺漏除外
SF	Sinking Fund 償債基金
	Semi-finished 半加工，半成品
	Special Fund 特別基金
sgd.	signed 已簽名，已簽署
SHEX	Sundays and holidays excepted 星期日、假日除外
shpt.	shipment 裝船
shr.	share 股份，股票
SIBOR	Singapore interbank offered rate 新加坡銀行同業拆放利率
SIC	Standard Industrial Classification 標準工業分類
Sig., SGN	signature 簽字，署名
S.K.D.	Semi Knock Down 半拆散

SL	Specific License 特別進口許可證
SLF	Savings and Loan Foundation 存放款基金會〔美〕
SMP	Semi-Manufactured Products 半製成品
S/N, s.n.	shipping note 裝船通知單
S.O., s/o	Seller's Option 賣方選擇權
	Shipping Order 裝貨通知單
SOD	Seller's option to double 賣方有權加倍
SOS	save our ship (souls) 船舶遇險求救信號
S.P.	Sales Promotion 推銷
	safe port 安全港
	stop payment 停止支付
S/P	Spare Parts 零件，備件
S.P.D., s.p.d.	steamer pays dues 船方支付稅捐
sq.in	square inch 平方英寸
sq. ft.	square foot 平方英尺
sq. yd.	square yard 平方碼
S.R.	ship's receipt 船方收貨單
SRCC	strikes, riots & civil commotions 罷工、暴動和內亂
SRD	Statutory Reserve of Deposits 法定存款準備率
S.S., s/s	steam ship 汽船，船名的前冠
ST	short ton 短噸，美噸
s.t.	stowed & trimmed 貨物進艙排列堆放整齊
Stge	Storage 短量
stk.	Stock 存貨
s.t.i.r.	subject to immediate reply 需立即答覆
stor.	storage 倉庫，棧租
Subs. Cap.	Subscribed Capital 認定資本
SUNFED	Special United Nations Fund for Economic Development 聯合國經濟開發特別基金
synd.	syndicate 辛廸加
SWIFT	Society for World-wide Interbank Financial Telecommunication 環球銀行間金融電訊協會

| T.A. | telegraphic address 電報掛號 |

	Technical Assistance 技術援助
	Technology Assessment 工藝鑒定
TAA	Technical Assistance Administration （聯合國）技術援助局
T/A	trade acceptance 商業承兌滙票
T.B.	treasury bill 國庫券
	trial balance 試算表
	Tariff Barriers 關稅壁壘
T.B.D. policy	to be declared policy 船運資料未確定保險單，暫保單
T.C.	telegraph collation 校對電報
	traveller's check 旅行支票
tc.	tierce 桶（盛 42 美加侖）
T.D.	trading department 貿易部
	treasury department 財政部
	［法］Tarif des Douanes 關稅率
	Time Deposit 定期存款
TDC	［法］Tarif des Douanes Communes 共同關稅率
TDP	Technical Development Plan 技術發展計劃
Tel.(No.)	telephone number 電話號碼
telex	teletypewriter exchange, teleprinter exchange 電傳，用戶電報，電報交換
tit.	title 稱謂，所有權
TKS	thanks 謝謝（電傳用語）
TLO, t.l.o.	total loss only 全損賠償
T.M.	telegram with multiple addresses 分抄或分送電報
	trad mark 商標
TMO	Telegraphic Money Order 電滙
t.o.	turn over 參照次頁，轉頁
TOB	Take-Over Bid 為控制某公司而購其股票的"出價"
T.O.P., t.o.p.	turn over, please 請推倒，請轉頁
TOU	Time of Usage 使用時間
TP	tax payer 納稅人
	top priority 最優先
	Treaty Port 通商口岸
	Trigger Price 起動價格，觸動價格
	Turn Point 轉折點
T.P.C.	Tax-Paid Price 完稅價

TPFC	Trans Pacific Freight Conference	全太平洋運費同盟
TPND	theft, pilferage and non-delivery	盜竊、提貨不着險
TQ, t.q.	[拉]tale quale = as they come	現狀條件
	Tariff Quota	關稅份額
T.Q.C.	Total Quality Control	全面質量管理
Tr., tr.	tare	皮重
	transfer	轉讓,過戶
	transportation	運輸
	transpose	調換
	translated	翻譯
T/R, TR	Trust Receipt	信託收據
	tons registered	註冊噸數
	telegramme restante	留交電報
TRS	terminal receiving system	外圍倉庫收貨制度
TS	transhipment	轉口裝運
T/T, TT, TT's	telegraphic transfer	電滙
TTB	Telegraphic Transfer Bought	電滙買進
TTS	Telegraphic Transfer Sold	電滙售出
TT selling	telegraphic transfer selling	電滙銀行賣價
TWA	Trans-World Airline, Inc	美國環球航空公司
TWC	total work cost	總生產成本

U

U.A.	Unit of Account	記帳單位
U/A	Undewriting Account	保險帳戶
UAPT	United Association for the Protection of Trade	貿易保護聯合會
UCC	Uniform Commercial Code	美國統一商法典
UDC	Universal Decimal Classification	國際十進位分類法
UEI	Unemployment Insurance	失業保險
U.K/C	United Kingdom or Continent	英國或歐洲大陸(海運用語)
U.K.F.O.	United Kingdom for order	英國沿岸之指定港口(海運用語)
ult., ulto.	[拉]ultimo = last month	上月

Un.	under bond　在保稅倉庫中
	underlying mortgage　優先抵押
	under Pay　少付工資
un.	undated bill　無日期票據
	underwriter　保險人
UNCDF	United Nations Capital Development Fund　聯合國資本開發基金
UNCTD	United Nations Conference on Trade and Development　聯合國貿易開發會議
UNIDO	United Nations Industrial Development Organization　聯合國工業發展組織
UNO, U.N.O	United Nations Organization　聯合國組織
UPU	Universal Postal Union　萬國郵政聯盟
URT	your telegram　貴方電報
u/w	underwriter　保險商

V

V., v	value　價值
	versus　對，對抗（法律、運動用語）
V., vid.	vide (= see, refer to)　參看
Va., val.	［拉］valuta (= foreight exchange)　國外滙兌，外滙
VA	Value Analysis　價值分析
VAT	Value Added Tax　附加價值稅
VC	Valuable Cargo　貴重貨物
	Visa Consulaire　領事簽證
VDR	Variable Deposit Requirements　可變存款條件
VE	Value engineering　價值工程
VFCR	Voluntary Foreign Credit Restraint Guidelines　外國銀行信貸自動限制規則（美國）
Viz.	［拉］videlicet (= namely)　即，就是，換言之
Vol.	Volume　容積，容量；卷，冊
VOP	Value as in Original Policy　照原保險價格
Voy.	voyage　航海
V.P.	vice president　副總統，副總裁，副董事長
v.s.	［拉］vide supra (= see above)　參見上面

W

W.A.	with average	單獨海損賠償
WACU	West African Customs Union	西非關稅同盟
WAEC	West African Economic Community	西非經濟共同體
WAMU	West African Monetary Union	西非貨幣聯盟
W.B.	Waybill	貨運單
	World Bank	世界銀行
W.C.	west coast	西海岸
	without charge	免費
W.C.A.	West Coast of Africa	非洲西海岸
W.C.F.C.	West Canada Freight Conferencc	西加拿大運費同盟
W.C.N.A.	West Coast of North America	北美西海岸
W.C.S.A.	West Coast of South America	南美西海岸
WFC	World Finance Corporation	世界金融公司
whf.	wharf	碼頭
W.G.	weight guaranteed	保證重量
W.I.	when issued	發行日期
W/M	weight or measurement	重量或體積（由船決定以較高者計算運費）
WOG	With Other Goods	與其他貨物合運
W.P.	weather permitting	雨天順延
W.P.A.	with particular average	單獨海損賠償
W.P.P.	waterproof paper packing	防潮紙包裝
WPT	Windfall Profits Tax	暴利稅，超額利潤稅
W.R., W/R	war risk	戰爭險，兵險
	warehouse receipt	倉庫收據
W.T.E.	war-time extension (clause)	如遇戰時則予展期（條款）
W.W., W/W	warehouse to warehouse	倉至倉（保險或條款）
	warehouse warrant	倉單
WWD, W.W.D.	weather working days	晴天工作日

X

X., x.	exchange	滙兌；交易所

	extension 電話分機，內線
XB	extra-budgetary 預算外
XC	Ex Coupon 除息票
Xcl.	excluding 不包括，免除
XD	Ex Dividend 除股息
X.in.	ex interest 除利息
X.n., X new	ex new 無權要求新股
X.P.	[法]express paye 快信
X.Rt.	Ex Right 無權利

Y., y., yd.	yard 英碼
Y., yr.	year 年
Y.A.R.	York-Antwerp Rules 約克一安特衞普(共同海損)規則
Y-day	yesterday 昨日
YT	your telex 你方電傳

Z

Z., z.	zero 零
	zone 區，地區
ZD	zero defects 無差錯，無缺憾
ZERT	[德]Zertifikat (= certificate) 證明書
ZI	Zone Interdict 禁區
ZL	Zero Line 零位線，基準線

附錄二
世界 50 家大銀行

（按中文筆劃排列）

銀 行 名 稱		國家或地區
中　文	**外　文**	
三井銀行	Mitsui Bank	日本
三和銀行	Sanwa Bank	日本
三菱銀行	Mitsubishi Bank	日本
大和銀行	Daiwa Bank	日本
大通曼哈頓銀行	Chase Manhattan Bank	美國
太平洋安全銀行	Security Pacific Corp.	美國
日本興業銀行	Industrial Bank of Japan	日本
巴西銀行	Banco Do Brasil	巴西
巴克萊銀行	Barclays Bank PLC. [①]	英國
巴黎國民銀行	Banque Nationale de Paris	法國
中國銀行	Bank of China	中華人民共和國
加拿大皇家銀行	Royal Bank of Canada	加拿大
加拿大帝國商業銀行	Canadian Imperial Bank of Commerce	加拿大
西太平洋銀行公司	Westpac Banking Corp.	澳大利亞
西亞那銀行	Monte Dei Paschi Di Siena	意大利
西德意志地方銀行（又稱“西德意志滙劃中心”）	Westdeutsche Landesbank Girozentrale	德國
多倫多自治領銀行	Toronto-Dominion Bank	加拿大
米蘭銀行	Midland Bank	英國
住友信託銀行	Sumitomo Trust & Banking	日本
里昂信貸銀行	Credit Lyonnais	法國
芝加哥第一國民銀行	First Chicago Corp	美國
阿比國民銀行	Abbey National	英國
東京銀行	Bank of Tokyo	日本
東海銀行	Tokai Bank	日本
花旗銀行	Citibank	美國
美洲銀行（全稱“美洲銀行國民信託儲蓄會”）	Bank America Corp（全稱 "Bank of America National Trust and Savings Associations"）	美國

銀 行 名 稱		國家或地區
中 文	外 文	
倫巴省儲蓄銀行	Cassa Di Risparmio Delle Provincie Lombarde	意大利
紐約化學銀行	Chemical New York Corp.	美國
紐約銀行家信託公司	Bankers Trust New York Corp.	美國
第一洲際銀行	First Interstate Bancorp	美國
第一勸業銀行	Dai-Ichi Kangyo Bank	日本
國民西敏寺銀行	National Westminster Bank PLC.	英國
國民勞動銀行	Banca Nazionale del Lavoro	意大利
梅隆國民銀行	Mellon National Corp.	美國
荷蘭通用銀行	Algemene Bank Nederland	荷蘭
荷蘭農業合作社中央銀行	Cooperatieve Centrale Raiffeissen-Boerenleenbank	荷蘭
都靈聖保羅銀行	Istituto Bancario San paolo Di Torino	意大利
富士銀行	Fuji Bank	日本
勞埃德銀行	Lloyds Bank PLC.	英國
意大利信貸銀行	Credito Italiano	意大利
意大利商業銀行	Banca Commerciale Italiana	意大利
瑞士信貸銀行	Credit Suisse	瑞士
瑞士銀行公司	Swiss Bank Corp.	瑞士
瑞士聯合銀行	Union Bank of Switzerland	瑞士
農業信貸國民銀行	de Caisse Nationale Credit Agricole	法國
滙豐銀行	HongKong and Shanghai Banking Corp.	香港
漢華實業銀行（又名漢諾威製造商銀行）	Manufacturers Hanover Corp.	美國
摩根保證信託銀行	Morgan Guaranty Trust Corp. of New York.	美國
德累斯頓銀行	Dresdner Bank	德國
德意志銀行	Deutsche Bank	德國

註① PLC 係 Public Limited Company 的縮寫。英國一些銀行根據英國《1980
年公司法》重新註冊，將 LTD 改為 PLC.

附錄三
世界各國貨幣名稱表

（按中文筆劃排列）

（一）亞洲

貨　幣　名　稱	縮寫或沿用的符號	國際標準化組織制定符號	輔　幣　及　進　位
土耳其里拉 Turkish Lira	LT	TRL	1 里拉 = 100 庫魯 (Kurus)
也門第納爾 Yemani Dinar	YD	YDD	1 第納爾 = 1000 費爾 (Fils)
日元 Japanese Yen	J¥	JPY	1 日元 = 100 錢 (Sen)
中國人民幣 Chinese Renminbi Yuan	RMb¥	CNY	1 元 = 10 角 (Jiao) = 100 分 (Fen)
巴林第納爾 Bahrain Dinar	BD	BHD	1 第納爾 = 1000 費爾 (Fils)
巴基斯坦盧比 Pakistan Rupee	PRS	PKR	1 盧比 = 100 派沙 (Paisa)
文萊元 Brunei Dollar	B$	BND	1 元 = 100 分 (Cents)
以色列鎊 Israel Pound	I£	ILP	1 鎊 = 100 阿高洛 (Agorot)
尼泊爾盧比 Nepalese Rupee	NRs	NPR	1 盧比 = 100 派沙 (Paisa)
卡塔爾里亞爾 Qatar Riyal	QR	QAR	1 里亞爾 = 100 迪拉姆 (Dirhams)
印度尼西亞盧比（通稱盾） Indonesia Rupiah	RP	IDR	1 盾 = 100 仙 (Sen)
印度盧比 Indian Rupee	Rs 或 I.Rs	INR	1 盧比 = 100 派士 (Paise)

貨　幣　名　稱	縮寫或沿用的符號	國際標準化組織制定符號	輔　幣　及　進　位
伊拉克第納爾 Iraqi Dinar	ID	IQD	1 第納爾 = 1000 費爾 (Fils)
伊朗里亞爾 Iranian Rial	Rls	IRR	1 里亞爾 = 100 第納爾 (Dinar)
老撾基普 Laos Kip	K	LAK	1 基普 = 100 阿特 (At)
沙特阿拉伯里亞爾 Saudi Arabian Riyal	SRls	SAR	1 里亞爾 = 100 哈拉拉 (Halalas)
孟加拉塔卡 Bangladesh Taka	TK	BDT	1 塔卡 = 100 派士 (Paise)
阿拉伯也門里亞爾 Arabian Yemen Riyal	YRL	YER	1 里亞爾 = 100 費爾 (Fils)
阿富汗尼 Afghani	Af	AFA	1 阿富汗尼 = 100 普爾 (Puls)
約旦第納爾 Jordanian Dinar	JD	JOD	1 第納爾 = 1000 費爾 (Fils)
敘利亞鎊 Syrian Pound	£s	SYD	1 鎊 = 100 皮阿斯特 (Piastres)
科威特第納爾 Kuwaiti Dinar	KD	KWD	1 第納爾 = 1000 費爾 (Fils)
香港元 Hongkong Dollar	HK$	HKD	1 元 = 100 分 (Cents)
韓國圓 Korean Won	W	KRW	1 圓 = 100 錢 (Chon)
馬來西亞林吉特 Malaysian Ringgit	M$	MYR	1 林吉特 = 100 分 (Cents)
馬爾代夫盧比 Maldivian Rupee	MAL Rs	MVR	1 盧比 = 100 拉雷 (Larees)
菲律賓比索 Philipine Peso	♀, P	PHP	1 比索 = 100 分 (Centavos)
斯里蘭卡盧比 Srilanka Rupee	SLRs	LKR	1 盧比 = 100 分 (Cents)

貨　幣　名　稱	縮寫或沿用的符號	國際標準化組織制定符號	輔　幣　及　進　位
越南盾 Viet-Namese Dong	D	VND	1 盾 = 10 角 (Ha'o) = 100 分 (Xu)
泰銖 Thai Baht	B	THB	1 銖 = 100 薩當 (Satang)
朝鮮圓 Korean Won	W	KPW	1 圓 = 100 分 (Jeon)
新加坡元 Singapore Dollar	S$	SGD	1 元 = 100 分 (Cents)
新台幣 Taiwan Dollar	NT$	TWD	1 元 = 100 分 (Cents)
塞浦路斯鎊 Cyprus Pound	£C	CYP	1 鎊 = 1000 米爾 (Mils)
蒙古圖格里克 Mongolian Tugrik	Tug	MNT	1 圖格里克 = 100 蒙戈 (Mungo)
緬甸元 Burmese Kyat	K	BUK	1 元 = 100 分 (Pyas)
黎巴嫩鎊 Lebanese Pound	LL	LBP	1 鎊 = 100 皮阿斯特 (Piastres)
澳門元 Macao Pataca	Pat	MOP	1 元 = 100 分 (Avos)

（二）歐洲

貨　幣　名　稱	縮寫或沿用的符號	國際標準化組織制定符號	輔　幣　及　進　位
比利時法郎 Belgian Franc	BF	BEF	1 法郎 = 100 分 (Centimes)
丹麥克朗 Danish Krone	DKr	DKK	1 克朗 = 100 歐爾 (Öre)
匈牙利福林 Hungarian Forint	Ft	HUF	1 福林 = 100 菲勒 (Filler)

貨　幣　名　稱	縮寫或沿用的符號	國際標準化組織制定符號	輔　幣　及　進　位
西班牙比塞塔 Spanish Peseta	Ptas	Esp	1 比塞塔 = 100 分 (Centimos)
德國馬克 Deutsche Mark	DM	DEM	1 馬克 = 100 芬尼 (Pfenning)
冰島克朗 Icelandic Krona, 複數 Kronar	IKr	ISK	1 克朗 = 100 奧拉 (Aurar)
希臘德拉克馬 Greek Drachma	Dr	GRD	1 德拉克馬 = 100 雷普塔 (Lepta)
法國法郎 French Franc	FF	FRF	1 法郎 = 100 分 (Centimes)
阿爾巴尼亞列克 Albanian Lek	Lek	ALL	1 列克 = 100 昆塔 (quintar)
波蘭茲羅提 Polish Zloty	ZL	PLZ	1 茲羅提 = 100 格羅希 (Groszy)
芬蘭馬克 Finnish Markka	Fmk	FIM	1 馬克 = 100 盆尼 (Penni)
保加利亞列弗 Bulgarian Lev	Lv	BGL	1 列弗 = 100 斯托丁基 (Stotinki)
南斯拉夫第納爾 Yugoslav Dinar	Din	YUD	1 第納爾 = 100 帕拉 (Paras)
英鎊 Pound Sterling	£ 或 £ stg.	GBP	1 英鎊 = 100 新便士 (New Pence)
馬耳他里拉 Maltese Lira	ML	MTL	1 里拉 = 100 分 (Centesimi)
挪威克朗 Norwegian Krone	NKr	NOK	1 克朗 = 100 歐爾 (öre)
荷蘭盾 Dutch Guilder or Florin	F 或 FL	NLG	1 盾 = 100 分 (Cents)
奧地利先令 Austrian Schilling	ASch	ATS	1 先令 = 100 格羅申 (Groschen)

貨　幣　名　稱	縮寫或沿用的符號	國際標準化組織制定符號	輔　幣　及　進　位
捷克克朗 Czechoslovakia Koruna	Kcs	CSK	1 克朗 = 100 赫勒 (Hallers)
意大利里拉 Italian Lira, 複數 Lire, Liras	Lit	ITL	1 里拉 = 100 分 (Centesimi)
瑞士法郎 Swiss Franc	SF	CHF	1 法郎 = 100 分 (Centimes)
瑞典克朗 Swedish Krona, 複數 Kronor	SKr	SEK	1 克朗 = 100 歐爾 (öre)
葡萄牙埃斯庫多 Portuguese Escudo	Esc	PTE	1 埃斯庫多 = 100 分 (Centavos)
愛爾蘭鎊 Irish Pound	£ Ir	IEP	1 鎊 = 100 新便士 (New Pence)
盧森堡法郎 Luxembourg Franc	Lux F	LUF	1 法郎 = 100 分 (Centimes)
羅馬尼亞列伊 Romanian Leu, 複數 Lei	L	ROL	1 列伊 = 100 巴尼 (Bani)
俄羅斯盧布 Russian Rouble	Rbs, Rub	RR	1 盧布 = 100 戈比 (Kopecks)

（三）非洲

貨　幣　名　稱	縮寫或沿用的符號	國際標準化組織制定符號	輔　幣　及　進　位
扎伊爾國扎伊爾 Zairian Zaire	Z	ZRZ	1 扎伊爾 = 100 馬庫塔 (Makuta) = 1000 森吉 (Sengi)
毛里求斯盧比 Mauritius Rupee	Mau Rs	MUR	1 盧比 = 100 分 (Cents)

貨　幣　名　稱	縮寫或沿用的符號	國際標準化組織制定符號	輔　幣　及　進　位
毛里塔尼亞烏吉亞 Mauritania Ouguiya	UM	MRO	1 烏吉亞 = 5 庫姆斯 (Khoums)
尼日利亞奈拉 Nigerian Naira	N	NGN	1 奈拉 = 100 考包 (Kobo)
加納塞地 Ghanian Cedi	¢	GHC	1 塞地 = 100 比塞瓦 (Pesewa)
布隆廸法郎 Burundi Franc	FBu	BIF	1 法郎 = 100 分 (Centimes)
安哥拉寬扎 Angolan Kwanza	KW	AOK	1 寬扎 = 100 勒韋 (Lwei)
利比里亞元 Liberian Dollar	Lib$	LRD	1 元 = 100 分 (Cents)
利比亞第納爾 Libyan Dinar	LD	LyD	1 第納爾 = 1000 廸拉姆 (Dirhams)
赤道幾內亞埃奎勒 Equatorial Guinea Ekuele	EK	GQE	1 埃奎勒 = 100 分 (Centimos)
岡比亞達拉西 Gambian Dalasi	DG	GMD	1 達拉西 = 100 布圖 (Butut)
肯尼亞先令 Kenya Shilling	K.sh	KES	1 先令 = 100 分 (Cents)
非洲金融共同體法郎 African Financial Community Franc	CFAF	XOF	包括：塞內加爾、貝寧、尼日爾、多哥、喀麥隆、乍得、中非帝國、加蓬、剛果人民共和國、科特迪瓦、布基納法索、馬里、赤道幾內亞。 1 法郎 = 100 分 (Centimes)
坦桑尼亞先令 Tanzania shilling	T.sh	TZS	1 先令 = 100 分 (Cents)

貨　幣　名　稱	縮寫或沿用的符號	國際標準化組織制定符號	輔　幣　及　進　位
佛得角埃斯庫多 Cape Verde Escudo	C.V.Esc	CVE	1 埃斯庫多 = 100 分 (Centavos)
阿爾及利亞第納爾 Algerian Dinar	DA	DZD	1 第納爾 = 100 分 (Centimes)
津巴布韋元 Zimbabwe (Rhodesian) Dollar	$Z	ZWD	1 元 = 100 分 (Cents)
突尼斯第納爾 Tunisian Dinar	D	TND	1 第納爾 = 1000 米利姆 (Millimes)
南非蘭特 South African Rand	R	ZAR	1 蘭特 = 100 分 (Cents)
烏干達先令 Uganda Shilling	USh	UGS	1 先令 = 100 分 (Cents)
埃及鎊 Egyptian Pound	LE	EGP	1 鎊 = 100 皮阿斯特 (Piastres) = 1000 米利姆 (Millimes)
埃塞俄比亞比爾 Ethiopian Birr	Br	ETB	1 比爾 = 100 分 (Cents)
馬達加斯加法郎 Madagascar Franc	FMG	MGF	1 法郎 = 100 分 (Centimes)
索馬里先令 Somali Shilling	SoSh	SOS	1 先令 = 100 分 (Cents)
莫桑比克梅蒂卡爾 Mozambique Metical	MT	MZN	1 梅蒂卡爾 = 100 分 (Centavos)
幾內亞比紹比索 Guinea-Bissau Peso	GP	GWP	1 比索 = 100 分 (Centavos)
幾內亞西里 Guinean Syli	S	GNS	1 西里 = 100 科里 (Cauri)
博茨瓦納普拉 Botswana Pula	P	BWP	1 普拉 = 100 西比 (Thebe)
塞拉利昂利昂 Sierra Leone Leone	Le	SLL	1 利昂 = 100 分 (Cents)

貨 幣 名 稱	縮寫或沿用的符號	國際標準化組織制定符號	輔 幣 及 進 位
摩洛哥廸拉姆 Moroccan Dirham	DH	MAD	1 廸 拉 姆 = 100 摩 洛 哥 法郎 (Franc) (centimes)
盧旺達法郎 Rwanda Franc	RF	RWF	1 法郎 = 100 分 (Centimes)
贊比亞克瓦查 Zambian Kwacha	ZK	ZMK	1 克瓦查 = 100 恩韋 (Ngwee)
蘇丹鎊 Sudanese Pound	Lsd	SDP	1 鎊 = 100 皮阿斯特 (Piastres) = 1000 米利姆 (Milliemes)

（四）美洲

貨 幣 名 稱	縮寫或沿用的符號	國際標準化組織制定符號	輔 幣 及 進 位
巴巴多斯元 Barbados Dollar	BDS$	BBD	1 元 = 100 分 (Cents)
巴西克魯薩多① Brazilian Cruzeiro	Cr$	BRC	1 克魯薩多 = 100 分 (Centavos)
巴哈馬元 Bahamian Dollar	B$	BSD	1 元 = 100 分 (Cents)
巴拿馬巴波亞 Panamanian Balboa	B	PAB	1 巴波亞 = 100 分 (Centesimos)
厄瓜多爾蘇克雷 Ecuadoran Sucre	S/	ECS	1 蘇克雷 = 100 分 (Centavos)
牙買加元 Jamaican Dollar	J$	JMD	1 元 = 100 分 (Cents)
古巴比索 Cuban Peso	Cub$	CUP	1 比索 = 100 分 (Centavos)
尼加拉瓜科多巴 Nicaraguan Cordoba	C$	NIC	1 科多巴 = 100 分 (Centavos)

貨　幣　名　稱	縮寫或沿用的符號	國際標準化組織制定符號	輔　幣　及　進　位
加拿大元 Canadian Dollar	Can$	CAD	1 加元 = 100 分 (Cents)
多米尼加比索 Dominican Peso	RD$	DOP	1 比索 = 100 分 (Centavos)
多米尼加聯邦東加勒比元 East Caribbean Dollar	EC$	XCD	1 元 = 100 分 (Cents)
危地馬拉格查爾 Guatemalan Quetzal	Q	GTQ	1 格查爾 = 100 分 (Centavos)
圭亞那元 Guyana Dollar	G$	GYD	1 元 = 100 分 (Cents)
委內瑞拉博利瓦 Venezuelan Bolivar	Bs	VEB	1 博利瓦 = 100 分 (Centimos)
阿根廷比索 Argentine Peso	$a	ARP	1 比索 = 100 分 (Centavos)
美元 United States Dollar	US$	USD	1 美元 = 100 分 (Cents)
玻利維亞比索 Bolivian Peso	$b	BOP	1 比索 = 100 分 (Centavos)
洪都拉斯倫皮拉 Honduran Lempira	L	HNL	1 倫皮拉 = 100 分 (Centavos)
特立尼達和多巴哥元 Trinidad & Tobago Dollar	TT$	TTD	1 元 = 100 分 (Cents)
海地古德 Haitian Gourde	G	HTG	1 古德 = 100 分 (Centimes)
格林納達東加勒比元 East Caribbean Dollar	EC$	XCD	1 元 = 100 分 (Cents)
烏拉圭新比索 Uruguayan New Peso	NUr$	UYP	1 新比索 = 100 分 (Centesimos)
哥倫比亞比索 Colombia Peso	Col$	COP	1 比索 = 100 分 (Centavos)
哥斯達尼加科郎 Costa Rican Colon	¢	CRC	1 科郎 = 100 分 (Centimos)

貨　幣　名　稱	縮寫或沿用的符號	國際標準化組織制定符號	輔　幣　及　進　位
秘魯因蒂② Peruvian Inti	I	PEI	1 因蒂 = 100 分 (Centavos)
智利比索 Chilean Peso	Ch$	CLP	1 比索 = 100 分 (Centesimos)
墨西哥比索 Mexican Peso	Mex$	MXP	1 比索 = 100 分 (Centavos)
薩爾瓦多科郎 Salvadoran Colon	¢	SVC	1 科郎 = 100 分 (Centavos)

（五）大洋洲及太平洋島嶼

貨　幣　名　稱	縮寫或沿用的符號	國際標準化組織制定符號	輔　幣　及　進　位
巴布亞新幾內亞基那 Papua New Guinea Kina	K	PGK	1 基那 = 100 托伊 (Toea)
西薩摩亞塔拉 Western Samoa Tala	WS$	WST	1 塔拉 = 100 分 (Sene)
所羅門羣島元 Solomon Islands Dollar	SI$	SBD	1 元 = 100 分 (Cents)
湯加潘加 Tonga Paanga	T$	TOP	1 潘加 = 100 分 (Seniti)
斐濟元 Fiji Dollar	F$	FJD	1 元 = 100 分 (Cents)
新西蘭元 New Zealand Dollar	NZ$	NZD	1 元 = 100 分 (Cents)
澳大利亞元 Australian Dollar	$A	AUD	1 澳元 = 100 分 (Cents)

註① 巴西於 1986. 2. 28. 發行新幣克魯薩多。每 1000 克魯賽羅舊幣換 1 個新幣。
　② 祕魯於 1986. 1. 1. 起使用新貨幣＂因蒂＂。舊幣＂索爾＂與新幣同時流通至 1989. 12. 31.

漢英國際經濟貿易詞典 = Chinese-English
dictionary of economics & international
trade／林燮寰主編. ‐‐臺灣初版. ‐‐臺北
市：臺灣商務, 1994 [民83]
　　面 ； 　公分
含索引
ISBN 957-05-0981-3（精裝）

1. 經濟 - 字典，辭典　2. 貿易 - 字典，辭典
3. 金融 - 字典，辭典

550.4　　　　　　　　　　　　　　83006303

漢英國際經濟貿易詞典
Chinese-English Dictionary of
Economics & International Trade

定價新臺幣 380 元

主　編　者　林　燮　寰
責 任 編 輯　劉　秀　英

出　版　者
印　刷　所　臺灣商務印書館股份有限公司
　　　　　　臺北市 10036 重慶南路 1 段 37 號
　　　　　　電話：(02)23116118 · 23115538
　　　　　　傳眞：(02)23710274 · 23701091
　　　　　　讀者服務專線：0800-056196
　　　　　　E-mail：cptw@ms12.hinet.net
　　　　　　郵政劃撥：0000165 － 1 號
　　　　　　出版事業
　　　　　　登 記 證：局版北市業字第 993 號

· 1993 年 9 月香港初版
· 1994 年 9 月臺灣初版第一次印刷
· 2001 年 7 月臺灣初版第三次印刷
本書經商務印書館（香港）有限公司授權出版

ISBN　957-05-0981-3(精裝)　　　　　　b　34672000